Practitioners, Practices and Patients

New Approaches to Medical Archaeology and Anthropology

*Proceedings of a conference
held at Magdalene College, Cambridge
November 2000*

Edited by

Patricia Anne Baker and Gillian Carr

Oxbow Books

Published by
Oxbow Books, Park End Place, Oxford OX1 1HN

© Oxbow Books and the individual authors, 2002

ISBN 1 84217 079 1

A CIP record for this book is available from the British Library

This book is available direct from
Oxbow Books, Park End Place, Oxford OX1 1HN
(Phone: 01865–241249; Fax: 01865–794449)

and

The David Brown Book Company
PO Box 511, Oakville, CT 06779, USA
(Phone: 860–945–9329; Fax: 860–945–9468)

or from our website

www.oxbowbooks.com

Cover images

Left column: Top, The *mangmani* of Pangma village, Nepal; Middle, A heathen shaman today, casting runes, (photo courtesy of R. J. Wallis and N. J. Johnson); Bottom, Gilber Chufandama, Jakwash shaman and primary health worker, propitiating an 'ancestor tree' marking his boundary of a colonisation area for his kindred.

Middle column: Top, Figure of TB spine in Anglo-Saxon individual from Bedhampton, Hampshire; Bottom, shaman's cache and other paraphernalia, Xaghra, Gozo, Malta.

Right column: Top, The rock crystal charm in its silver mounting of the Stewarts of Ardsheal (MOSP53) (reproduced with permission of the National Museum of Scotland); Bottom, Etruscan dental appliance from museum in Copenhagen (reproduced with permission of the National Museum of Denmark).

Back cover: Roman scalpels, after Jackson 1990, fig. 1, numbers 6–8.

Printed in Great Britain at
The Short Run Press, Exeter

To
Josh and Sal

CONTENTS

Introduction vii

1. Medical anthropology, material culture, and new directions
    in medical archaeology (*Elisabeth Hsu*) 1

2. Diagnosing some ills: the archaeology, literature and history
    of Roman medicine (*Patricia Anne Baker*) 16

3. Tuberculosis: a multidisciplinary approach to past and current
    concepts, causes and treatment of this infectious disease
    (*Charlotte Roberts*) 30

4. A preliminary account of the doctor's grave at Stanway,
    Colchester, England (*Philip Crummy*) 47

5. A time to live, a time to heal and a time to die: healing and
    divination in later Iron Age and early Roman Britain (*Gillian Carr*) 58

6. A computer simulation of Mambila divination (*David Zeitlyn*) 74

7. Beer, trees, pigs and chickens: medical tools of the Lohorung
    shaman and priest (*Charlotte Hardman*) 81

8. Healing here, there and in-between: a Tamu shaman's experience
    of international landscapes (*Judith Pettigrew and Yarjung Tamu*) 109

9. The Xaghra Shaman? (*Simon Stoddart*) 125

10. Tobacco and curing agency in Western Amazonian shamanism
    (*Françoise Barbira Freedman*) 136

11. Magic, healing, or death? Issues of Seidr, 'balance', and morality in past and present (*Jenny Blain*)... 161

12. Of crystal balls, political power, and changing contexts: what the clever women of Salerno inherited (*Christopher Knüsel*).......................... 172

13. Lithic therapy in early Chinese body practices (*Vivienne Lo*) 195

14. Kill or cure: Athenian judicial curses and the body in fear (*Ralph Anderson*) 221

15. Etruscan female tooth evulsion: gold dental appliances as ornaments (*Marshall Joseph Becker*).. 238

INTRODUCTION

A fortunate first meeting of the editors took place at the Theoretical Archaeology Group meeting in Cardiff, December 1999, which led to discussions on a shared interest in ancient medicine. The editors met again at the Theoretical Roman Archaeology Conference in London in April 2000. Here, they considered a variety of issues about the field of archaeology and medicine and the approaches taken in scholarly works. One of the main concerns noted was that little interdisciplinary discussion seemed to be taking place between archaeologists who were interested in medical care of past societies and anthropologists who study modern societies' understandings of medicine. From an archaeological point of view (both editors are archaeologists), it was felt that rather limited explanations and interpretative methods were being used towards an understanding of medicine in the past. These methods generally take a narrow definition of the subject. One method that has provided much information has been the field of palaeopathology, which has developed the study of disease, injury and pathology from skeletal remains (e.g. Boddington, Garland and Janaway 1987; Roberts and Manchester 1995). From palaeopathological evidence it is often possible to determine how a patient might have been cared for, for example, from the study of the lifespan of the severely physically impared, or from examining how well a bone has healed. Another field within medical archaeology is palaeobotany, used to recognise possible medical plants which played a role in healing. It goes without saying that both are necessary studies towards understanding medicine and healing procedures in the past, but, at the same time, they cannot always inform us of the cultural perception of healing procedures, although paleopathology can sometimes provide information about a particular cultural viewpoint of disease. Unfortunately, both studies are generally not concerned with answering questions about the type of healer who had helped, or attempted to help, the patient. In some cases the medical tools used on a patient can be identified from close examination of the skeleton; however, the remains of medical instruments are generally studied by archaeologists who are interested more in material culture than biological anthropology. Among those who study medical instruments used in past societies, the majority of work is concentrated on the Classical and Arabic worlds. These studies are firmly grounded in comparisons with the literary evidence of the periods (e.g. Bliquez 1985; Gilson 1978, 1981; Jackson 1990; 1994; Kunzl 1983; Albucasis trans. Spink and Lewis [1973]). In classical scholarship, assumptions are often made that medical treatment was homogeneous throughout their periods, and that all of their medical practices and practitioners performed their art according to the works of medical writers such as Galen, Celsus and the Hippocratic writers (Baker 2001 and this volume). The only instruments that tend to be identified are those that are outlined in the medical texts and their function is always described as being practical and 'rational', without any discussion of possible variations in medical practice or understandings about the body. What we found to be missing in many of these studies, especially the works focused on material culture, was a consideration of the medical anthropological literature and communication between the disciplines. We also realised the importance of asking anthropologists to consider the material culture of healing and to determine the roles, functions and cultural meanings behind what is used for healing. Often in anthropological studies the tool being used is noted, but its importance is frequently overlooked in favour of other issues about the processes and descriptions of the disease and healing. Thus, collaboration between the two areas of study was, and is, believed by the editors to be important for scholars, as a means of realising the complexities of medical ideologies, beliefs and understandings about the body in sickness and its cure. Because little discussion seemed to be occurring, we felt that a conference including papers by archaeologists and anthropologists would be beneficial to widening the interpretations of health care. This volume is, therefore, the outcome of a conference held in Magdalene College, Cambridge in November 2000 that brought together these diverse means of interpretation.

Because of the nature of the conference and the disciplines with which we were dealing, a concentration upon the material culture of healing was at the forefront of discussion at the conference. However, it was intended that authors would take a broader definition of instrumentation beyond just medicaments, their preparatory tools and western ideas of medical instruments. Artefacts such as divination and 'shamanic' tools were also included. Contextual studies of material culture as a means of determining attitudes towards objects relating to disease, healing and medicine were welcomed. Moreover, consideration of the many different types of healers was deemed necessary for expanding interpretations of healing practice. Incorporated in many of the papers in both the conference and the volume were considerations of the cultural constructions of the body in sickness and health.

Papers presented in this volume are interdisciplinary, some to such an extent that it was difficult to categorise them according to the disciplines of archaeology or anthropology, let alone into sub-divisions of embodiment, healing, divination and so forth. During the process of editing, it became apparent that there were no easy means by which we could organise papers into specific sub-categories. The papers are arranged simply next to those that share similiarities; although any one could be rearranged to fit with other papers.

Hsu's paper was chosen as the first because it discusses general aspects of medical anthropology, which might be considered of primary importance to medical archaeologists. The paper was commissioned to discuss various issues including culture-specific forms of illnesses, diagnosis, 'therapeutic efficacy' versus 'therapeutic success' and the notion of 'placebo'. Baker's contribution was also chosen as an introductory paper, as it discusses problems in the archaeological interpretation of medical tools. It specifically questions scholarship on Roman medical instruments and its uncritical reliance upon classical medical texts. To remedy the situation Baker suggests looking at the remains in their archaeological context to determine cultural meanings of instruments not discussed in the textual information. Although a period-specific paper, the methods suggested could be used for other periods explored through archaeology.

Roberts' paper on tuberculosis discusses the disease in the present and in many historical contexts as well its social and cultural contextual meanings. She pays attention to the cultural construction of the disease and the ways in which people and their carers in different societies dealt with it.

A case study cited by several authors in this volume is presented here by Philip Crummy, the original excavator of the 'Doctor's Grave' at Stanway in Colchester, Essex (UK). Crummy describes various elements of the grave including the surgical tools, the gaming board, the 'divination' rods and the strainer bowl. A number of authors have interpreted these finds in various ways throughout the volume.

On the subject of divination we also have papers by Carr and Zeitlyn. Zeitlyn examines the spider divination among the Mambila of Cameron, discussing computer simulation (and its inherent problems) of the divination process. Zeitlyn outlines how Mambila divination can be used to determine whether an illness should be treated by conventional western-style allopathic medicines, or by 'traditional' healing.

Carr considers the possible roles of divination, shamanism, concepts of auspicious and inauspicious time and human sacrifice in British Iron Age healing rituals. She then considers the effect of Roman doctors and their medicines on the indigenous people and their reaction to it, drawing parallels with other societies where western medicine has been brought into communities which previously relied only upon their own native healers.

The tools of healing are discussed in the paper by Hardman, who examined the Lohorung of eastern Nepal. Her paper looks at how the (what would be considered unusual by archaeologists) material culture related to healing, such as beer, pigs and chickens, is regarded and used.

Pettigrew and Tamu, like Carr, also examine the working of medicine in the context of colonial contact, and discuss what happens when a Nepali shaman joins the British army as a gurkha and is posted overseas. Ritual journeys made by shamans searching for lost souls go over a named local geographical landscape, so how do shamans perform their work in other countries? Can they heal people in other geographical landscapes? How can their ancestors help spirits find these distant healing locations?

Stoddart works on several levels in his discussion of the Xaghra shaman of Gozo in Malta, mentioning cosmological landscapes, but homing in on the demarcated shamanic space, indicated by specific material culture. He works specifically in the arena of mortuary ritual as a means of identifying the possibility of shamanic practices in Malta.

Barbira Freedman describes the role of hallucinogenic plants including tobacco (and its smoke) and *ayahuasca,* as shamanic diagnostic and healing tools. These narcotics aid the shaman by inducing visions and dreams, which impart knowledge and also enable communication with plant spirits.

Blain discusses modern shamanic practices ('seidr') which have been reconstructed by drawing on the practices of Icelandic shamans as described in the sagas coupled with information from the archaeological record. She also examines evidence for past

and present trance, healing and spirit working in northern spiritual contexts, as well
as bringing out the complexity, diversity and multivocality of modern shamans who,
like shamans in traditional societies, are inventive and creative.

Knüsel also examines shamans in the archaeological record. Specifically he looks
for funerary evidence for pre-Christian shamanesses, especially in the early medieval
period. He homes in on the role of the crystal ball and its changing role from the pre-
Christian to Christian era as a tool of healing to a symbol of power, and from the
female to the male sphere.

Lo explores early Chinese lithic therapy and has found recurring patterns in the
techniques of mortuary ritual, self-cultivation and medical theory and practice. She
has looked at how minerals such as arsenic, cinnabar and jade were used to preserve
the body in life and in death. These minerals and stones were also scattered around
the corpse to delineate a sacred space to protect the body.

Anderson also considers embodiment in his discussion of the role and use of
Athenian judicial curse tablets in 'binding' a person to produce a state akin to fear in
victims. He discusses the user of the curse (*defigens*), who planted the tablets in
sanctuaries or in graves of the untimely dead to give him/her supernatural assistance
with harming in the context of the Athenian legal system.

Becker discusses the use of gold dental appliances by south Etruscan women. He
argues that these were not replacements for decayed teeth, but were instead cosmetic
and took the place of healthy teeth that had been deliberately removed. The paper
warns us that medical and cosmetic procedures can be performed in the same manner,
but have very different meanings.

To conclude, we hope that this book will be an important contribution to the field
of medical archaeology, anthropology and history. The conference generated much
discussion between the speakers and audience. The editors certainly found that the
interdisciplinary nature of the conference produced thought-provoking and innovative
papers, thus pointing the way forward.

We would like to thank David Brown at Oxbow Books for publishing this volume;
Dr. Simon Stoddart for helping us to acquire the room at Magdalene College
Cambridge; and Elizabeth Hsu and Chris Knüsel for agreeing to act as discussants.
We would also like to thank the referees, and all the people who attended, both as
speakers and as audience, and who created wonderful discussion. A number of papers
were received from people who did not attend the conference, including: M. Becker, F.
Barbira Freedman, C. Hardman and J. Pettigrew. We would like to thank them for
their interest.

Bibliography

Albucasis on surgery and instruments, M.S. Spink and G.L. Lewis (Trans.) 1973. London:
    Wellcome Institute of the History of Medicine
Baker, P. 2001 'Medicine, culture and military identity' pp. 48–68 in G. Davies, A. Gardner and
    K. Lockyear (eds), *TRAC 2000: Proceedings of the tenth annual theoretical Roman archaeology
    conference*, Oxford: Oxbow Books.
Bliquez, L. 1985 'Λιθουλκος, Κιρσουλκος' *American Journal of Philology* 106, 119–121.

Boddington, A., Garland, A.N. and Janaway, R.C. 1987 *Death, decay and reconstruction: approaches to archaeology and forensic science*, Manchester: Manchester University Press.

Gilson, A. 1978 'A doctor at Housesteads' *Archaeologia Aeliana* 6 (series 5), 162–165.

Gilson, A. 1981 'A group of Roman surgical and medical instruments from Corbridge' *Saalburg Jahrbuch* 37, 5–9.

Jackson, R. 1990 'Roman doctors and their instruments: recent research into ancient practice' *Journal of Roman Archaeology* 3, 5–27.

Jackson, R. 1994 'The surgical instruments, appliances and equipment in Celsus' *De Medicina*' pp. 167–209 in *La Médecine de Celse*, Saint-Étienne: Publications de l'Université Saint-Étienne.

Künzl, E. 1983 *Medizinische Instrumente aus Sepulkralfunden der römischen Kaiserzeit*, Cologne: Rheinland Verlag GmbH.

Roberts, C.A. and Manchester, K. 1995 *The archaeology of disease*, Gloucester: Sutton Publishing.

Patricia Baker and Gillian Carr

1. Medical anthropology, material culture, and new directions in medical archaeology

Elisabeth Hsu

The field of medical anthropology has been rapidly expanding since the late seventies, when journals in the field were first published. It has since ramified into many different subjects (Johnson and Sargent 1990), and apart from being taught at anthropology departments and medical schools as part of university education (Good 1994), short-term courses are offered for health personnel, development workers and, recently, even dance therapists, with the aim of improving health care provision. Work in applied medical anthropology is in demand, quite rightly, even though researchers like Taussig (1980) and Young (1982), and many more, have long pointed to the potential danger of medical anthropology becoming a sub-discipline of biomedicine if research is conducted merely with the goal to enhance the effectiveness of health care. All of us bring unquestioned assumptions to our work, yet given the current prestige and centrality of the medical establishment in contemporary society, this seems to be especially true in the area of medicine. In order to be critical and reflective of attitudes to personhood, health and illness, ideas about life and death, and medical practice that is either taken for granted or put off as strange, research in medical anthropology should remain broad in perspective, firmly grounded in social theory and based on long term ethnographic fieldwork. Medical anthropology performed in this way will not only account for the diversity of existent practices but may also, if sensibly applied, ultimately lead to new ways of thinking about, and living with, illness and disability.

Even though material culture, as used in medical practice, has not been a theme much discussed in medical anthropology, insights derived from long-term partici-pation in contemporary medical practice may prove useful to those who, confronted with fragments of material culture, wish to gain an understanding of medicine in the past. As every archaeologist knows, this is an undertaking fraught with dangers because social practice involves material culture in different ways, and can only rarely be traced through written records. To the medical archaeologist it is perhaps an advantage that medical practice often involves specialised artefacts and the application of specific material substances, like drugs. Moreover, remains of human bones and tissue contain information of biological and medical interest. Accordingly, this article will discuss, firstly, the use of artefacts in diagnostics and therapeutics, secondly, some culture-specific forms of illness, which may interest primarily, but not only, palaeopathologists and, thirdly, some selected themes widely discussed in medical anthropology.

PARAPHERNALIA USED IN MEDICAL TREATMENT AND DIAGNOSIS

Medical treatment: material culture plays a conspicuous role in medical treatment. Specific instruments used for minor surgery, obstetrics, bone setting, trepanation, cataract operations, and the like, are found in many cultures, of materials as diverse as stone, bone, bronze and other metals, earthenware, ceramics, porcelain, wood, bamboo, raffia, silk, wax, and many more. Archaeologists have been confident in identifying specific medical instruments such as scalpels, forceps, probes, tweezers, scapuli, the gynaecological speculum or saws for sawing bones, to name just a few of the objects used for medical treatment. In addition, even forms of therapeutics that merely involve the laying on of hands, manual manipulation or massage, may leave material traces, due to the fats and perfumes used.

Most wide-spread in therapeutics is probably the administration of drugs, which can be identified in minute quantities through chemical residue analysis. Some drugs are ingested, some externally applied; the ways in which they are administered vary enormously. The drugs themselves are derived from minerals, plant and animal parts, often through complicated and highly sophisticated procedures of preparation. Sometimes the whole plant or animal is processed into a drug, yet more often people differentiate between the specific effects of its parts – the roots, leaves, petals or whole flowers, fruits, seeds, bark or the blood, nails, hair, skin, various organs like the liver or gall-bladder, and the like. Depending on the mode of preparation, different illnesses are treated. Thus, the bark of the mahogany tree among the Fra Fra in Ghana, if pounded into powder, is considered effective in treating boils on the body surface and, if boiled in water and ingested, is used for treating stomach aches and diarrhoea (workshop on ethnobotany in Northern Ghana, 2000). Not only the modes of administering a drug, but also the procedures of drug preparation can be very complex, and often involve specialised artefacts. There are also cases where the pharmaceutical procedure cannot be distinguished from the culinary one. It is well known that in Chinese cultures there is a close interrelation between the preparation of medicinal decoctions and meals in form of a soup,[1] but this is in no way particular to Chinese cultures and elsewhere one encounters similarly complex procedures of drug preparation and cooking.

In some cases the chemical compounds considered to make these drugs efficacious have been identified; in others the medicines seem to derive their effectiveness primarily from their symbolic value, such as in cases where virility is strengthened through the ingestion of snake blood, rhinoceros-horn powder or tiger-penis liquor (fieldwork in China 1988–89 and Taiwan 1999). Thus, medicines like talismans, certain jewellery (copper rings against headaches, amber necklaces against the pain infants have when teething), charms written onto paper and pasted onto the pillar of one's house, stones placed on altars or also by the door step, liquors, or simply water, sprinkled or spat onto a patient and his or her homestead, are considered to be imbued with protective and/or healing powers. These objects and substances are often not considered efficacious in themselves but only if prepared and used in the right way (for instance, if collected at the right time of day during the right season or if applied while murmuring spells).

Archaeologists are only all too aware that material culture cannot reveal the full complexity of the cultural practices within which they were used, and the fragments unearthed in an archaeological site reveal even less. How could an archaeologist recreate, when confronted with fragments of brush and ink, and perhaps a shard of porcelain in which there are traces of rice-paper ashes, the religious practice of Daoist priests, who wrote with red ink Chinese characters in beautiful calligraphy onto yellow paper, burned them into ashes and had people ingest them with water, thereby spreading their protective and healing powers to the members of their community (Schipper 1993, 73)? Even though some artefacts and substances have a well-defined and specific medical usage, the fieldworker has learned that materials used for medical treatment are often efficacious primarily in a meaning-oriented way.

Diagnosis: modern medicine makes use of very specific instruments and artefacts for establishing a diagnosis through investigation of bodies and corpses, to the extent that patients have much deplored the loss of human contact during a medical consultation. In his classic account, Reiser (1978) shows that it was in the 19th century that techniques of auscultation with the stethoscope, visual technology with lens and microscopes, and laboratory tests were developed within medicine; then, with the invention of electricity, ECGs and EEGs came into fashion, and soon also X-ray photography, and all this altered physicians' interests, shifted their attention away from the patient as a person, and fundamentally altered the nature of the clinical encounter.

Before the rise of diagnostic technology in Europe, the patient's narrative, in combination with the doctor's observation and sometimes a physical examination, formed the basis of diagnosis. At that time, pulse diagnostics which allowed physicians to maintain a very direct and personal contact with their patients, was practised in many different parts of the world. Culture-specific forms of it had been recorded in the third century BC by Hellenistic physicians, and in the second century BC by Chinese ones, and Galen's teachings of the second century AD eventually spread to Arab countries (9th century AD) and India (13th century), and also Meso- and South America (16th–17th centuries), and in each of these places they were modified as they became integrated into local practice.

Although one may think that physicians engaging in pulse diagnostics do nothing more than laying their hands around the wrist of the patient, sometimes barely touching it with their fingertips, and even though the procedure itself would not seem to demand it, pulse diagnostics involves also the use of artefacts, to varying degrees. In contemporary China, for instance, the doctor usually takes the patient's pulse inside a room while being seated on a chair at a table, onto which is laid a little square cushion on which patients lay their hands (Farquhar 1994, 138–140). In nineteenth century Japan doctors would not make use of chairs and tables but characteristically crouched on a mat (Kuriyama 1999, 58–59). Tibetan doctors, by contrast, who work for a Socialist village health care station and undertake to make home visits, engage in a pulse diagnostics that does not involve any artefacts at all. The patients they visit, inside or outside their house, roll back the sleeves, hold the forearm vertically up into their air, and let the doctor put his or her hand around it (Parfionovich *et al* 1992, 54–61). Although all three forms of pulse taking have family resemblances, the artefacts alone – the chairs, table, and little square cushion or the mat or a nothing – provide no clue that all involve a common basic practice.

The above examples show that artefacts used in the medical context may sometimes have a whole variety of different functions, some of which no one would regard as medical – such as the chairs and table – or sometimes only one very specific function – such as the little square cushion. In general, it is fair to say that the more limited the range of a medical artefact's usage, the greater the certainty of there being a specific medical practice and theory. On the other hand, the function of an artefact cannot be deduced solely from its appearance. This seems to apply in particular to artefacts used in the context of divination.

Diagnosis need not only be body and person-oriented (Young 1976), and divination can be viewed as a form of diagnosis and prognosis with highly developed specialised techniques which often, though not always, is used for identifying the cause of the illness outside the body, in social relations or in the spirit world. The artefacts used, such as bundles of stalks of similar height, dice, a handful of cards, heaps of stones with different colours, suggest that they are meant to generate random results; the production of unpredictable events is an important feature of many divinatory practices. However, sometimes artefacts involved in divination are unrecognisable as such, for instance, who would recognise the use of two wooden sticks for the termite oracle among the Azande that Evans Pritchard (1937, 356) describes? Who would think that a gourd rattle found in a building identified as a 'divining hut' and two grass sheaves in its centre were used within the same divination séance? The former is shaken rhythmically until the diviner goes into a state of crying, belching, growling and snorting where spirits start speaking to him about the cause of the client's problem and the latter represents the male and female aspect of 'the divination thing', which in those moments sometimes speaks through the medium of the diviner to his clients directly (Whyte 1997, 61–64). In those cases, as in many others, it is the spatial closeness of the artefacts and the context in which they are found which provide clues for the archaeologist. It would be futile to try to derive their combined use in social practice from their appearance alone.

In this volume David Zeitlyn discusses a divinatory practice among the Mambila in Cameroun, which shows dangers of instantly ascribing function to structure: leaves and a spider are put on the sandy bottom of a pot, the pot is then covered, and the spider is expected to move the leaves when it crawls about; the position of these leaves to each other determines the response to the questions posed to this oracle. Some of these leaves have distinctive colours and forms drawn onto them, but Zeitlyn tells us that for the Mambila these symbols on the surface of the leaves have no significance in divination.[2] It is important for the archaeologist to acknowledge that, among the Mambila, the drawings on these leaves nowadays have nothing to do with their function in divinatory practice. Although conspicuous in appearance, these drawings have no function.

Diviners do not only use artefacts marked by a certain regularity, like two sticks of the same length, or dice with six identical square surfaces, to produce random results. They also may investigate natural phenomena and focus on irregularities: the shape of clouds; the occurrence of lunar and solar eclipses or the appearance of other unusual stellar events such as comets or supernovas; bird flight and other animal behaviour. Diviners may interpret these events in the universe at large as relevant to the events in the human realm; changes in the former, the macrocosm, are conceived as analogous to those in the latter, the microcosm. Such divinatory practices are known to us not only through ethnographic accounts, but also through written records of the actors themselves and artefacts that often consist of charts of numbers and other signs, arranged in an order based on numerological calculations. The chart used for the Naxi frog horoscope (Fig. 1.1), for instance, shows pictographs of the four directions and the corresponding elements of wood, fire, metal and water and, in circular alignment concentric to those, the twelve animals of the zodiac, and in the centre, which corresponds to the element earth, there is a needle pierced through a frog, which looks as though it were swirled around like a compass needle (card at exhibition, see Oppitz and Hsu 1998). Charts of a similar kind are also used in other forms of medical diagnostics, which straddle the boundary between divination and diagnostics, such as inspection of the urine, iris, tongue, complexion, or also, the feeling of the pulse mentioned above.

In summary, medical diagnosis and treatment often involves the use of artefacts and *materia medica*, and this has made possible extensive documentation of medical paraphernalia. The archaeologist interested in exactly how these were applied in medical practice can learn from anthropology that their preparation and application involves complicated procedures, which are difficult, if not impossible, to detect solely from the study of objects. While in general one may guess the function of an artefact from its appearance and structure, one has to bear in mind that not every structure has function for the practice investigated, even if it is as conspicuous as the symbols drawn on the leaves of the Mambila spider oracle. In addition, similarity in social practice, such as pulse diagnostics in different cultures, need not be directly evident from the material culture that it involves. On the other hand, artefacts that initially seem to have no bearing with each other can be shown to have been used within one and the same medical or divinatory procedure due to their spatial vicinity and the context in which they are found.

PALAEOPATHOLOGY AND CULTURE-SPECIFIC FORMS OF ILLNESS

Medical archaeologists have long been interested in the epidemiological profile of ancient populations and the kind of diseases from which people suffered. Features such as deformations in bone structure and teeth, unusual tissue (in mummies for instance), and the chemical composition of hair can all inform us about the general status of health among a population, on their nutrition and the ailments and diseases from which they suffered. Medical anthropology emphasizes that the illnesses people experience are not merely biological processes; culture always plays a role in shaping them.

Elisabeth Hsu

Figure 1.1. Naxi frog horoscope.

Illness is neither a purely biologically determined nor an entirely culturally constructed event, and in order to draw awareness to this, terms like 'disease' and 'illness' were coined. This was twenty years ago when medical anthropology had to bring across a new message to the medical world, and the definition of these two terms, which differed between authors, sparked off extended and partly futile debates. As a result, many medical anthropologists today refuse to acknowledge the significance once imputed into these terms and many now use the terms 'sickness', 'illness', and 'disease' interchangeably. It has to be borne in mind that in contrast to the difference anthropologists make between 'sex' and 'gender' in gender studies, where 'sex' refers to the biologically given anatomy of being either male or female and 'gender' to the culturally constructed form of being man or woman, it would be absurd in medical anthropology to make the distinction between 'disease' as the biologically given and 'illness' as the culturally constructed. And yet this continues to be taught in many introductory classes on medical anthropology.[3]

A variety of physiological processes are particularly prone to being reinforced through the meaning that is attributed to them. For instance, heart palpitations tend to get worse if such palpitations are considered indicative of a more serious condition. Thus, heart palpitations that may ordinarily occur when a woman takes the contraceptive pill have been shown to lead to heart distress among women in Iran, so-called *natiye qalb* (Good 1977). Another frequently recorded example of a physiological process which, if stigmatised, can be reinforced is increased vaginal discharge or leucorrhoea. Discharge need not always be a sign of an acute inflammation or a highly pathological condition like cancer; it may occasionally be released in larger quantities for no apparent reason, and can become heavy in stressful life situations. In Korea in the 1950s marriage contracts were dissolved because leucorrhoea was considered indicative of the 'cold', a primarily bodily condition which could extend to emotional coldness and sexual frigidity (Kim *et al.* 1982). Likewise, occasional nocturnal emissions rarely alarm a man in the West, yet in many Asian contexts they are highly stigmatised; men suffering from so-called 'semen loss' are typically associated with symptoms of lethargy and a general loss of vitality (Obeyesekere 1985). In the early eighties it was fashionable to call these conditions 'culture-bound syndromes', a term that has since been criticised for its emphasis on 'otherness', which would mask the fact that all pathological conditions are culture-bound. The reason these examples are raised here is that bodily processes, which can suddenly occur and disappear again, sometimes without being noticed, can become reinforced and pathologised by the culture-specific meaning and stigma with which people imbue them.

One is inclined to believe that the meaning-making process affects particularly mental conditions. However, it is important to recognise that not only mental conditions, but also somatic ones, such as infectious diseases, can manifest themselves and be experienced in entirely different ways depending on the cultural context or on the social standing of a person in that culture. Influenza, which sends well-nourished citizens in our latitudes into bed for only a few days can kill if people lack sufficient sheltering and nutrition, a phenomenon that often depends on income and/or class more than anything else. This effect is quite distinct from the biological factors, which made it to a lethal disease among many indigenous peoples before they had had contact with Europeans. Likewise, tuberculosis as experienced by the nobility in 19th century in Europe (Sontag 1979) and as a disease of poverty and 'structural violence' (Farmer 1998), in southern Africa, for instance, is hardly experienced as the same illness event. This is especially the case now where AIDS patients often suffer from tuberculosis, and 'tuberculosis' tends to be the term which is used as a substitute for the more stigmatised 'AIDS' (fieldwork in Tanzania, 2001). It is not just the meaning-making process that can shape physiological and pathological processes, but also the nutritional status and environmental factors, which in turn often depends on political stability, economic factors, climate and ecology. Many diseases manifest themselves not only in culture-specific, but also in class-specific or population-specific ways.

Some conditions are pathologised in some cultural contexts and sanctified in others. Anorexia nervosa is one such condition. It is well-documented that in the northern hemisphere anorexia nervosa arose in an epidemic-like fashion during the eighties, and it is presented as a typical phenomenon of the 'body politic': bodily processes of an individual – starving and weight loss – are an expression of invisible forces of social control, triggered off and maintained through expectations about gender roles. Admittedly, becoming ill with anorexia does not affect women only and is a complex process that involves individual psychology, genetic constitution and family constellations. Yet, its epidemic-like occurrence cannot be denied to be culture-bound and gender-specific (Bordo 1993).

In mediaeval Europe, there also were women who consciously went into prolonged states of starvation. They did it in a religious context, and their starving was viewed as a form of asceticism, which was interpreted as purifying, enabling them to transcend their worldly boundedness (Bynum 1987). It would be wrong to speak in that case of 'anorexia nervosa', for that form of starvation and weight loss was not medicalised, but sanctified. Here it is noteworthy that elsewhere too, in China for instance, self-starvation and weight loss have been pathologised in the medical context, and sanctified in the context of basically religiously motivated 'self-cultivation practices'. Thus, the *Yellow Emperor's Inner Canon*, which was first compiled in the first century BC or AD, describes a condition of starvation and weight loss as pathological.[4] Yet, in Daoist circles of Late Imperial China, manuals were printed which instructed people, women in particular, on how to engage in bodily techniques of so-called 'inner alchemy' in order to reduce their weight and breast size, stop their menses and attain the state of so-called 'pure *yang*' (Despeux 1990)

It would be absurd to refer to all four of the above processes of starvation and weight loss as 'anorexia nervosa', since each form of starvation manifests itself in different cultural settings quite apart from being conceptualised differently by the actors themselves. It would be even more absurd to consider 'anorexia nervosa', which is a *biomedical* notion, an underlying *biological* process, which only in the non-Western contexts is shaped by culture. While some may find it useful to refer to biomedical nosological entities as 'diseases', it is important to see that these disease entities are, just like others, culturally constructed; the biomedical term 'anorexia nervosa', for instance, dates to the 19th century. These examples show that palaeopathologists, in interpreting the health of populations, have the exciting task of considering their findings in the light of what is known about the manifestation of illness and health in the culture in question.

Themes in medical anthropology

One of the prime reasons that may have motivated researchers to engage in what some now call 'interpretive medical anthropology' and to investigate, in particular, the meaning-making processes surrounding questions of health and illness is that this meaning-making process is often crucial for the outcome of medical treatment. Successful treatment often depends not only on the biomedically ascertained efficacy of treatment but more importantly on the patient and his or her entourage's perception of the changes and transformations effected both in the patient as a person and in interpersonal relations.

'Therapeutic efficacy' versus 'therapeutic success'

This is not to deny that the efficacy of treatment can be biomedically ascertained (for instance, through double-blind randomised clinical trials). However, treatment that is clinically ascertained as biomedically efficacious need not always enhance the well-being of the patient in question. Some differentiate between the patient's 'subjective' experience of the treatment and its assessment with 'objective' criteria ('objective' meaning that which is acceptable as 'objective' to the clinician). Such a distinction is, however, unsatisfactory in that it accounts for the problem in a rather one-dimensional way. In particular, it underplays the importance of the entirety which forms the patient's lived experience (Csordas 1993), and his or her social entourage and cultural embeddings, which play an important role in shaping the outcome of the treatment (e.g. Lindenbaum and Lock 1993).

The 'success' of an artist is well-known to be a phenomenon of fashion and timeliness that may depend on interpersonal dynamics, and social and cultural factors, more than on anything else, the 'quality' of his or her work itself being an aspect of his or her success that is difficult to assess. Similarly, one may view the 'success' of a treatment as being dependent not only on the chemical activities of the ingredients of a drug in a diseased body or on the effectiveness of words on a patient, but on a whole host of interpersonal dynamics, as well as on the macro-social context. These may not only be decisive in shaping the patient's physiological/pathological processes and his or her subjective experience of the treatment, but also in the evaluation of the treatment by others who accordingly will treat the patient as ill, disabled, handicapped, or just normal (Hsu 1996).

The above distinction between biomedically ascertained 'therapeutic efficacy' and 'therapeutic success' appears in the first instance reminiscent of Arthur Kleinman's (1980, 82) distinction between the 'curing of disease' and the 'healing of illness', the latter being attained through 'the provision of personal and social meaning for the life problems created by sickness'. However, this distinction between curing and healing draws on a contrast of the biological and the psycho-social which implicitly seems to invoke the artificial distinction between 'disease' as a biological event and 'illness' as a psycho-social one. The distinction made here between efficacy and success differentiates between the frameworks of evaluation applied; the former is biomedical, the latter social scientific.

The notion of 'placebo' and its limitations

Although not all treatment consists of the administration of drugs, many people speak of 'placebo' as though it were useful to evaluate the outcome of medical treatment by focusing on the effectiveness of drugs. As every general practitioner knows, the effectiveness of a drug cannot be reduced to the pharmacodynamics and pharmacology of the substances in a drug alone and one may address the problem by proposing to assess a so-called 'total drug effect' and accordingly investigate, apart from the chemical activity of the drug's ingredients, its appearance and packaging (its colour, shape, size, texture, smell, etc.); the dispenser, beliefs about his status and his/her belief in the drug; the recipient and his/her beliefs; and the micro- and macro-context in which the drug is consumed. The 'total drug effect' is thus composed of the drug's chemical effect and the positive or negative effects of belief on physical, physiological and social well-being; in short, the positive 'placebo' or negative 'nocebo' effects (Helman 1990, 170).

The above way of accounting for the clinical encounter from the point of view of the drug is enticing for its simplicity and clarity. It differentiates between 'real' as opposed to 'believed' effects, and testifies to a worldview which gives priority to the reality of processes that can be assessed through the methods of the biomedical sciences. Medicine, which is all about the 'real' world, thereby delegates to anthropology the task of accounting for 'belief'. Needless to say that this is a rather medico-centric way of assessing the effects of treatment. The placebo effect is 'noise' in the process of testing new drugs, a nuisance for the medical scientist. 'Placebo-induced therapeutic changes are specifically those successes which are illegitimate for official scientific medicine' (Sullivan 1993). The history of the notion 'placebo' shows how the term was appropriated and modified in the course of consolidating biomedicine as a profession; it was a tool for institutionalising a normative medicine over heterodox practices and unconventional healers (Kaptchuk 1998).

Rather than belittling 'placebo', one could feel inclined to appropriate the term for defining a field of anthropological inquiry. However, by doing so, the anthropologist unnecessarily restricts research to a domain artificially delimited by medical concerns; a medicine's effects on a bodily state, particularly if the effects are instant, may be crucial for assessing a social interaction, such as the process of building up the patient's trust in the practitioner. Moreover, since the term 'placebo' tends to be associated primarily with the psychology of the patient and 'belief', it bears the danger of covering up the importance of institutional conditions, financial constraints, and social dynamics for the outcome of treatment. Therefore many anthropologists avoid using the term.

Patient-practitioner relations

It is indeed the case that medical treatment often involves the administration of drugs, or the use of other objects like the talismans, which are considered to transmit and ensure well-being. Yet, as mentioned earlier, there are also other aspects of the clinical encounter, which contribute to a successful therapeutic intervention and these also involve material culture. Thus, the success of treatment depends largely on successful communication between practitioners and patients, whatever that may imply: it may be obtained through using a common vocabulary which typically indigenous healers and their clientele tend to share more than biomedical physicians and their patients do, or it may happen without depending on the exchange of words, but on certain gestures, like the laying on of hands.

Patient-practitioner relations are typically marked by some form of inequality; practitioners generally enjoy high status, and this is the case not only for biomedical doctors, but also for shamans and healers. The status of doctors, shamans or healers is often evident in the material culture that surrounds them: the dress worn (from a shaman's 'armour' to a physician's white coat), the location inhabited (from shrines and cult centres to charity hospitals, clinics, leprosaria, and the like), and the medical instruments or religious paraphernalia used (from crystals and swords to the pens and pagers). One would expect that this manifestation of status in material goods is meant to influence credibility and trust, which in itself can work towards the success of treatment. For medical archaeologists this means that not only medical instruments and drugs, but also the location of healing, clothes and other status symbols become relevant in their account of the medical practices investigated.

Patients and practitioners form a relationship that 'is not dyadic, though it may appear to be so' (Budd and Sharma 1994, 3); for they are actors among a larger group of people. Doctors have assistants, students, or nurses, who surround them; shamans have helpers, human or animal; patients rarely seek medical advice on their own. Often they are accompanied by at least one person. Sometimes they are represented by someone else and they themselves are never seen by the healer. Frequently, issues of medical concern become a matter of discussion among various people in the patient's entourage – Janzen (1978) spoke of the 'therapy managing group'. Among healers, the healer's assistant or wife often fulfils tasks essential for the treatment. Where his status demands that he always appear humorous and kind, she may be the one who quarrels with the patients, if necessary and ensures that they do what he requires (Hsu 1999, 60). Or while a healer is welcoming and friendly to every client, his wife complains how he is being laboured and overworked (Roseman 1992, 76–78). Or while the healer is standing and listening to the spirits of the clients in trance and interprets their wailing, his wife who seated next to the clients has the task of discussing details in the social conflict which brought them to the healer (fieldwork in Tanzania, 2001). This complementarity between wife and healer may manifest itself also in items of material culture like clothes, masks, or the positioning of the two within the arena in which the healing ritual is performed.

In summary, treatment involves more than patient and practitioner. Doctors and healers are often imbued with such authority to the extent that their dependency on their entourage is not seen and is often neglected, even in ethnographic accounts. The importance of the patients' social entourage for the outcome of treatment is, by contrast, widely acknowledged although patient culture still tends to be insufficiently researched. For the medical archaeologist this means that both the medical specialist's paraphernalia as well as patient culture are worth investigation.

'Medical pluralism' and inequalities in the distribution of medical services

Rarely is a serious illness treated in only one encounter. Patients seek treatment from a whole variety of different practitioners; they may seek their advice in sequence and also simultaneously. The notion 'medical pluralism' counters the biomedical profession's claim to 'exclusive competence' in health care (Freidson 1970), legitimates other medical practices as based in coherent 'systems' of thought (Leslie 1976), and points to the wide range of choices patients have, when seeking for treatment (Nichter 1996). Medical practitioners span a wide range of activities, from the herbalist, who knows a single recipe for a single problem, to spirit mediums, shamans and learned doctors (Leslie and Young 1992). In general, doctors and healers are aware of other doctors and healers, and may occasionally refer a patient to each other, yet close co-operation between doctors and healers is very rare indeed (Last and Chavunduka 1986).

While some have emphasized medical pluralism, others have pointed to inequalities in the provision of health services. This applies not only to the distribution of biomedical resources and institutions, as particularly authors with a Marxist orientation have pointed out (e.g. Waitzkin 1982), but also to the distribution of indigenous forms of health care. Choices are restricted not only by cultural outlook, class, or status but also by geographical locality; in societies with distinctive urban centres, urban-rural divisions are blatant. Some consider diversification, specialisation and uneven distribution of different medical practices an exclusively modern phenomenon, but others have documented it for antiquity (Lloyd 1983). It is to be expected that in any given society more than one type of medical specialist was at work, and that archaeology can reflect this.

Health and everyday life

So far, medicine has been presented as being concerned primarily with treatment, and the issues discussed above have been motivated by a therapy-oriented outlook. However, life-style and diet and many other issues that fall in biomedicine under the rubric of 'preventive medicine and hygiene', are just as much a matter of concern to medical anthropologists. Social tensions, as sometimes evident in the spatial positioning of the parties involved, may lead to the victimisation of single individual. Deviant behaviour and crime can become medicalised: totalitarian states have a tendency to turn 'bad' to 'mad', and the 'civilising process' has more than once contributed to the instigation of witch-hunts which largely went against 'wise women's' knowledge.

If one starts thinking of daily 'self-care', diet, and hygiene, self-presentation through dress, ornamentation, tattoo, and hair style, one moves into domains of everyday culture, from combs and tooth picks to soaps and perfumes, mirrors, water supplies, drains and sewers, cooking pots, and other objects of daily life. Not only ritual space and layout, but also architectural design, such as the direction in which houses are positioned, is often motivated by ideas of fortune and misfortune, health and illness (taking account of predominant winds may be synonymous with an awareness of illness-bringing demons). In this way, material culture of everyday life can be seen as relating to issues of medical concern. Archaeologists know that this material culture of daily life is often found in graves; the treatment of the dead – whether they are mummified or crouching in a cabinet, whether covered with jade armour or thrown into a ditch – reveals not only attitudes to death and the other world but also ideas about life and personhood in everyday culture.

Conclusion

Specialised instruments for diagnosis and treatment or bones and teeth have long attracted attention from medical archaeologists and palaeopathologists, and the above themes discussed in medical anthropology may add new perspectives. Examples were raised from observation of highly sophisticated drug preparation to discussion of culture- and class-specific forms of illness to explorations of the evaluation of treatment. Many more could be listed. Medical anthropology emphasizes that it is the meaning people attach to their actions which matters, and this meaning that people attribute to social practice motivates also their production and use of artefacts.

Notes

1 The following recipe quoted from a manual of the late 3rd century BC, unearthed at Mawangdui in mainland China, was used for treating a urine retention: 'To treat it, boil three *sheng* (litres) of black soy beans in three ... of fine gruel vinegar. Cook rapidly. When it bubbles, stop the fire. When the bubbling subsides, cook again, stopping after it bubbles for the third time. Sieve to obtain the liquid. Use one portion of oysters and three of finely pounded poisonous *jin* (Aconitum sp.? or Corydalis sp.?), altogether two substances –. Take one three-fingered pinch reaching to the knuckles, put it into lukewarm gruel vinegar, ... drink it. (Harper 1998, 253, with modifications).

2 From a historical point of view, the similarity of these symbols compared to others found among the more southern Yamba, among whose divinatory practice they may have had some function, would suggest that the Mambila copied the ornamentation of the leaves from the Yamba without knowing for what it was used.

3 Some may find it useful to speak of 'diseases' when one refers to the biomedical understanding of a pathological condition, i.e. 'disease' refers not to the biological event itself but the biomedical understanding of events that both biological and social processes shape. Researchers who use the term 'disease' in this way are aware that biomedicine, despite its highly sophisticated language for accounting for illness events, is like any other science culturally embedded; and that the biomedical understanding of 'disease' is thus ultimately also a cultural construct. This definition of 'disease' that is currently most frequently used was already formulated by Gilbert Lewis (1975, 129); the debates in the 1980s were largely engendered by Arthur Kleiman's (1980) use of the term.

4 'The Yellow Emperor said: "There are cases where a person is prone to hunger yet has no appetite, what kind of *qi* brings them about?" Qi Bo said: "If the essential *qi* unites with the spleen, hot *qi* stays within the stomach. When there is stomach heat, then it devours the grains. There is a wasting of the grains, hence the patient is prone to hunger. When stomach *qi* inverts and rises, then the stomach pit gets cold. Therefore one has no appetite"' (quote from *Ling shu* 80).

Bibliography

Bordo, S. 1993 *Unbearable weight: feminism, western culture and the body*, Berkeley: University of California Press.

Budd, S. and Sharma, U. 1994 *The healing bond: the patient-practitioner relationship and therapeutic responsibility*, London: Routledge.

Bynum, C.W. 1987 *Holy feast, holy fast: the religious significance of food in Medieval women*, Berkeley: University of California Press.

Csordas, T.J. (ed.) 1994 *Embodiment and experience: the existential ground of culture and self*, Cambridge: Cambridge University Press.

Despeux, C. 1990 *Immortelles de la Chine ancienne. Taoisme et alchimie féminine*, Puiseaux: Pardès.

Evans-Pritchard, E.E. 1937 *Witchcraft, oracles and magic among the Azande*, Oxford: Oxford University Press.

Farmer, P. 1998 *Infections and inequalities: the modern plagues*, Berkeley: University of California Press.

Farquhar, J. 1994 *Knowing practice: the clinical encounter of Chinese medicine*, Boulder: Westview Press.

Freidson, E. 1975 *The profession of medicine: a study in the sociology of applied knowledge*, New York: Dodd, Mead.

Good, B.J. 1994 *Medicine, rationality, and experience: an anthropological perspective*, Cambridge: Cambridge University Press.

Good, B.J. 1977 'The heart of what's the matter. The semantics of illness in Iran' *Culture, Medicine, and Psychiatry* 1, 25–58.

Harper, D. 1998 *Early Chinese medical literature: the Mawangdui medical manuscripts*, London: Routledge.

Helman, C.G. 1990 *Culture, health and illness*, 2nd ed. Oxford: Butterworth-Heinemann.

Hsu, E. 1996 'The polyglot practitioner: towards acceptance of different approaches to treatment evaluation' pp. 37–53 in S. Gosvig Olesen and E. Høg (eds) *Studies in alternative therapy III. Communication in and about alternative therapies*, Odense: Odense University Press.

Hsu, E. 1999 *The transmission of Chinese medicine*, Cambridge: Cambridge University Press.

Janzen, J.M. 1978 *The quest for therapy in Lower Zaire*, Berkeley: University of California Press.

Johnson, T.M. and Sargent, C.F. (eds) 1990 *Medical anthropology: a handbook of theory and method*. Westport, CT: Greenwood.

Kaptchuk, T. 1998 'Intentional ignorance: a history of blind assessment and placebo controls in medicine' *Bulletin of the History of Medicine* 72, 389–433.

Kim, Y.K. *et al.* 1982 '"Naeng": a Korean folk illness' pp. 129–149 in H.J. Diesfeld (ed.) *Medizin in Entwicklungsländern*, Bern: Peter Lang.

Kleinman, A. 1980 *Patients and healers in the context of culture: an exploration of the borderland between anthropology, medicine and psychiatry*, Berkeley: University of California Press.

Kuriyama, S. 1999 *The expressiveness of the body and the divergence of Greek and Chinese Medicine*, New York: Zone Books.

Last, M. and Chavunduka, G.L. (eds) 1986 *The professionalisation of African medicine*, Manchester: Manchester University Press.

Leslie, C. and Young, A. (eds) 1992 *Paths to Asian medical knowledge*, Berkeley: University of California Press.

Leslie, C. 1976 *Asian medical systems: a comparative study*, Berkeley: University of California Press.

Lewis, G. 1975 *Knowledge of illness in a Sepik society: a study of the Gnau, New Guinea*, London: Athlone.

Lindenbaum, S. and Lock, M. (eds) 1993 *Knowledge, power, and practice: the anthropology of medicine and everyday life*, Berkeley: University of California Press.

Lloyd, G.E.R. 1983 *Science, folklore and ideology: studies in the life sciences in Ancient Greece*, Cambridge: Cambridge University Press.

Nichter, M. 1996 'Popular perceptions of medicine: a south Indian case study' pp. 203–249 in M. Nichter and M. Nichter (eds), *Anthropology and international health: Asian case studies*, Amsterdam: Gordon & Breach.

Obeyesekere, G. 1985 'Depression, Buddhism, and the work of culture in Sri Lanka' pp. 134–152 in A. Kleinman and B. Good (eds) *Culture and depression: studies in the anthropology and cross-cultural psychiatry of affect and disorder*, Berkeley: California University Press.

Oppitz M. and Hsu E. (eds) 1998 *Naxi and Moso ethnography. Kin, rites, pictographs*, Zürich: Völkermuseum.

Parfionovich, I.M., Dorje, G., Meyer, F., and Sans-rgyas-rgya-mtsho, S. (1653–1705) 1992 *Tibetan medical paintings: illustrations to the Blue Beryl treatise of Sangye Gyamtso (1653–1705)*, London: Serindia.

Reiser, S.J. 1978 *Medicine and the reign of technology*, Cambridge: Cambridge University Press.

Roseman, M. 1991 *Healing sounds from the malaysian rainforest: Temiar music and medicine*, Berkeley: University of California Press.

Schipper, K. [1982] 1993 *The Taoist body*, Berkeley: University of California Press.

Sontag, S. 1979 *Illness as metaphor*, New York: Farrar, Straus & Giroux.

Sullivan, M.D. 1993 'Placebo controls and epistemic control in orthodox medicine' *Journal of Medicine and Philosophy* 18, 213–231.

Taussig, M.T. 1980 'Reification and the consciousness of the patient' *Social Science and Medicine* 14B, 3–13.

Waitzkin, H. 1983 *The second sickness: contradictions of capitalist health care*, New York: Free Press, London: Collier Macmillan.

Whyte, S.R. 1997 *Questioning misfortune: the pragmatics of uncertainty in Eastern Uganda*, Cambridge: Cambridge University Press.

Young, A. 1976 'Internalizing and externalizing medical belief systems: an Ethiopian example' *Social Science and Medicine* 10, 147–156.

Young, A. 1982 'The anthropologies of illness and sickness' *Annual Review of Anthropology* 11, 257–285.

2. Diagnosing some ills: the archaeology, literature and history of Roman medicine

Patricia Anne Baker

INTRODUCTION

Those interested in Roman medicine are fortunate in that there survives a variety of medically related material in the literary and archaeological records, from which one is able to make informed interpretations on the subject. However, when it comes to the interpretation of the material remains, archaeologists interested in Roman medicine generally tend to narrow the focus of their scholarship to two main areas of consideration: one being the discussion of buildings that have been identified as *valetudinaria,* or hospitals, in Roman fortifications (e.g. Charlesworth 1976; Dolmans 1992; Dyczek 1995; Jettner 1966; Press 1988); the second, and seemingly more popular area, concentrates on the identification and description of objects that have been recognised as Roman-style medical tools (e.g. Braadbaart 1994a, 1994b; Bliquez 1985; Bliquez and Oleson 1995; Gilson 1978, 1981; Jackson 1988, 114–124, 1994a, 1994b, 1995; Künzl 1983, 15–29, 1996; Milne 1907). It is the latter which shall be the focus of discussion for this paper. It must be mentioned here that the terms *Roman medicine* and *Roman-style medical tools* used throughout this paper are not intended to imply that medical care was the same in all areas of the empire. The term Roman medicine is merely used to indicate medical treatment during the Roman period. Whilst the term Roman-style medical instruments refers to medical tools found in the provinces that are similar to those from Roman Italy, no implication should be made that the uses and the meanings of the tools were the same across the Roman empire. What is extraordinary about this particular sphere of archaeology is that in spite of the concentration on the artefactual remains, there is hardly any mention or awareness of current scholarly theories on material culture. Through studies of material culture it has been demonstrated in other areas of archaeology, such as prehistory and post-medieval archaeology, that it is possible to gain a strong insight into perceptions of past societies by the study of the context of material remains (e.g. Hodder 1982, 2000; Jones 1997, 129, 131; Shanks and Tilley 1987, 79–80, 107). Although contextual studies can provide archaeologists with detailed information not available in the literature about specific finds, the papers on medical tools never offer comment on depositional interpretation with the exception of perhaps mentioning the provenance. When the instruments are discussed from known archaeological sites they are simply listed with possible descriptions mentioning their function as presented in the Greco-Roman medical literature (e.g. Deringer 1954; Döderlein 1973; Gilson 1978, 1981; Hauff 1993/94; Künzl 1983). These studies remain deeply entrenched in their understanding of instrument function on the basis of the information provided in the written record. The answer to why this area of archaeology continues to be examined in this manner is clearly stated by Salazar (2000, 230) who says in her book on the literature of war wounds in antiquity:

> 'In addition to the literary evidence, there is also a fairly large amount of archaeological evidence. Although on its own this material would be open to numerous, contrasting, conjectures, it can be used along with literary evidence and in comparison with it.'

So the view is, that on its own, archaeological evidence is inadequate. To be fair, Salazar is not a trained archaeologist; yet her statement is consistent with the general belief in classical studies, as has been pointed out by Shanks (1996, 154), that material remains are somehow secondary to the literature. Even if the two sources of evidence demonstrate opposing points of view, as Salazar says they sometimes do, her comment still insinuates that without literary sources to support the material remains there is no point in interpreting meanings from artefacts. The narrowness of this approach is obvious because the literature does not tell us everything about past societies, it is biased to the author and it seems fair to say that even as a source of material culture the literature is open to just as many 'numerous, contrasting conjectures'.

If material remains are assessed within their own context more can be understood about their functions, meanings and role in social practices. This idea that material culture is the commonly quoted 'hand maiden to history', meaning that it can only be supported by historical evidence, has long since been argued against by historical archaeologists (e.g. Deetz 1977; Johnson 1999, 154; Morris 2000). For example, in the 1970s Deetz discussed the problems with relying on literary sources for the one and only interpretation of archaeological remains in Colonial America. It was pointed out that often the written evidence only provided a small or partial amount of information concerning life in Colonial times (Deetz 1977, 10). Quite often mundane events and culturally understood actions are not recorded. Consequently, another means of gaining an awareness of practices and societal or cultural cognition is to scrutinise the non-literary genre of remains to discern meanings about past societies. Though, a word of warning must be given and that is not to ignore the literature all together, but to use it critically. For example, in reference to material remains, Morris states that classical literature provides a wealth of descriptions about the purpose and significance of many objects that are readily found and identifiable in the archaeological record (2000, 26). It is possible that an archaeologist might accept one idea presented in writing about a particular artefact, when there may be other literary sources that state something completely different. The numerous meanings represented in the written works indicate the probability that there may be more meanings and understandings about an object that have not been discussed in the literature, and these might be discerned from the archaeological evidence. Thus, one should aim to distinguish meanings from the literature, but to realise that not necessarily all the ideas about a particular object can be gained from this one means of context.

A further difficulty with basing archaeological studies of medical instruments on the literary sources alone is that the conclusions formed tend to be built upon sources that were written by doctors or people familiar with medicine who lived in Italy, Greece and the eastern Mediterranean (e.g. Celsus, Galen, the Hippocratic writers, Soranus and Paul of Aegina). From these sources generalisations are made about the entire empire. The difficulty with this is that no account is made for the fact that many areas in the Roman empire where the medical instruments have been found are essentially proto-historic, such as the provinces of Britain, Gaul and Spain as well as those on the Rhine and Danube. These are areas where Latin and/or Greek, the languages of the extant medical texts, were not necessarily always spoken or read. It is also possible, and should be taken into consideration, that many people practising medicine may not have had the ability to read (Galen *De libris propriis* 19.9 K). Nonetheless, there seems to be an underlying assumption, though nothing is clearly stated, in archaeological scholarship, that all Roman doctors would have been skilled in reading. Or if the illiteracy problem is pointed out, as Jackson (1995, 190) does, the issue is not considered beyond the statement. No questions are raised about whether or not conceivably illiterate doctors might have had the opportunity to learn information provided in the texts. More specifically, considerations are not proffered about how an illiterate doctor might have understood the use of an instrument in accordance to how classical medical writers described them. Nor is a provision made for the possibility of variations in the therapies prescribed and treated by doctors across the empire if they may not have had access to, or understood, what was written in the medical texts (Braadbaart 1994a, 1994b; Jackson 1988, 114–24, 1995; Künzl 1983, 15–29, 1996; Milne 1907).

Another related issue to be addressed here is that of medical teaching. There was no regulated medical teaching and training in the classical world. There were many ways in which a person could have become a doctor: some might have visited the medical libraries at Cos and Alexandria, whilst others may have been trained as an apprentice (Drabkin 1944). The absence of regulated or standardised teaching again alerts one to the likelihood of differences in medical practice across the empire. Similar to the problems with reading, no ideas are suggested or analysis made about what the differences in teaching meant to the use of medical tools. It is not simply the question of how the knowledge of medicine was disseminated, but, more significantly, who was to have access to medical information. In Greco-Roman medicine there almost seems to be an expectation that knowledge was open to the public and that information would have been fairly standardised, because we are aware that there were libraries and bodies of medical literature available in the Mediterranean and assume that they were accessible to anyone interested. On the other hand, information is not always intended for common consideration; medical knowledge is sometimes only in the control of a select few people. One demonstration of this surreptitious approach to the disclosure of medical knowledge is seen amongst the healers of the Azande, a group of people living in the Sudan and Zaire. Evans-Pritchard observed that the Azande taught their knowledge of healing practices to students piecemeal over a long period of time, and what was being taught was considered knowledge only to be given to a select few, rather than open to everyone (1976 [1937], 90–1). There is no intention to make a direct analogy from this anthropological example to the Roman world, as this is from a society with very different views and practices of healing than those we might expect of Roman medicine. It does, however, force one to consider whether such practices might have occurred in medical treatment in different areas and perhaps different periods of time in the Roman empire. Even if the information is too scarce to support some possibilities, nevertheless it is interesting to speculate how ideas were passed on in the empire. Perhaps doctors/healers in certain societies of the provinces did not consider healing to be open to everyone and they endeavoured to keep knowledge of it secret. It may even have been that the practices of folk healers living in the Mediterranean, where it is believed 'rational' or 'scientific' medical information was widely available, did not allow their techniques to become common knowledge. These suggestions are simply provided for the consideration of other possibilities in the dissemination of medical ideas and practices. In an area where illiteracy was common and no standardisation of medical teaching is known, one should not expect uniformity in medical practice and the use of medical tools. Rather, one should bear in mind that these differences most likely indicate a variety of medical understandings and practices, and differential access to medical information across the Roman empire.

RELIABILITY OF THE MEDICAL LITERATURE

Since the identification and function of instruments are tied to the literature, it must also seriously be considered whether the sources used to identify the instruments are accurate. For the scholarship on instrument descriptions, sources related to the topic of medical care such as Celsus, Galen, the Hippocratic writers, Oribasius, Paul of Aegina and Soranus are frequently consulted and used as handbooks for tool identification. It is appropriate that these sources should be consulted as they do provide evidence for a function, or a couple of functions, of Roman-style medical instruments. Morris (2000, 6–7, 27) points out that ancient literature is a form of material evidence, but one that must be critically appraised by the archaeologists who use it for the identification of artefactual remains. Those using the sources should not simply apply the information presented in the literature, but be familiar with criticisms in philology and historiography. Even if an archaeologist is not a specialist in a particular area they are using to support their argument, such as classical literature, it is beneficial for one to at least have an awareness of problems faced in that particular field. The same, too, can be said for philologists and historians using archaeological material. The more one is willing to delve into the scholarship of the source material one is using, the more critical judgements will be about the past.

Yet, as mentioned, there is a lack of critical discussion about the accuracy and relevancy of the literature being used for instrument identification. A potential explanation for this lack of rigorous interpretation is that the functions of the tools are described in the literature in a practical manner, as they deal with surgical procedures and not the more abstract philosophical discussions on the functions and anatomy of the body and the curing of disease. The practicality of the descriptions lend themselves to be understood as objective and functional, and are taken by scholars as a 'hard' science, or fact. This viewpoint is likely to be related to modern appreciations of science in western societies. Science-based ideas are often assumed by both laymen and scholars to be objective, pragmatic and rational, something that has irrefutable foundations, rather than theoretical and culturally influenced ones. Specifically related to this paper, the supposition of objectivity in modern science is reflected onto understandings of the seeming practicality of Roman surgical procedures, rather than being questioned as something that might have been speculative and subjective. In support of this view towards science in the modern world is a study by Toumey, an anthropologist who made an examination of how people living in the United States conceptualise scientific study, and found that most are quite gullible to the scientific word. If a scientist endorses something it is believed to be an objective truth (1996, 3–6). This is mainly because, as Mascia-Lees and Black point out, 'scientific research is so valued in contemporary society it is often difficult to accept that it is affected by external factors' (Mascia-Lees and Black, 2000, 19). Science is as much subjective and hypothesis-based today as it was in the past. Archaeologists of Roman medicine must learn, first of all, that even if something appears quite practical, and commonsensical, that the understandings of how an instrument was to be used would be grounded in contemporary understandings of the body; thus, not as is understood in the modern western world. This is not to suggest that scholars disregard the functions mentioned in the texts, but consider how they relate to medical ideas of the time and possible variations in medical practice. They must also consider that there may have been different perceptions and uses of the instruments that seem 'irrational' to us, but 'rational' to people living within the Roman empire, a point that will be returned to and discussed in greater detail below.

In a recent work on medical doxography and historiography in Classical Antiquity, van der Eijk argues that ancient sources relating to medicine are not to be recognised as indisputable (1999, 5–6). Although the volume is concerned with examining the histories of medicine made by classical writers about their predecessors rather than the more practical elements of medical treatment, it provides a relevant warning that there are limitations with the written medical sources just as one would expect with other forms of literary sources. A general problem recognised in classical medical history is that the authors at times took certain liberties in their accounts. Occasionally they employed the use of literary characteristics to promote 'vividness, clarity and involvement with the audience in their writing' (van der Eijk 1999, 6), which could have not only distorted modern, as well as ancient, understandings about the life of a particular physician, but the ideas and philosophies under which they worked. If it is possible to detect problems in the historical descriptions of medicine, then one should expect them in the more esoteric as well as practical works on medicine. Moving away from the strict doxographical work of van der Eijk, one can borrow from it to begin to question how classical medical writers might have used their predecessors' works as manuals for procedures of treatment and the problems that might arise from this. An example of possible misunderstandings and interpretations in medical texts is presented by von Staden (1995) in his study on metaphor in Galenic writings. He discusses Galen's belief as a medical writer that any scholar of medicine had to be an historian of the subject and of the language in which it was written. The reason behind understanding the language is to comprehend the exact meaning of a text to enable the teasing out of meanings of a particular figure of speech or analogy used by medical predecessors. Galen himself would have been making these interpretations, and he may not have grasped the original idea of earlier medical writers. With this, one sees that ancient medical writings are interpretations and understandings by an author on the work of another – a doxographical hermeneutic – rather than straightforward and universally understood meanings. The same can be said of writings on surgical procedures. One can expect that alterations to medical literature on surgical procedures could have been made by a writer recording surgical functions of medical tools described by his or her predecessor. Alterations could have been made on a conscious level, as if the writer might not have agreed with what had been said earlier, or if new ideas and/or practices had come into play. Subconscious changes to the literature are also possible in that perhaps the writer misunderstood the intended function of a medical tool. In relation to medical instruments one does not need to look far to begin to notice a variety of descriptions in the written medical sources about their surgical uses. By perusing the standard work of Milne (1907) on medical instruments it becomes immediately apparent that one medical writer would often describe an instrument as having a different function to that provided by another medical writer. In some cases even a different name for the tool is provided. The trephine (Milne 1907, 131–2), for example, is named in the Hippocratic texts as priwn and in Galen as χοινικίς and Celsus refers to it in Latin as a *modiolus*. Each writer describes a different purpose for the tool as well. The archaeological descriptions of the instruments will always mention the variety of functions discussed by the different writers, but even here no issue is raised about whether Roman doctors understood all of the functions mentioned in the various texts. Some doctors might not have been familiar with the many different recorded uses of an instrument. Simply the fact that there were different names and functions mentioned for one tool by different writers implies that there were different perceptions and understandings of an instrument. It also indicates that there may have been a variety of understandings not mentioned in the literature, a general idea discussed above.

Changes in ideas through time are also never considered. Milne, for example, used the many different sources that mention the use of medical tools, listing the various possibilities for the use of a tool, but did not question whether all the uses were understood at the same period in time. Each author he uses was writing in a different period and was influenced by the understandings of medical practice at the time. It is possible that something said in the Hippocratic corpus may not have been agreed with by Galen and other doctors of Galen's time. To support this further, the trephine is described by Paul of Aegina, who wrote in the seventh century AD, as something that should not be used as it did not cure the problems mentioned by the earlier writers (Milne 1907, 132), demonstrating that ideas about medical tools were not static. Scholarly work must take this aspect into consideration when making statements about tool function.

Other hindrances

As mentioned, what was written in the Mediterranean about Roman medicine may not have been read, understood or agreed upon in other areas of the empire where groups of people may have had contact with the Romans, but were not necessarily adopting Roman life-styles. It is not simply the manner in which archaeologists use the literary sources that inhibits interpretations of medical care in the past, but their elementary understandings of how the Roman world functioned. This point is germane to the argument because, although it is argued above that the use of literature as a context for archaeological material is not without its problems, when the literature is used it is done so in the context of ideas of Romanisation. The basis of the theory is that any indigenous population with whom the Romans came into contact would have aspired to have a Roman life-style, because modern scholars have portrayed it as superior to that practised by indigenous local populations (e.g. Cunliffe 1984, 126–127). For medicine it cannot be stressed enough that there is an underlying assumption that what is said in the literary sources by Mediterranean writers was understood and used by every doctor across the empire, hence medicine was Romanised. Unfortunately this view is rather narrow. Studies in colonialism have demonstrated that different societies react differently to the culture with which they have come into contact. Some societies reject all new influences, others adopt or adapt certain aspects, and often the invading colonial power will be affected by the indigenous population (e.g. Dietler 1995, 90–91; Jones 1997, 132; Woolf 1998, 6). It is becoming far less easy to argue for Romanisation, as there is much evidence for resistance to a Roman life-style on the part of the conquered peoples (e.g. Clarke 1999). This theory is yet another obstacle in the way of rigorous scholarly interpretations in relation to medical archaeology. One example of how Romanisation has influenced interpretations of medicine is seen in Wilmanns' work on the Roman army medical corps (1995, 36, 133–4). She argues that Roman medical practices would have been spread to the native populations through the army, but a problem arises in assuming that the Roman army was homogeneous and that all practices, be they medical or other, would have been uniform throughout the military. Through the examination of archaeological remains this assumed standardisation in medical practice has been brought into question. Although there is not a substantial amount of evidence, cultural variations in medical practice within the Roman army can be detected (Baker 2001). Moreover, Wilmanns argues that there would have been a greater acceptance of Roman medical treatment (1995, 133–134) in the second and third centuries AD because more inscriptions mentioning medical personnel have been found in the western frontiers from these times. Yet the numbers of inscriptions are not much higher than for the first century. In fact, Wells (1999, 197–198) has demonstrated that there is ample evidence, especially from metalworking, of a resurgence of indigenous identities during the second and third centuries AD in the western provinces. Rather than becoming increasingly Roman, many societies in the western empire were actually reverting to their former life-styles. The Roman empire did not consist of a homogeneous culture, but of numerous societies with different beliefs and understandings about their world and how it functioned (for discussions on this see Clarke 1999; Jones 1997; Wells 1999; Woolf 1998). Even if people borrowed or used Roman-style medical instruments, the practices of their use must have varied.

In relation to this one may again turn to the anthropology of medicine to question whether there are similar understandings of the body and medicine, as well as acceptance of new ideas about medical treatment in other areas of the world. There are many case studies that repeatedly remind us that amongst traditional societies we should not expect to find the same form of medicine or understandings of the body and illness as that of the West. As people have different understandings of illness and its treatment they will not always adopt the practices of another simply because the medicine of one society appears 'superior' (e.g. Kleinman 1980; Morley 1978). Kleinman, for example, noticed in his studies of Taiwanese medical practices that even when people have been introduced to the perceived superior western-style medical practices, they continue to use their own forms of medical treatment. Sometimes the two disparate practices are combined, but he notes that there seems to be a general suspicion of the western medical tradition (1980, 205–206). This account provides one cross-cultural example of how societies view and accept or reject medical practices that differ from their own, even when they might appear 'beneficial' and 'scientific'. A similar occurrence may have taken place in the Roman world. In the context of Roman military medicine it is noticeable that Roman-style instruments and inscriptions mentioning doctors were not found in all fortifications, perhaps implying localised patterns of acceptance or rejection of Roman-style medical instruments (Baker 2001).

EXAMINING MEDICAL INSTRUMENTS FROM AN ARCHAEOLOGICAL PERSPECTIVE

With the understanding that historical and archaeological sources have underlying problems, it is here that I would like to propose how an archaeologist of medicine could examine the remains of medical instruments from both a literary and non-literary perspective. The vaginal speculum will be used as a demonstration of how medical tools have a number of meanings and functions that can be discerned independently from both the archaeological and literary records. Before discussing the instrument in its archaeological context, its mention in the medical literature will be presented. First of all we do not, as far as I am aware, have an accurate description of the tool's appearance until the Arabic period. The tool for the most part is only mentioned, not described, in the literature. It is known as a *dioptera* (vaginal speculum) or as *organum* (the instrument) and is mainly discussed in association with gynaeco-logical problems (see Longfield-Jones 1986 for a full discussion). Sometimes the speculum is not mentioned, but an instrument like it would, it seems, have been required in many of the medical treatments for gynaecological problems. It is with this assumption that one may point to how simple it is to make immediate assumptions about the type of tool used in a medical procedure. Here the presumption is that the tool without a name must have been a speculum – it makes sense to the modern reader, especially with our understandings of gynaecology. This tool, however, may not have been what the authors had in mind when they were discussing the treatment. Perhaps they considered another instrument, maybe something unknown to us, to be better suited for the treatment, instruments that were commonly understood to them, but not to the modern reader, and, thus, our assumptions may not be correct. However, turning from this digression, the speculum was more clearly discussed in some of the ancient literature. There is an excerpt from the late Roman period that describes how the tool is to be used (Paul of Aegina 6. 73) that provides some indication of its appearance. Yet, the main source of information about the tool is provided by the Arab writer Albucasis, who described two types of specula, one being like a 'book press' which has two screws and the ends of two pieces of wood, but it is more slender than that of a proper book press (Chapter 77, Spink and Lewis 1973, 486). There is no evidence for this style of instrument in the extant finds. The second discussed by him is similar to those found in the archaeological record for the Roman period, which consists of two handles with a worm screw between them and a priapiscus on the utility end of the instrument. The screw is turned to open the three or four pronged priapiscus. Roman specula are not common in the archaeological record, and some are only found in parts. There is the possibility that perhaps the 'book-press' instrument described by Albucasis was frequently used and it has not been identified in the archaeological record. Furthermore, the material from which they were made might account for their scarcity. According to Albucasis they were made from ebony and boxwood (Chapter 77, Spink and Lewis 1973, 486). Since the instruments are complex they would have been expensive to make in metal and wooden ones may have been more common. Wooden instruments are unlikely to survive, except in exceptional preservational circumstances. Those specula that have been found are made of a copper-alloy. Moreover the classical literature does not provide us with much information about how the patient, doctor or maker of the tool would have perceived it in the context of contemporary attitudes towards the body.

From an archaeological point of view, one way to gain an insight into the understanding of objects that were associated with an ill body, and a female body in the case of gynaecological instruments, is by examining the context in which they were found. However, typically for Roman archaeology, when instruments are described their provenance is sometimes mentioned, but frankly little consideration is given to its importance. Furthermore, the place of deposition is often uncritically taken to locate a place of medical practice. The find spot need not necessarily be the place of use; it may simply be the location of final loss or discard of refuse. Context can indicate a different function for a medical tool; for example, the leather workshop located outside the Roman legionary fortress at Bonn has produced a few scalpels (van Driel-Murray and Gechter 1984). They are described as medical tools, but the essentialist view that an object can only have one function is clearly indicated by the description of these instruments. It is not wrong to describe them as medical tools, but in their context they appear to have been used for another purpose, that of leather working. It is possible that the instruments could have had their function changed; they may have started out as medical tools, but were reused for leather working. In both cases the tools were used for cutting skin, animal and human.

Bliquez (1995) made a study of specula and other gynaecological instruments found in Pompeii. The basis of his work was to locate the original provenance of the instruments excavated in the nineteenth century, with very poor recording of their location or their associated finds. He argues that the find spot is indicative of the place where gynaecological practice would have taken place. With this he makes two assumptions: first that the tools were used for a specific form of medical treatment based on knowledge gained from the literary evidence; and secondly that their provenance indicates places of use (1995, 219). These presumptions narrow the focus of the questions that could be considered, and impair the possibilities of making further inquires about the tool. Rather than assuming that the tools examined were strictly used as vaginal specula, Bliquez could have examined them in relation to their associated finds to see if they might have had other functions. He mentions that they were found with other instruments, but elaborates no more. Nor are we told if the instruments were found with other artefacts, such as amulets, statuettes, or votive offerings, that might lead us to understand other aspects of medical care that the modern western tradition would not see as scientific, as there were aspects of 'non-rational' healing that were present in the ancient world. So this could tend to downplay the aspects of Roman medical practice, which we might regard as irrational. The only other consideration given to the provenance is to indicate the place of manufacture, but little is said about this (Bliquez 1995, 221). Other archaeological examples demonstrate that the location of instruments show that they were perceived as having other meanings besides the function of healing in a 'rational' sense. In some instances medical instruments have been found in good condition, discarded in post-holes and at the entrance of Roman fortifications (Baker 2001). There is evidence of Roman soldiers making votive offerings, quite often with objects associated with the body, such as shoes and armour. Many times the offerings are located on the boundaries of sites or in the foundations of buildings. The instruments might have been discarded in such places because of their associations with the body. Objects associated with the body appear to have been thought of as having 'magical' powers that could have been used in ritual deposition. Thus the condition and location of instruments can bring other possible meanings.

To provide another example of how meanings can be discerned from archaeological contexts, one can examine other finds of specula and the condition in which they were found. In some instances the specula were found in graves. One from Merida in Spain came from an area that has, exceptionally, four burials containing medical instruments (Künzl 1983, 102–103). The tomb in which the speculum was found also contained a balance. In this burial the speculum was in perfect condition, but this is not the case for all of the specula found in tombs. Some are found broken, for example, parts of one were found in a burial at Verona, Italy. Peculiarly, its associated finds were in good condition, such as scalpel handles, glass vessels and other medical tools (Künzl 1983, 104). It is not clear what part of the speculum survived, but it is more interesting to speculate why the rest of the instruments are in good condition and this one is not. This same pattern appears amongst objects from a grave in Varna, Bulgaria (Künzl 1983, 112), where only the screw of the speculum was found. It is again interesting to note the occurrence of specula in fragmentary condition from tombs with other instruments and objects (that may or may not have had a medical function) in good condition. A good example of how meanings can be drawn from instrument condition can be demonstrated from medical tools deposited in the Schutthügel, a large water-logged deposit of finds located outside the legionary fortress of Vindonissa, in

Switzerland, thought to be a place for refuse disposal. A number of instruments have been recovered from this area in what could be considered a good functional condition. Since they appear to be in working order it is necessary to question why they were discarded. One can speculate on a number of reasons why this had been done. It is possible that the instruments were seen to have been polluted, perhaps having been used on someone quite ill, or who had died. Perhaps they were used in the treatment of an illness considered to have been taboo, much like many modern westerners think of objects that have come into contact with people suffering from contagious diseases. As much as people today might try and hide their prejudices, objects can still be avoided because of their associations.

Returning to the specula, they too provide us with information about other possible meanings. As with grave goods, objects are frequently employed to create an identity for the dead person, in these instances instruments perhaps denoting that of a doctor, healer or midwife. Secondly, a close association between healers and the tools of their trade could make these objects inalienable and unsuitable for use by anyone else. However, more explicit symbolic and metaphorical meanings may have been stressed through burial. Given that specula are closely associated with the treatment of female reproductive problems they might carry with them explicit meanings related to reproduction, birth and the facilitation of life. Breaking specula and placing them in graves could, conversely, evoke meanings to do with the termination (breaking) of life. Alternatively, burial might have been an action designed to negate any inherent pollution perceived to be associated with the object. In the case of gynaecological instruments sex-related pollution taboos are likely to have been strong.

Many questions can be raised about why instruments were buried in tombs and why they are found in a range of conditions. For example, did those who employed these instruments consider them to be polluted if they were used on a patient with a certain illness, or on one who died? How did the patients themselves regard the instruments? What did they do with them if they though the doctor was incompetent? Did they see them as being taboo if they were associated with an ill or dead person? Were they considered to be appropriate votive offerings because they were associated with the body?

Conclusion

What is needed to expand an understanding of these instruments is a critical evaluation of both literature and archaeological sources without undue preference being given to the literature. More attention should be given to the archaeological context of the instruments. The functions of tools might change through their use-lives, including their final uses as grave goods or votive objects. Tools might be employed in ways that diverged from those in the literary sources, and given the complex cultural mix of the Roman world this is likely. We are only aware of those tools that have medical functions because of their description in medical texts. There is no guarantee that the full range of tools integral to medical treatment is known. An example of this is the possible use of divining rods from the tomb found at Colchester, Essex (Crummy this volume). If these tools were divining rods, or even another form of medical instrument with which we are unfamiliar, the example demonstrates the possibility that Roman medical practice did not always conform to the expectations of Western science.

Overall, what I hope to have pointed out in a historical archaeological context in ancient medicine is that archaeologists do not have to rely wholly on literary sources to understand the material remains and their functions. One can, of course, use such sources in a far more critical manner than has been done to learn about one function, yet at the same time use archaeological contexts to determine the full range of use, function and social understandings of the tools, information that is not readily available in the textual sources.

Acknowledgements
I would like to thank Dr. J. Pollard and Professor Ph. van der Eijk for their helpful comments, although all mistakes are the author's own.

Bibliography

Ancient Sources

Albucasis   Spink, M.S. and Lewis, G.L. 1973 *Albucasis on surgery and instruments*, London: Wellcome Institute of the History of Medicine.
Celsus   A. Cornelii Celsi *Corpus Medicorum Latinorum* (vol. I), F. Marx (ed.) 1915 Leipzig: B.G. Teubner.
Galen   *Claudii Galeni opera omnia* C.G. Kühn (ed.) 20 vols. in 22 1821–1833 Leipzig: Cnobloch.
Oribasius   *Collectionum medicarum reliquiae* (vols. I and II), I. Raeder (ed.) 1928–31 Leipzig: B.G. Teubner.
Paul of Aegina   *Paulus Aegineta*, I.L. Heiberg (ed.) 1921–24 Leipzig and Berlin: B.G. Teubner.
Soranus   *Sorani Gynaecia*, J. Ilberg (ed.) 1927 Leipzig: B.G. Teubner.

Modern Sources
Baker, P. 2001 'Medicine, culture and military identity' pp. 48–68 in G. Davies, A. Gardner and K. Lockyear (eds) *TRAC 2000: proceedings of the tenth annual theoretical Roman archaeology conference*, Oxford: Oxbow Books.
Bliquez, L. 1985 'Λιθουλκος, Κιρσουλκος' *American Journal of Philology* 106, 119–121.
Bliquez, L. and J.P. Oleson 1994 'The origins, early history and applications of the *pyoulkos* (syringe)' pp. 83–103 in G. Argoud (ed.) *Science et Vie Intellectuelle a Alexandri*, Saint-Étienne: Publications de l'Université de Saint-Étienne.
Bliquez, L. 1995 'Gynecology in Pompeii' pp. 209–224 in Ph. J. van der Eijk, H. Horstmannshoff and P.H. Schrijvers (eds) *Ancient medicine in its socio-cultural context*, Amsterdam and Atlanta: Rodopi Press.
Braadbaart, S. 1994a 'Medical and cosmetic instruments in the collection of the 'Rijksmuseum van Oudheden te Leiden', The Netherlands' *Oudheidkundige Mededelingen uit het Rijksmuseum van Oudheden te Leiden* 74, 163–175.
Braadbaart, S. 1994b 'Romeinse medische instrumenten' *Geschiedenis der Geneeskunde* 1 (5), 51–55.
Clarke, S. 1999 'Contact, architectural symbolism and the negotiation of cultural identity in the

military zone' pp. 36–45 in P. Baker, C. Forcey, S. Jundi. and R. Witcher (eds) 1999 *TRAC 98: proceedings of the eighth annual theoretical Roman archaeology conference, Leicester 1998*, Oxford: Oxbow Books.

Charlesworth, D. 1976 'The hospital: Housesteads' *Archaeologica Aeliana* (Series 5) 4, 17–30.

Cunliffe, B. 1988 *Greeks, Romans and Barbarians: spheres of interaction*, London: Guild Publishing.

Deetz, J. 1977 *In small things forgotten*, New York: Anchor Press/Doubleday.

Deringer, H. 1954 'Die Medizinischen Instrumente des Ennser Museum' pp. 144–155 in *Forschungen in Lauriacum* 2: 1952: Linz.

Dietler, M. 1995 'The cup of Gyptis: rethinking the colonial encounter in early-Iron-Age western Europe and the relevance of the world-systems model' *Journal of European Archaeology* 3(2), 89–112.

Döderlein, G. 1973 'Medizinische Instrumente aus Vindonissa und Aquae Helveticae' *Medizinische Monatschrift* 27, 409–412.

Dolmans, M.Th.R.M. 1992 'De medische verzorging van de Romeinse soldaat' *Hermeneus* 64, 1–11.

Drabkin, I.E. 1944 'On medical education in Greece and Rome' *Bulletin of the History of Medicine* 15(4), 333–351.

Dyczek, P. 1995 'The *valetudinarium* at Novae: new components' pp. 365–372 in *Acts of the 12th international congress on ancient bronzes* (NAR) Amersfoort.

Evans-Pritchard, E.E. 1976 [1937] *Witchcraft, oracles, and magic among the Azande* E. Gillies (abridged), Oxford: Clarendon Press.

Gilson, A. 1978 'A doctor at Housesteads' *Archaeologia Aeliana* 6 (series 5), 162–165.

Gilson, A. 1981 'A group of Roman surgical and medical instruments from Corbridge' *Saalburg Jahrbuch* 37, 5–9.

Hauff, E. 1993/94 'Die Medizinische Versorgung von Carnuntum' *Carnuntum Jahrbuch* 10, 89–196.

Hodder, I. 1982 *Symbols in action*, Cambridge: Cambridge University Press.

Hodder, I. (ed.) 2000 *The meaning of things: material culture and symbolic expression*, London and New York: Routledge.

Jackson, R. 1988 *Doctors and diseases in the Roman empire*, University of Oklahoma Press: Norman and London.

Jackson, R. 1990 'Roman doctors and their instruments: recent research into ancient practice' *Journal of Roman Archaeology* 3, 5–27.

Jackson, R. 1994a '*Styphylagra, staphylocaustes*, uvulectomy and haemorrhoidectomy: the Roman instruments and operations' pp. 167–185 in A. Krug (ed.) *From Epidauros to Salerno: symposium held at the European University Centre for Cultural Heritage, Ravello, April 1990*, Rixensart: Pact Belgium.

Jackson, R. 1994b 'The surgical instruments, appliances and equipment in Celsus' *De Medicina*'. pp. 167–209 in *La Médecine de Celse*. Saint-Étienne: Publications de l'Université Saint-Étienne.

Jackson, R. 1995 'The composition of Roman medical instrumentaria as an indicator of medical practice: a provisional assessment' pp. 189–208 in Ph.J. van der Eijk, H.F.J, Horstmannshoff and P.H. Schrijvers (eds) *Ancient medicine in its socio-cultural context*, Amsterdam and Atlanta: Rodopi Press.

Jettner, D. 1966 'Geschichte des Hospitals', *Sudhoffs Archive für Geschichte der Medizin und der Naturwissenschaften 11*, Wiesbaden: Franz Steiner Verlag GmbH.

Johnson, M. 1999 *Archaeological theory: an introduction*, Oxford: Blackwell Publishers.

Jones, S. 1997 *The archaeology of ethnicity*, London and New York: Routledge.

Kleinman, A. 1980 *Patients and healers in the context of culture*, Berkeley: University of California Press.

Künzl, E. 1982 'Römische Medizin im Spiegel archäologischer Funde', *Archäologie in Deutschland* 1 (Jan-März), 14.

Künzl, E. 1983 *Medizinische Instrumente aus Sepulkralfunden der römischen Kaiserzeit*, Cologne: Rheinland Verlag GmbH.

Künzl, E. 1996 'Forschungsbericht zu den antiken medizinischen Instrumenten' *Aufstieg und Niedergang der romischen welt II, 37. 3*, 2433–639.

Longfield-Jones, G.M. 1986 'A Graeco-Roman speculum in the Wellcome Museum' *Medical History* 30, 81–89.

Mascia-Lees, F.E. and N. Johnson Black 2000 *Gender and anthropology*, Prospect Heights, Illinois: Waveland Press.

Milne, J. 1907 *Surgical instruments in Greek and Roman times*, Oxford: Clarendon Press.

Morley, P. 1978 'Culture and the cognitive world of traditional medical beliefs: some preliminary considerations' pp. 1–18 in P. Morley and R. Wallis (eds) *Culture and curing: Anthropological perspectives on traditional medical beliefs and practices*, London: Peter Owen.

Morris, I. 2000 *Archaeology as cultural history*, Oxford: Blackwell Press.

Press, L. 1988 'Valetudinarium at Novae and other Roman Danubian hospitals' *Archeologia* 39, 69–89.

Salazar, C. 2000 *The treatment of war wounds in Graeco-Roman antiquity*, Leiden: Brill.

Shanks, M. and Tilley, C. 1987 *Social theory and archaeology*, Cambridge: Polity Press.

Shanks, M. 1996 *Classical archaeology of Greece: experiences of the discipline*, New York and London: Routledge.

Toumey, C.P. 1996 *Conjuring science: scientific symbols and cultural meanings in American life*, New Brunswick, New Jersey: Rutgers University Press.

van der Eijk, Ph.J. 1999 'Introductory chapter one: historical awareness, historiogaphy and doxography in Greek and Roman medicine' pp. 1–32 in Ph.J. van der Eijk (ed.) *Ancient histories of medicine: essays in medical doxography and historiography in Classical Antiquity*, Leiden: Brill.

van Driel-Murray, C. and M. Gechter 1984 'Funde aus der Fabrica der legio I Minerva am Bonner Berg' *Beiträge zur Archäologie des Romischen Rheinlands 4*, Cologne: Rheinland-Verlag GMBH.

von Staden, H. 1995 'Science as text. science as history: Galen on metaphor', pp. 499–518 in Ph.J. van der Eijk, H.F.J,Horstmannshoff and P.H. Schrijvers (eds), *Ancient medicine in its socio-cultural context*, Amsterdam and Atlanta: Rodopi Press.

Wells, P.S. 1999 *The Barbarians speak: how the conquered peoples shaped Roman Europe*, Princeton: Princeton University Press.

Wilmanns, J.C. 1995b *Der Sanitätsdienst im Römischen Reich*, Hildesheim, Zürich and New York: Olms Weidmann.

Woolf, G. 1998 *Becoming Roman the origins of provincial civilisation in Gaul*, Cambridge: Cambridge University Press.

3. Tuberculosis: a multidisciplinary approach to past and current concepts, causes and treatment of this infectious disease

Charlotte Roberts

INTRODUCTION

> 'Interest in tuberculosis is at an all-time low which is striking if deaths are at an all-time high' (Farmer 1999).

Tuberculosis (TB) is an infectious disease of considerable importance as a health problem in our world today, and increasingly so (Snider *et al.* 1994). Brown *et al.* (1996) likens TB to malaria in that it has re-emerged to 'plague' populations because of the results of human behaviour. Its fascination for medical historians and researchers working in biological anthropology and, specifically, on the history of disease as identified in human remains, i.e. palaeopathology, lies in its complexity as a disease reflecting so many facets of a population's lifestyle. Clinicians and medical anthropologists working with people with TB in developing and developed countries see the disease as multifactorial in aetiology, and increasing in frequency at a rate difficult to comprehend. Described as a disease of poverty, TB has been with human and other (non-human) populations for many thousands of years, and looks set to remain in the world for the foreseeable future.

Like so many research areas in the history of medicine and disease, there has been a strong tendency over the years for researchers interested in TB to consider their particular evidence (documentary evidence or human remains) as being of primary importance, and capable of telling the story of TB. Too often we work in our own research worlds with little consideration of other perspectives. This rather short-sighted view is highlighted by the discipline of medical anthropology (McElroy and Townsend 1996), which considers health problems in a very broad sense, taking into account all aspects of a person or population's experience of 'their disease' into the final interpretation. In effect, it is the person or group of people who are the centre of concern, not the disease itself, unlike in many clinical contexts today where TB is treated (Curry 1968). In this holistic approach, where humans are viewed as 'biological organisms with a long evolutionary history, as social persons who organise systems of health care, (and) as beings who communicate and maintain cultural systems' (McElroy and Townsend 1996, xxi), much more can be learnt of how people experience disease, what they understand about it, how they deal with it, and what the future holds. It is this broad outlook on TB that is the focus of this paper – an outlook that hopefully may encourage cross-discipline collaboration in tracing the history of disease in the future.

The aims of the paper are to consider what TB is, how frequent it is today and was in the past, what factors are important for its appearance in a population, concepts of how and why TB occurs, and how it was, and is, treated. The ultimate aim is to illustrate how it is much more fruitful, by using multiple forms of evidence, to explore the impact of TB on past populations rather than concentrating on one piece of evidence. Tuberculosis is a multifaceted disease, which, in palaeopathology, is difficult to interpret using only the evidence from human remains.

TUBERCULOSIS: THE DISEASE

Tuberculosis, an infectious disease of mammals and birds, is caused by the organisms *Mycobacterium tuberculosis* and *Mycobacterium bovis* in humans. Along with *M. africanum* and *M. microti*, these four organisms make up what is called the *Mycobacterium tuberculosis* Complex (Aufderheide and Rodríguez Martin 1998, 119). However, there are many other mycobacteria, including *M. leprae*, the organism that causes leprosy in humans. Additionally there are also what are called atypical mycobateria, but their ability to infect humans is low; they are usually encountered in people with suppressed immune systems or in organs already affected by disease (Aufderheide and Rodríguez Martin 1998, 119). *M. avium* is one such atypical organism – one that primarily affects birds; in humans infection of bones and joints may occur (Resnick 1995, 2486). It is now recognised as a source of tuberculosis in humans (Kelley and Lytle-Kelley 1999), and is one of the organisms in the *M. avium* Complex (with *M. intracellulare* and *M. scrofulaceum*). Kelley and Lytle-Kelley (1999, 185) describe this Complex (MAC) as being 'the most common of the nontubercular mycobacteria'. The MAC has not only been associated with a number of conditions such as healed and active TB and chronic bronchitis, but has been isolated in soil, water, food, dust and other animals. Therefore, it could have been a threat to people in the past (as today) via these potential infective sources.

Tuberculosis is contracted via the lungs or tonsils through inhaling droplets containing the organism (*M. tuberculosis* and *M. bovis*), or via the gastrointestinal route through infected meat and milk of animals (*M. bovis*). This infectious disease kills three million people a year worldwide (Table 3.1). The World Health Organisation estimates that one third of the world's population is infected with TB, that there are eight million new cases each year, and that by the year 2020 it will be the fourth leading cause of death (WHO 2000).

Many factors are believed to contribute to the appearance of TB in human populations past and present (Table 3.2). Poverty, poor living conditions, and a settled way of life with high population density living in close contact with each other and infected animals, promoted the disease's appearance in the past. Travel and migration also

Table 3.1. The leading causes of death worldwide. Data from the World Health Organisation, Annual Report, 1997 (in Grange 1999).

Disease	No. of deaths annually (millions)
Coronary heart disease	7.2
Cancer (all types)	6.3
Cerebrovascular disease	4.6
Acute lower respiratory infection	3.9
Tuberculosis	3.0
Chronic obstructive pulmonary disease	2.9
Diarrhoea (includes dysentery)	2.5
Malaria	2.1
HIV/AIDS	1.5
Hepatitis B	1.2

Table 3.2. Risk factors in tuberculosis (past and present).

Risk factor	Modern	Identifiable in past populations?
Poverty	+	√
Animals	+	√
Overcrowding	+	√
Poor hygiene	+	√
Poor diet	+	√
Occupation	+	√
Travel/migration	+	√
Disasters	+	√
HIV/AIDS	+	X
Multidrug resistance	+	X
Ethnicity	+	√
Older and younger people	+	√
Build	+	√
Concept of disease	+	√
Immunosuppressive therapy	+	X

√ = identifiable using primary or secondary evidence
X = not relevant in the past or difficult to identify

exposes people to new diseases they may not have any resistance to, including TB, and migrants today often live in poverty in temporary housing (Davies 1995). Migrants also take TB to new places and expose new populations to the infection. Along with other possible predisposing factors such as a hereditary predisposition, the influence of age, sex, ethnicity, and occupation (Bowden and McDiarmid 1994), TB proves itself a complex disease. Today the main factors responsible for an increase in frequency are poverty, the presence of HIV (Human Immunodeficiency Virus) and AIDS (Acquired

Immune Deficiency Syndrome) in a person, which compromises the immune system (Raviglione *et al.* 1995), resistance to antibiotics and lack of access to health care facilities. In developing countries, contact with infected animals and their products (dung, meat, milk and blood) is also a potential way the infection can enter a human population. However, only two of these contemporary factors, poverty and contact with animals and their products, are of course relevant for the past as far as is known.

It is suggested that tuberculosis first appeared in human populations with the advent of agriculture and the domestication of animals (Steinbock 1976, Roberts and Manchester 1995). In fact, Hare (1967) suggests that the human variety of TB is a mutant of the bovine form, although this has not been supported by any definitive evidence. Whilst there have been no reports of TB in skeletal remains from hunter-gatherer populations, it is possible that TB in hunted wild animals may have been transmitted to humans during hunting and the butchery and consumption of their meat. Furthermore, some hunter-gatherer populations today are reported to have TB (Truswell and Hanson 1976). Many mammals, including humans, can be affected (O'Reilly and Daborn 1995) and, while cattle have been targeted in the past to be the animals that, once domesticated, transmitted the infection to humans, there are clearly other early domesticates such as sheep and goats that could equally have been responsible. In addition, today in Britain, badgers in the south-west of England have been labelled as transmitting TB to cattle, thus initiating a badger cull in recent years (Corbett and Harris 1991). Furthermore, it is now known that the bovine form of the disease cannot only be transmitted through eating infected meat and drinking infected milk and blood, but also by droplet infection (Grange *et al.* 1994). Tuberculosis may also be transmitted via dung from infected animals when that dung is used for fuel or as a building material. It is known that the disease-causing organisms can survive for some time outside the animal (Cosivi *et al.* 1995 and Table 3.3). Therefore, in antiquity, it is relevant to think not only of domestication of animals facilitating infection of humans, but also sharing of living space with animals. This would promote droplet infection of humans from their animals, and the use of dung for a variety of purposes. It has also been proved that humans can infect animals (Cosivi *et al.* 1995). The epidemiology of this disease is thus complex.

Table 3.3. Survival time of M. bovis under different environmental conditions (from Cosivi et al. 1995).

Contaminated material	Conditions	Survival time
Purulent emulsion	Direct sunlight	>10h but <12h
	Diffuse sunlight	At least 30 days
Cattle dung	Direct sunlight	>6h but <37h
	Diffuse sunlight	14–150 days
	Covered	365–730 days
Pasture	Temperate climate	Depends on season and climate (7–63 days)
Water (experimentally contaminated)	–	18 days

THE EVIDENCE FOR TUBERCULOSIS IN PAST POPULATIONS

Diagnosing tuberculosis today is a little easier than trying to identify it in past populations. Sophisticated diagnostic tests have developed over many years, particularly since the discovery of the tubercle bacillus and X-rays at the end of the nineteenth century. Since those discoveries, and in recent years, biomolecular methods of diagnosis have come to the fore, as they have in archaeology (e.g. Salo *et al.* 1994), which makes diagnosis a little less problematic (see below). Recognising tuberculosis in the past, however, relies not only on the archaeological evidence, but also on historical data in the form of written records and illustrations, which also provide us with a window on this infectious disease. Nevertheless, all the forms of evidence used for reconstructing the evolution and history of TB have their limitations.

Identifying the macroscopic evidence rests mainly on the skeletal evidence from archaeological sites. This is especially focused on the presence of destruction of the bony structure of the spine or Pott's disease (see Fig. 3.1), similar changes in the major weight-bearing hip and knee joints, and other features that may be the result of TB (Resnick 1995). What we assume was the disabling nature of the spinal changes is difficult to confirm due to the many vagaries affecting interpretation of disability in

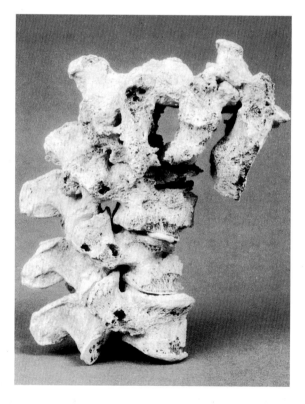

Figure 3.1. Figure of TB spine in Anglo-Saxon individual from Bedhampton, Hampshire.

the past (Roberts 2000). However, diagnosis relies (preferably) on a complete skeleton (often not always possible in archaeology), and the consideration of all the possible different disease processes that could cause the changes (i.e. providing a differential diagnosis). Nevertheless, only 3–5% of people with the infection will develop the bone changes (1940s and 1950s figures – Resnick 1995, 2462), and therefore consideration of this macroscopic evidence can only reveal the tip of the iceberg of the tuberculous problem in the past. However, there is some dispute about the diagnostic criteria used for TB, i.e. there is a possibility that the clinical criteria usually accepted in palaeopathology may be flawed (e.g. see Roberts *et al.* 1998, Roberts *et al.* 1994, Roberts and Buikstra, in review). Furthermore, there is indeed an 'osteological paradox' in attempting to infer health from the skeleton (Wood *et al.* 1992). This landmark paper in 1992 brought together much data on the problem of identifying, analysing and interpreting the evidence of disease in skeletal remains. Many points were discussed and these included the problem of identification of disease in fragmentary remains; differentiating pseudopathological lesions, sample representivity, individual frailty and immune response in a population and its effect on the manifestation of disease in a person and their skeleton; the fact that people may die before bone damage occurs and, finally, diseases affecting the soft tissues would not be recognised solely by examining the skeleton.

Despite these limitations, developments in biomolecular methods of diagnosis have allowed previously undiagnosed tuberculous individuals to be identified (Haas *et al.* 2000). The use of ancient DNA and other biomolecules specific to a disease-causing organism, such as *M. tuberculosis* or *M. bovis*, as a method of diagnosis in palaeo-pathology has recently come to the fore over the last ten years. In theory, should these biomolecules survive the burial process and if there is no modern DNA contamination (see Brown and Brown 1992 for a discussion), then they may be utilised to diagnose disease. For example, a disease that does not leave its mark on bone may be identified (e.g. malaria – Taylor *et al.* 1997), and disease that killed a person before bone damage occurred may also be recognised (Haas *et al.* 2000). Ancient DNA analysis may also help confirm a possible case of TB, although proof of the presence of TB aDNA does not mean specific lesions in the skeleton were caused by the infection. More recently, methods have developed to the extent where it has proved to be possible to determine which organism of the *M. tuberculosis* Complex caused TB in the skeleton (Mays *et al.* 2001). Another development in the use of other biomolecules to diagnose TB has been the analysis of ancient mycolic acids. These molecules appear to survive better than aDNA and have been used to confirm, with DNA, a diagnosis of TB (Gernaey *et al.* 2001).

Historical data also has its problems, particularly in inferring whether tuberculosis is in fact being described or illustrated. Many terms used in past literature have been accepted as describing TB. These include consumption, the King's Evil, scrofula, phthisis, tissick, and tabes. Whether all these terms, and at all times, actually describe what we believe today to be TB is debatable. In addition, when signs and symptoms describing this infectious disease are used as an indicator of the presence of TB, controversy arises because of the clinical features not being particularly patho-gnomonic, i.e. specific, to tuberculosis. For example, coughing up blood may indicate lung cancer, and shortness of breath could relate to a number of pulmonary diseases. Likewise, the illustrations of deformities of the spine may indicate not necessarily TB of the spine, but other conditions such as osteoporosis-induced collapse of the vertebrae or brucellosis. Nevertheless, medical historians have inferred the presence and, sometimes, frequency of the disease from these data (e.g. the Egyptian figurine with a deformed back – Morse *et al.* 1964, and descriptions of TB – Meinecke 1927). However, people working in palaeopathology have always maintained that there is a lack of correlation between the frequencies of TB cited by historical sources and those revealed in skeletal remains (e.g. Roberts *et al.* 1998, 56). The fact that only a few percent of people with TB develop bone damage may be part of the explanation, but inappropriate diagnostic criteria may be another. Are the historical sources right, i.e., did the writers and artists always get the diagnosis right? Or are the frequency rates seen in the macroscopic evidence for TB in skeletons more realistic? Perhaps a rate between the two may be more acceptable, but perhaps biomolecular analysis of large numbers of skeletons in the future will potentially provide us with the real figure.

TUBERCULOSIS IN THE PAST: OLD AND NEW WORLD EVIDENCE

The primary evidence for tuberculosis comes in the form of changes in skeletal and mummified remains. If the evidence for lesions believed to be tuberculous is undisputed, i.e. by other experienced researchers, then there is near certainty of a diagnosis of tuberculosis. Of course, diagnosis is not that easy, as discussed above and also highlighted by Waldron (1994), and Miller *et al.* (1996). Written and illustrated evidence are no more reliable, because descriptions and illustrations of people with the infection are problematic in interpretation. Did that person really have TB of the spine or something else? These forms of data also rely on the author and artist getting their diagnosis right. For example, the London Bills of Mortality, which were recorded from 1562 to 1837, and chart births and deaths for parishes inside and outside of London's walls (Molleson and Cox 1993, 206), record tuberculosis (consumption) as a lead cause of death, especially in the seventeenth century AD. Were all these deaths said to be caused by consumption really TB? And was everybody who was touched for the King's Evil (believed to be TB) during the post-Medieval period a victim of TB (see below)? Cause of death data in the past (and even today) is often criticised (Evans 1998; Hardy 1994; Payne 2000). After the discovery of the tubercle bacillus and X-rays at the end of the nineteenth century, diagnosis and frequency rates may have become more accurate (although see above). Prior to this time, without efficient methods of diagnosis, TB rates may have been either over-inflated or less than the real figure.

Figures for TB in Old and New World populations over the last few thousand years rely primarily on diagnosis of TB in skeletal and mummified remains and usually also destructive lesions of the spine, as described above, on a case-by-case basis. Already we have noted that only a few percent of people with TB develop changes in their skeletons, and, therefore, absolute rates cannot be established, although it is possible to estimate a minimum number. Researchers thus report cases as 'individuals affected in the population' rather than numbers of, for example, spines affected compared to the number available for study (Larsen 1997, 102). Nevertheless, the latter is the method most advocated for presenting data on frequency rates for disease in past human remains (see Waldron 1994 for a discussion).

The first evidence for TB in human remains from the Old World comes from Italy and is dated to 5,800 ±90 BP (Canci *et al.* 1996). The cave site of Arma dell Aquila also had contemporary evidence that suggested a population who were sedentary farmers who had domesticated animals and a settled lifestyle, thus suggesting that contact with animals led to TB occurring in the human population. While skeletal evidence for TB has been recorded earlier in the Old World from Jordan and dated to the eighth millennium BC (El Najjar *et al.* 1997), the evidence is not undisputed (Roberts and Buikstra in review). Many European countries, including Britain, saw increases in this infection in the later Mediaeval period (from the twelfth century onwards) when urbanism had developed and populations were living in close contact with each other, thus enabling the human form of the disease to be transmitted by droplet infection. Continuous ingestion of infected meat and milk in both urban and rural areas, and sharing of living space between humans and their animals, would also have added to the tuberculosis load in populations. Wild animals are also known to be a potential reservoir of tuberculosis and, thus, hunting and gathering groups could also have potentially have contracted TB during slaughter, butchery and consumption of hunted animals. While this is posed as a possible source of infection for earlier populations, no evidence yet has come from archaeologically derived hunter-gatherers. However, in some parts of the world, skeletons of hunter-gatherers are rather scarce, especially in the U.K., and therefore absence of evidence does not necessarily mean evidence of absence.

In the New World tuberculosis definitely appears in a pre-Columbian context (i.e. prior to AD 1492). There is a widespread distribution of cases east of the Mississippi in North America, all post-dating AD 700 (probably reflecting archaeological activity and therefore more data), a virtual absence in Mesoamerica, but also data from South America dating to as early as AD 290 in northern Chile. Thus, TB seems to have occurred first in South America and spread to North America, arriving as early as AD 1000 (Roberts and Buikstra in review). However, where are the cases from Meso-america if transmission was south to north? Interestingly, all Mexican examples are in the west, and it is suggested that trade along the western coast from South to North America via Mexico could have left TB in its wake as people travelled north. These data, of course, also indicate that Europeans could not have brought TB to the New World, because by that time it was well established in the Americas.

TB was undoubtedly present in both Old and New Worlds pre-Columbus, although large parts of the world still have yet to reveal their tuberculous secrets, mainly because little palaeopathological analysis is being undertaken in areas such as China, sub-Saharan Africa, India, and Russia where some of the earliest evidence for agriculture and domestication is found. The pattern of tuberculosis, and its rise and fall in humans over several thousands of years, seems set to change in future years as more data emerges. Furthermore, as more biomolecular analysis of skeletal and mummified remains, with and without TB, is undertaken with the aim of generating positive results for the *Mycobacterium tuberculosis* complex, our numbers of cases will increase, and perhaps approach the figures suggested by historical data.

TUBERCULOSIS IN ANIMALS OTHER THAN HUMANS

We know that TB affects many animal species (O'Reilly and Daborn 1995), but if TB was originally contracted from animals then where is the evidence from non-human remains? Little of this evidence is forthcoming, but it may be unrecognised, and therefore it is unknown whether animal populations actively suffered chronic TB in the past. Domesticated animals today may show skeletal TB but it is not well described in the literature (Brothwell *pers. comm.*). However, apart from the problem of only having dis-articulated non-human remains to study in archaeology, an animal may not have lived long enough for the skeletal changes to occur, depending on what the animal was used for. Clearly, to have a knowledge of the impact of TB in non-human populations (and thus its effect on humans) requires an understanding of how TB affects the non-human skeleton – an area that is not high on the archaeozoologist's agenda, although some have promoted the study of animal palaeopathology (Brothwell 1991). Furthermore, the veterinary clinical literature is less useful for the analysis and interpretation of animal remains compared to that utilised by clinicians dealing with sick humans, and veterinary scientists do not see animals with bone changes characteristic of chronic disease. This is usually because animals are slaughtered before this can occur. Again, biomolecular analysis may identify those animals with TB but no bone change. For example, an *as yet unconfirmed* case of TB has been reported in bison bone dated to 17,000 BP from North America where the DNA of *Mycobacterium tuberculosis* complex was isolated (Martin *et al.* 2000). It should be stated that this result has not been subject to scientific peer scrutiny. However, if this analysis is accepted and verified by researchers, we have a very early case of tuberculosis in non-human remains, well before the first evidence in North America in humans.

The impact of TB on human populations around the world, according to historical data, has been very debilitating, causing great mortality and suffering. That being true, then how did people manage when the skeletal changes took their toll on the spine, hip and knee? Did people have difficulty getting about and carrying out particular tasks, or did they adapt and manage the situation well? Did they have any access to care and treatment of any sort? Did they know how they contracted the illness that caused them a problem in their lungs and affected their breathing? Did they link the debilitating changes in their spine with the disease in their lungs? Concepts of how a disease is caused often bears a direct relationship to the treatments administered and/or accepted in a population.

WHY TUBERCULOSIS OCCURS IN POPULATIONS: CONCEPTS OF CAUSATION, PAST
AND PRESENT

Although the main factors today leading to TB have been discussed already, these
factors may or may not be recognised or accepted by people in both developed and
developing countries. It is often the case that reasons generated about how and why
the disease was contracted will be determined both by a population's culture and the
many facets that make up that culture (Rubel and Garro 1992, and Table 3.4). Indeed,
some diseases may have an associated stigma such that people diagnosed may be
ostracised from their communities, and their marriage and work prospects damaged
forever. This is especially so if contracting the disease is believed to be via sinful
behaviour, or is thought to run in families. On the one hand, diagnosis (preferably
early in the disease's history) potentially 'nips in the bud' its progressive development,
but on the other a person may suffer considerably within their social context. This
latter scenario may thus lead to people who think they have the infection avoiding
diagnosis, and therefore making their prospects for a recovery negligible. Ethnographic
studies suggest that some groups today stigmatise individuals with TB (Hudelson
1999; Khan *et al.* 2000; Rangan and Uplekar 1999). It is seen as a disease of poverty and
as a result of social and immorally unacceptable behaviour. Doctors were, and are,
often loathe to diagnose the infection because they realise(d) the consequences for the
patient. One wonders, therefore, whether any frequency rates for TB that were, and
are, cited were, and are, accurate. A similar picture emerges with the past and present
diagnosis of leprosy, another infectious disease. The stigma associated with leprosy
today has even led to treatment aimed at correcting deformities so that people can
return to their villages and towns and continue with their lives, not recognised as
being leprous.

Sontag (1991) describes TB as a disease compared to cancer, which consumes the
body and is rapid in its progression. In the past TB was associated with romanticism,

Table 3.4. Sidama population's concepts of tuberculosis (from Vecchiato 1997).

Category	Frequency	Responses (%)
Excessive work	103	33.4
Contagion	51	16.5
Malnutrition	35	11.3
Airborne	27	8.8
Ranta	18	5.8
Natural disease (kalaqamunni)	16	5.2
Exposure to sun	10	3.2
Hereditary	4	1.3
Decreased blood level	3	1.0
Evil spirits	3	1.0
Evil eye	1	0.3
Other	6	1.8
Don't know	32	10.4
Total	**309**	**100.0**

with many characters in opera and theatre portrayed with TB (Lutwick 1995). In addition, artists and authors were apparently better at their trade if they had TB, which was allegedly supposed to inspire genius (Stirling 1997). However, at the time when these people were drawing, painting and writing, TB was a very common condition (Dormandy 1999). Therefore, it was more a coincidence that they were 'performing' and suffering from TB at the same time. Such was the case that a direct link between genius and TB was established. In addition, despite the comments above referring to the avoidance of TB diagnosis, there was a strong feeling, particularly in the Victorian period, that for young women to have TB was advantageous for marriage. To eat well was considered rude, but to appear pale, thin and weak was considered attractive to the opposite sex (Howe 1997; Sontag 1991), and people with TB were often portrayed in paintings in this way.

Focusing on Britain, for the earlier periods (i.e. before the Victorian period) it is difficult to interpret what people thought with respect to how disease was contracted and whether stigma was associated. We know, however, that Graeco-Roman physicians believed that disease was generally caused by an imbalance of one or more of the four humours, which were later equated with the seasons of the year and elements (fire, earth, water and air). Too much or too little of one or more of blood, black or yellow bile or phlegm necessitated restoration of the balance (Evans 1998). However, gods and goddesses, magical forces and other potential predisposing factors were also relevant at that time and influenced treatment (Scarborough 1969). During the Anglo-Saxon period in England, populations saw a mixture of possible causes of disease: elf-shot (arrows shot into the body by a demon); contagion (a body part affected by substances in contact with it or near it); intrusion of an object; or by poison from a creature ((flying venom) – Grattan and Singer 1952, 3). Appropriate treatments developed. Once Europe moved into the later and post-Medieval periods, religion played a strong part in people's beliefs about causation of disease. It was seen as something that had to be endured, often as a punishment for sin (Alford 1979, 389). Concepts of disease causation in the west revolved around Greek and Arabian medical traditions, which had all been translated by the fourteenth century AD (Mettler 1947, 362). Naturally, these different concepts need to be considered with respect to treatment, whose development and evolution (and success, both past and present) would have been very much influenced by them (Gatchel et al. 1989).

HEALING THE SICK: TREATMENT OF TUBERCULOSIS: PAST AND PRESENT

Today, where you live and how much money you have mainly determines whether you get access to treatment. Politics will, overall, prevent or enable populations to get care and recover from TB (Walt 1999, 68). Furthermore, whether a person adheres to the treatment regime is often influenced by many factors. For example, a person may feel better before the full course of antibiotics has been taken, and therefore will not take the rest of the therapy (Rubel and Garro 1992, 627). The general feeling, however, is that those least able to comply with treatment are those most likely not to. Preventative measures such as the administration of the BCG vaccine (O'Reilly and

Daborn 1995), improvement in living conditions, reduction of poverty, and treatment using multiple antibiotics to combat the infection (through Directly Observed Therapy (Short Course) or DOTS – Squire and Wilkinson 1998) are the main features of therapy for people today (Porter and Grange 1999). Traditional medicines based on herbs also feature highly in some groups (e.g. Vecchiato 1997). However, multi-drug resistance (MDR) has become a major problem today (Grange 1999).

It is difficult to assess exactly what treatments specific people with TB were exposed to in the past because direct evidence for treatment of any disease or trauma is rare in the archaeological record (Roberts and Manchester 1995). Access to care in general is also an aspect of treatment, which is unknown and was probably determined by age, sex and social status. In the past a medley of therapies appears to have been present for the treatment of disease. General therapeutic regimes included herbs, cautery (Meinecke 1927), and bloodletting (Smith 1988). However, specific herbal remedies such as lungwort (*Pulmonaria officinalis*), a herb with leaves that appear similar in appearance to lung tissue affected by tuberculosis, was one such herb recommended for TB, as indicated by both ancient and modern herbals (Potterton 1983). Resin/oil mixtures from trees, e.g. yellow amber and myrrh, also formed many bases for medicines for TB (Roberts and Buikstra in review), and turpentine, gold, iodine, copper, phosphorus and magnesium were also recommended (Bates 1992; Evans 1998; Pesanti 1995).

Diet was also important in many treatment suggestions. Often this involved ingestion of meat and milk from animals (Daniel 1997; Pease 1940). It is possible that if an animal had TB, then ingestion of it may have (if in small enough doses) induced immunity in the person. People also travelled to access a better environment, for example to the Alps (Bryder 1988), and the act of travel was also supposed to help (Daniel 1997). Sanatoria (meaning 'to heal') also developed from the seventeenth century AD to deal (some believe) with tuberculosis. They provide an environment, preferably at altitude, with lots of fresh air, a healthy well balanced diet, and graded exercise (Bates 1994; Bryder 1988; Dormandy 1999; Evans 1998). Surgery was practised in some, for example, lung collapse therapy (to rest affected lungs) and rib resection (Evans 1998). In effect, it provided a place of hope for families with relatives with the disease, and care for those afflicted. Whether they were actually effective in relieving their infection is still being debated (Evans 1998, 13). While a healthy well-balanced diet with lots of meat was advocated in sanatoria, other more unconventional dietary regimes included snails and snake excrement (Smith 1988). Another environment that people felt was beneficial to those with TB was Mammoth Cave in Kentucky, U.S.A. A constant temperature and humidity apparently provided a good healing place for people, and stone and wooden huts were built inside the cave. Unfortunately this treatment regime was not very successful (Mohr and Sloane 1955). Inhalation of various substances, including tobacco and burning dung, were also recommended, but in most cases were probably not very effective (Meinecke 1927). A treatment that was commonly available for people with TB in England and France was 'Touching for the King's Evil'. The king or queen of the time, from the later Medieval period onwards, was believed to be able to cure people with the disease; a gold touch-piece was provided to those touched, but if they lost it then TB would return to haunt them

Table 3.5. Ethnobotanical remedies against tuberculosis in Ethiopia (from Vecchiato 1997).

Sidama culture plant name	Scientific name	Effects
Arghisa	*Aloe megalacantha*	Emetic
Basu Bakula	*Cucmis ficifolius*	Emetic
Bullancho	*Labiatae*	Emetic
Daguccho	*Podocarpus gracilior*	Emetic, expectorant
Gambela	*Gardenia Iovis totantis*	Emetic
Garamba	*Hypericum lanceolata L.*	Emetic, expectorant
Gatame	*Sheffelera abyssinica*	Emetic, expectorant
Ghidincho	*Discopodium penninervium*	Emetic
Ma'disisa	*Trichcladus ellipticus*	Emetic, expectorant
Malasincho	*Clutia robusta*	Emetic
Nole		Emetic

(Daniel 1997; Crawfurd 1911). It is debatable whether the many thousands touched had the disease but, again, this form of treatment may have given people hope.

Clearly, treatments today could be more effective if people were not resistant to the antibiotics used, and all had equal access to medical care. Furthermore, if everybody lived in healthy environments (in their broadest sense) and were not malnourished, this may prevent the disease increasing in frequency. In the past, antibiotics were not available so less effective forms of treatment were followed, based on a population's concepts of how and why the disease occurred. Today, in traditional groups, more alternative methods of treatment are used (Table 3.5), even in situations where antibiotics are readily available, thus reflecting how much culture affects the outcome of disease.

CONCLUSIONS

TB is with us today and will be for many years to come until poverty is tackled, and effective therapy is developed and introduced into both developed and developing countries, with access for all. TB in the past is also seen and dates from at least 6,000 years ago; it has been with us for a long time.

Studying disease in the past necessitates a broad outlook in order to understand how people perceive the disease, its impact on populations, and why specific treatments are used. In order to do this, multiple forms of evidence must be utilised in order to provide a window on diseases that plagued our ancestors. Use of one form of evidence can bias the final picture; all forms have their limitations and must not be regarded as the final answer and explanation to all the questions we might have. Tuberculosis, as has been shown here, is one of the most complex of infectious diseases, affecting many birds and mammals, including humans, and its appearance is influenced by a wide variety of predisposing factors. In addition, the reasons suggested as to why it has occurred have varied through time and place, and this still continues to be the case. Treatment regimes have also varied and have been very much dependent on theories of causation. Medical anthropology, clinical medicine, palaeopathology, documents and art all provide a small window on this important disease in the past but none provides the whole story. Until researchers accept this as a fact, then the history of the disease will be all the poorer. Very recent data actually now suggests that *m. tuberculosis* did not directly evolve from *m. bovis* (Brosch *et al.*, 2002).

Acknowledgements

I would like to thank the two reviewers for highlighting improvements in the text.

Bibliography

Alford, J.A. 1979 'Medicine in the Middle Ages: theory of a profession' *Centennial Review* 23, 377–396.

Aufderheide, A.C. and Rodríguez Martin, C. 1998 *Cambridge encyclopedia of human palaeopathology*, Cambridge, University Press.

Bates, B. 1994 *Bargaining for life. A social history of tuberculosis, 1876–1938*, Pennsylvania: University of Pennsylvania Press.

Bowden, K.M. and McDiarmid, M.A. 1994 'Occupationally acquired tuberculosis: what's known' *Journal of Occupational Medicine* 36(3), 320–325.

Brosch, R., Gordon, S.V., Marmiesse, M., Brodin, P., Buchrieser, C., Eiglmeier, K., Garnier, T., Gutierrez, C., Hewinson, G., Kremer, K., Parsons, L.M., Pym, A.S., Samper, S., Van Soolingen, D. and Cole, S.T. 2002 A new evolutionary scenario for the *Mycobacterium tuberculosis* complex. Proc. National Academy Science 99 (6): 3684–3689.

Brothwell, D. 1991 'On zoonoses and their relevance to palaeopathology' pp. 18–22 in D.J. Ortner and A.C. Aufderheide, (eds) *Human palaeopathology. Current syntheses and future options*, Washington D.C.: Smithsonian Institution Press.

Brown, P.J., Inhorn, M.C. and Smith, D.J. 1996 (revised edition) 'Disease, ecology and human behavior' pp. 182–218 in C.F. Sargent and T.M. Johnson (eds) *Medical anthropology. Contemporary theory and method*, London: Praeger.

Brown, T. and Brown, K. 1992 'Ancient DNA and the archaeologist' *Antiquity* 66, 10–23.

Bryder, L. 1988 *Below the magic mountain. A social history of tuberculosis in 20th century Britain*, Oxford: Clarendon Press.

Canci, A., Minozzi, S. and Borgognini Tarli, S. 1996 'New evidence of tuberculous spondylitis from Neolithic Liguria (Italy)' *International Journal of Osteoarchaeology* 6, 497–501.

Corbett, G.B. and Harris, S. 1991 (3rd edition) *The handbook of British mammals*, Oxford: Blackwell Science.

Cosivi, O., Meslin, F-X., Daborn, C.J. and Grange, J.M. 1995 'Epidemiology of M. bovis infection in animals and humans with particular reference to Africa' *Rev. Sci. Off. Int. Epiz.* 14(3), 733–746.

Crawford, R. 1911 *The King's Evil*, Oxford: University Press.

Curry, F.K. 1968 'Neighbourhood clinics for more effective outpatient treatment of tuberculosis'. *New England J. Medicine* 279, 1262–1267.

Daniel, T.M. 1997 *Captain of death. The story of tuberculosis*, Rochester: University of Rochester Press.

Davies, P.D.O. 1995 'Tuberculosis and migration' *J. Royal College of Physicians of London* 29, 113–118.

Dormandy, T. 1999 *The white death. A history of tuberculosis*, London: Hambledon.

El-Najjar, M., Al-Shiyab, A. and Al-Sarie, I. 1997 'Cases of tuberculosis at Ain Ghazal, Jordan' *Paléorient* 2(2), 123–128.

Evans, C.C. 1998 (2nd edition) 'Historical background' pp. 1–19 in P.D.O. Davies (ed.) *Clinical tuberculosis*, London: Chapman and Hall Medical.

Farmer, P. 1999 *Infections and inequalities. The modern plagues*, University of California Press.

Gatchel, R.J., Baum, A. and Krantz, D.S. 1989 (2nd edition) *An introduction to health psychology*, New York: McGraw Hill.

Gernaey, A.M., Minnikin, D.E., Copley, M.S., Dixon, R.A., Middleton, J.C., and Roberts, C.A. 2001 'Mycolic acids and DNA confirm an osteological diagnosis of tuberculosis' *Tuberculosis* 81(4), 259–265.

Grange, J.M. 1999 'The global burden of tuberculosis' pp. 3–31 in J.D.H. Porter and J.M. Grange (eds) *Tuberculosis: an interdisciplinary perspective*, London: Imperial College Press.

Grange, J.M., Daborn, C. and Cosivi, O. 1994 'HIV related tuberculosis due to M. bovis' *European Respiratory Journal.C:* 7, 1564–1566.

Grattan, J.H. and Singer, C. 1952 *Anglo-Saxon magic and medicine*, Oxford: University Press.

Haas, C.J., Zink, A., Molnar, E., Szeimies, U., Reischl, U., Marcsik, A., Ardagna, Y., Dutour, O., Palfi, G. and Nerlich, A. 2000 'Molecular evidence for different stages of tuberculosis in ancient bone samples from Hungary' *American Journal of Physical Anthropology* 113, 293–304.

Hardy, A. 1994 'Death is the cure of all diseases. Using the General Register Office cause of death statistics for 1837–1920' *Social History of Medicine* 7(2), 472–492.

Hare, R. 1967 'The antiquity of disease caused by bacteria and viruses: a review of the problem from a bacteriologist's point of view' pp. 115–131 in D. Brothwell and A.T. Sandison (eds) *Diseases in antiquity. A survey of the diseases, injury and surgery of early populations*, Springfield, Illinois: Charles C. Thomas.

Howe, G.M. 1997 *People, environment, disease and death*, Cardiff: University of Wales Press.

Hudelson, P. 1999 'Gender issues in the detection and treatment of tuberculosis' pp. 339–355 in J.D.H. Porter and J.M. Grange (eds) *Tuberculosis: an interdisciplinary perspective*, London: Imperial College Press.

Kelley, M.A. and Lytle-Kelley, K. 1999 'Considerations on past and present non-human sources of atypical and typical mycobacteria' pp. 183–187 in G. Pálfi, O. Dutour, J. Deák and I. Hutás (eds) *Tuberculosis. past and present*, Szeged, Hungary: Golden Book Publisher Ltd. and Budapest: Tuberculosis Foundation.

Khan, A., Walley, J., Newell, J. and Imdad, N. 2000 'Tuberculosis in Pakistan: socio-cultural constraints and opportunities in treatment' *Social Science and Medicine* 50, 247–254.

Larsen, C.S. 1997 *Bioarchaeology. Interpreting behavior through the skeleton*, Cambridge: University Press.

Lutwick, L.I. 1995 'Introduction' pp. 1–4 in L.I. Lutwick (ed.) *Tuberculosis*, London: Chapman and Hall Medical.

Martin, L., Rothschild, B.M., Leu, G., Khila, G., Becovier, G., Greenblatt, C., Donoghue, H.D. and Spigelman, M. forthcoming '*Mycobacterium tuberculosis* complex from an extinct bison dated 17,000 BP' *Abstracts of the Paleopathology Association Annual Meeting, San Antonio, Texas.*

Mays, S., Taylor, G.M., Legge, A.J., Young, D.B. and Turner-Walker, G. 2001 'Paleopathological and biomolecular study of tuberculosis in a medieval skeletal collection from England' *American Journal of Physical Anthropology* 114, 298–311.

McElroy, A. and Townsend, P.K. 1996 *Medical anthropology in ecological perspective*, Oxford: Westview Press.

Meinecke, B. 1927 'Consumption (tuberculosis) in Classical antiquity' *Annals of Medical History* 9, 379–402.

Mettler, C.C. 1947 *History of medicine*, Philadelphia: Blakiston Company.

Miller, E., Ragsdale, B. and Ortner, D.J. 1996 'Accuracy in bone diagnosis: a comment on palaeopathological methods' *International Journal of Osteoarchaeology* 6, 221–229.

Mohr, C.E. and Sloane, H.N. 1955 *Celebrated American caves*, Rutgers University Press.

Molleson, T. and Cox, M. 1993 *The Spitalfields Project. The anthropology. The middling sort*, York: Council for British Archaeology Research Report 86.

Morse, D., Brothwell, D.R. and Ucko, P.J. 1964 'Tuberculosis in ancient Egypt' *American Review of Respiratory Disease* 90, 524–541.

O'Reilly, L.M. and Daborn, C.J. 1995 'The epidemiology of Mycobacterium bovis infections in animals and man: a review' *Tubercle and Lung Disease* 76 (Supplement 1), 1–46.

Payne, D. 2000 'Death keeps Irish doctors guessing' *British Medical Journal* 321, 468.

Pease, A.S. 1940 'Some remarks on the diagnosis and treatment of tuberculosis in antiquity' *Isis* 31,380–389.

Pesanti, E.L. 1995 'A history of tuberculosis' pp. 5–19 in L.I. Lutwick (ed.) *Tuberculosis*, London, Chapman and Hall Medical.

Porter, J.D.H. and Grange, J.M. (eds) 1999 *Tuberculosis: an interdisciplinary perspective*, London: Imperial College Press.

Potterton, D. (ed.) 1983 *Culpeper's herbal*, London: W. Foulsham and Co. Limited.

Rangan, S. and Uplekar, M. 1999 'Socio-cultural dimensions in tuberculosis control' pp. 265–281 in J.D.H. Porter and J.M. Grange (eds) *Tuberculosis: an interdisciplinary perspective*, London: Imperial College Press.

Raviglione, M.C., Snider, D.E. and Kochi, A. 1995 'Global epidemiology of tuberculosis morbidity and mortality of a worldwide epidemic' *Journal of the American Medical Association* 273(3), 220–226.

Resnick, D. (ed.) 1995 *Diagnosis of bone and joint disorders*, Edinburgh: W.B. Saunders.

Roberts, C.A. and Manchester, K. 1995 *The archaeology of disease*, Gloucester: Sutton Publishing.

Roberts, C.A. 2000 'Did they take sugar? The use of skeletal evidence in the study of disability in past populations' pp. 46–59 in J. Hubert (ed.) *Madness, disability and social exclusion. The archaeology and anthropology of 'difference'*, London: Routledge.

Roberts and Buikstra (in review) *Tuberculosis. Old disease, new awakening*, University of Florida Press.

Roberts, C.A., Lucy, D. and Manchester, K. 1994 'Inflammatory lesions of ribs: an analysis of the Terry Collection' *American Journal Physical Anthropology* 85, 169–182.

Roberts, C.A., Boylston, A., Buckley, L., Chamberlain, A. and Murphy, E.M. 1998 'Rib lesions and tuberculosis: the palaeopathological evidence' *Tubercle and Lung Disease* 79(1), 55–60.

Rubel, A.J. and Garro, L.C. 1992 'Social and cultural factors in the successful control of tuberculosis' *Public Health Reports* 107(6), 626–636.

Salo, W.L., Aufderheide, A.C., Buikstra, J.E. and Holcomb, T.A. 1994 'Identification of Mycobacterium tuberculosis DNA in a pre-Columbian mummy' *Proceedings of the National Academy of Science* 91, 2091–2094.

Scarborough, J. 1969 *Roman medicine*, London: Thames and Hudson.

Smith, E.R. 1988 *The retreat of tuberculosis 1850–1950*, London: Croom Helm.

Snider, D.E., Raviglione, M. and Kochi, A. 1994 'Global burden of tuberculosis' pp. 3–11 in B.R. Bloom (ed.) *Tuberculosis: pathogenesis, protection and control*, Washington D.C.: American Society for Microbiology.

Sontag, S. 1991 *Illness as metaphor*, New York: Farar, Straus and Giroux.

Squire, S.B. and Wilkinson, D. 1998 (2nd edition) 'Directly observed therapy' pp. 469–483 in P.D.O. Davies (ed.) *Clinical tuberculosis*, London: Chapman and Hall Medical.

Steinbock, T.T. 1976 *Paleopathological diagnosis and interpretation*, Springfield, Illinois: Charles C. Thomas.

Stirling, G. 1997 'Tuberculosis and 19th and 20th century painters' *Proceedings of the Royal College of Physicians of Edinburgh* 27, 221–226.

Taylor, G.M., Rutland, P. and Molleson, T. 1997 'A sensitive polymerase chain reaction method for the detection of *Plasmodium* species DNA in ancient human remains' *Ancient Biomolecules* 1, 193–203.

Truswell, A.S. and Hanson, J.D.L. 1976 'Medical research among the !Kung' pp. 166–195 in R.B. Lee and I. DeVore (eds) *Kalahari hunter-gatherers. Studies of the !Kung San and their neighbours*, Harvard: University Press.

Vecchiato, N.L. 1997 'Sociocultural aspects of tuberculosis control in Ethiopia' *Medical Anthropology Quarterly* 11(2), 183–201.

Waldron, T. 1994 *Counting the dead. The epidemiology of skeletal populations*, Chichester: Wiley.

Walt, G. 1999 'The politics of tuberculosis: the role of power and process' pp. 67–98 in J.D.H. Porter and J.M. Grange (eds) *Tuberculosis: an interdisciplinary perspective*, London: Imperial College Press.

Wood, J.W., Milner, G.R., Harpending, H.C. and Weiss, K.M. 1992 'The osteological paradox: problems of inferring prehistoric health from skeletal samples' *Current Anthropology* 33, 343–370.

World Health Organisation 2000 *Global tuberculosis control*, Geneva: World Health Organisation.

4. A preliminary account of the doctor's grave at Stanway, Colchester, England

Philip Crummy

INTRODUCTION

Stanway was a remarkable funerary site for a select group of high-status Britons who died in the late Iron Age and early Roman periods. Among the dead was a doctor or surgeon whose remains were interred with his surgical instruments. Other objects in the grave that may have had a medical function consist of a strainer bowl, which had been used to make a tea-like infusion with *artemisia*, and a set of rods. Most of the surgical instruments lay on top of a wooden gaming board on which gaming pieces had been laid out as if at an early stage in a game.

The site was excavated intermittently between 1987 and 1997 by the Colchester Archaeological Trust. A full report on the results is being prepared as I write, and it is hoped that this will be published around 2003/4. The dates given below are provisional: they are likely to be modified once the finds and sequencing have been fully studied.

THE SITE

The Stanway site lies to the south west of modern Colchester (Fig. 4.1). It is situated just outside the defended part of *Camulodunum*, a kilometre west of the farmstead at Gosbecks, which was the focal point of the whole pre-Roman settlement (Hawkes & Crummy 1995, 95–8).

The site was in the form of five enclosures (Fig. 4.2), which were laid out sequentially. Enclosure 2 was the smallest and earliest of the enclosures. It formed the core of a farmstead dating from the around the second century BC. Enclosure 1 was laid out in the first century BC followed by Enclosures 3 to 5 between *c.* AD 25 and *c.* AD 60. Unfortunately, no traces of any round houses survived inside Enclosure 2 because of the effects of modern deep ploughing, but there were finds such as loom-weights and distinctive pits which only occurred inside this enclosure and showed it to have had an agricultural function. Enclosure 1 may have been laid out as an agricultural enclosure, but later was used for funerary purposes.

The site was large, being about 200 m. square, yet it only contained graves for

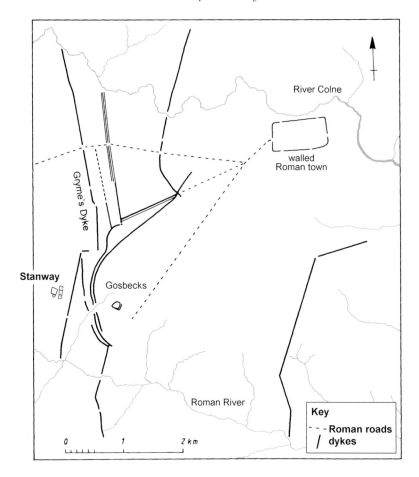

Figure 4.1. Plan showing the location of the Stanway site in relation to the Iron Age settlement and the Roman town.

eleven or so people. The most important of these were associated with four wooden chambers placed axially in four of the enclosures (i.e. Enclosures 1, 3, 4, and 5). The grave goods in the chambers had been deliberately broken, and fragments were deposited with small amounts of human cremated bone in the otherwise empty chambers. Two of the chambers, if not all of them, were each covered by an earthen mound.

In addition to the chambers, there were at least seven secondary burials. The burial rite in these cases did not involve the ritual smashing of the grave goods, and none of the graves had wooden chambers. Three of the secondary burials are of particular interest because their grave goods seem to signify something about the occupation or status of the dead person. One of these was the grave of the doctor or surgeon. Another was that of a presumed 'warrior' because it contained a spear and possibly a

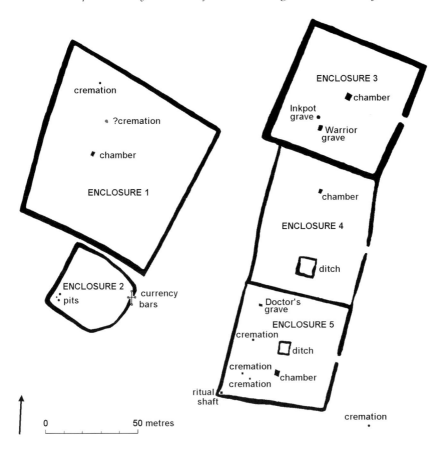

Figure 4.2. Plan of the Stanway site.

shield, and the third grave appears to have contained the remains of a person who could read and write because it included an inkpot.

Other activities inside the enclosures are indicated by smashed pottery at or near the corners of Enclosure 5 and a possible ritual shaft in the southwest corner of the same enclosure.

THE DOCTOR'S GRAVE

The surgical kit is a significant discovery, because it suggests that the dead person had practised surgery. However, the Doctor's Grave is notable, not just for the surgical instruments, but for some of the other objects which were in it (Fig. 4.3).

In addition to the instruments, there was a folding wooden gaming board, a set of glass gaming counters, a dinner service of eleven Gallo-Belgic vessels, an amphora (a

Philip Crummy

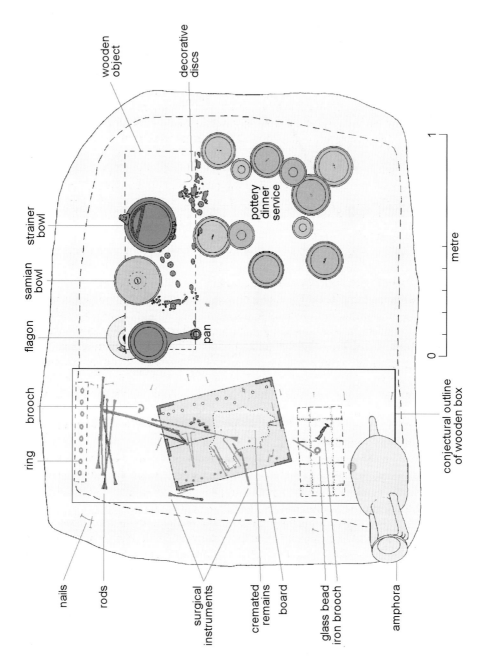

Figure 4.3. Plan of the doctor's grave.

wooden
object

decorative
discs

strainer
bowl

samian
bowl

flagon

pan

pottery
dinner
service

metre

0   1

brooch

ring

nails

rods

surgical
instruments

cremated
remains

board

glass bead
iron brooch

amphora

conjectural outline
of wooden box

Beltrán 1 *salazon*), a ceramic flagon, a samian bowl, a copper-alloy pan, a copper-alloy strainer bowl, three brooches, a glass bead, a set of eight rods, eight copper-alloy rings, various fragments of wood and textiles, and cremated human bone. Unfortunately the soil is too acid for unburnt bone to survive, so no evidence survived for the deposition of animal parts. The grave is dated to *c*. AD 50–60.

An interesting feature of the grave was the clarity of the evidence for the placing and arranging of the objects in it. The dinner service was grouped at one end, with metal vessels, the flagon, and the samian bowl grouped to one side of it. The vessels were upright as if they had contained food or drink (as is commonly the case in graves of this kind). The gaming board was opened up and the glass counters laid out on top of it as if at an early stage in a game. The cremated remains were then placed in a heap on one half of the board. Three of the rods were laid carefully end-to-end to overlap the board, and the rest were placed to one side in a bundle. The instruments were then spread out so that ten were on top of the board and the others were nearby. Everything in the grave appears to have been complete and intact when buried except for a surgical saw. This instrument had been broken into five pieces and the fragments placed in a tight group near the centre of the board.

The metal element of the surgical kit consisted of thirteen instruments (Fig. 4.4; Jackson 1997). These are: two one-piece iron scalpels, two combined sharp and blunt hooks (one iron and the other copper alloy), a smooth-jawed copper-alloy forceps, a pointed-jawed iron tweezers/forceps, a set of three iron handled needles graded in size, a copper-alloy scoop probe, what appears to have been a double hook of some kind, and a small iron saw with a tiny handle of copper alloy and bone. The thirteenth instrument was too corroded to determine its form or identity. In addition to these thirteen instruments, the kit is likely to have contained items made of organic materials, which have not survived. The missing element would presumably have included dressings and bandages, and instruments made of materials such as wood, reed, feathers, and textile. Together these instruments and the other items would have made a kit, which would have allowed the doctor/surgeon to perform a wide range of surgical procedures (Jackson 1997).

All but one of the one-piece iron instruments from Stanway have a distinctive knobbed terminal at one end which seems to mark them out as a cohesive group. The exception is the iron double hook, but this presumably also belongs to the group, and simply lacks the knobbed terminal because it is double-ended.

The scoop probe is a standard Roman type, and is the sort of instrument that routinely occurs in Roman medical kits on the continent. Otherwise, although the instruments are clearly related in terms of function and general form with contemporary Roman instruments, there are differences that betray other influences on their origin and development. In particular, one-piece scalpels and the predominance of iron instruments are not typical of Roman kits, but are features which are reminiscent of a small group of earlier instruments which have been found in Iron Age sites of central and eastern Europe (Künzl 1991).

Another interesting find in the grave was a copper-alloy strainer bowl (Fig. 4.5). The distribution of these objects (Sealey 1999, 122) shows them to occur broadly in Britain and central and northern Europe, not around the Mediterranean. Thus the

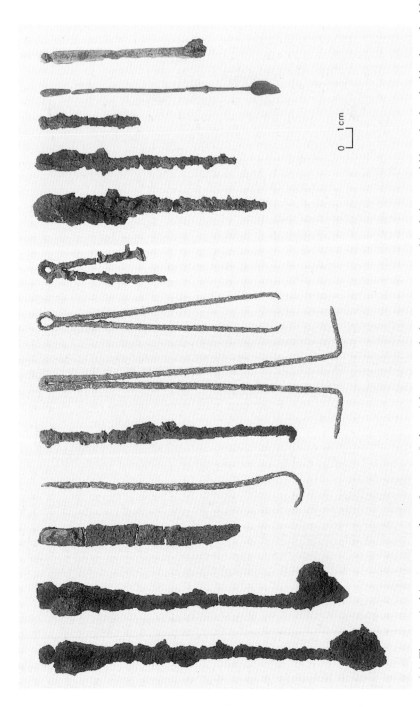

Figure 4.4. The surgical instruments from Stanway. Left to right: two scalpels, saw, two combined sharp and blunt hooks, double sharp hook?, smooth-jawed fixation forceps, pointed-jawed tweezers/forceps, three handled needles, scoop probe, and the handle of an incomplete object.

Figure 4.5. Replica of the strainer bowl from the doctor's grave. Approximately 300 mm wide (maximum diameter) and 110 mm high.

Stanway strainer bowl, like nearly all of the surgical instruments, is likely to be of 'Celtic', if not British, manufacture.

There is a debate surrounding the function of the vessels. J.V.S. Megaw (1963, 35) suggested in the 1960s that they were wine strainers, but Paul Sealey has more recently argued that they were for flavouring ale or mead (Sealey 1999, 123–124). Fortunately, a plug of organic material survived inside the spout of the Stanway strainer, and pollen analysis by Patricia Wiltshire has shown this to consist largely of the plant artemisia. The bowl has three feet soldered on to its underside. The method of attachment suggests that the vessel could not have been subjected to direct heat from a fire, because the solder would have melted and the feet would have fallen off. It is very unlikely, therefore, that decoctions were made in the vessel. Thus either the bowl was for making infusions, or it was for straining decoctions or (less likely) infusions prepared elsewhere.

Artemisia was and is still widely used for medicinal purposes (e.g. Grieve 1973, 858–9, Dioscorides in Riddle 1985, 69–70), so that its presence in a grave with a surgical kit could be taken to indicate that the dead person had administered herbal remedies. The drink could therefore have been a medicinal tea, made with artemisia, boiling water and possibly honey to counteract artemisia's exceptionally bitter taste. The medical properties of the brew (perceived and real) would depend to a degree on the species of artemisia, but unfortunately the latter cannot be determined from the pollen. Artemisia might also have been used as a means of flavouring ale or wine. Mugwort (*Artemisia vulgaris*) was widely used in Britain as a flavouring for ale before the introduction of hops, and it was still being added to some country home brews as late as the 19th or early 20th centuries (Grieves 1998, 556). Writing in the 1st century AD,

Pliny the Elder explained how, in Greece, artemisia was used to flavour wine (*Historia Naturalis*, XIV, 109). Artemisia, presumably *Artemisia absinthium,* was added to must (wine concentrate) and the mixture was reduced by boiling until it was one third of its original volume. The result was an early form of absinthe, which Pliny tells us would be added to wine a spoonful at a time. However, as explained above, the strainer bowl could not have been used for boiling liquids, in which case, if the artemisia was indeed for flavouring wine or ale, then presumably the liquid was boiled up with the plant in a more suitable vessel, and then strained through the strainer bowl as it was being served.

Patricia Wiltshire has yet to complete her study of the artemisia and the other pollens from the spout of the strainer bowl, and she may be able to clarify some of these issues in due course.

In addition to the strainer bowl, there is also the set of rods, which needs to be considered in case they also were linked to medical practice in some way. There are eight rods in total: four in iron and four in an alloy of copper (Fig. 4.6). They are all the same shape but in two different sizes, such that there are two large iron rods, two

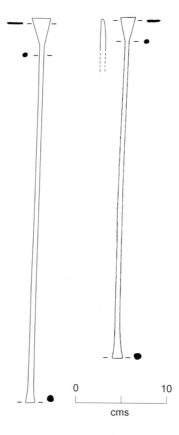

Figure 4.6. Schematic outline drawings showing the two forms of rods from the doctor's grave.

large copper-alloy rods, two small iron rods, and two small copper-alloy rods. Eight copper-alloy rings lay close to the rods. The function of the rings is also uncertain, but given their number and their proximity to the rods, there is a possibility that the rings and the rods were functionally linked.

No parallel has as yet been found for the rods, and their function remains obscure. A puzzling feature of these items is their replication in two different metals: it is as if there were two sets of four rods, one in iron and the other in copper alloy.

Of the possible uses for the rods, the most likely would appear (at least at present) to be divination. The rods could have been cast on the ground and the resultant configuration of all eight rods 'read'. Alternatively, just a few of the rods could have been somehow 'selected', and the composition of the selection interpreted. The fact that three of the eight rods had been extracted and laid on the gaming board separately from the others lends support to the latter explanation. The total number of possible combinations for a selection of three is only sixteen, which seems rather small, unless the rods were marked in some way. However it was done, divination could certainly explain the duplication of the rods in a second material. For example, the characteristics of the metals might have been interpreted in terms of gender or personality. Iron being hard might have been seen as male and having masculine attributes, whereas copper alloy is relatively soft and could be seen in opposite terms. Similarly size could be viewed in the same way, i.e. large as masculine and small as feminine.

Another explanation for the rods is that they were cauteries. Although there are no good known Roman parallels, the rods are reminiscent in form to much later examples (Karen Howell *pers. comm.*) such as shown here in Figure 4.7. Interestingly the man in the illustration is shown working with a pair of cauteries. One is in his hand and another is in the fire as if he is continually swapping them over. The Stanway rods are in effect pairs of rods of different sizes and materials, and so if used in pairs as cauteries, they would have offered a choice in the size of the working area of the instrument and the amount of heat which could be applied at any one time. However, the heated end of these later cauteries took the form of a small flat plate or pad which was offset and at right angles to the shaft (Fig. 4.7).

If the Stanway rods were indeed used in this way, they would have been rather clumsy instruments by comparison.

In the same vein, Dr Alan Richardson (*pers. comm.*) has kindly suggested that the rods might have been used for pin-firing horses. This is a technique whereby the flat elongated tips of heated irons rather like the Stanway rods are applied in a zig-zag pattern to the tendons in the animal's leg. He further suggests that the rings may have been part of the equipment needed to hobble the horse before starting to work on the problem leg. According to the system he describes, nine rings would have been needed to bring the animal down and keep it still on the ground, but it is questionable if the Stanway rings were large enough to accommodate the ropes or straps which would have had to pass through them.

The relationships between the Britons at Camulodunum and the incoming Romans remains to be fully explored and understood. The doctor was one of a group of Britons who, in AD 43, choose to stay in Camulodunum despite the Roman take-over. Many of his contemporaries decided otherwise and left to fight under Caratacus, who, of

5. A time to live, a time to heal and a time to die: healing and divination in Later Iron Age and early Roman Britain

Gillian Carr

INTRODUCTION

Who were the native healers of later Iron Age and early Roman Britain, and what happened to them when the Romans, with their own doctors and healing practices, arrived after the conquest? A consideration of British Iron Age medicine and its fate is entirely absent from archaeological literature. No research has been conducted exclusively on medical practitioners and practices during this period, with the exception of references to druids and their roles as healers by Green (1997). We also have references to medical practices made in passing by the Roman authors (e.g. Caesar's *Gallic War* VI, 16, where human sacrifice was performed to appease the gods to spare the life of the sick; and in Pliny's *Natural History* XVI, 95, where mistletoe was gathered for its use in healing). It is the role and fate of these healers (which most likely included the druids) and their medicine that I wish to discuss in this paper.

Given that the Romans suppressed and persecuted the druids (e.g. Pliny *Natural History* 30, 4; Suetonius *Claudius* 25, 5), driving them underground (Webster 1999), were the native methods of healing also driven underground? Was there tension and competition or peaceful co-existence between native and Roman healing methods and between the healers? Did the ordinary native Britons remain loyal to their native medical treatments and healers or did they also use Roman doctors? And did native healers adopt any of the practices of 'Roman' medicine (akin to a 'Romanisation' of medicine)?

METHODS OF HEALING

Medical archaeologists do not often feel comfortable discussing or acknowledging healing in the past through anything other than that which is 'recognisably' medical, such as herbal medicine. 'Medical' instruments are not often recognised as such in the archaeological record unless they resemble our own to a certain extent (e.g. Roman or Greek instruments, from which our own ultimately derive). Indeed, it is *because* the Roman and Greek instrumentation and some of their medical practices are ancestors of our own, that we refer to 'medicine' and 'doctors' in these periods, and use anthropological terms to describe healing and healers in prehistory. By using the loaded term 'medicine', we are falling into the trap of suggesting that it was rational, familiar and 'just like ours'.

'Medical' treatment and methodology is often only recognised from examination of bones and pathologies, which reveal past injuries and diseases or corrected abnormalities. Medical anthropologists, however, have long recognised the role of healing through song, dance, narrative, shamanistic trance, divination and sacrifice. It is archaeologically 'unconventional' or 'alternative' healing methods such as these which were likely to have been 'conventional' in the past. Here, I will argue that divination (and its sometimes-associated shamanistic trance) and sacrifice (which can also be related to divination) can perhaps be recognised in the archaeological record, and so it is these practices which will be considered here before going on to discuss the impact of Roman medicine. Before continuing, however, it must be made clear that most of what is suggested here has to remain, by its very nature, speculative and conjectural.

A NOTE ON THE CRITICAL USE OF CLASSICAL REFERENCES

Our information on native British healers (who were likely to have included the ritual specialists referred to as 'druids') comes from two sources: the classical authors and the archaeological record, although it must be emphasised that most of the classical authors describe druidic practices in Gaul and not Britain. However, I have chosen to include these because some of the artefacts associated with medical practices, which I describe in this paper, also come from Gaul. It is also possible, therefore, that the later Iron Age / early Roman transition in British medical practices, which I describe, may not have been broadly too dissimilar to those in Gaul. Because the evidence is limited, however, this paper remains a general overview rather than a contextual study.

I would like to make it clear here that I would not advocate an uncritical use of classical sources: they are likely to be biased and reflect the personal agendas of those who wrote them. In addition, it is likely that they used certain literary topoi to make the native Britons seem barbaric and uncivilised (Stewart 1995). The Roman authors would also have only an 'etic' or outside perspective of the people they met, and so would not have fully understood what they saw, not being members of that society. Finally, the use of classical sources has, in the past, often encouraged a 'top down' approach to studying the archaeological record, rather than a 'bottom up', i.e., because we are told that the Britons performed human sacrifice, we look for it in the archaeological record – rather than starting with the archaeological record itself and interpreting it with an open mind. In this paper I have tried to use the sources simply to help point the way to areas which might benefit from further study; however, it is often inevitable that they are sometimes used in a 'top down' manner. I have nevertheless tried to be critical in my use of them, and not to accept them at face value. I have thus also employed anthropological case studies to help understand the potentials of the archaeological record without relying entirely on the classical texts to direct my search.

DIVINATION

What evidence do we have for divination in the Iron Age, and how would it have been used in medicine and healing? Divination can be performed in many ways, and can broadly be divided into 'mechanical' and 'emotive' (see Devisch 1985; Zeitlyn 1987). Emotive divination typically involves some sort of 'possession', where there is perceived to be contact between the operator and spirits (e.g. the Tibetan Nechung oracle). This kind of divination often involves a shamanistic trance, which will be discussed later. Mechanical divination, on the other hand, involves simply the mechanical use of the divinatory objects/procedures, e.g. the Azande *'benge'*, 'three sticks' or 'rubbing board' oracle (Evans-Pritchard 1937), or Mambila divination (Zeitlyn 1987; this volume). These latter forms of divination or oracles can be consulted to give 'yes' and 'no'/'true' and 'false' answers, as discussed by Evans-Pritchard (1937) in his classic study. Questions can be posed such as 'will my sick daughter die?', 'shall I take her to the healer today?' or 'is witchcraft making my daughter ill?'. Zeitlyn tells us that divination is often used to decide whether to use traditional remedies or to go to the state dispensary (1987, 32).

Divination can also take other forms, such as 'sortilege', or divination by lots, which must be performed and 'read' by the diviner. Divination by lots is performed among the Ndembu of Zambia, who toss up a heap of symbolic objects in a flat, round winnowing basket. The diviner ostensibly makes his diagnosis on the basis of examining the configuration of objects on top of the resulting pile (Turner 1975, 244–245). Another example of sortilege is given by Tacitus, who tells us that the Germans used to cast lots by cutting down a tree branch, slicing it into strips, and marking each with a different sign. These were then thrown at random onto a white cloth, three strips were picked up without looking, and the meaning read from the signs scored upon them (*Germania* 10).

Specialist knowledge was also needed for other divinatory techniques, such as the studying of entrails (performed by haruspices) or augury (the cries and flights of birds) described by Cicero (*On Divination* 1, VI, 12). The druids were also credited with divination by animal and human sacrifice (discussed later) and augury (Dio Chrysostom *Orationes* 49; Diodorus Siculus *Library of History* V, 31, 2–5). In the Roman bathing and healing temple complex of Sulis Minerva at Bath, there is an altar stone dedicated by Lucius Marcius Memor, a *haruspex*, a Roman cult official whose job it was to divine the future by examining the liver and entrails of sacrificed beasts. This is the only recorded instance of a haruspex in Britain. It is unknown whether or not this is the only example of where Roman and native practice overlaps. However, it is possible that, where practices were similar, native Britons may have been happy to use, or had faith in, divinatory techniques practised by Roman practitioners.

What artefacts do we have from the archaeological record that suggest a divinatory use? Perhaps the most notable recent possibility are the 'divination' rods from the 'doctor's grave' at Stanway, Colchester (Crummy 1997; this volume). The grave, dating to AD 50, is thought to be that of a doctor because a range of Roman-style medical equipment has been found in the grave. Medical kits are very rare in Britain (in fact there is only one other example in Britain, and that is problematic). Out of the thirteen instruments in the grave, twelve of them differ subtly from Roman types.

Also found in this grave were eight metal rods, cylindrical in section – four of iron and four of copper alloy. There were two small and two large of each, and they were found associated with eight copper-alloy rings. The two terminals of the rods are also different: one end flattens and splays out into a triangular shape, and the other end is knobbed. It is not known exactly how they may have been used, if indeed they were used in divination, but it has been suggested by Crummy (*pers. comm.*) that, after asking a question, the rods were cast upon the ground in such a way that they could be 'read' by those who knew how.

There is also a small range of artefacts in the Iron Age which seem to relate to *time* (although it must be pointed out that not all of the artefacts are found in Britain), including at least one artefact which suggests that time was divided into auspicious and inauspicious time: the Coligny Calendar. The implication I am making here is that the time for rituals, including healing rituals, was probably very important in Iron Age society.

The Coligny calendar is from France and dates to the third century AD (Duval and Pinault 1986, 24–6; although Green (1997) dates it to the first century AD). It appears to be a calendar of religious festivals and cult events and is quite different from the Roman Julian calendar. It is clear that the concepts it represents are indigenous: although it is written in the Latin script, the language is Gaulish, and it records good and bad days. At the start of each of the twelve months the name of the month is given, followed by either MAT(U) meaning 'good' or complete, and ANM(ATU) meaning 'bad' or incomplete; also ATENOVX, which means 'returning night', marking the division of the month into a bright half (full moon) and dark half (new moon); in fact, the calendar reckons time in nights rather than days, in keeping with what we are told by Caesar (*Gallic War* VI, 18), who mentioned that the Gauls also marked time in nights rather than days.

The division of time into good and bad, auspicious and inauspicious, could help one determine when was a good time for healing or a healing ceremony to be performed; whether it is a good time to submit yourself to the surgeon's knife; and whether it is a good time to consult the 'spirits' and ask them for help. Presumably, if a patient arrived at a bad time, he or she would have to go away and come back later. Only certain things can be done at certain times and on certain days.

Time is also important in healing practices in other societies. Zeitlyn (1990, n8) points out that in emotive divination, where the diviner is possessed, possession at the wrong time of day can lead to a wrong prediction. Evans-Pritchard (1937) tells us that, among the Azande, when using the poison oracle, consultation may take place on any day except the day after a new moon. In addition, evenings are the prescribed time for consulting the three-stick and termite oracles. Among the Gnau of West Sepik Province, Papua New Guinea, the bamboo divination takes place at night (Lewis 2000). The following artefacts suggest to us that night-time and certain times of the month may also have been the time for divination in the Iron Age.

Two specific artefacts might be considered as having potential for divination. They both bear images of the moon, reminding us that time was marked in nights rather than days, at least among the Gauls. The first of these two artefact types is the anthropomorphic, hilted short sword. This rare and specialised weapon is made throughout Europe during the La Tène phase of the Iron Age, and is distinctive for its handle, which is in the shape of a human figure. The standard typology of these swords was established by Hawkes (Clarke and Hawkes 1955), but Fitzpatrick (1996) has discussed the small number (*c.* 15%) which have on their blades up to four distinctive 'stamps' which are inlaid with alloys or precious metals (although no swords with inlays have yet been discovered in Britain). The 'stamps' usually take the form of a vertical line (which is in line with the rib or centre of the sword and thus its centre of gravity) with a circle to the left of it and, to the right, a crescent. Other symbols are sometimes present, but these can also be interpreted as images of the moon in one of its phases. Fitzpatrick notes that the identification of these stamps is highly dependent on the preservation of the swords at the time of their discovery, and their subsequent curation.

Fitzpatrick suggests that the stamped line on the swords should be interpreted as representing a distinction between the waxing and waning moons and the link between the lunar phase and lucky or unlucky time as suggested by the Coligny calendar. He goes on to suggest that the swords themselves were involved in practices or ceremonies associated with making and keeping the time by counting nights, and determining what were propitious days.

Fitzpatrick suggests that these short swords or daggers were used specifically to establish when certain events (including healing) were to take place by people who had calendrical or astronomical knowledge, such as druids or other ritual specialists (Green (1998b) also suggests that these specialists ritually controlled and measured time). They were also the same people who practised animal and human sacrifice and divination (*ibid.* 1996). Fitzpatrick also suggests that the use of a specialised blade would be appropriate on these occasions. It is possible, then, that the anthropomorphic sword was actually the ritual dagger used in human sacrifice, as suggested by the shape of the handle.

The other artefact bearing images of the moon in its different phases is a rare type of bronze 'spoon' with circular handles, usually occurring in pairs, catalogued by Craw (1923–24). The bowl of one 'spoon' is always marked by a cross, and the bowl of the other always has a small hole. Craw suggested that the perforation acted as a strainer, but beyond that, not much else is known about them. Fitzpatrick (1997) has suggested that they were used in divination, although he points out that, beyond this speculation, not much more can be said. However, he suggests that each of the four quadrants of the spoon represent the four phases of the moon. At least one spoon, from Penbryn near Cardigan, has been found to contain inlays (or the remains of inlays) in all four quadrants, one of which was gold. Fitzpatrick (2000) suggests that each inlay represents images of the moon.

Quite how these spoons may have worked in divination is unknown and will remain that way, but if we were to speculate, we might imagine the practitioner using them to let some substance (perhaps a powder or liquid) fall from one spoon to the other via the hole, letting it fall upon one quadrant or the other. Presumably some force other than the practitioner was thought to control where the substance fell (an example of emotive divination?). The quadrant of the spoon containing the substance may have indicated the auspicious phase of the moon in which to carry out a certain activity, which may have included performing a healing ritual.

Divination through sacrifice

In the past, archaeologists have been extremely wary of using human sacrifice in their interpretations. Although many have not believed that human sacrifice actually took place during the Iron Age and Roman period, this is slowly changing, as shown by recent research (e.g. Green 1997, 1998a; Isserlin 1997).

The literary evidence that human sacrifice may have happened in the Iron Age includes the writings of classical authors such as Caesar (*The Gallic War* VI, 13); Strabo (*Geography* 4, 4); Diodorus Siculus (*Library of History* V, 31, 2–5); and Pomponius Mela (*Chorography* III, 18–19). However, we should be aware that these writings were biased and influenced by literary convention and personal agendas, such as the desire to project a stereotypic image of uncivilised barbarians.

We must also be aware that the classical authors' accounts of the activities of ritual specialists changed through time. There is a striking difference between the comments made by writers in the first century BC and those of the first century AD. Caesar, Strabo and Diodorus Siculus project a positive image of the druids engaged in official capacities as judges, teachers and presiders over ritual matters including sacrifice. But if we examine the testimony of Tacitus, Lucan, Pliny and Pomponius Mela, all of whom wrote in the first century AD, we find new notes creeping in: the association of the druids with secret places such as forests (reflecting the new status of druids as an underground movement following state proscriptions), and more pejorative, emotive descriptions of savage rites (Webster 1999). Were the druids becoming more 'extreme' in their practices, more 'impressive' to convince and win over an audience who had begun to abandon them, or who had begun to investigate other options?

Whatever the druids' reasons for employing human sacrifice, we must investigate the role of sacrifice in healing ceremonies before we go on to consider the archaeological evidence in Britain for such practices.

Although there are many kinds of sacrifice that are performed for a variety of reasons (see Bourdillon and Fortes 1980; Girard 1972), sacrifice can also be performed as part of a healing ritual. Evans-Pritchard tells us that the Nuer sacrificed on many occasions, including when a man is sick. Nuer sacrifice falls into two broad classes: collective sacrifice made at rites of passage, and individual sacrifice. The latter prevents danger hanging over people, or is made to appease an angry spirit or to get rid of misfortune that has already fallen, as in times of acute sickness. These sacrifices involve ideas of propitiation and expiation (Evans-Pritchard 1956). Among the Tallensi of Northern Ghana, somebody's fault, a sin committed and unatoned, lies behind misfortune such as an illness. Sacrifice is believed to remedy this sin (Fortes 1975).

Green (1998a) suggests that, crucial to the determination of sacrifice is the act of giving, which may have a number of functions including a request to the spirits for something to happen or not to happen; it may take the form of appeasement or propitiation, and it may also take the form of a thanks-offering for, e.g. recovery from illness. Caesar tells us that Gauls who were seriously ill employed druids to sacrifice human victims, because unless 'for a man's life, a man's life be paid', the gods would not be appeased (*The Gallic War*, VI, 14).

Green (1998a) follows Girard (1977) in suggesting that ritual aggression is an important element in the symbolism of sacrifice because of the energy associated with violence: the more violent and aggressive the sacrifice, the more efficacious the outcome. There is evidence to suggest that, in the Iron Age, the *violence* or force associated with the slaughter of sacrifice was the important feature of the sacrifice rather than the killing *per se*.

This can be seen in the ritual destruction of some artefacts, e.g. at the Folly Lane cremation in St Albans (Niblett 1999), and the Lexden tumulus in Colchester (Foster 1986), both of which seem to have been conducted with unnecessary savagery prior to their deposition. This is also visible in the 'overkill' factor, which can be seen on some Iron Age bodies. The most notable example can be seen in Lindow Man in Cheshire, who was garrotted, had his throat slit, his skull fractured, was strangled, stabbed in the neck and torso, and may also have been poisoned as evidenced by the grains of mistletoe pollen in his stomach, which could have been toxic if he ate enough of it (Stead *et al* 1986). However, as such a very small amount of mistletoe pollen was found, it is possible that it was used medicinally instead. Mistletoe is well known in the early modern pharmocopeia as being efficacious for ailments such as gout, hypertension and some tumours (Nyberg 1993).

There are other examples of potential human sacrifice (although other interpretations are possible) seen in funerary practices of the period. Green (1998a) noted that, at the Iron Age hillfort of Danebury in Hampshire, some of the bodies in pits have their arms placed tightly together as if bound, and some bodies were smashed and / or weighted down by large blocks of flint or chalk. This is something we also see in some of the animal bone deposits at Danebury, and could well reflect a similar sacrificial practice.

Other possible examples of human sacrifice can be seen at Maiden Castle, excavated by Sharples (1991), where some skeletons have been found 'tightly flexed' (indicative of having been bound), buried face down, or covered by slabs (or combinations of all three). It is possible that some in the famous 'war cemetery' at Maiden Castle, where so many of the occupants had head and arm wounds, were also sacrificed. One woman's head was 'dislocated at the time of death' and another woman had her 'spine severed above the fifth lumbar vertebra at death'.

We might also consider the skeletons of 120 to 130 individuals found in a ditch at Spettisbury Rings in Dorset, piled together with no evidence of ceremonial burial. Although many of these casual burials have previously been interpreted as excarnation by exposure (Carr and Knüsel 1997), or a deposit akin to the ossuary seen at some Gaulish sites (Fitzpatrick 1984, 186), I would not rule out the possibility that some are the result of sacrifice.

Divination through shamanic trance (emotive divination)

As mentioned above, divination can take the form of 'emotive' divination, where there is direct contact between the diviner and the spirits, so that the diviner is often possessed. The diviner will thus go into a trance to communicate with the spirits. In the case of a healing ritual or trance, the healer will ask the spirits what is wrong with the patient or how to heal him or her. The healer may also go into a trance so the spirits can speak through them and reveal the causes of the client's misfortune. Either the spirit itself speaks or the shaman translates his trance-induced babble later. Peters and Price-Williams (1980, 397) identify shamanic ecstasy as a 'specific class of altered state of consciousness involving (a) voluntary control of entrance and duration of trance, (b) post-trance memory, and (c) transic communicative interplay with spectators'. This means that the shaman is able to remember what he/she has said and experienced during the trance.

There are many ways the shaman can go into a trance: through chanting or focusing intently; through music or dancing; or through ingestion of hallucinogenic substances or alcohol, all of which make the shaman receptive to spiritual contact (hallucinogenic substances available in Iron Age Britain are discussed in Creighton 2000, 52).

A possible piece of evidence for trance states achieved through ingestion of hallucinogenic substances can be seen in the above-mentioned 'doctor's grave' from Stanway, just outside Colchester. Among other objects, a spouted strainer bowl was found in this grave, previously thought to have been used for straining alcohol such as ale, mead or some other native drink (Sealey 1999, 123–4). However, in the spout of the strainer bowl, a plug of organic material was found. This has been analysed and identified as pollen of the artemesia plant – but which artemesia is unknown.

Artemesia comes in many forms, all of which are medicinal: *Artemesia abrotanum* or southernwood, aids menstrual flow; *Artemesia cina* or santonica gets rid of worms; *Artemesia vulgaris* or mugwort is a digestive stimulant; and *Artemesia absinthum* or wormwood is good for indigestion, worms and fever (Hoffmann 1996). However, in the past, wormwood was used to flavour absinthe and can be poisonous. It also has hallucinogenic properties. According to folkloric herbals, wormwood was burned in incenses designed to aid in developing psychic powers. It was also used to summon spirits. Mugwort was often drunk before divination and was said to aid in psychic working and induce prophetic dreams (Cunningham 1985).

It would seem, therefore, that the strainer bowl could have been used for boiling, straining and pouring medicines of some sort. Examination of other examples of strainer bowls, such as the one from Sheepen in Colchester, show us that some are decorated around the spout with animal faces, such that the spout forms the muzzle or mouth. Some of the animals are almost identifiable as, perhaps, foxes or frogs. Could there be a meaning behind these animals or the choice of animals? One might speculate that they could represent the shaman's spirit helpers; or that the shaman could be endowed with the properties of these animals after drinking the liquid. It is also possible, however, that they are just simply decorations.

Other archaeological evidence for shamanic trance is highly speculative to say the least, but if one were to consider other possible evidence, one might include Aylesford Bucket. This is a funerary bucket from Kent decorated with copper alloy bands. The uppermost band is decorated with fantastic animals, which initially appear to be horses. However, they also have antlers, curling lips, unusual tails – and the legs of humans. Fitzpatrick (2000) has suggested that these images could represent priests in ecstatic trances taking on the shape of an animal in order to make contact with the spirits.

If we were to speculate even further, we might include such artefacts as mirrors in our list of divinatory equipment. Through focusing intently on the surface of a mirror, which may have been covered in a layer of water to make the surface smoother and more reflective, the shaman could have entered a trance, probably with the aid of hallucinogens. This may have worked using the same principal as scrying using a crystal ball or a bowl of water, the method Nostradamus tells us he used. Mirrors have properties that make them objects of mystery in many cultures. Any image has left and right transposed, while the viewer can see forwards and backwards at the same time. It has been pointed out many times that the abstract style of 'Celtic' art, with its tendrils and swirls, contain many hidden animal and human faces and eyes which swim in and out of view. One might suggest that, were these mirrors also used in divination, these images might represent spirits. Green (*pers. comm.*), on the other hand, has suggested that the 'bug eyes' seen in many of the hidden faces in 'Celtic' art might represent the bulging eyes of shamans in a state of trance.

ROMAN 'MEDICINE'

So far we have discussed the possible forms of Iron Age healing methods through divination. Some of these seem to emphasise an auspicious and inauspicious time for rituals, which could have included those of healing, or spirit consultation on the health of the sick. What happened to these forms of healing when the Roman soldiers arrived in Britain with their own doctors? How much access did native Britons have to Roman doctors? If they had access, did the Britons *use* Roman doctors? Did the Romans use British healers?

Jackson (1988) tells us that the work of military doctors would not have been restricted to soldiers alone, and that either on a formal or informal basis, people from the surrounding farms, villages and small towns may have visited the Roman forts for treatment. He also says that, in the long term, some of the military doctors would have become part of the local community themselves after retirement from the army, and continued to practise in a civilian setting. In this way, the army spread Roman medical knowledge and techniques, but also collected fresh information from locals. However, Jackson also mentions that few surgeries or consulting rooms have ever been positively identified, so these assumptions are not backed up by archaeological evidence.

We must ask, however, why would an ordinary native Britons wish to visit a Roman doctor as opposed to one of their own healers? As is well known in medical anthropology, illnesses and diseases are culturally determined, experienced and understood – as is diagnosis, method of treatment, and cause of sickness. Anything that the Roman doctor could have said or done to or for the native Briton may have made little sense to them in terms of their own cultural 'logic'. This would also have worked in reverse, for any Romans that wished to use native healers.

Baker (2001) asserts that Romanocentric readings of the past have created the belief that any culture would have adopted a Roman way of life, including Roman-style medical practices, because of its inherent 'superiority'. In addition, variations in medical practice differed between cultural groups in the Roman empire, just as they did within Roman medicine itself. She points out that Roman medicine was not a standardised system; it was not understood or practised in the same way throughout the empire, despite the idea of homogeneity being intrinsic to the study of Roman military medicine. It is likely that, as military doctors in the army were able to retain some form of their cultural identities in military matters (Saddington 1997, 496), then it is possible that they could have retained other aspects of their society, including their traditional medical practices.

NATIVE HEALTH CARE PLURALISM

Whatever their cultural identity, or the medical understandings and beliefs of the Roman doctors, why would the native Britons put Roman-style medical knowledge above that of their own healers, if indeed they did? Let us consider cases where western medicine has been brought into communities which previously only relied upon their own native healers.

Among the Manus of the Admiralty Islands, Melanesia, despite the popularity of European-American culture, western medicine is losing ground. It actively competes with traditional medicine and is not seen as complementary. It is often the last resort and, thus, when the patients eventually seek help from the local Aid Post Orderlies (APOs), it is often too late, and thus western medicine has a reputation for failure. Which system is chosen depends upon the Manus' classification of illness rather than their perception of what each medical system can do. There is a loyalty to their traditional sicknesses (i.e., the way in which they define the sickness and its cause), because disease is a category defined by the language of the native culture. Therefore, only a traditional medicine can cure a traditional sickness. The 'white man' is perceived as neither affected by, nor able to cure, native illnesses (Romanucci-Ross 1977).

In lower Zaire, western and native medical systems play a complementary rather than a competitive role. Western medicine is not regarded as competent to deal with dimensions of illness caused by anxiety, anger, social conflict, witchcraft and magic, as it denies the reality and validity of some of these. By this denial, western medical practitioners communicate to their clients the limited nature of western medicine. Once again, some illnesses could only be dealt with by one of the medical systems. There was no competition (Janzen 1978).

The Ningerum of Papua New Guinea, in contrast to their response to other western innovations, rapidly and eagerly accepted western medicine. Every Ningerum person uses western medicine, though not necessarily for every illness, and western and traditional medical treatments are used together in a complementary fashion and are not seen as conflicting. Self-diagnosis is typically the rule among the Ningerum, based on general knowledge. Patients select practitioners for specific kinds of treatment, based on their own self-diagnosis. Individual practitioners are believed to have specific therapeutic powers which require esoteric knowledge; no Ningerum practitioner can treat every illness. The practitioner is selected based on the self-diagnosis, and does not do the diagnosis him or herself. Sometimes western medical practitioners are used, sometimes native practitioners, and sometimes both simultaneously for best results if one is deemed insufficient (but never ineffective). However, western medicines are not deemed effective in exorcising spirits or removing sorcery packets, and so the APOs are not called upon to perform these procedures (Welsch 1983).

What we can learn from these examples is simply that, whether the systems are in conflict or complementary, traditional medical systems are consulted for some types of illness, such as spirit possession, sorcery and witchcraft, and western medicine is consulted for other sorts of problems, depending on what is deemed to be wrong with the patient. It can be suggested that this is probably what happened in the early Roman period. The native healers were consulted for some illnesses, and the Roman doctors for others. Even if the native healers or druids were driven underground, it is probable that the local people knew where to find them and still consulted them (although it should be noted that not all druids everywhere were driven underground or 'hushed up'. In the *Scriptores Historiae Augustae Aurelian* 44.4 and *Numeranius* 14, the author tells us that female druids were openly foretelling the imperial succession; in fact, Aurelian himself consulted female druids in Gaul).

It is unlikely that the druids were the only healers in the community. Pliny (*Natural History* 30, 13) tells us that, under Tiberius (A.D. 14–27), a decree of the Senate was issued against druids and related diviners (*vates*) and healers (*medici*). In addition to druids (probably Kleinman's 'professional sector', Kleinman 1980), there would have been a mixture of common knowledge, traditional home remedies or 'old wives' tales', advice from family, friends and neighbours, and from people with experience of sickness (Kleinman's 'popular sector'). It is likely that other individuals who specialised in forms of healing, such as the midwife, 'wise person', tooth extractor, or herbalist existed (Kleinman's 'folk sector'). All of these sources may have been consulted concurrently.

THE NATIVE PERCEPTION OF ROMAN 'MEDICINE'

It was mentioned above that the cultural logic of Roman-style medicine was unlikely to have made sense to the native Britons. It has been suggested elsewhere that, for native Britons, Roman culture was loaded with negative connotations (Clarke 1999). Clarke found that, among the native community around the Roman fort at Newstead, the architecture of the houses was round (a native feature), but within the fort the houses were exclusively rectangular (a Roman feature). Clarke suggested that this lack of cultural convergence was a deliberate choice and part of the expression of cultural identity. For the Britons, Roman culture had negative connotations because the fort's extramural settlement was ritually unclean and polluting with large amounts of careless on-site accumulations of rubbish (unlike native settlements), and they were divorced from the wider indigenous landscape (unlike native settlements).

Taking Clarke's suggestion that Roman culture was sometimes seen as unclean and polluting, and adding to that the importance of auspicious and inauspicious time in native medical rituals and healing – something which was unlikely to have been important to the Romans – we can see that there is no clear reason why the native Britons might ever have consulted Roman doctors in the early Roman period. There is no reason why they might have considered Roman-style medicine to be effective if it did not employ the ritual conditions that they may have considered necessary.

It may have been hard for them to have faith in such a foreign medical system. The Kanty people of Siberia, for example, found it hard to understand how a cure for the body had to be divorced from a cure for the soul under the Soviet medicine system. Their own traditional shamanic cures are directed at 'spiritual' ailments of patients, usually believed to take the form of lost or stolen souls. When they returned from the Soviet hospital, they often asked a shaman to make sure that the cause of the symptoms had been treated as well as the symptoms themselves (Balzer 1983), thus reflecting a lack of faith in an unfamiliar medical system that did not accord with their notions of the body and health.

THE NATIVE PERCEPTION OF NATIVE MEDICINE AFTER THE ROMAN PERSECUTION OF NATIVE PRACTITIONERS

If the druids were the main medical practitioners of the time, did Roman oppression and persecution of these people have any effect on the native perception of druids and their ability to be effective medical practitioners?

We can perhaps see a parallel in the case of the Siberian Kanty shamans, who were discredited and persecuted by Soviet authorities. An absolute prerequisite for an effective shamanic cure is faith. Given that Soviet persecution had turned faith in shamanic power to fear, failure of traditional medicine became a self-fulfilling prophecy (Balzer 1983). Kanty belief in shamans as either curers or sorcerers is waning, and they are now considered to be deceivers as well as doctors. The shamans now often go underground, and hide their profession (and are hidden by the Kanty), as later Iron Age / early Roman druids may also have done. Balzer also reports that some shamans are resorting to unconventional practices, such as blood-letting, covert séances, and the use of weapons (1983, 65), although she labels such practices as attributable only to disreputable shamans. During the time of Roman persecution of druids, we hear of their practices also becoming more extreme and unconventional, as discussed above. Balzer suggests that disreputable behaviour among shamans is due to disillusionment to the point of despair at the ridicule of their knowledge. It is possible that something similar happened to native druids, whose knowledge had been described as 'idle superstition' by the Romans (Tacitus, *The Histories* 4, 54).

CONCLUSION: THE FATE OF NATIVE MEDICINE AND HEALERS

What was the fate of native medicine? Did the native healers or druids 'die out' as a result of Roman oppression? Roman accounts of druids are recorded up to the fourth century, so it is likely that they continued to exist, but as an underground movement (Webster 1999). I have argued that, in the early Roman period, it is unlikely that native Britons consulted Roman doctors (except, perhaps, where practices converged, as with entrail consultation). Roman-style medicine is not likely to have employed the 'correct' ritual circumstances or methods (i.e. divination at certain special times) necessary for healing according to native mentality. It is also unlikely that Roman-style medicine was believed to be able to cure native categories of illness and disease.

Later on, any acceptance of Roman-style medicine, or rather, the medicine as practised by Roman doctors, need not have weakened native belief in the effectiveness of their traditional methods. The traditional healers and the Roman doctors may have been consulted at the same time, with the Britons resorting to Roman doctors for some complaints and the native specialists for others.

How, then, are we to understand the unique 'doctor's grave' at Stanway? This grave seems to contain elements of both Roman (the medical instruments) and native (the strainer bowl and 'divination' rods) medicine. Does this unique grave represent a 'Romanisation' of medicine? Does it represent a native healer who 're-trained' in Roman medicine in order to be acceptable to the Romans, or in order to treat 'Romanised' élite Britons? Did the healer merely adopt certain new medical practices from the Roman doctors? I would suggest another alternative.

Underwood and Underwood (1981) tell us of untrained 'injectionists' such as the *sahi* or health worker in Raymah, Yemen Arab Republic, whose practice consists mainly of giving injections of various western drugs. They have little training (usually a brief association with a health professional; in one case a month's work as a hospital cleaner), and limited diagnostic skill. To the inhabitants of Raymah, however, the *sahi* practices what is considered to be the quintessence of western medicine: the treatment of illness by injections.

I would suggest that the 'doctor' from Stanway, in a similar way, employed 'Roman' medical instruments as a quintessence of Roman-style medicine. Like the *sahi*, he may not have used the instruments in the way that they were intended. In fact Roman medical tools need not imply the practice of Roman-style medicine (Baker 2001). Like any form of material culture, such tools might be adopted and transformed in accordance with local understandings; 'Roman' artefacts were often incorporated into existing spheres of use and meaning for indigenous practices (c.f. Carr 2001). This position is further supported by the fact that these 'Roman' medical instruments did not 'conform closely to standard Roman types' (Crummy 1997, 7), as mentioned above, suggesting that the native healer made them simply to resemble what he thought were quintessentially 'Roman' instruments, perhaps because he was losing ground to Roman-style medicine. It is likely that they were used in native healing rituals in an entirely native way, or were perhaps adapted to a native understanding of how to use them. In addition, Baker (2001) reminds us that the modern identification of them as surgical tools need not exhaust the range of functions that they may have performed. If this doctor's grave is in any way typical of what was happening in the early Roman period (despite being the only example of its kind), it is possible that it represents, not a 'Romanisation' but a 'creolization' of medicine in early Roman Britain (c.f. Webster 2001).

Acknowledgments
I would like to thank Andrew Fitzpatrick and Miranda Green for their comments on this paper. I would also like to thank Philip Crummy, for letting me examine the

Stanway Doctor's medical instruments, and Paul Sealey, for discussing strainer bowls with me. All mistakes are my own.

Bibliography

Baker, P. 2001 'Medicine, culture and military identity' pp. 48–68 in G. Davies, A. Gardner and K. Lockyear (eds) TRAC 2000: Proceedings of the Tenth Annual Theoretical Roman Archaeology Conference, London 2000, Oxford: Oxbow Books.

Balzer, M.M. 1983 'Doctors or deceivers? The Siberian Kanty shaman and Soviet medicine' pp. 54–76 in L. Romanucci-Ross, D. Moerman, L. Tancredi (eds) The Anthropology of Medicine: from culture to method, Massachusetts: J.F. Bergin.

Bourdillon, M.F.C. and Fortes, M. 1980 Sacrifice, London and New York: Academic Press.

Carr, G. 2001 "Romanisation' and the body' pp. 112–124 in G. Davies, A. Gardner and K. Lockyear (eds) TRAC 2000: Proceedings of the Tenth Annual Theoretical Roman Archaeology Conference, London 2000, Oxford: Oxbow Books.

Carr, G. and Knüsel, C. 1997 'The ritual framework of excarnation by exposure as the mortuary practice of the early and middle Iron Ages of central southern Britain' pp. 167–173 in A. Gwilt and C. Haselgrove (eds) Reconstructing Iron Age Societies: new approaches to the British Iron Age, Oxford: Oxbow Monograph 71.

Clarke, R.R. and Hawkes, C.F.C. 1955 'An anthropoid sword from Shouldham, Norfolk with related British and continental weapons' Proceedings of the Prehistoric Society 21, 198–227.

Clarke, S. 1999 'Contact, architectural symbolism and the negotiation of cultural identity in the military zone' pp. 36–45 in P. Baker, C. Forcey, S. Jundi and R. Witcher (eds) TRAC 1998: Proceedings of the Eighth Annual Theoretical Roman Archaeology Conference, Leicester 1998, Oxford: Oxbow Books.

Craw, J.H. 1923–24 'Two bronze spoons from Burnmouth, Berwickshire' Proceedings of the Society of Antiquaries of Scotland 10, 143–160.

Creighton, J. 2000 Coins and Power in Late Iron Age Britain, Cambridge: Cambridge University Press.

Crummy, P. 1997 'Britain's earliest doctor?' Rescue News 73, 7.

Cunningham, S. 1985 Cunningham's Encyclopedia of Magical Herbs, St Paul, Minnesota: Llewellyn Publications.

Devisch, R. 1985 'Perspectives on divination in contemporary sub-Saharan Africa' pp. 50–83 in W. van Binsbergen and M. Schoffeleers (eds) Theoretical Explorations in African Religion, London: Routledge and Kegan Paul.

Duval, P.-M. and Pinault, G. 1986 Recueil des Inscriptions Gauloises, 3: Les calendriers (Coligny, Villards d'Héria), Paris: Supplément à Gallia 45.

Evans-Pritchard, E.E. 1937 Witchcraft, Oracles and Magic among the Azande, Oxford: Clarendon Press.

Evans-Pritchard, E.E. 1956 Nuer Religion, Oxford: Clarendon Press.

Fitzpatrick, A. 1996 'Night and Day: the symbolism of astral signs on Later Iron Age anthropomorphic short swords' Proceedings of the Prehistoric Society 62, 373–398.

Fitzpatrick, A. 1997 Who were the Druids?, London: Weidenfeld and Nicolson.

Fitzpatrick, A. 2000 'Les Druides en Grande-Bretagne' L'Archéologue Hors-Série 2, 47–49.

Fortes, M. 1975 'Tallensi Prayer' in J. Beattie and G. Lienhardt (eds) Studies in Social Anthropology: Essays in memory of E.E. Evans-Pritchard by his former Oxford Colleagues, Oxford: Clarendon Press.

Foster, J. 1986 The Lexden Tumulus: a reappraisal, Oxford: British Archaeological Reports British Series 156.

Girard, R. 1977 *Violence and the Sacred*, London: Johns Hopkins.

Green, M.J. 1997 *Exploring the World of The Druids*, London: Thames and Hudson.

Green, M.J. 1998a 'Humans as ritual victims in the later prehistory of Western Europe' *Oxford Journal of Archaeology* 17(2), 169–189.

Green, M.J. 1998b 'The Timelords: ritual calendars, druids and the sacred year' pp. 190–202 in A. Gibson and D. Simpson (eds) *Prehistoric Ritual and Religion*, Gloucestershire: Sutton Publishing Ltd.

Hoffmann, D. 1996 *Complete Herbal: a safe and practical guide to making and using herbal remedies*, Shaftesbury: Element Books.

Isserlin, R.M.J. 1997 'Thinking the unthinkable: human sacrifice in *Roman Britain*?' pp. 91–100 in K. Meadows, C. Lemke and J. Heron (eds) *TRAC 96: Proceedings of the Sixth Annual Theoretical Roman Archaeology Conference, Sheffield 1996*, Oxford: Oxbow Books.

Jackson, R. 1988 *Doctors and Diseases in the Roman Empire*, London: British Museum Press.

Janzen, J. 1978 *The Quest for Therapy in Lower Zaire*, Berkeley: University of California Press.

Kleinman, A. 1980 *Patients and Healers in the Context of Culture*, California: University of California Press.

Lewis, G. 2000 *A Failure of Treatment*, Oxford: Oxford University Press.

Niblett, R. 1999 *The Excavation of a Ceremonial Site at Folly Lane, Verulamium*, Society for the Promotion of Roman Studies, Britannia Monograph Series No. 14.

Nyberg, H. 1993 'Celtic ideas of plants' pp. 85–114 in H.P. Hultinen and R. Latvio (eds) *Entering the Arena. Presenting Celtic Studies in Finland*, Helsinki: University of Helsinki.

Peters, L.G. and Price-Williams, D. 1980 'Towards an experimental analysis of shamanism' *American Ethnologist* 7, 397–418.

Romanucci-Ross, L. 1977 'The hierarchy of resort in curative practices: the Admiralty Islands, Melanesia' pp. 481–487 in D. Landy (ed.) *Culture, Disease and Healing: studies in medical anthropology*, New York: McMillan Publishing Company Inc.

Saddington, D.B. 1997 'The 'politics' of the auxilia and the forging of auxiliary regimental identity' pp. 493–6 in W. Groenman van Waateringe, B.L. van Beek, W.J.H. Willems & S.L. Wynia (eds) *Roman Frontier Studies 1995*, Oxbow Monograph 91, Oxford: Oxbow Books.

Sealey, P.R. 1999 'Finds from the cauldron pit' pp. 117–24 in N.R. Brown (ed.) *The Archaeology of Ardleigh, Essex*, Chelmsford: Heritage Conservation, Essex County Council in conjunction with Scole Archaeological Committee 1999, East Anglian Archaeology Report No. 90.

Sharples, N. 1991 *Maiden Castle: excavation and field survey 1985–6*, London: English Heritage Archaeological Report 19.

Stead, I.M., Bourke, J.B., Brothwell, D. 1986 *Lindow Man: the body in the bog*, London: British Museum Press.

Stewart, P.C.N. 1995 'Inventing Britain: the Roman creation and adaptation of an image' *Britannia* 26, 1–10.

Turner, V. 1975 *Revelation and Divination in Ndembu Ritual*, London: Cornell University Press.

Underwood, P. and Underwood, Z. 1981 'New spells for old: expectations and realities of Western medicine in a remote tribal society in Yemen, Arabia' pp. 271–97 in N.F. Stanley and R.A. Joshe (eds) *Changing Disease Patterns and Human Behaviour*, New York: Academic Press.

Webster, J. 1999 'At the end of the world: druidic and other revitalization movements in post-Conquest Gaul and Britain' *Britannia* 30, 1–20.

Webster, J. 2001 'Creolizing the Roman Provinces', *American Journal of Archaeology* 105, 209–225.

Welsch, R.L. 1983 'Traditional medicine and western medical options among the Ningerum of Papua New Guinea' pp. 32–53 in L. Romanucci-Ross, D. Moerman, L. Tancredi (eds) *The Anthropology of Medicine: from culture to method*, Massachusetts: J.F. Bergin.

Zeitlyn, D. 1987 'Mambila divination' *Cambridge Anthropology* 12(1), 21–51.

Zeitlyn, D. 1990 'Professor Garfinkel visits the soothsayers: ethnomethodology and Mambila divination' *Man* (ns) 25(4), 654–66.

6. A computer simulation of Mambila divination

David Zeitlyn

INTRODUCTION

The archaeological record includes a wide variety objects associated with divination, ranging from the tortoise-shells that pre-figure the Chinese I-Ching, the stalks of the I-Ching itself, through to heated scapulae[1] in North America to the engraved pieces of lead in Roman shrines. Where written sources exist they can help the identification and understanding of the objects, and such is the case in two of the three examples just listed. Without such contextualising information it is far harder to establish that an object or objects have a divinatory purpose. An example is the metal rods found in the doctor's grave in Colchester (see Crummy this volume). To consider the odd one out in the list above, it is doubtful whether an excavated scapula could be identified as being associated with divination were it not for the records of contemporary divinatory practice.

The Mambila people of Cameroon and Nigeria use a variety of different types of divination to assist them when making decisions that range from the mundane and trivial through to those of a more serious nature. Among these are guilt in criminal cases such as theft or witchcraft and the appropriate course of action for an illness. As an illness becomes progressively more serious, those concerned with its treatment may use progressively more reliable types of divination. A common question, taken to be answered through divination, concerns whether an illness should be treated by conventional western-style allopathic medicines or by other methods of 'traditional healing.' This paper concerns the most important type of Mambila divination: the one that is locally regarded as the most reliable, and hence that used when matters of the greatest import are at issue: spider divination.

I have been working with Mambila Spider divination since 1985. I was formally initiated into its practice in March 1986 by the late Wajiri Bi, a senior Mambila Diviner. I have published several accounts of analyses based on this work at a more or less general level (Zeitlyn 1990; 1993). One paper (1990) involves a detailed analysis of a single divinatory session. In practice, it proved to be extremely difficult to document such sessions consistently, including details of the outcome in every case. I explain some of the reasons for this below. Here, I report on some data that mark a new avenue in research in this sort of divination: the use of a computer-based simulation.

Basic set-up

I have described the system of Mambila Spider Divination in detail elsewhere (Zeitlyn 1993 and online at http://era.anthropology.ac.uk/Divination/). The essential idea is that a spider that lives in a hole in the earth emerges from its burrow and disturbs a set of marked leaf 'cards'. The area around the hole is cleared and covered over with a broken pot with a lid, since the spider prefers to emerge in darkness. A binary (yes/no) question is answered by seeing whether the cards have been pushed by the spider near to or onto a stone and stick which the diviner places near to the hole. Since it is possible for some cards to be placed on one, both or neither markers, a complex set of responses is possible despite the ostensible simplicity of the system. It should be noted that the pots and lids could easily enter the archaeological record. In fact, some sets of the leaf-cards have been collected and are now housed in the Pitt Rivers Museum in Oxford, among others. Objects in such collections are hard to interpret. The cards pose a particularly telling example of the difficulty.

As was said above, each card has a pattern cut in it, for example, sun, moon, path, man, woman, chief and so on (see the illustrated lists in Gebauer 1964). Many groups in Cameroon refer to these meanings in their systems of spider divination, but not the Mambila. Mambila diviners know the meanings of the patterns on the cards and insist that the cards must have the symbols correctly depicted. However, the meanings of individual cards were never referred to in any of the sessions that I have witnessed (nor in the simulation).

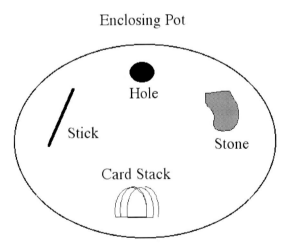

Figure 6.1. Nggam Dù set-up.

75 5555555

5 5

5 5 5

555 5 5

Problems in the field

I have long been a passionate advocate of the detailed and systematic collection of field case studies. Indeed, my first papers on the subject revolve around one session recorded in January 1987. Although I have documented other sessions, I have not published any more cases. The reasons why it is hard to document a complete session form an important part of why, with the help of Michael Fischer, I have recently started using a simulation of the divination set up to elicit cases.

For the researcher, Mambila spider divination is difficult to study, since when in action the diviners move quickly. The lid is raised slightly to see if the spider has in fact emerged and provided a response by disturbing the leaf cards. If it has, the lid is lifted off or pushed to one side. The diviner either pronounces the answer, or if it is less than clear, he may gesture at a particular area so the client can see what he is talking about. He inspects, removes the leaves and begins to pose the next question in perhaps 15 seconds. It is hard for the attendant anthropologist to photograph even with the most automatic of cameras or even attempt to make a drawing.

My tape recordings are full of my voice saying 'mɔm yə, mɔm yə kwa mì wə né foto'. [Wait, wait let me take a photo]. Worse still, the enclosing pots make a deep pool of shadow so it is hard to see clearly. If the camera is held at an angle it can easily focus on the top rim not the leaves at the bottom. Finally leaves may be invisible, hidden under the rim, visible only if one peers from the side – sometimes leaves are left on opposite sides so no single view point will reveal *all* the leaves (see example below). Although drawing would be better than photographs there is barely time even for the hastiest of sketches.

Clearly, the field researcher in such circumstances has a dilemma: either to interfere with the normal process of divination by intervening so as to get good photos or drawings, or accept that the natural flow of events is such that the documentation will be far from perfect. Since my initial interest was socio-linguistic I was happy to settle for the latter, relying on imperfect photos in conjunction with the tape recording of what was said. The sessions I have documented (not all of which have been published) have incomplete or patchy visual documentation. If the diviner said the pattern was 'like so' I was happy to accept it. In other conversations with diviners, patterns would be drawn in the dust to explain typical configurations and their interpretation so I was not too surprised – where I could see what was going on the interpretation appeared to be consistent with the official abstract accounts. It should be said that knowledge of the basic principles of interpretation is widely distributed – most adult men have at least a basic knowledge of how to read the pattern of the leaves.

Collaboration with my colleague Mike Fischer (the Director of the Centre of Social Anthropology and Computing at University of Kent, Canterbury) presented a solution to the problem – to make a simulation of divination in which the patterns could be recorded so giving a way of understanding more about how the interpretations are constrained by the patterns. This also has the potential capacity to document the processes in which divinatory objects, of the kind that may be found later in the archaeological record and in museums, are embedded.

In the field the procedure was as follows: we pilot-tested the procedure with a few

Figure 6.2. Examples of bad and good photos.

people to confirm my assertion that the meanings of the individual cards are not referred to in normal divination. There was a choice available in the logging as to whether a click would open a window showing the detailed image of the card clicked upon (the original setting) or, alternatively, if it would tick a box in the list on the left, to assist analysis. In the end, the latter method was selected. In the course of discussion with DZ, the diviner would talk about certain cards and, as he did so, DZ tried to click on the card in question, thus creating a list of salient cards.

In order to facilitate comparison, the programme used in the field was set so that the first five card selections and positions were identical in all cases. After the first five selections the numbers of cards shown, their position and orientation were chosen randomly by the programme. The number of cards was constrained to be between three and six. There are a few unusual options such as when a card is drawn down into the hole (signifying a death, possibly of a human) or when a card is pushed partially under the edge of the surrounding post. Special images of a crumpled/ folded card and of a half-card were prepared. An extra routine was introduced to show these options occasionally. In the end, after pilot testing, we removed these options. The image of the 'half-card' (half pushed under the pot) proved hard to interpret and the card in the hole did not occur often enough to feature in the trial cases that we encountered.

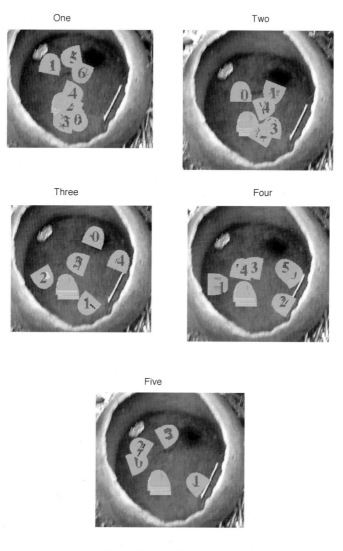

Figure 6.3. The first five patterns.

The results both confirm my field observations and demonstrate how the principles which had been explained to me were acted out in practice. More than that, they demonstrate the benefits of age and experience. Put simply, younger and less experienced diviners are more prone to dismissing a result as 'not saying anything' than their seniors. An experienced diviner can interpret an ambiguous leaf-pattern as giving a subtle and complex answer to a question that was misleadingly simple.

Conclusions

Computer research aids such as the ones I have described are not a panacea. Even using this tool, several datasets were unusable – in one case the programme was not reset so a long and intricate session with an experienced diviner does not contain any of the initial fixed patterns for comparison. In another case, I forgot to start the log and so the records are incomplete, and, since starting the log resets the sequence of fixed patterns, there is a mismatch between the sound recording and the log. Such is the reality of undertaking technologically complex research.

What I have learned, I believe, is something that I had gathered but could not justify or explain. Essentially this is how the rules of interpretation which seem so cut and dry when explained starkly, out of the context of actual divinatory praxis (for example, to a neophyte or an anthropologist), constrain the interpretations of diviners but do not fully determine them. The diviner and their clients are thinking through problems. The technology employed, here a spider and some leaf cards (or their electronic counterpart), acts as an external buffer, something to think with or against. It may be a prompt to consider previously neglected avenues of research, or it may confirm a set of pre-existing prejudices. The technology may constrain but it does not prevent negotiation from taking place. This is now familiar territory in the study of divination (e.g. Parkin 1979, Whyte 1991 and 1997, Shaw 1991). What we have been discussing is a means of achieving a more detailed study of how diviners and their clients respond to and incorporate the external constraints upon their negotiations, which may conclude in the choice of treatment for a sick child.

Notes

1   The cracks that appear on shoulder blades (scapulae) after they have been placed in a fire are used in divination by some native American groups (see Moore 1957 and Vollweiler and Sanchez 1983). The early Chinese system was similar: tortoise shells were heated and the resulting pattern of cracks was interpreted (Keightley 1978).

Bibliography

Gebauer, P. 1964 *Spider divination in the Cameroons*, Milwaukee: Milwaukee Public Museum.
Keightley, D.N. 1978 *Sources of Shang history. The oracle-bone inscriptions of Bronze Age China*, Berkeley: University of California Press.

Moore, O.K. 1957 'Divination – a new perspective', *American Anthropologist* 59, 69–74.

Parkin, D. 1979 'Straightening the paths from wilderness: the case of divinatory speech' *JASO: The Journal of the Anthropological Society of Oxford* 10(3), 147–160.

Shaw, R. 1991 'Splitting truths from darkness. Epistemological aspects of Temne Divination' pp. 137–52 in P.M. Peek (ed.) *African Divination systems – ways of knowing,*Bloomington: Indiana University Press.

Vollweiler, L.G., and Sanchez, A.B. 1983 'Divination – "adaptive" from whose perspective?' *Ethnology* 22 (3), 193–209.

Whyte, S.R. 1991 'Knowledge and power in Nyole divination', pp. 153–72 in P.M. Peek (ed.) *African divination systems – ways of knowing*, Bloomington: Indiana University Press.

Whyte, S.R. 1997 *Questioning misfortune: the pragmatics of uncertainty in eastern Uganda*, Cambridge and New York: Cambridge University Press.

Zeitlyn, D. 1987 'Mambila Divination', *Cambridge Anthropology* 12(1), 21–51.

Zeitlyn, D. 1990 'Professor Garfinkel visits the soothsayers. Ethnomethodology and Mambila divination' *Man (n.s.)* 25(4), 654–66.

Zeitlyn, D. 1993 'Spiders in and out of court or "the long legs of the law." Styles of spider divination in their sociological contexts' *Africa* 63(2), 219–240.

7. Beer, trees, pigs and chickens: medical tools of the Lohorung shaman and priest

Charlotte Hardman

In much of the world the tools of the western medical practitioner are all too well known – the white coat, stethoscope, the prescription pad, thermometer and surgical instruments. Diagnosis of disease in biomedical terms is accepted and the taxonomy of the medical profession orders and interprets most health problems that occur. In Kathmandu, Nepal pharmacies are as full of antibiotics, aspirin, paracetamol and indigestion tablets as they are in London, but instead of the homeopathic alternatives there are ayurvedic ones from India. Yet for many people in Nepal, Kathmandu included, pains and symptoms are not primarily understood and experienced according to the assumptions of scientific medicine or in ayurvedic terms, but in terms of angry gods, evil spirits, ancestors and hungry ghosts or human witches. This is even more noticeably the case in rural East Nepal, with which I am concerned in this paper.[1] Even where some 'Western' medicines or hospitals can be reached within a few days walk, biomedical cures are often viewed with ambivalence. The logic is that, unless the primary source is dealt with by appeasing the ancestor or the angry spirit, the 'Western' cure cannot work and might make symptoms worse by aggravating the superhuman realm. Once problems with the superhuman realm have been addressed, then the non-traditional medicine can work.

But why should this be of archaeological concern? How can ideas about symptoms and cures in the Eastern hills of the Nepal Himalayas be of interest to those digging in the Amazon, Africa or Siberia? First, although the notion of 'Rai culture' is an anthropological device, an abstraction, embedded in it are certain views about illness which are more widely relevant to other groups. Their ideas about illness are intimately connected to cosmological ideas or a worldview which could be, at least in part, characterised as 'shamanic', 'animistic' and related to 'ancestor worship' and have an astonishing similarity to ideas and practices existing all over the world (see Eliade 1964; Hoppál and Howard 1993; Baldick 2000). Care, of course, needs to be taken not to over-generalise these terms and also in emphasising the diversity across cultures. Anthropologists from van Gennep's writing in 1903 to Kehoe in 2000 have argued at length the view that is shared by many anthropologists that the terms 'shaman' and 'shamanism' should be restricted to the peoples of Siberia, from whom the name derives. Nevertheless, a broader interpretation has suggested a universal phenomenon and it may be helpful for archaeologists to consider the cosmological components of 'shamanic' cultures, a point already put forward by the archaeologist Richard Bradley (2000, 32) writing about the archaeology of natural landscapes,

> 'The shamanic experiences are important for our purposes because these sensations may become associated with particular kinds of location in the landscape. Eliade writes of 'holes' or 'openings' and this is an apt description of the caves and rock fissures that play such a major part in the sacred geography of the Arctic and Classical worlds. He discusses the sensation of flight that is naturally associated with the trees and mountains that reach into the sky'.

Understanding shamanic experiences of ecstatic flight may be significant, as Bradley suggests, in throwing light on features of the natural landscape. This landscape of rivers, mountains and rocks is mapped as much by shamanic ritual journeys as by geography. In an altered state of consciousness ritual journeys are undertaken to encounter ancestors, spiritual beings and lost souls and these 'journeys' are perceived by practitioners to visit actual geogaphical locations. What should not be forgotten by archaeologists, however, in their haste to focus on content and not process, or from an inability to emerge from dualistic thinking, is the particular *attitude* to the natural landscape central to 'shamanism'. Although varying from culture to culture, all or parts of the natural landscape are understood as being imbued with some kind of power or 'spirit', but, as we shall see, this does not necessarily mean they are seen as 'sacred'. The centrality of this attitude in appreciating the medical tools of some cultures is a theme of this paper. Therefore, secondly, although this paper is concerned with specifically understanding the medical tools and instruments of Lohorung Rai [2] practitioners, it also aims to clarify this particular kind of attitude to the world, sometimes misinterpreted as being a sacralizing attitude, or crudely epitomised as 'animistic'.

Epitomising the Lohorung Rai view of the world as 'shamanic' and 'animistic' is vastly over-simplistic. What it does, however, is focus on a view, common in Nepal, that there are different ways of 'knowing' and 'understanding' the world and that the way to understand the 'true' nature of things is by means of those shamans and priests who can relate to a spiritual and ancestral world and who understand the spiritual forces at work in the cosmos. It also focuses on understanding the complicated and subtle ideas about the existence of a power or quality which endows a vitality or power to certain material and natural objects. The three hearth stones, beer and trees, for example, as well as pigs and chickens have this quality and are crucial to restoring well-being when sickness and misfortune occur [3]. These objects and animals are central to the curative process but understanding their role and significance as healing tools must present a problem for the archaeologist. Firstly, what bestows power on the tools is nothing intrinsic to the objects or animals themselves, but is conceptual and, therefore, not immediately accessible to the archaeologist. The second problem is the impermanence of the tools. In most healing rituals, the healing tools specific to that ritual are obliterated: some are left to rot, some are destroyed in sacrifice and others are taken away by the household to be consumed by the living. Nothing is left for posterity. Re-creation is a central component of the ritual activity and the subsequent obliteration of material evidence is therefore of its essence. However, if archaeologists have evidence of people who are replicating the nature of human life in this world in their conception of another world in the way, for example, that the dead are catered for just like the living; if they have evidence of 'shamanism' whether in rock art or artifacts such as drums or headgear and if there are no permanent temples or shrines to be found, then it might not be too much of a leap of the imagination to infer the significance of natural places as ritual places and natural objects as healing tools. What I want to elaborate in this paper is how these tools are viewed. Doing so involves understanding 'animism' by which I mean, following 'a relational (not a failed) epistemology' (Bird-David 1999, 69); a way of knowing that is common to human beings everywhere, but which in the modern state has lost much of its authority. This way of relating to the world is important for any archaeologists interested in understanding the different ways in which natural objects and the natural landscape can have significant value in the conceptual framework of a culture.

In the first sections in this paper I explain how Lohorung Rai practitioners and their tools are classified and how Lohorung divide the material world into those objects. Certain animals, trees and plants have ritual names and can, therefore, be used as medical instruments; certain ones cannot. The middle section looks at several performances, the symbolism and meaning of the shrines, the ritual objects and animals, the healing ritual itself and how these and the construction of a shrine reveals Lohorung attitudes to health and disease. The final part of the paper suggests some interpretations of the rituals and the significance of the tools.

Classifying the world

Three factors dominate the lives of Lohorung and other Kiranti, these sedentary agriculturalists; the saturation of their lives with spiritual beings; a tendency to embody these beings in objects and images, to give concrete shape to an ancestor in a shrine, in the kind of beer, tree and food he or she desires; and thirdly the pre-eminence of the 'ancestral order'.

It is this last factor that I wish to discuss first since it is the key frame of reference to be understood in relation to Lohorung beliefs and ideas about illness and in their classification of the world, including their classification of which tools can be used in healing rituals and which cannot. For Lohorung to maintain 'good health' they consider it essential to recreate the 'natural' ancestral order, the original primeval order as recorded in myths, and to reaffirm the unity between nature, superhuman beings and human beings. They have what Herzfeld (2001, 102) calls a 'structural nostalgia', a view that the world was once a place of perfect balance and reciprocity, untouched by the corruptions of time. Even if not absolutely perfect, then it is at least undeniably powerful, since failure to recreate and maintain relations with the ancestral world leads to depression, increased sickness, possibly death, and ensuing chaos. In contrast, repetition of ancestral words and adherence to ancestral order acts as a way of recharging the cosmos. It brings vitality.

It is all three factors which lie behind the Lohorung propensity to divide the world into those objects considered 'ancestral' and those which are 'not ancestral'. Animals, trees, plants and objects that have an 'ancestral ritual name' (*samek*) are distinguished from those which do not; only phenomena with *samek* names can be used as ritual tools or as we might say 'medical instruments'. Only they 'belong' to primeval time. The trees to which the ancestors are called, the branches used as weapons, the places where they sit, the pillars of the house, the three stones of the hearth, the plants and bamboo, water pitchers, gourds of beer, the ladder of the house, the sacrificial chicken or pig used in a ritual all have *samek* names and have a relationship with ancestors. Everthing with a ritual *samek* name is tribal, traditional and ancient. They are the continuation of ancestral time, thereby ensuring its immortality. In spite of the global trend towards modernisation (the Lohorung, too, like modern Indian fabric, mirrors and radios), they still conceive of the strength, support and protection of their clans and society as coming from the primeval past.

Samek is, then, the 'original' or proto-name and is linked to a whole body of myths and knowledge about Original Beings and ancestors. That tradition which is understood by most Kiranti groups to be partially shared by all of them is referred to as *mundhum* or *muddum*, though local terms also apply. The significance of this ancestral ritual name in terms of healing is the power that medical instruments derive from their connection with this ancestral past. They are attributed with a quality which makes them 'alive' in the sense that it gives them strength and a kind of vitality, which is as vulnerable to loss as it is among humans. The attribution of human characteristics such as vitality and consciousness to these material and natural objects shifts people's attitudes towards them, particularly in ritual situations, but it does not make them 'sacred' in themselves. The special kind of ancestral vitality or force is also shared by humans. It binds together humans and these natural entities with ritual names in a relational sense. The 'quality' or 'vital strength' that bonds them among Lohorung Rai is called *saya*. The concept is not easy to translate, and I have dealt with it in depth elsewhere (Hardman 1981). In brief it is more than vitality and more than a 'soul', which does convey its metaphysical aspect. *Saya* could be called a life force and a 'power', almost like a magical energy, its power deriving from its link with the ancestral past. It is like an ancestral spirit or a powerful principle infusing all persons and some natural and material objects with an energy. Unless *saya* is flourishing people lose all vitality and the will to live; plants and trees droop, stones become brittle. *Saya* is also 'power' in the sense of resistance to misfortune and disease and an inner resource to face the world with head held high, deriving from and depending upon good relations with ancestors. All 'medical tools' used by shamans and priests, whether inanimate objects or natural phenomena, possess this key quality.

A female shaman (*mangmani*) from the village of Pangma (see Fig. 7.1) explained to me that if there were no ritual names (*samek*), people could not talk to ancestors. With *samek* names ancestors understand, experience and can therefore act; they relate to the names and objects they are familiar with, that is, *samek* is the ancestral language and can therefore raise and strenthen *saya*. Objects with *samek* names and the vital *saya* energy 'belong' to the ancestors. The shaman said,

> 'So it is that all trees, leaves, *singlung* have an ancestral name. That is 'green grass', that is 'stone'. We are 'man'. We became rich by grass and stone.

Figure 7.1. The mangmani *of Pangma village.*

> Once it was all free, and as people claimed it they named it: that green grass
> also has *samek*. It is owned. Everything had a *samek*, making it a separate
> kind; fire has *samek*, door has *samek*; we call maize *lingkhama*, rice we call
> *rungkhama* and millet *wekhama*; money is *pekhama*, bamboo is *yangli'powa'*
> With these names the ancestors claimed ownership.'

Objects like the hearth-stones, trees like *waiphu*, animals like pigs and birds like
chickens exist in a different order of reality from objects like tea or ploughs that are
relatively new to the Nepalese hills. Beer, trees, pigs and chickens can be used as tools
to communicate with ancestors and therefore as tools to cure because they already
have a relationship with ancestors. They were brought into being, or valued, by the
creators of Lohorung society (see also Allen 1974; Gaenszle 1991, 1993). As a necessary
part of its creation, and as part of its history, myths and traditions each of these
natural entities has a necessary part in its continuation and has a role to play in
healing rituals. In present times, the attribute of *saya*, the vital ancestral power,
functions metaphysically as the transcendent unity connecting human beings, natural
objects and material objects with ancestors and the primeval past, acting as an
energising force. This is not how it used to be in the original primeval order. Then,
beer, trees, stones, water springs, plants, birds, pigs and chickens (all things now

possessing *saya* and a *samek* name), could speak and understand humans. This was at the time when ancestors were still establishing clan territories and they could communicate with the spirits and the objects of the natural landscape. So ancestors of one clan could say 'so now you are our water spring (*chawa*)' and it became theirs, protecting them and giving them an identity. Now, in this new age, man has lost these powers, leaving only the *yatangpa* (local priests) and *mangpa* (shaman) to act as the mediums. Only they really know the old language, only they can 'see' the cosmic paths to find the ancestors, or angry ghosts of the dead, and therefore only they who can restore balance and good health when misfortune or illness strikes, still using, however, the tools of the past.

In this section we have already begun to see that the order of existence of Lohorung medical tools is connected to their animated status in myth and their relationship with the culture heroes and powerful, creative ancestors. Beer, trees, pigs and chickens all have *samek* names, all are connected to mythical stories and to particular ancestors, and all possess the vitalising quality of *saya*. We cannot apply any apparent intuitive distinction between 'animate' and 'inanimate'. For Lohorung these primary ontological categories are not key. Instead, they focus on different ways of being in the world. Beer has a way of being in the world, which links it to trees and chickens. All three are treated with respect not because they are seen as 'animate', but because they are associated, through the quality of *saya*, with the mythical realm and this gives them a kind of consciousness. Clearly there are differences (e.g. beer does not have 'breath', *sokma*). In ontological terms what all of them share is the key essence of *saya* which gives them a special relationship both to living humans and the ancestors.

THE 'PRACTITIONERS'

The cosmology of Lohorung Rai, as of their neighbouring Rai and Limbu 'brothers' (and a key feature of most shamanic cultures), is based on a view of the universe that is divided into three worlds: an upper, a middle and a watery lower world. Humanity lives in the middle world. The lower world is associated with the primeval snake ancestors living mainly in rivers and mountain springs. The ancestors and well-integrated dead (*sammang*) live in the upper world, separate, however, from spirits or ghosts resulting from unnatural or inauspicious death, who are excluded from the land of the dead and destined to roam hungry, thirsty and lonely which forces them to attack humans and inhabit the middle world (for a detailed description of these different spirits and ancestors see Hardman 2000, 59–101).

Illness and misfortune are associated with the spiritual beings inhabiting all three realms. To deal with the illnesses are two classes of ritual practitioner (as there are among other Kiranti), the local priests (*yatangpa*) and shamans called *mangpa*. These act as the main intermediaries between the world of the living and the 'other worlds', the world of the ancestors, ghosts of the dead, spirits and gods who intermittently interfere with the bodies, minds, vitality, crops and world of the living. Although it is common knowledge in Nepal that everyone can reach the 'other world' by means of their dreams, Lohorung, like other Rai, Limbu or Tamang, talk about the need for special practitioners to act as experts, whose work is in understanding and manipulating powers in this and the other worlds. They are understood to have their own ways of knowing and working. Their skills lie in diagnosing, divining, becoming possessed or making shamanic journeys, often in a trance state. My Lohorung friend Anuma was worried that I would not have access to either *yatangpa*, local priests or shaman, *mangpa*, in England. Given her understanding of the powers of superhuman beings to interpenetrate the lives, bodies and world of the living, I was in considerable danger. Having initiated a relationship with them, if I did not attend to them, pay them respect, feed them I would be ill and without anyone to communicate with them for me.

Of the two key Lohorung ritual officiants with knowledge to use the medical tools, the *yatangpa* is considered to be the most important; the *mangpa*, the shaman, is more dramatic, being like the pan-Nepali *jhānkri* (N). The *yatangpa* is essential for performing rites of passage, birth, marriage, death and responsible for the ancestors, performing the annual renewal of the house shrine, and the ritual at the harvesting of first crops; the annual rite to all ancestors. He is able to maintain a harmonious relationship with the most important superhumans, their own ancestors, who are almost like deities, and when disorder occurs in the form of sickness or misfortune, he is the most sought after officiant. Every Lohorung household must have access to a *yatangpa* – their doctor, priest, psychopomp, and diviner all in one. Chitra Bahadur, a Gurkha now living in England, told me that no Lohorung could envisage life without one. On the other hand, Lohorung 'illness' is often the unwanted anger and hunger, desires and feelings of all kinds of spirits and ghosts of the dead and to deal with these the more ecstatic *mangpa* (female *mangmani*) shamans, and the pan-Nepali *jhānkri*. Nepali speaking shamans may be called in to help. *Mangpa* and *mangmani* deal with the broadest spectrum of superhuman beings – Lohorung ones and the deities, ghosts and spirits of other tribes such as Tamang, Gurung, and Sherpa, and those of the Hindu Chetrī and Bahun.

The key skill of the Lohorung specialists has to do with altered states of consciousness, 'seeing' and performing, in contrast to knowing the right things, and talking and writing the right way, like the Western doctor. The Western doctor relies on a skill to diagnose and on knowledge of a biomedical or surgical cure. The skill of the tribal *mangpa* and *yatangpa* is as mediators between the spirit world and the human world, dependent on their ability to 'see' – hence their name *khangkhuba* 'ones who can see' – and on their ability to communicate with the ancestral and spirit world using their 'medical tools'. Like other shamans all over the world (see Winkelman 2000) they have the ability to go into altered states of consciousness at will and perceive what is for most human beings normally an intangible and invisible dimension. This is the upper world or lower world, dimensions where ancestors can be encountered, where mediating officiants can communicate with natural phenomena like trees, mountains, or rivers connected to the ancestral world. Understanding this dimension means accepting a mystical interconnectedness of phenomena, which are linked to culture heroes and primordial ancestors; and that their medical tools have a powerful resonance in this dimension which helps to facilitate communication.

One *yatangpa*, the oldest in Pangma village, explained the power of 'seeing', so crucial to healing, as lying deep in the belly and as coming from deep in his memory, mind, and consciousness (the oldest and most secret bits conceived as residing in the belly). 'Seeing' is also understood in terms of *lemmang* and *semmang*. What we can see when awake – in waking vision (*lemmang*) is limited. In another vision (*semmang*) restrictions of time and space and the divisions of the world disappear. It is explored by everyone in their dreams, and by *mangpa* and *yatangpa* who have been chosen to 'see' that aspect of the world. Since other human beings have lost the ability to 'see' and talk to this other reality, the ability of shamans and priests to 'see' is accepted as a valuable and authoritative way of knowing the world. The medicinal tools of beer, trees, pigs and chickens are not only material and visual connections between these two different worlds, they are perceptible forms that make the mysteries of the ancestral reality and the primeval world more accessible to the patient.

What I would like to show is the context and use of these 'medical' ritual instruments and how they are used to help Lohorung shamans and priests return a patient to health.

PRIESTS AND THEIR MEDICAL TOOLS

Earlier in this paper I mentioned the close relationship existing between ancestors and those natural objects possessing a ritual *(samek)* name and an animating life force *(saya)*. To obtain a diagnosis of any illness the tools used must possess these two elements. Ginger and leaves are the most favoured tools for divination. When the *yatangpa* divines he throws uncooked rice and then pieces of ginger onto banana leaves. If the ginger falls the right way up, with the newly cut side showing, then that ancestor is not angry and could not be involved in the illness. If it falls upside down, this is understood as a clear indication that the ancestor is hungry and angry. When Nanda, the woman of the house I was living in fell ill early on in fieldwork, the divination to find out what was wrong didn't take long. The divination with ginger was done and the *yatangpa* announced it was *pappamama'chi*, 'grandfather-grand-mother' ancestor. These are the guardian grandparents including all the Lohorung's remotest and closest ancestors who have died a natural death and including the 'kings' and 'queens' who created the cultural order and institutional models to which society should adhere today. If angered, these beings need a grand sacrifice to pacify them. This ritual needed one pig, six chickens and twelve eggs. The leaves were carefully wrapped up by her husband in a cloth. The woman of the house already seemed better. She had stopped moaning and could talk and drink a little *dibu* (millet beer). The *yatangpa* was given warm beer in a *tongba*, a bamboo container with a thin bamboo pipe to suck up the liquid, the form of hospitality indicating respect. This is the way that beer is most often given to ancestors.

It should be said here that alcohol in general is valued and regarded as a 'powerful' (meaning 'clever', *ichuba*), agent. There is a story about how the early ancestors, 'forest people' discovered the effects of alcohol, 'They dried the leaves of the creeper called *habektangma*, crumbled them to dust and put it in the water and drank it. They found they were a little drunk and very strong. They did much work and felt good: 'our bodies are good now. They tried adding it to maize, then to millet and then later to rice and it tasted good. But if people drank just a little too much then they cried like a dog, if they drank more, they fought like a bear and if they drank even more they lost their mind and slept like a snake'.

It is only women who know how to make beer and only they who brew, store and serve it, including for medicinal purposes such as during labour. Beer is offered, following a complex code of hospitality, to all human guests and offerings of beer are made in all indigenous Lohorung rituals to ancestors and ghosts of the dead. Given the unequivocal pleasure it offers, its 'medicinal' value for priests and shamans lies in its ability to lure or coax ancestral and spiritual beings and at the same time indicate respect.

On another occasion when Nanda was sick the *yatangpa* sat with a branch of *sibung* in Lohorung, or *titepāti* (Mugwort, *Artemis vulgaris*). This is a medicinal tool and a medicine. It is a medicine for bellyache and for aching knees. As an instrument it offers protection for women who carry sprigs of it when they walk anywhere away from the safe areas of the compound and the immediate village, and even within the village if they are out at night. They wear the leaves tucked into their wide waist bands and occasionally mutter words commanding the spirits to stick to their own path and not to wander into those of the living. As a tool of the *yatangpa* during diagnosis it offers protection from ghosts of the dead. Nanda brought the *yatangpa* a metal plate and some ginger. He stuck one end of each piece of ginger into some ash and waived the branch of *titepāti* over the plate. Shaking gently in his cross-legged position he seemed to enter momentarily an altered state of consciousness; he threw each piece of ginger in turn onto the plate naming each ancestor. If it were to fall with the clean side facing up then this would be a good sign, if ash-side up then it would show the source of the sickness. On this occasion the problem lay with *Chawatangma*, the most fickle and difficult of the ancestors, requiring three chickens, one for *Chawatangma* herself and two for *Sikāri* her constant companion.

Lohorung in Pangma village talked constantly about how bad pain is until *Chawatangma* is promised her ritual. Once recognised as 'queen' (*hangma*), her status reaffirmed and the offerings of chickens promised, the pain from *Chawatangma* usually lessens. Since Nanda was ill for another week, the *yatangpa*, who had diagnosed the hunger of *pappamama'chi*, came several times more and found 'the house ancestor' (*khimpie*) was angry as well and would have to be offered two chickens.

Let us now look at how the ritual tools for different causes of illness relate to the characteristics of the offending ancestor and how the shrines and tools of *Chawatangma* differ from those of *pappamama'chi* or other ancestors whose ritual is performed in the house. Why is she so feared? Why are so many illnesses associated with her? In terms of characteristics *Chawatangma* is perceived as the most creative of all the ancestors having fashioned the natural world from which her names derive. She has over twenty names, each indicating an area of her powers, an attribute or role, such as *bakhatangma*, owner/woman of the soil, *tapnamtangma*, owner/woman of the forest, *serepmotangma*, youngest one, *singtowatangma*, owner/woman of the trees, *lungtongtangma*, owner/woman of stones and rocks. As *khewama* she gives cotton to *mangpa* shamans; as *lilaoti*, *goanleni*, she is a village spirit, as *dewatangma*, a mother goddess. Her proper name is

Yagangma and she is described as being an old woman, having breasts so long that they fall down her legs. When she walks she throws them over her shoulder to keep them out of the way.

As well as being the most creative ancestor, however, *Chawatangma* is also the archetypal 'wild' ancestor, amoral, greedy, jealous and untamed. On purpose, she ignores Lohorung traditions and social institutions created by the culture heroes of the myths and works, instead, to undermine morality. Typifying everything that is anti-social she is the opposite of the guardian grandparents (*pappamama'chi*), and the ancestors of the house shrine (*Khammang/Yimi*), and is known as once being the teacher of human witches. She attacks people's minds so they do not know right from wrong; they cannot behave 'properly', and eventually lose their senses. She entices away the *lawa* (essence of life, vital soul) of adults and children, putting her victims in danger of death. Typically, *lawa* is lost through fright and so *Chawatangma* frightens a child, the *lawa* leaves and she hides it under a tree, stone, at the top of a bamboo tree, in the depths of water or under the wing of a chicken. When she is simply 'angry' or hungry the human symptoms are sore eyes, nose, throat, or aching limbs and bellyache.

As owner of the forests, trees, the animals living there, and of all the natural landscape – rivers, stones, rocks, fields – *Chawatangma* is seen as having enormous power over men and women. Having created the natural world and the variety of species within it she demands recognition of her ownership, respect for her domain and seeks revenge if it's not given, such as keeping animals hidden from hunters or causing injuries when people try to fell her trees without permission. If bribed she can bring wealth in the form of plentiful crops of rice, maize and millet. Her price? Lavish offerings must be made of beer, pigs and chickens, sacrificed in secret in the privacy of the household domain, within the compound or inside the house. The key to the success of these rites lies in their secrecy. No other lineage member shares the sacrificial offering or the ensuing meal and since no one can know about it but the household members, they perform it in the middle of the night without any priest or shaman. What we have here is the antipathy of core Lohorung values: lack of sociability and egalitarianism, lack of honesty and openness to the lineage group, and a household acting just for its own greed, but, as we have seen, *Chawatangma* encourages these. Once such an intimate relationship with *Chawatangma* has started she can hold the household to ransom using sickness of a household member as the ransom. During fieldwork in 1980 one boy had lost his mind (*niwa*), his sense of right and wrong; he was eating his own faeces and had lost his hearing. The village talked of how the household performed *Chawatangma* rituals in secret.

The appropriate location for the *Chawatangma* ritual is on the outskirts of the forest or in a dense bamboo grove on the outskirts of the village. She is part of the 'wild' and the location of her shrine in the forest reflects her ability and desire to undermine the 'civilised' world and its social institutions. A ritual 'house' or shrine is constructed for *Chawatangma*. Significantly, the 'house' is a miniature of the shelters Lohorung make for themselves in the forest, not a 'civilised' house like some of the ancestral shrines, which are made closer to the image of their own homes (see Fig. 7.2). *Chawatangma's* house shrine consists of a semi-circle of branches from the *chigaphu* tree (N. *patle katuj*) or *yangsingphu* tree (N. *chilaune*)[4], with the leaves creating a kind of roof. *Chawatangma's*

Figure 7.2. Shrine for Pappamama'chi.

companion, however, one of the *sikāri* hunters, who is always given a shrine alongside the Old Woman, has a more civilised 'house' made of the *sigaphu* tree, often used in housebuilding. A feature of Lohorung stilt homes and a symbol of Lohorung 'culture' is the wooden house ladder. The *sikāri* hunter's shrine boasts a symbolic representstion – a miniature house ladder. We can see here how the male companion is represented as a civilising influence. A hunter, he is also guard and companion to the ancestor and armed with a bow and arrow. Bamboo, for Lohorung and other Kiranti, in the form of the bow and arrow, is another symbol of a civilising force, a symbol of cultural order which can be overturned by the wild and uncontrolled primaeval ancestors (see Hardman 2000, 113–120).

The structure, form, and location of *Chawatangma's* shrine creates a tangible and visible image of her essential characteristics for those involved in the ritual. In the same way shrines for other ancestors similarly reflect their key characteristics. From a Kiranti perspective houses reflect who you are. The household is the key economic, political and ritual unit, not an individual. The significance of the house relates to a key myth describing the founding elements of Rai culture, namely housebuilding and house initiation, as well as agriculture, and theft by marriage. Houses are fundamental

Figure 7.3. A destructible, temporary shrine.

to the nature of personhood. Reflecting this, houses must be built in a particular way and the microcosm of the 'civilised' Lohorung house is found in the house shrine for *Khammang* and *Yimi*, made symbolically just as a house is made. These are the ancestors who are guardians of what is spiritually and morally correct and their shrine hangs in a secluded corner of the house, located on the 'uphill' 'front' wall behind and above the hearth, or on the same wall but in the attic. This space is associated with that which is male, the patriline.

We can see how the forest or bamboo grove, a 'natural place' has ethnographic significance in Lohorung ritual. Bradley comments, 'Natural Places have an archaeology because they acquired a significance in the *minds* of people in the past. That did not necessarily make any impact on their outward appearance, but one way of recognising the importance of these locations is through the evidence of human activity that is discovered there' (2000, 35). The problem, is what kind of remains might be discovered? The difficulty for the archaeologist, as mentioned at the beginning, is that these tree 'houses' which are in essence destructible, temporary shrines, act to house and, at the same time, represent the ancestral spirits only for as long as the ritual lasts (see Fig. 7.3).

These ritual shrines create mediated relations with the ancestor. We might say that they encode memory, to assist in representing and recreating mythical stories. We might also see them as the 'surgical setting', made in the correct form for the particular cure to take place. In this sense the trees (*sing*), or rather the branches which must be fresh and 'alive' (*hingkrikpa*), are key 'tools' in any cure. Belonging to the world of ancestors, who are mostly 'forest people' (*tapnam yapmi*), the tree shrines can suggest ideas of creating the 'other' world of the past. Without them ancestors could not be summoned. The trees provide the framework or structure around which the other medicinal tools, the beer, and pig or chicken, can be placed. They stage the event. For *Chawatangma* fire is brought to the clearing as well as the other key ingredients for the curative process –cooked rice, two eggs, ginger, a vessel of water, beer (in the form of a bamboo *tongba* and a gourd full of thick millet beer), lentils and soya beans (because *Chawatangma* used to grow them) and the chickens. All must come from the house of the patient: ancestors only accept offerings of the household's own produce, the fruits of the labours of their own hands and animals raised by their own clan.

Lohorung attitudes to the natural landscape, the jungle and forests, rivers, lakes and mountains are closely associated with *Chawatangma*. Women in particular fear and avoid the forest, never going through one alone and always carrying a protective weapon, such as branches of *titepāti* (Mugwort, *Artemis vulgaris)* and offerings of beer. The jungle, associated with *Chawatangma*, is the symbolic opposite of the house; it represents danger, the 'wild', the uncontrolled and uncivilised from which the roots of their society were born. To enter the dense jungle is almost to enter primordial time. The landscape is primordial and ancestors may be given respect there, but it would be a misinterpretation to apply the word 'sacred' to the geography or the landscape. To imply that certain spaces are 'sacred' and others are 'profane' (following Durkheim) misunderstands that space can be both at the same time or neither. For example the forest belongs to *Chawatangma*. It symbolises her values; nature rules, not culture. She rejects traditional values and behaviour and the complete opposite of the guardian ancestors *(pappamamma'chi)* who represent moral perfection and civilisation as created by the culture heroes. Mostly the forest is neither sacred nor profane. For a while, during a ritual, however, space in the forest is seen as 'apart' from the rest of the world; Lohorung see it as being 'closed off' from 'this world' for the duration of the rite. What sacralizes that space is the attitude of the priest (*yatangpa*) or shaman (*mangpa)* and those involved for the duration of their activities in which communication is made with the other cosmological realms and with ancestral beings. This attitude shifts ritual objects as well as space onto a metaphysical plane in which time and space and categories of the ordinary no longer apply and everything imbued with the power of *saya* is revitalised.

Central to this process of revitalisation in each ancestral ritual is the 'ritual journey' made by the *yatangpa*. The journey could be mapped onto the lanscape and the path for each ancestor is a defining feature of their ritual. The officiant – whether *mangpa* or *yatangpa* – is in a trance state but never in these ancestral rites is he or she in an ecstatic state involving dancing, drumming, hyperactivity and visual hallucinations. Rather, officiants experience more meditative type trances. The shaman or priest concentrates on the shrine, the tree houses, the offerings laid out, the beer and the sacrificial chickens; they then journey on a mental or imaginary flight, much as one might in Western visualisation, but here reenacting a stylized and traditional journey that has power in its very reenactment.

Speaking in ritual language, using the *samek* names and describing all the objects, the officiant begins at the shrine. There is a real sense here of the magical power of words, that the ritual is not only about something, but does something (Austin 1962), its efficacy depending on a rhetorical power of words. In this case the efficacy depends on demanding the attention of the ancestors and communicating the presence of the

Figure 7.4. The yatangpa *plays a plate (like a drum) to help him on his ritual 'journey'.*

house construction and all the offerings of beer, ginger, etc. and transporting them into the superhuman realm by means of ritual language.
The shaman or priest chants:

> *telladam lasudam* (the leaf on which offering placed)
> *kasudam tambodam,* (the copper bowl, the pitcher)
> *sakbalitham pi'malitham* (the tongba beer vessel and the thin pipe)
> *subi'ma lam, kongbi'ma lam* (ginger)
> *sibungma mabungma (titep~ðti* Mugwort)
> elawahangma choyahangma yo! (Chawatangma)
> *me'lo'wa lam chekchekwa lam* (the bird path)

Starting at the shrine (*thān*) the journey follows the 'path of the earth'. Specifically, this follows 'the way under the earth, arising up at springs', then goes under white earth, then red earth emerging at the nearby town of Dingla. Emerging from the earth the *yatangpa* flies as a bird and comes to a lake, but then searches for the clan's own spring (*chawa*) drinks and sours up to the high Himalayas, to a gold lake where he can communicate with *Chawatangma* and *Sikāri* and give them respect.

singtang'so anam'no, lungtang'so anam'no (you own all the trees, all the stones).

The ancestors are offered the beer, the rice and the chicken, and the ritual name of the sick patient gives her identity:

> 'we offer beer and liquor of all kinds; this is the *lawa*, this is the piece of clothing belonging to a *wekhama* (the sick female member of *hangkhim* clan)'.

Chawatangma is told 'even if you don't feel like eating and drinking, eat and drink'. It is made clear who is talking to her, what clan the *yatangpa* belongs to, what clan the patient belongs to; he names the season and the path they are following to encourage her not to feel angry or neglected. Dealing with her firmly he asks her to :

> make clear the *lawa*, tell (me) and make clear the paths of my dreams, give well-being and good fortune! Give comfort and fortune; raise their *saya* as high as the snowy mountains; if our *saya* has grown small, make these *saya* tall! Protect us from the evil spirits, ghosts, spirits of dead ancestors, from bad gods who give diseases, from male witches.
>
> *Bakhatangma*, eh! yo!, *tapnamtangma, serepmotangma*, yo! Saya of ginger, *saya* of all the things laid out on the leaf in front of the shrine, and the *saya* of the ginger again, yes the *saya*, ye! *saya* of the raksi liquor, *saya* of the beer, ya:y! ha:y! (we have) protected and enclosed the *saya* of the chicken, oh yes, up until now we have! the female hen, the chosen one, we have covered with a basket, yes, we have protected them.

At this point the hen is hit on the back with a wooden stick and killed. The *yatangpa* describes this in ritual language going on to describe how he directs a few drops of blood from the chicken's mouth to fall into the middle of the liquor, *raksi*. If *Chawatangma* is offered a pig it is sacrificed by being shot in the heart with an arrow. The objective is to lose as little blood as possible – a point I will return to below – but enough to prove to *Chawatangma* that the animal has been killed. She is asked to accept the offering, whether a pig or a chicken, and is asked in return that she keep to her own place:

> 'Take it! Take the blood, take the chicken/take the pig, take it!'

And again the *yatangpa* describes the path that he is following in his journey in his trance state, the season, his ritual clan name and again requests clear dreams, health, good fortune, well-being, wealth, and ends by saying:

> 'From today onwards take away bad omens, tears coming from the chicken, water from its nose; protect us with the splayed out peacock's tail, surround us with it, protect us.'

For some ancestors, the *yatangpa* in his trance state has to take 'the path of the rivers'; for another it may be 'the flower way', which is one of the hardest mystical journeys. The rivers and the flowers are associated with the transition to another world. In every *sammang* the officiant has to describe in ritual language whatever material objects are being offered at the beginning and end of the journey. The ancestors would not understand just the spoken words; for them beer is *sakbalitham pi'malitham*, 'egg' is *bombulu*, 'pig' is *sopakma hangpasa*, 'chicken' is *pichali'wa sampongli'wa* and so on. To take an outsider's view for a moment, the knowledge that the words spoken have the power to communicate with the very ancestors connected to their pain may be, for a Lohorung patient, as powerful a relief as taking a pill that will deal directly with the source of pain even if the pill is a placebo. Certainly some Lohorung describe relief once the words have been spoken. For us, too, instilling or rekindling hope is a central part of the healing process (see Spiro, 1998).

Offering blood increases the hope of cure since blood sacrifice is also recognised as the most effective way to change the mood of the ancestors. Blood is the essential 'medical tool' in all *sammang* ancestral rituals. It is the symbol of fertility and prosperity. Both menstrual blood and the vital ancestral force of *saya* are symbolised as flowers. Blood and flowers are closely associated with a vital force amongst several Kiranti peoples (e.g. see Sagant 1991[1981]). We could also say that ancestors need to see the blood to realise the continued closeness of blood brothers, to see that the blood ties are renewed. Moreover, from the blood, ancestors know that meat is being offered and to eat meat is to feast. To eat a lot of meat is seen as good for health: meat is a symbol of wealth. However, to appreciate the full significance of blood as a 'medical tool', the myth of origin needs to be mentioned. By offering blood, human beings originally achieved their desired goal of emerging from the Primal Lake. In the myth a bird takes the place of a human blood offering. Birds are mythically the closest and most 'natural' substitute for humans. In Lohorung, Thulung Rai, Mewahang Rai and Dumi Rai mythology, human characters are at times represented as birds – that is, as part of the natural world and not separated from it (Allen 1976a, b & c; Gaenszle 1991; Hardman 2000). The characters are as if human but their other 'natural qualities', like their ability to fly, make it clear that they are bird-like. Reflecting this close identification with birds, each clan also has a bird that it cannot eat – the bird that is seen as an identifying feature of the clan. The black bird *kālo jureli*, known in Lohorung as *kerokpa*, is not eaten by the Lamsong clan; *yangkoama* is not eaten by Yangkhrung; *lelo'wa* by Dekhim, and so on. Given this closeness to birds it is not surprising that just as Lohorung do not sacrifice human beings, nor do they sacrifice birds – with just one exception. It is the domesticated fowl living alongside humans, which is sacrificed. One reason, I was told, that they are chosen to be sacrificed 'in our place' is that – like humans – chickens cannot fly and can therefore be easily caught. Pigs are also seen as being bonded to humans. They live under their stilt houses; like humans they suckle their young. According to Lohorung tradition, pigs and chickens made a pact with the ancestors migrating from the Primal Lake and agreed to this fate, knowing the importance of blood in manipulating successful outcomes. As the old man from Diding told me,

> 'Chickens and pigs are offered in our place. *Sammang* rites had to be done as they migrated, and it was with chickens and pigs that they made a promise. 'I'll go in your place' said the pig and so did the chicken. In place of human offerings we took their blood instead. It was same as offering our sister.'

Lohorung sacrifice is the ritual killing of substitutes as a way of ensuring contact and communication with ancestors. They employ the symbolism of killing, the shedding of blood in minute quantities, to recreate the links with the ancestors. This in turn brings about rebirth of the original order and revitalization, which in turn will raise the *saya*, the vital energy, of all concerned. The efficacy for Lohorung and other Kiranti lies in two things: the appearance of blood and not watery saliva (*makwa*), and the correct performance of the communication which, along with the offerings, has the regenerative effect of restoring the vitality of the patient and countering the demoralization of the ancestor – by raising *saya* (see Sagant 1991 for a description of a similar Limbu ritual).

The efficacy of the original rite, a blood sacrifice, made by the original Kiranti brothers, the mythical ancestors, to leave the Primal Lake, laid the model for later rites which work by communicating with the ancestors with the appropriate blood offering. This Lohorung rite can be compared with Vedic and classical Indian sacrifice, in which every act of sacrifice refers back to the creation of the world: 'every sacrifice may be said to replicate the primal act of Prajapati who produced creation by the sacrificial dismemberment of his own body ... *Any* sacrifice, then ... maintains or repairs the cosmic order ... It therefore represents a renewal of time' (Parry 1982, 77; see also Eliade 1964, 11). The effectiveness of the communication, which is linked to its correct performance, is similar to the Brahmanic tradition in which 'in its very carrying out, the order of the world is reproduced and maintained. The right order of sacrifice is, and assures, the right order of the world' (Herrenschmidt 1982, 26).

Blood must not flow in any great quantity in any indigenous Lohorung ritual: what is important is just a few drops. If the sacrificial chickens are very small their heads have to be chopped off to produce the drops of blood. Larger chickens produce drops of blood from the mouth when killed by hitting them hard on their spine with a stick. If we look at the way in which the order of the world is linked to sacrifice, the key to it is in the myth in which the primal ancestors emerged from the Primal Lake but also in the notion that blood is connected to the vital force (*saya*). The order of the world is maintained and restored to harmony when the correct sacrifice and correct ritual chant, re-enacting the original ritual, are performed so that *saya* is raised. Sacrifice is an act of universal regeneration. The restoration of a mystical union through sacrifice was of course also one of the key elements to sacrifice noted in the anthropological essay by Hubert and Mauss ([1899] 1964). For Lohorung the order of the world is based on a mystical union between living and ancestors in the form of *saya* and links explicitly to sacrifice since, correctly performed, this is how *saya* is raised, and the connection accounts for its effectiveness.

It is important to remember that sacrifice is both useful and an obligation: sacrifice as a form of gift creates an obligation: 'if he gives it is partly in order to receive ... Disinterestedness is mingled with self-interest. That is why it has so frequently been conceived as a form of contract' (Hubert and Mauss[1899] 1964, 100). Lohorung have expectations that the offering of their own domestic chickens or pigs, symbols of the original sacrificial victim, will placate the ancestors and restore the sick person to health. We can see here how crucial pigs and chickens are as medical tools.

The shape of their shrine and the material objects laid out for the ancestors is both a model *of* what they as living human beings liked best and a model *for* controlling them. In other words, the idea of the rituals and the tools is twofold: first to please and placate and persuade the ancestors back into a strong relationship with the household and, secondly, to regain control of the ancestors. The location of the shrine is significant, as well as how the trees are used to give it shape and meaning. Every human being and every 'ancestor' (*sammang*) has some material tool which is, for them, the most useful and important thing they own and from which they gain both security and identity. It is something with which they are so familiar, knowing all its uses, potentialities and powers and, knowing more about it than others, it gives them power and, therefore, protection. These 'weapons', as Lohorung told me, are also their source of strength. A woman's 'weapon', for example, is cotton, her weaving shuttle and sickle, a man's, his kukri knife and bow and arrow. The forest is *Chawatangma's* weapon. 'Flowers', *bung*, are for another ancestor *waya warema* what particular trees or types of bamboo are for other *sammang*. They told me mine was my pen. For the 'house ancestor' *Khimpie* it is the largest kind of bamboo called *sakbaphu* (*Tama bans* in Nepali), one of the most important components of house building. The ritual shrine for *Chawatangma* is a model of what she likes best – the shelter in the forest using trees, which are her 'weapons', the thick millet beer, the lentils and soya beans which she used to grow as well as the chickens. It is also a model for relating to and pleasing the ancestor who created the natural order and is still part of the wild.

A ritual of a shaman

Rituals of the *mangpa* are often performed on the verandah and in the yard of a household, in the public sphere. Those of the *yatangpa* are performed either far away from the house or inside the house in spaces that are 'closed' from the rest of the community. The more public rituals of the shaman have a different atmosphere to those performed by the *yatangpa*. Watching the shaman from Rawa Khola was like watching an all night-long performance of mime and pantomime, of laughter, dancing, drumming and buffoonery. The audience watched and responded to the theatrical acts, the ritual actions and demands of the shaman. The seriousness of the healing process was almost incidental to the theatricality of the performance. From the beginning there was laughter on the verandah of the house of a villager named Tara Bahadur. It was already dark when they started preparing the shrine (*thān*) against the wall of the verandah. The shrine had been laid out by Tara Bahadur (see fig 7.5).

Eight small leaf plates; three large leaf plates with money and uncooked rice in them; a pitcher of water with a piece of ginger and five peisa piece inside, and branches of three trees – *komphu* (N. *kahula*), *waiphu* (N. *musure katuj*) and *suphu* (N. *sal*, *Castanopsis tribuloides*). The water, the ginger, the money, the rice and the tree branches are at this point the main tools of the *mangpa*. Lohorung talk of them as being the 'weapons', *silli*, the powerful instruments to make things happen. The reality of the power of the primeval ancestors and the myths about them are again represented symbolically in these tools. The tools not only have to change the mood of the ancestors and gods called and thereby the well-being of the household, but also that of the patient, who is a microcosm of the household.

The performance went on all night with numerous diagnoses and curative rites. Only a brief description of one small section of the activities will be given here. The

Figure 7.5. The ritual objects.

youngest member of the household had been ill and firstly the *mangpa* decided to raise her links with the ancestors by raising her *saya*. He put some ginger in each plate containing rice, took a bundle of *semphu* leaves in his hand and put a knob of ginger in his shirt for protection and then waived the bowl of burning incense around his body. He threw some rice at both sides of the metal plate, put more incense on the fire and, folding his hands together, began to pray to his *guru* master spirits; he began to shake a bit and started to dance, playing one of the copper plates like a drum. Trembling increasingly, he took two bundles of leaves in each hand, shook the house door, put some water in his mouth and shoved one of the bamboo *gungring* in his mouth followed by a lighted piece of rolled cotton to reach communion with his master spirits. The *Sansari mai*, the pan-Nepali divinities responsible for epidemics, had to be reached and the path had been laid our for them in the form of the cotton wound around the pitcher of water and two bamboo *gungring* tied together. He put ash on his forehead to assist their arrival and played himself into a trance, using the metal plate as a drum, stopping occasionally to drink beer from the *tongba* bamboo vessel, now calling on *Dache Lama*, a Tibetan divinity. When the spirit came to the shaman he started trembling more. Finally, with assistance from one helper who held up high the *tongba* on one side of the *mangpa*, and another on the other side holding up high the water and branches of trees, the three hopped and danced around the verandah shouting in ritual language to raise the youngest daughter's *saya*, her vital spirit, her connections with the ancestors.

The *mangpa* tucked *semphu* into his trousers and became possessed briefly by the ancestor of a neighbouring Rai group. It is important for the *mangpa* to protect his body with ginger and branches of protective leaves. Illnesses, according to Lohorung, are often the attachment to the body of the desires and anger of ancestors or spirits. Unless protected, shaman or priest may absorb their anger and suffer in turn the bellyaches, cramps or diarrhoea, which are evidence of angry ancestors or jealous witches. This vulnerability of humans makes sense where bodies are not 'bounded' in the way they are often viewed in the West, but viewed as being open to the emotions of others. The ancestors themselves do not penetrate the body, but their desires and emotions can. Preventive rituals can build up the strength of the boundaries of the body and pacify possible negative emotions by pleasing ancestors with the right kind of hospitality.

Divining again – this time with leaves – the *mangpa* sliced the bundles of *komphu* and *waiphu* (trees used in house building and associated with ancestors). The more leaves fall the right way up the more likely the household is to be healthy. What should be noted here is that the *mangpa* divined not for one individual but for the whole family. The household, rather than the individual, is a key unit in relations with the ancestors and, therefore, in restoring health when they are seen as the cause. At times it is not the household but the lineage or clan that is the significant unit and rites are done accordingly. Divination can foretell whether a household will have good fortune and well-being depending whether the majority of leaves fall right side up or upside down. To appreciate this we have to remember the reality of a connection between leaves (or trees) and ancestors. There is a relational connection going back to mythical times: the intuition that humans have lost is retained by the metaphysical connection between the shaman and the divining objects, the ginger or the leaves. The ginger and the leaves have *saya*, that vital energy which links them to the ancestral world.

The ritual to raise the *saya* of the head of the household required two bamboo containers (*tongpa*) full of matured and fermented millet, and two gourds containing the strong, thin beer which is squeezed from similar millet; one *mana* of husked rice grown in one's own fields; one crowing cock; ginger; a turban, which is tied around the head of the person whose *saya* needs raising; and a kukri knife placed in the same person's hand. The elders of the village sat to the left and the right of the 'sick' person and in a small earthen oil lamp some *siwali* (a water plant, *Blyxa octandra*) or *titepāti* (*Artemisia vulgaris*) flowers were placed before the lamp was lit. The lamp was placed on top of the husked rice. The *mangpa* took the cock under his right arm, and began to shake a little as he recited. The elders joined in at the end.

> O raise the saya of this *kechaba* of the *lamawa* spring. If an enemy has lowered his *saya*, if his father, mother, wife, children, brothers or sisters, have lowered his *saya*, today you raise it; on the right and on the left we elders are sitting so you raise his *saya*; from today make his *saya* strong and walk close to your enemies, make them wander and run away.

As the *mangpa* said *mechirayo meruku*, the assistant killed the cock by striking it on its back with a stick and, as the drops of blood came out, everyone shouted, '*saya* has been raised!' (*saya pogayo!*). Everyone present then had to jump up and make the 'patient' jump up as well, shouting very loudly as they did so. Again, the shaman examined the chicken's blood to foresee the fortune of the family. If no blood comes from the mouth, but instead water from the eyes or nose, the rite has failed and the patient remains demoralised. This time there was just a drop of blood from the chicken.

We have already seen the significance of the blood of pigs and chickens in the ancestral rituals of the *yatangpa*. The ritual tradition that symbolically links blood with the good state of *saya*, links blood with the ancestors and with success, prosperity and a healthy life is powerful in the rituals of both officiants. As Allen says about the neighbouring Thulung Rai 'the health and fortune of an individual Thulung and his relationship to his ancestors are fused in a single concept … health is only an aspect of a concept of good order which embraces the properly cooperative ancestors' (1976b, 510). Good health for Lohorung is certainly social as well as physical, but the necessary sociality and hospitality must be directed as much to superhuman beings as to living neighbours. The loss of connections and the lowering of *saya*, whether brought about by insult or ill-health, leads to a demoralized condition which can be cured with the rite as described above. Central to Lohorung understanding of illness and health lies in the connection with founding ancestors, who established the harmonious good order upon which all their traditions are derived, and in the concept of *saya*, the 'ancestors within' or 'ancestral spirit'. Without the medicinal tools of trees, beer, pigs and chickens the rituals to re-connect with the ancestral world could not be performed. Moreover, unless those involved in the ritual show the necessary respect to the medicinal tools, the rite could not work. In this sense it is the attitude of those involved which creates their power. We have seen how everything that has *saya* belongs in reality to the ancestral world and must be viewed with the reality that existed at that time. Then, trees, plants and animals could communicate with ancestors. In rituals they should still be treated in the same way 'as if' commmunication was possible, respecting their own unique power and value, their own way of being in the world, and within the appropriate framework. Outside of the ritual space no such metaphysical attitude is required.

Everyone, both man and ancestor, needs high *saya* for well being, and from the very beginning of the order of the world the force of vitality could be conveyed to ancestors and balance restored simply on the sight of a drop of blood. The transmissibility of substances, qualities and emotions are apparent in Nepali ideas of the body and can be compared to early Western ideas about of the power of the witch to invade the confines of the body. 'Witchcraft was, among other things, a form of power which involved exchanges between bodies' (Purkiss 1996, 119). In Nepal the jealous evil eye of the witch can invade the body and bring about acute diarrhoea in their victim. Whereas in early modern England the power of the boundless and formless female body was threatening and its spillage serious because there was an ideal of a more solid, whole and bounded body, among the Kiranti there is no such cultural construction. The Lohorung notion of person, male and female, is not a fixed, bounded entity but more like that of the Hindu idea in which it is 'permeable, composite, partly divisible, and transmissible. Processes internal to the person are ... continuous with processes of exchange between and among persons' (Marriott 1976, 194). Transmissibility of substances and emotions is inevitable. The anger of *khimpie*, the house ancestor, is not just a feeling, but can communicate through the unbound body in the form of paralysis or wounds. In a similar way the quality of the drop of blood is transmitted to *sammang*. The force of the blood can enter the bodies of the ancestors as easily as blood is spilled. Whether from a chicken or a pig, just a drop is enough to raise the vital connections between living and *sammang*, to raise the source of energy, courage, and self-respect so that balance is restored to the order of the world.

INTERPRETATION

So far I have mainly discussed the Lohorung's own attitudes to health and illness and their understanding of how their 'medicinal' tools work, though for the purposes of this paper I have used biomedical terminology ('medicinal tools', 'doctor', 'surgical setting', 'health management'). I would like to consider here the effectiveness of these tools using non-indigenous criteria. A clear distinction should be made between the rituals of the *yatangpa* priest and those of the *mangpa* shaman. In the former there is no performance, no interaction between the audience and the officiant, and the focus remains directed at the ancestor in question. The efficacy of the rituals of the priest lies in part in the way in which the superhuman world is given a powerful material presence in the forms of the shrines to which each ancestor or spirit is enticed. Each of these shrines, as a medical tool, represents a powerful material presence, a material object to assist the patient's ability to visualise their 'journey to health'. In each ritual the patient knows that the shaman or priest is going into a trance state and undertaking a mystical journey for them, specifically addressing their illness and the mood of the ancestor. The way that the rituals are structured means that, even if the language used in the rituals is not totally understood, the very notion of the journey and the special mood of the event must bring about in the patient some experience of a process taking place. The medical tools, the erected house shrines and offerings act to mediate between the personal experience and a highly charged social meaning. Most important, the moment of sacrifice, the moment of divination from the blood, is seen as a renewal. As I mentioned above, just a drop is enough to raise the vital connections between living and *sammang*, to raise the source of energy, courage, and self-respect. Lohorung can see the drop and understand the meaning. It is common knowledge that blood is an indication of fertility, health and prosperity and the drop can evoke a visualisation of that curative moment, a revitalisation from a demoralised state, in a most dramatic way. This is not so far from our own experiences of recovery. Western medical anthropologists talk about 'journeys to recovery' and the importance of 'domains of significance' for a cure to take place. For example, Mattingley (2000) tells the story of the actor Oliver Sacks, recovering from a leg injury and infuriated by the medical expression 'uneventful recovery'.

> 'What damned nonsense! Recovery ... was a 'pilgrimage', a journey in which one moved, if one moved, stage by stage, or by stations. Every stage, every

station, was a completely new advent, requiring a new start, a new birth or beginning. One had to begin, to be born again and again. Recovery was an exercise in nothing short of birth ... unexpected, unexpectable, incalculable and surprising. Recovery uneventful? It *consists* of events' (2000, 206).

Mattingley comments how many patients and healers may agree that 'recovery 'consists of events' ... [with] powerful motives to transform therapy time into a domain of significance, one that acquires phenomenological weight because it creates a present which is threefold, which embodies connections to past and, especially, to future' (2000, 206).

For Lohorung the sight of the trees, shaped to house a particular *sammang* ancestor, and the beer laid out with the other offerings, along with the sound of the ritual language, may act as a reassuring sign that the ancestor causing pain has been contacted. The shrine heightens the visualisation of the presence of the ancestors and the journey to recovery, while the sacrifice of the pig or chickens reinforces the absolute signficance of the event for the patient.

Desjarlais (1992) has argued against intellectualist and symbolist approaches to understanding healing rituals in Nepal, whereas I would consider the possibility of both in understanding Lohorung medical tools. From the symbolist point of view the tools can work by 'provoking transformations of the worldview' of a patient, for example, watching the sacrifice of the pig or chicken, or experiencing the rite to raise their own *saya*. The symbols fire the imagination and the emotions so that they become personal experience; the invisible world is made manifest and the patient placed within that reality; the reality of this world becomes enmeshed with that of the 'other world'. The symbolic category of *saya*, which in part may define the experience of the patient, transforms from low to high in the process of the ritual entwining of realities. Desjarlais argues that though 'transformation of experience' is part of the answer (1992, 208); the rite works because the shaman 'changes how a body feels by altering what it feels. [The] cacophany of music, taste, sight, touch, and kinesthesia activates a patient's senses. This activation has the potential to 'wake' a person, alter the sensory grounds of a spiritless body and change how a body feels. A successful soul-calling rite recreates the sense of 'presence' intrinsic to Yolmo experiences of well-being' (Desjarlais 1992, 206). My own feeling is to allow for the possibility of any of these working, as well as other reasons to do with catharsis, externalisation of problems, and resolution of social conflict. Though scorned by many in the medical profession, the placebo effect is one of the most powerful tools in Lohorung medicine to trigger the body's ability to heal itself.

In adopting an intellectualist approach to the medical tools, I would argue that they may well encourage patients to think differently about their condition; they may, for example, rekindle hope by seeing that effective and appropriate action has been taken. After all, the practices in rituals are rational as well as visual or 'symbolic'. Given the essentially human or anthropomorphic view of ancestors that the Lohorung hold, we cannot understand Lohorung statements about *sammang* and the kinds of trees they need to build their houses, statements about *sammang* and their 'hunger', simply as symbolic statements. Undoubtedly, their rituals include symbolic action. The shrines are, as we have seen, symbolic representations of their houses, there are numerous symbolic or mimetic qualities to the enactment of past events performed by the *mangpa*, and the sacrificial chicken or pig is symbolic. But the activity is instrumental and pragmatic and should be effective given the framework within which they understand illness. The medical tools are empowered with the vital substance of *saya*, enabling communication with ancestors and facilitating a return to a stable relationship. The *yatangpa*, *mangpa*, and participants perform the ritual because their knowledge of the *sammang* and the symptoms of the person indicate to them that relations with a particular *sammang* have become unbalanced. Experience and divination tell them that this person's acute pain and dizziness is an indication that (for example) *Pappamamma'chi* are enraged. Given the web of reciprocal obligations upon which their relationship with their ancestors is based, given their knowledge of the mythical sacrificial model and given their understanding of the nature of ancestors' lives in the past, their needs and desires are not really different from their own. For the patient attending any ritual and for those performing it, there is inevitably some intellectual expectation that each ritual will be effective. Lohorung do not carry out their curative rituals expecting them to fail! Moreover, evidence certainly suggested that patients came away thinking differently about their condition. Whether in the West or in Nepal we are all involved in a system of belief. As Thomas (1971, 800) points out,

> The modern working-class woman who remarks that she doesn't believe in doctors is acknowledging the fact that the patient still brings with him an essentially uninformed allegiance. Usually he knows no more of the underlying rationale for his treatment than did the client of the cunning man. In such circumstances it is hard to say where 'science' stops and 'magic' begins.

Sometimes cures do not happen and Lohorung can understand why. Mistakes are made. The paralysis may indicate that *Khimpie* is responsible when, in fact, it is *Chawatangma* playing tricks trying to look like a *Khimpie* paralysis. Diagnosis goes wrong, but there is always a reason, whether based on the complicity of the *sammang* to mislead the *yatangpa*, the inability of the *yatangpa* that day to 'see', or some mishap leading to an incorrect performance. When diagnosing they say, 'It is *Khimpie*' or '*Chawatangma* is hungry' or 'she is angry' or 'the mind of *pappamamma* hurts, we must raise their *saya*'. They know *sammang* have mind (*niwa*) from the evidence that they 'feel' and have 'wants'. The word they use for the desires of the superhuman beings is *luchakmi*. The human equivalent is '*minchakmi*', with much the same meaning: 'wanting to do/eat something,' 'to feel like something', 'to feel ... ' *Sammang*, however, 'feel' and 'want' (*luchakmi*) in a more selfish, dramatic way than adult human beings. They compare the wants or possessiveness of the *sammang* with those of children in their sudden intensity, using this to explain the sudden onset of certain illnesses. The rituals can only work if they satisfy the *sammang*. If they are performed incorrectly the pain simply redoubles.

I argue here against the view that rituals for Lohorung are essentially expressive and crucially different from 'practical' action in the way classically suggested by Beattie (1966). Rituals are, of course, 'showing' and 'saying' in all kinds of expressive ways exactly what the ritual is enacting. But what the ritual actually did and meant to the participants, I found was based on firm notions about how ancestors and humans behave, how they respond to coercive offerings, how anger can be counteracted with satisfying food, and how *saya* rises when compensations ease the insult. Once *sammang* have been satisfied, Western medicines will bring the most speedy cure in humans. The focus in the ritual was always on bringing about a change in the feelings of *sammang* and as a consequence restoring the relationship between humans and ancestors. Illness associated with *sammang* was always understood as requiring a restoration of the balance between the living and the ancestors by raising *saya*. As with pregnancy, one cannot be 'a little bit ill from *sammang*'. If *sammang* are involved, the relationship has to be addressed but once that has been done it is recognized that Western medicine can sometimes be very effective in dealing with other levels of the illness. Without initial ritual sacrifices, however, the Western medicines cannot work. Some did, however, say that taking Western medicines could be dangerous if it increased the anger of the *sammang* involved. Whether the practices of the priest or those of the shaman are to be considered their efficacy was not to be found in their social status. According to my own informants it had to do with each household's trust in the 'trueness' of the officiant's relations with the spiritual world, and inevitably people's opinions differed. The intuitive experience of one household led them to place their trust in the *mangmani*, that of another in the local *yatangpa* and another in the wild Rawa Khole *Mangpa*. In this sense the role of material tools in the healing process is supportive: as elements in the ritual action, however, they are crucial.

CONCLUSIONS

The unquestioned efficacy of biomedicine and the Cartesian mind-body split was rejected early on in the natural childbirth movement by Balaskas (1983), and more generally by Illich (1974) and others in alternative/complementary medicine. This was followed by medical anthropologists and sociologists demonstrating the need for a more cross-cultural approach (e.g. Helman 1984) and an approach which included the importance of locating the patient in a social and personal environment (e.g. Turner [1987] 1995). What I have tried to show in this paper is that in some cultures, such as that of the Lohorung Rai in East Nepal, there is an approach to the nature of human life in the world which differs from these views and demonstrates a more social and relational view of the body, accepting as it does crucial links between natural, spiritual and human existences. Integral to their understanding of health and illness, is the view that well-being is dependent on respectful relationships with the living, with the ancestors and with the world that is seen as belonging to them. Illness and misfortune are indications of the problems that inevitably occur given the tangled way in which natural, spiritual and human existences interpenetrate. Although in the West the importance of human relationships in health is increasingly explored, the notion of the significance of spiritual relations or bonds with natural phenomena are still paid little attention.

One further point emerges from this paper which is the focus the Rai healing rituals give to the experience of demoralisation or depression. A common side effect of illness and suffering found all over the world is the feeling of dejection, dispiritedness, melancholy or despair, particularly in severe or chronic illness, disfiguring radical surgery, physical disabilities, illnesses connected to moral issues (such as AIDS, alcoholism), in mental illness connected to unemployment or defeating work situations, in illness preventing functioning in the community, leprosy – the list has only just begun. As Kleinman says (1988, xiv) 'one of the unintended outcomes of the modern transformation of the medical care system is that it does just about everything to drive the practitioner's attention away from the experience of illness.' In spite of some improvements in this area since the 80s, it is still the case that the despair and demoralisation experienced by patients may well be given insufficient attention. In contrast, dealing with demoralisation is central to Lohorung healing rituals. According to their view of the person each individual inevitably loses vitality, self-esteem and experiences the fall of *saya* when suffering from the attack of any ancestor. This expresses itself in lack of sociability, and sometimes even alienation from cultural values. In the Lohorung understanding of being human each person and every household needs to keep alive their relationship with their community and the ancestors and creators, who lie at the core of their indigenous traditions. This is the only way to control feelings of distress, demoralisation and despair, which can lead to death. The importance of this is reflected in the way that relationships are institutionalised in the concept of *saya*, a spiritual presence in the body. It is also reflected in the way that all Lohorung indigenous rituals are concerned to restore the key relationship with *sammang* ancestors and raise *saya*. This restores a sense of self esteem and vitality which disappears when the relationship is broken. Loss of vitality or demoralisation are both evidence of, and a condition for, ill health. For Lohorung, restoration of health primarily involves dealing with demoralisation. The beer, trees, pigs and chickens assist as much in raising the *saya* of the patient as they do in pleasing and controlling and raising the *saya* of the ancestors. The problem for the archaeologist must be that the 'cleverness' of the 'medicinal tools' and the power of the places in which the rituals are performed is only maintained so long as there are the priests and shamans to re-enact the scenes of the primeval past. Apart from any chicken bones not scavenged by hyenas there will be no physical traces left for posterity.

Notes

1   Most of the ethnographic data here was collected in roughly 30 months fieldwork (1976 to 1980) that was funded by the Social Science Research Council and the American Association of University Women. There has been a brief visit since but most subsequent contact has been maintained with written communications with two key informants.

2   Lohorung Rai, speaking a Tibeto-Burman language, live in Eastern Nepal to the south of Mount Makalu. Although much of the material for this paper refers to one group, the Lohorung Rai, similar attitudes to illness exist throughout East Nepal amongst other Rai and Limbu groups, collectively known as Kiranti. In terms of general culture Rai and Limbu are close. The Kiranti are sedentary agriculturalists, subsistence farmers, growing rice, maize and millet. Lohorung live in dense villages in houses built on stilts. In the space underneath the house live the livestock, mainly pigs, chickens and goats, oxen and

water buffalo. Unlike their Hindu neighbours few Lohorung can afford tea and prefer to drink liquor, mainly beer of various kinds and strength, hence the Nepali term for them of *matwali,* people belonging to a class of Alcohol Drinkers, making them ritually inferior.

3   For a detailed discussion of how this attitude is embedded in Lohorung notions of self and emotion see Hardman 2000.

4   Indigenous terms in the text followed by N. are Nepali; all other indigenous terms are Lohorung.

Bibliography

Allen, N. 1974 'The ritual journey: a pattern underlying certain Nepalese rituals' pp. 6–22 in C. von Furer-Haimendorf, (ed.) *Contributions to the anthropology of Nepal*, Warminster: Aris and Phillips.

Allen, N. 1976a *Studies in the myths and oral traditions of the Thulung Rai of East Nepal*, Oxford: Unpublished D. Phil Thesis.

Allen, N. 1976b 'Shamanism among the Thulung Rai' pp. 124–140 in J.T. Hitchcock and R. Jones (eds) *Spirit possession in the Nepal Himalayas*, Warminster: Aris and Phillips Ltd.

Allen, N. 1976c 'Approaches to illness in the Nepalese hills' pp. 500–552 in J. Loudon (ed.) *Social Anthropoloy and Medicine*, London: Academic Press.

Austin, J. 1962 *How to do things with words*, Cambridge, Mass: Harvard University Press.

Balaskas, J. 1983 *Active birth*, London: Unwin Paperbacks.

Baldick, J. 2000 *Animal and shaman: ancient religions of Central Asia*, London: I.B. Taurus.

Beattie, J. 1966 'Ritual and social change' *Man* (n.s.) 1, 60–74.

Bird-David, N. 1999 'Animism revisited' *Current Anthropology* Vol 40, 67–91 (February Supplement).

Bradley, R. 2000 *An archaeology of natural places*, London and New York: Routledge.

Desjarlais, R. 1992 *Body and emotion: the aesthetics of illness and healing in the Nepal Himalayas*, Philadelphia, University of Pennsylvania Press.

Eliade, M. 1964, *Shamanism: archaic techniques of ecstacy* (Translated from the French by Willard Trask), Princeton: Princeton University Press.

Gaenszle, M. 1991 *Verwandschaft und Mythologie bei den Mewahang Rai in Ostnepal. Eine ethnographische Studie zum Problem der "ethnischen Identität"*, Wiesbaden-Stuttgart: Franz Steiner Verlag.

Gaenszle, M. 1993 'Interactions of an oral tradition: changes in the *muddum* of the Mewahang Rai of East Nepal', pp. 164–175 in G. Toffin (ed.) *Nepal: Past and Present*, New Delhi: Sterling Publishers Private.

Gennep, A.van 1903 'De l'emploi du mot 'chamanisme', *Revue de l'Histoire des Religions* 47, 51–57.

Hardman, C. 1981 'The psychology of conformity and self-expression among the Lohorung Rai of East Nepal' pp. 161–180 in P. Heelas and A. Lock (eds), *Indigenous Psychology*. London: Academic Press.

Hardman C. 2000 *Other worlds: notions of self and emotion among the Lohorung Rai*, Oxford: Berg.

Helman, C.G. 1984 *Culture, Health and Illness*, Oxford: Butterworth Heinemann.

Herrenschmidt, O. 1982 'Sacrifice: symbolic or effective?' pp. 24–42 in M. Izard and P. Smith (eds) John Leavitt (translator) *Between belief and transgression: structuralist essays in religion, history and myth*, Chicago: University of Chicago Press.

Herzfeld, M. 2001 *Anthropology: theoretical practice in culture and society*, Oxford: Blackwell.

Hoppál, M and Howard, K. (eds) 1993 *Shamans and cultures*, Budapest: Akadémiai Kiadó and Los Angeles: International Society for Trans-Oceanic Research.

Hubert, H. and Mauss, M. 1964[1899], *Sacrifice: its nature and function* (trans. W.D. Halls), Chicago: University of Chicago Press.

Illich, I. 1974 *Medical nemesis*, New York: Bantam .

Kehoe, A.B. 2000 *Shamans and religion: an anthropological exploration in critical thinking*, Illinois: Waveland Press.

Kleinman, A. 1988 *The illness narratives*, New York: Basic Books.

Marriot, M. 1976 'Hindu transactions: diversity without dualism' pp. 109–142 in B. Kapferer (ed.), *Transaction and meaning*, Philadelphia: Institute for the Study of Human Issues.

Mattingly, C. 2000 'Emergent narratives' in *Narrative and the cultural construction of illness and healing*, pp. 181–211 in C. Mattingly and L.C. Garro (eds), Berkeley: University of California Press.

Parry, J. 1982 'Sacrificial Death and the Necrophagus Ascetic' pp. 74–110 in M. Bloch and J. Parry (eds), *Death and the Regeneration of Life*, Cambridge: Cambridge University Press.

Purkiss, D. 1996 *The witch in history: early, modern and twentieth-century representations*, London and New York: Routledge.

Sagant, P. 1991 (1981) 'With Head held high: the house, ritual and politics in East Nepal' pp. 129–154 in G. Toffin (ed.), *Man and his house in the Himalayas: Ecology of Nepal*, New Delhi: Sterling Publishers Private.

Spiro, H. 1998 *The power of hope: a doctor's perspective*, New Haven and London: Yale University Press.

Thomas, K. 1971 *Religion and the decline of magic*, London: Weidenfeld.

Turner, B.S. (1995 [1987]) *Medical power and social knowledge* London: Sage.

Winkelman, M. 2000 *Shamanism: the neural ecology of consciousness and healing*, Westport, Connecticut and London: Bergin & Garvey.

8. Healing here, there and in-between: a Tamu shaman's experience of international landscapes

Judith Pettigrew and Yarjung Tamu

Shamans and their clients have been studied almost exclusively within their local environment or at least within their country of origin (see for example, Atkinson (1989); Desjarlais (1994[1992]); Holmberg (1989); Laderman (1991). Although there is a significant literature on shamans who practice in the urban centres of their home country (Balzer 1993; Kendall 1996; Humphrey 1999), a literature on the relationship between shamans and practitioners of other traditions (Mumford 1990; Ortner 1978; Pignède 1993[1966]) and a small number of publications on indigenous shamans who treat their non-indigenous neighbours (Joralemon 1990; Villoldo & Jendresen 1990; Young, Ingram & Swartz 1989) there does not appear to be a literature on shamans who practice transnationally[1]. We do not know what challenges are faced by shamans who provide treatment for people of diverse cultural backgrounds in distant lands. Nor are we aware of the processes through which a local healing practice – which is embedded in a culturally specific belief system and spiritual landscape – is transported across vast distances and used to treat people whose belief system and understanding of the world are totally different.

What happens, for example, when a Nepali shaman joins the Gurkhas, is posted overseas, and is consulted by people of his own and other ethnic groups? How does he negotiate the differences of culture and landscape? At rituals in Hong Kong does he see the spirit world of Nepal or of Hong Kong? What landscapes does he journey over during rituals for people of different nationalities in diverse locations across the globe and how do his ancestors and helping spirits find these distant healing locations? How does he explain culture-specific concepts and practices to people who have no knowledge of them? What ritual use can he make of the flora and fauna of distant places? Can he, for example, metamorphose into an English fox and a Nepali tiger when working in England or can he only take on the characteristics of a Nepali animal in Nepal and an English one in England? Can a Nepali shaman encounter and tame the spirits that inhabit such diverse places as Hong Kong, Brunei, suburban England and rural Ireland?

This paper examines transnational shamanic practice through a dialogue between a Nepali shaman and an anthropologist. Yarjung Tamu is a Tamu[2] *pachyu chiba* [head *pachyu*[3] shaman] and ex-Gurkha soldier from western Nepal who currently lives and works in the United Kingdom. During the last ten years Tamu has collaborated with anthropologists and archaeologists in the United Kingdom, Switzerland and Nepal on a series of projects on Tamu shamanic material culture, ritual and healing, ethno-history and archaeology. Tamu is a founder member of the Tamu Pye Lhu Sangh religious and cultural organisation whose self-appointed mandate is the preservation of shamanic religion and its associated cultural traditions and knowledge. He is one of the few remaining fluent speakers of the Tamu shamanic language *Chõ Kyui* and is presently engaged on a long-term project to computerise his oral chants so that they will be accessible to future generations of Tamu-mai. Judith Pettigrew, who is Tamu's partner, is an Irish anthropologist. She has undertaken research on shamanic healing, the politics of cultural preservation and ethno-history among the Tamu-mai since 1990 and has collaborated with Tamu since 1991 (Pettigrew & Tamu 1994; 1999; forthcoming).

We approach the question of the transportability of Tamu's practice by discussing his past experiences of healing in the British Army and contemporary experiences of conducting consultations and rituals in Europe in this paper. In particular, we pay attention to the question of how a shaman adapts to practising in different geographical and spiritual landscapes with people from diverse cultural backgrounds as well as relating this to the anthropology of shamanic healing.

The first section of the paper focuses on Tamu's experiences of practising as a *pachyu* in Hong Kong in the late 1970s and 1980s. It describes how it became public knowledge that he was a shaman and the circumstances under which he was permitted to treat soldiers and their families. The paper also pays attention to Tamu's experiences of working as a regimental first aider, first aid instructor and doctor's assistant.[4] The overriding focus, however, is the material world of healing. Specifically, we explore the manner in which Tamu negotiated the spirit landscape of healing when based in Hong Kong. These themes are then taken up in a discussion of Tamu's contemporary practice of shamanism in Europe. Although practical matters currently prohibit Tamu from conducting major healing rituals he frequently conducts consultations and minor rituals.[5] While the main focus of his work outside Nepal is in the United Kingdom, he has also conducted rituals and consultations in Germany, Switzerland, Siberia and Ireland.

INTRODUCTION TO THE NARRATIVE

This narrative is based on a lengthy conversation that took place in English between the authors in the spring of 2001 and was expanded upon during short subsequent conversations. Prior to the original discussion, Pettigrew prepared a list of questions that were added to during the dialogue. As Tamu requested that the conversation not be taped, Pettigrew used a shorthand technique that aimed to record his responses as fully as possible. As the emphasis was on acquiring a detailed rendering of Tamu's words, the resulting transcript does not have a complete record of Pettigrew's questions. To facilitate reading, the partial list has been removed from the narrative. The presentation of the narrative in a chronological manner is based on the format followed in the original conversation; however, the narrative has been subject to considerable editing by Pettigrew. In particular, Tamu's idiosyncratic way of talking has been rendered into standard English in order to avoid the possibility that he be viewed as anything other than an intelligent, articulate man. Italicised comments by Pettigrew, which aim to highlight, clarify or elaborate on specific points, are interspersed with the narrative. In common with Humphrey's comments (1996, 19) concerning her collaboration with Daur Mongol, Urgunge Onon, Tamu's recollections 'during our conversation we were not distanced by the act of thinking them into ... anthropology. That task was for me', [the European anthropologist]. To this end an analytical section written by Pettigrew – which Tamu subsequently read and commented upon – follows the narrative. Responsibility for the content of this section is solely that of Pettigrew as is responsibility for the overall shape of the chapter.

YARJUNG TAMU

I am a Tamu and a member of a shamanic family from the village of Yangjakot in western Nepal. Nowadays I live mainly in the town of Pokhara and also in England. All my male ancestors have been *pachyu* shamans and many of the women in our family know a lot about the tradition although they do not work as shamans.[6] From the time I was a small child until I was 25 I studied to be a *pachyu*. Then I decided that I would like to try to join the British Army [Brigade of Gurkhas]. Our family did not have a tradition of joining the Gurkhas and so I was the first to become a soldier.

I did my basic training in Poklihawa [in the south of Nepal]. *Pachyus* can't eat pork or buffalo but my *gulla* [recruiter] told me that as I was now in the army and was going overseas I would leave my gods and goddesses behind in Nepal and I could eat what I liked. I believed him and so I ate the delicious fried meat in the cookhouse. I didn't check what it was – I just ate it. And so sometimes I ate buffalo and pork. One evening after I had eaten pork I became possessed. For three days I shook under a mosquito net in my tent. I could not go on parade. The regimental first aider came to see me but his medicines did not work. Then they brought some local shamans to see me. They did some small rituals and I got a bit better but I did not completely recover. I changed my mind about the army and said to my *gulla* 'I am a shaman, I pray to lots of gods, maybe my gods don't want me to go into the army. Sorry, but I can't go to Hong Kong.' The *gulla* gave a report to the Gurkha major [most senior Nepali officer in the Battalion]. He suggested that I write to my father and ask him to try to control the gods and also suggested that I should try Hong Kong. He said that if I became more sick in Hong Kong then I could return to Nepal. My report did not go any further than the Gurkha major. The British officers were not told and so I was able to stay in the army. If they had been told I would probably have been asked to leave immediately, as they would have considered me to be a sick man. Why would they have kept me when there are thousands of fit men wanting to join who did not get a chance?

I wrote to my father and told him that I had made a mistake, had eaten pork and had become possessed and was now ill. I asked him to please make the gods happy.

I told him that if I was not well when I reached Hong Kong I would return to Nepal. I also promised him that I would never again eat polluted food or buffalo or pork. My father immediately did a *phai lu* ritual [to honour and appease ancestral and protective deities]. After that I left for Hong Kong and when I got there I completely recovered and finished my nine months of training without any problems. Because of that incident people knew that I was a *pachyu*. As many of them did not know the word *pachyu* as they did not speak Tamu language they called me a *lama* [Buddhist priest]. I was called the 1st 2nd *ko lama* [lama of the 1st 2nd Battalion of the Brigade of Gurkhas].

As the first shaman from his family to join the Gurkhas, Tamu did not have a blueprint for how he should behave as a shaman-soldier (see below for a discussion of shamans in the army). He accepted his recruiter's comments that his gods and goddesses would remain in Nepal and that by becoming a soldier he had become a different type of person – one who could violate the prohibitions he observed as a shaman. By violating taboos, however, he discovered that this was not so – his deities had accompanied him into the army. Tamu's request to his father and his father's ability to control gods at a distance gave Tamu his first experience of 'long-distance' shamanising.

HEALING IN THE GURKHAS: HONG KONG

I did a lot of healing in Hong Kong. I treated people in the evenings in the married quarters. I saw children, women, men, people with all kinds of problems – skin infections, headaches, stomach ache, children with worms, people whose minds had cracked, people who did not want to eat, those who had become possessed. Witches had possessed some of these people and others had become possessed because their ancestral gods were not happy with something they had done.

The first person I treated was my section commander's wife. She had very bad skin problems. Her skin was irritated, she had many pimples and her body was itching all over. I conducted a ritual for her one evening after work in her home. This ritual included treatment with boiling water and fire. I was able to do the boiling water treatment because I found *rudru po*, the special plant I needed for that treatment in the jungle. I was quite surprised to find that it grew in Hong Kong. Afterwards I discovered that many plants I needed for healing grew in Hong Kong, but I had to go deep into the jungle to find them. My section commander and his children would not stay in the room when I was doing the fire treatment. He said to me that if I burned his wife it was my responsibility! The ritual was successful and she was cured. She was very pleased as she had been unwell for a long time and although she had seen many doctors she had not been able to find a cure. The family thanked me and after that it became widely known that I was a strong *pachyu* and could cure people. Lots of people asked to see me.

Many of Tamu's clients were from other Nepali ethnic groups who have shamanic traditions similar to the Tamu-mai. This does not necessarily mean that they would be knowledgeable of shamanic procedure. Some people consult shamans even though they are highly sceptical or ignorant of their methods. Treatment seeking is usually pragmatic and pluralistic and more about perceived efficacy than about shared belief or an understanding of techniques. It is common for clients to consult a range of healers either sequentially or at the same time.

I was not the only shaman in the Gurkhas based in Hong Kong at that time. A few years later after I had moved to another camp a young shaman arrived and did some rituals in the camp that I had previously been stationed in. During a ritual he fought a witch but he didn't win. He returned to his barracks and told his friends that he lost a battle with a witch and that the witch had taken his heart. Shortly afterwards he began to have heart pain and three days later he died in the British Military Hospital. The witch had swallowed his heart [his 'heart soul' which meant that it could not function properly] and so he couldn't survive.

Witches are the prime antagonists of shamans and much of the task of a ritual involves invoking and fighting them. There are actions, objects and clothing that a shaman can use to protect against a witch attack but many of these forms of protection would be unavailable to a soldier conducting part-time healing in Hong Kong. Stories about the defeat of shamans are told by lay people and shamans alike and form part of the discussion concerning the power and status of practitioners.

There is no literature on shamans who heal in the Gurkhas. Tamu states that at any one time there are very few shamans in the army and those that are recruited have usually not completed their apprenticeship. Because of this they are reluctant to practice and when questioned will often downplay their knowledge. Tamu in contrast was considerably older than his stated age on recruitment, had completed his training as a pachyu and was prepared to practice. The topic of shamanic practice in the Gurkhas requires further research. On a recent fieldtrip to a Gurkha camp in Brunei, I was told of a Tamu klehbri shaman who does not practice; however, as I was unable to interview him I did not discover why. Klehbris, who are death specialists and not healers, are less in demand on a day-to-day basis than pachyus and this may account for his non-practice.

If someone wanted healing, first of all they had to ask permission from the Gurkha major [GM] in their battalion. If the GM gave permission then it was passed down through the ranks to me. From the GM the permission was passed to my company commander. From him it came from the company 2IC [second in charge], and then he told the platoon commander who told the sergeant who told the corporal who told me! I would be told that I had to go to such and such a place at a certain time to heal. If they lived close by then I went to their quarters by foot, if they lived far away I was taken by Land Rover. The ritual would start about 6 pm and end at midnight. The Land Rover would come at midnight to collect me and drive me back to my barracks. Soldiers have to get permission to go to another camp at night and so if I was doing a ritual in another camp and it was going to go on until late then permission had to be given by a senior British officer. I don't know exactly what they were told but they did give permission and so some of the British officers knew that I was doing healing in the camps. When I was based in Brunei I was asked directly by a British officer to give shamanic advice. A friend of mine had got lost in the jungle during exercises. Everybody thought that an animal had killed him. The British second in charge and a Nepali officer came to see me and asked me if he was dead or alive. I told them that he was alive and that the jungle spirits had hidden him. I was right, as after a week he was found alive. They were surprised but they didn't give me thanks. I should have had a letter of thanks, but I didn't get anything.

There appears to be tolerance of Tamu's healing activities on the part of British officers as he is provided with some institutional support. This support, however, seems to be implicit rather than explicit. On the one occasion when he has an opportunity to openly demonstrate his abilities in the course of his army work and does so, his skills are not given public recognition.

As part of one of my medical training courses I worked in the British Military Hospital in Kowloon for a while. I also worked in the health centre as a doctor's assistant. This gave me a chance to watch doctors at work. I was interested in their techniques; especially pulse taking. I was surprised, as all they did was listen to the heartbeat. Our system is extremely complicated and difficult to learn. You have to be very sensitive, as there are many different types of pulses. Some of the pulses we take are vibrating and you have to work out the type of vibration, for example, is it a continuous vibration or not. As taking pulses is so difficult we sometimes consult other shamans. This is the same as doctors who talk together about their patient's problems. We can tell a lot of things from the pulse including whether or not a person has been attacked by a witch or a spirit and if they have or have not lost a soul [soul loss is a major cause of illness. Men are believed to have nine souls and women seven (see below)].

There were other things that I was interested in. I noticed that doctors use lots of painkillers. If a soldier complained of pain they would give him a painkiller but if that didn't help then they would up the dose. If that did not work they would change the medicine and try another one. This is a bit like our system. For example, if a small ritual does not work then we do a bigger ritual. In both systems the power is upgraded. Often doctors do not seem to know exactly what works but they do not like to send people to other systems. I thought that this was a bit strange as we often send patients to doctors if they have a problem that is not due to spirits. For example, when I was stationed in Brunei I had a knee problem. I went to the doctor and got painkillers but they did not work. Some of my friends had a similar problem and had been treated effectively by acupuncture and so I said to the doctor 'Sir, can I have acupuncture?' He replied, 'No, it is just like a painkiller. You can not have acupuncture.' I sat there quietly but I felt fed up inside. Six months later I left the army. I took voluntary redundancy.

For Tamu the army experience was riddled with frustrations. By choosing to become a regimental first aider/doctor's assistant he placed himself in a position where he could make comparisons between his healing tradition and those of biomedicine. Proximity, however, brought disappointment as he discovered that biomedical practitioners were intolerant of other traditions. Thus the lack of status he experienced as an un-promoted soldier was reproduced in the interaction with army doctors.

When I was in Hong Kong the British army doctors told patients they couldn't cure to go to see their witch doctor. That is how I discovered that they called people like me witch doctors. I do not know if they respected shamans or not but they did tell people to see us if they could not sort out their problems. I healed people from all the different ethnic groups – Gurungs (Tamu-mai), Rais, Limbus, Newars – all except British people. I did not treat British people because they did not ask me for treatment. I treated Chinese people who worked in the camp but usually I only gave them first aid. Sometimes if I was called to provide first aid and if I saw that there was a spirit problem I would treat that as well. For example, if a person had a headache and the pills didn't work then I would say a *mantra* [incantation]. I didn't always tell them what I was doing. There was no need to tell.

While Tamu treated people from different Nepali groups on request and Chinese people with spirit problems covertly, he did not treat British people. This was not only because they did not ask for treatment, but also because, as a first aider, he did not encounter British people with spirit problems. If he had he would have treated them. According to Tamu, British people suffer from spirit problems but as they don't have a system of rituals to counteract malevolent spirits, they suffer ill health and die unnecessarily from these problems.

I did not have much equipment with me in the army. I only had my *premphu* and my *prumain* [nine sacred Himalayan herbs collected on special days]. *Premphu* are made from the seeds of the *Prem* tree, which are collected, dried and then strung together. They can also be made from the wood of the *Prem* tree. *Premphu* that have been used by a strong shaman are very powerful. My father's, for example, are especially powerful. *Premphu* have many uses: they are protective, they can provide information about a person's illness or about the spirit world; they can be used for counting when chanting; they can be placed over a sick person's body for healing; they can be used to fight spirits or witches. *Premphu* have many other *secret* uses that I cannot discuss. They are mainly worn around the neck but they can also be placed around the wrist or on top of the *kaidu* rice statues [see below]. In Hong Kong I did not have a drum with me, but I did use *kaidu*. *Kaidu* are rice statues that represent gods or evil spirits. Statues that represent gods are white and they are made out of boiled rice that is moulded by hand. Statues representing evil spirits are brown/black and they are made from boiled millet. As I did not have all my equipment with me, I was not able to do big rituals. Actually I did not need lots of equipment, as I was not asked to do big rituals. I only did small rituals that were not so dangerous. For example, I could not change into an animal to enable me to fight evil spirits, as I did not have the bones or beaks that represent those animals with me.

Nepalis are affected by the same kinds of spirit problems in Hong Kong as they are in Nepal. In Hong Kong there are ghosts, witches, evil spirits, cemeteries [malevolent spirits who reside in cemeteries can cause the living harm]. It is not different. Everywhere the spirit world is the same. The spirits all have the same behaviour and cause problems for people. I healed people with witch problems, spirit problems and so on. In Hong Kong and also in the UK there are many witches. People do not admit that they are a witch but the trouble is there. Other people are witches but do not know it and they give curses without knowing it. Those that know can recognise a shaman. Those that don't know are from families that used to have a reputation for witchcraft. They cannot help it – giving a curse comes naturally to them. In the past people in the UK knew about witches – you can see this if you visit some of the museums – nowadays people here have half beliefs; their beliefs are mixed up.

Tamu believes that his model of the supernatural world has universal application. To him this is the way the world is and those who do not recognise it as such have either lost the knowledge to appreciate it or they are unaware of it.

When I needed my ancestors during a ritual they came easily. There was no need for a map. In the United Kingdom I use a map [a written list which contains the names of the countries his ancestors have to pass over en route from Nepal to the UK], but actually I can bring them directly. It is just not as easy or as fast for them. With a map they come directly. In some rituals I to go to Nepal to collect them and in other rituals I call them and they come alone. When I collect them I go physically to get them. I can travel across the world in a second. For example, when I am chanting and say the name of a place then I am in that place. You will see me in front of you playing my drum and chanting, but I am in Nepal. Although the ancestors pass over many lands they do not have problems with bad spirits on the journey. Ancestral spirits are not like humans and they do not get danger from things along the route. I know this because they always arrive okay. Their world is different from ours. Maybe they fight with other spirits or ancestors but we don't know. Maybe they laugh and joke also!

When I was healing in Hong Kong I did not often have to go on shamanic journeys. It depended on the ritual. If I had to go on a journey that required me to go to Nepal then I went directly there. Hong Kong is close to Nepal so its not very different physically and culturally. I felt that it was the same land so there was no problem. Sometimes I went on journeys to other worlds, for example, to the nine planets called *sōku mōku*. These are the planets that circle around the earth. They are places where gods and spirits live. So it doesn't matter if you are in Nepal or Hong Kong or somewhere else as some of the journeys are to completely different worlds.

RITUALS AND CONSULTATIONS IN THE UNITED KINGDOM

Rituals can be done anywhere. For example, if I do a ritual in Coldham's Lane [Cambridge], I collect the local spirits and call them to the ritual. If I am here I see here, if I am in Afghanistan I see Afghanistan, if I am in Hong Kong I see Hong Kong. You can't do healing or other rituals without the help of the local *sildo naldo* [gods of a local area]. If I pray then within a second I can see the local *sildo naldo*. Wherever I am I can see *sildo naldo*. Some are powerful and some are not. I have not found any powerful *sildo naldo* in Cambridge. I do not know why. Maybe there are some, but I haven't met them yet. In Ely [cathedral city 15 miles from Cambridge] there are powerful *sildo naldo*. It is a very old place and a good place for them. It is a kind of a base for *sildo naldo*. I have visited Ely on foot and have also visited it during rituals [while on a shamanic journey]. I feel that there is a special kind of power there.

When necessary I can turn into an animal. If I meet a devil spirit in a ritual I can change into a tiger, lion or a leopard and either fight or run away fast. If I meet a hunting spirit I can change into a vulture and can fly in the sky. I can fly miles up into the sky and look down at the earth. It is very nice. If a different type of spirit attacks I can move into the middle of the sea and they cannot follow me. This is why *pachyus* use crystals as they can represent the sea. You cannot change into something unless you have a text [oral chant] to change you. I cannot change into a hare, rabbit or mouse, as I do not have texts for these animals. I do not need them. There are so many animals in the world that it is impossible to have texts for them all. I cannot make up new texts as *pachyus* only chant the texts that our ancestors created a long time ago. The texts make the objects that represent the animals or the elements come alive. During the early stage of a ritual I chant the texts to get them ready to be used if I need them later on. When I need them I say a *mantra.* Ordinary people look at me and just see a person, but the spirits do not see a person. To them I look like a tiger or a lion so they get very frightened. The people at the ritual hear my drum rhythm change but they still hear drumming, whereas the spirits hear it another way; they hear the roar of a lion. I can change into a wasp or a bee. Wasps are poisonous and so they are very protective against evil spirits. People in the UK want to get rid of a wasp's nest, as they are worried that they or their children will get stung, but they do not realise the protective role that wasps play against spirits. There is no problem turning into an animal that doesn't exist in the place I am working in as long as I have something that represents that animal like a bone, tooth or feather.

Rituals are accompanied and narrated by the chanting of multiple-purpose, often lengthy, 'oral texts' (pye). Essentially these texts narrate action – activities cannot occur without first being described. An animal representative cannot become 'alive' unless it has previously been chanted 'alive'. Pye tell of the origins of people, animals, plants, shamanic paraphernalia and sacred substances. Others recall stories of gods, ancestors, famous shamans, shamanic travel, shrines, demons, witches, stars, luck, illness and death. The pye were created by the ancestors and cannot be expanded or updated. The emphasis in ritual chanting is on exact repetition which according to Strickland (1983: 260) experienced Tamu shamans come very close to achieving.

Spirits are all the same, they don't have ethnicity. Every religion has its own way to call gods and spirits – Muslims, Christians, us, but it's all the same. The only thing that is different is the way to call. Spirits understand spirit language. They all speak the same language. It is just as easy for me to recognise ghosts in Ireland, where I did a recent consultation, as it is for me to recognise them in Nepal. Ghosts do not like change and the ghosts in the house in Ireland were causing problems as the owners had done renovations and that is when the problems started. Ghosts in Nepal would do exactly the same thing. Although there are different types of spirits, they belong to the same species, just like humans. For example, we do not have tails or three legs and three arms. Spirits have some kind of special society, but I do not think that they have families or clans or a system like that. Actually, I do not know. When we are dead we will know.

The bad spirits never beat the gods: the power is in the words. For example, 'Amen'. We say *ombet.* The spirits can't beat the word. If the shaman does not have powerful words then the evil spirits can beat them. It's like a lock/unlock system. If you don't have the key you will be killed. If you are drunk in a ritual the spirits won't come, you will be vulnerable and could be killed. It is very important to get the words of a chant right as otherwise you are wasting your time and could even bring danger to yourself. This is why so much time and attention is paid to the way student shamans' chant the texts.

All humans have seven or nine souls. There is the body soul and other souls but they are secret. I know where and how souls leave a person's body but this is also secret. Witches can steal souls. One of the main reasons that people become ill is because they have lost a soul. Souls can easily leave the body. For example, a soul can leave with a dead person during a funeral or can get lost in water. Children's souls leave particularly easily and spirits that live in water often attract them. If you lose more than half of your souls you become crazy, your brain goes, you become *mind cracked* [mad]. If you lose all your souls you die.

Tamu's universalist model of the supernatural extends to his model of the body and the mind, the vulnerability of humans and the causes of illness. Just as spirits are cross-culturally similar so are people, their afflictions and their potential to be cured.

I have done lots of rituals in the UK but I find it difficult to work here. It is hard to get the information I need. For example, when I am doing a ritual I need to know where the water source is, who the ancestors of the area are and the name of their original village. This information is important as I need to evaluate the power that exists in the area so that I know what power is available to assist me and what bad spirits I might have to fight. People here don't know these things, or they only know them approximately. I need exact information as otherwise it gets difficult. It's a bit of a cocktail here so it's hard for me to find lost souls. I have most of my equipment with me, which is good. I have my one-sided drum that was made on an auspicious day from the wood of a special tree and is covered with goatskin. I also have a bell and a conch shell. In the past *pachyus* blew the horn of a deer. Nowadays deer horns are hard to get so most of us use conch shells as they do the same job. The conch shell gives messages to the spirit world. I put power into the sound that the evil spirits can't tolerate: it breaks their ears. All the instruments I use, for example, the drum, bell, cymbals and conch shell have their own role to play but they also work like a team.

An important aspect of conducting a major healing ritual is the presence of colleagues and assistants. Assistants and/or members of the audience play instruments and undertake supporting tasks. Other essential participants are people familiar with trance who can judge if and when it is necessary to assist the pachyus leave an altered state and can provide the necessary assistance. Although Tamu emphasises that he cannot conduct major rituals in the UK as sacrifice is prohibited, the absence of knowledgeable assistants is also a limiting factor.

I have the beaks of several birds with me in England and other things like my porcupine quills, which are my main weapons. They are very powerful and are used for fighting, for protection and also other secret uses. All of these things are in the Museum [Cambridge University Museum of Archaeology and Anthropology].[7] I have a special arrangement with the curator and I can take out my objects if I need them for a ritual or if I am giving a talk. Most of the rituals I do in the UK are protective rituals for people who are going on long journeys, or people who have bad luck or have had something bad happen to them. I also do astrological consultations, protective rituals for people who are in dangerous astrological positions and good luck rituals. Sometimes people come to see me because they think they have been cursed or because they want to know if their house is haunted or if they have a spirit problem. I see adults, children and babies. A couple of years ago I was invited to Germany to do a good luck ritual for a friend's baby.

I do not advertise my healing and most of the people I see in Europe are friends, acquaintances, and friends of friends or people I meet when I give a talk at a university or a museum. I see anybody who asks but mostly those who ask know a bit about shamanism and have respect for it. I can treat people who don't believe but they don't usually come. I often give people protective amulets. There are many types of amulets made out of different types of paper on which secret symbols are written on special days. I write the symbols in different types of ink depending on what power I want to put into the amulet. For example, if I want to prevent the spread of a transmitted disease like chicken pox then the amulet must be written with the blood of a monkey. The monkey does not have to be killed; I just need a little of its blood. Amulets can also be written using ink made from herbs, human blood, or ink made from the charcoal of cremated human remains. Amulets can be written on things other than paper including the bark of a special tree or even a piece of a person's clothing. This is used when someone wants to bring back a husband or wife who has left. If the amulet is worn then the person who has left will return within 15 days.

It is very different working with English people as the culture is different. Nepalis know what questions to ask and what not to ask but English people ask questions all the time! Sometimes I get fed up with all the questions. It is complicated here, as after a ritual, you must not take money out of the house for three days, but people here do not have that idea and they find this very difficult to organise. They ask me if they can withdraw money from the cash machine or if they can take a cheque out! Well, the ancestors cannot answer that question so I have to decide myself. As long as money does not go out of the door I think it is okay but it is hard these days to know exactly what money is. In the past there was no paper money in Nepal, only coins, and so *pachyus* told people not to take coins out. Then the paper money came and *pachyus* had to tell people not to take paper money out and now there are cheques and cash machines and we have to make decisions about these.

While most Nepalis that Tamu treats have some knowledge of ritual content, and have a similar cultural style regarding question-asking, there is more diversity than might first be apparent. Knowledge of rituals among second and third generation urban-dwellers is limited compared to their parents and grandparents, and interactional styles are changing.

I haven't done big rituals here but the small ones I have done have been just as successful as those that I do in Nepal. While it is much harder for me to work here, when I overcome the problems I face, the end result is similar. I have done lots of protective rituals for people going to do fieldwork in remote overseas locations and each of these have been successful. A couple of years ago I saw a teenage girl whose mother brought her to see me as she had had a series of bad accidents. She was in a very vulnerable astrological position and I gave her an amulet. Some months later her mother phoned back to let me know that she was well and that her bad luck had ended. I have seen people who had psychological problems caused by soul loss and in each case I have been able to help them. With problems like depression it takes time and people usually need repeat rituals but immediately after the rituals these people improved. A couple of times I have been asked to do a ritual for a family but the person with the most problems didn't turn up. In a situation like this it is extremely difficult to find lost souls. It takes extra time, extra work and even then it may not be possible to locate them.

Most Nepalis who consult a shaman have to a greater or lesser extent been enculturated into a 'shaman-patient interactional model'. They know, for example, that while doctors ask detailed questions about the course of an illness a shaman requires detailed information about the local landscape, deities, ancestors and the local history of habitation. Clients in a shamanic culture also know that they will be party to certain restrictions after the ritual. Most Europeans know none of these things and while they expect to be asked about the nature of their problem and in turn to ask detailed questions concerning the course and prognosis of their complaint they do not expect to be asked to give a reading of the local landscape based on knowledge that they do not have. Neither are they prepared for the post-ritual restrictions. Although Tamu is aware of the cultural differences the success of a ritual depends on knowledgeable and compliant patients, which many of his European clients cannot be: consequently he is frequently frustrated. Clients on the other hand are usually very positive about their consultation, but are often at a loss initially to know what is expected of them and how to behave. They are frequently overly reverential and are surprised by the quick shifts between ritual actions and lively social interaction interspersed with the consumption of alcohol.

ANTHROPOLOGICAL COMMENTARY: JUDITH PETTIGREW

Tamu's narrative addresses a range of themes including: 1) the view of western medicine from a shaman's perspective; 2) the comparison between biomedical practice and shamanic practice; 3) how expatriate Tamus and Nepalis from other ethnic groups use both systems; 4) the interchangeability of some healing systems versus the incompatibility of others; 5) problems of place and geography in shamanic practice in a mobile society and 6) the adaptation of an ancient healing systems to a modern world. While each of these themes merits attention, analysis in this paper focuses primarily on two central issues: 1) how Tamu adapts to practicing in a different geographical context and with people from different ethnic groups; 2) what this mean in terms of the anthropology of shamanic healing.

Most accounts of shamanism focus on a practitioner healing in their local setting or at least within their country of origin. In contrast, this chapter presents an insider's account of shamanic practice in a variety of transnational and cross-cultural situations. Tamu discovered as a new recruit that being a soldier did not mean that he was no longer a *pachyu*. His gods and ancestors and, therefore, his shamanic powers, went with him into the army. With the responsibility to attend to his deities and ancestors came the privileges of retaining his ability to practice.

Practising transnationally with people of different cultural backgrounds poses a range of problems. Tamu believes that all landscapes are cosmically the same, however, despite his ability to read the nuances of spirit behaviour in the townscape of Cambridge, Tamu's ability to successfully conduct rituals is made more difficult by his clients' lack of information concerning specific aspects of their local landscape. Most urban Europeans cannot accurately provide the required information that includes details such as the local water source and the names of the original inhabitants of the area. The answer that Tamu has been given by clients in Cambridge that 'the local water source is Anglian Water' [the local water company] creates a problem that can make a ritual unsuccessful. The onus is then on Tamu to adapt his practice. Although he has the scope to use some alternative approaches it is not possible for him to develop new techniques, as his tradition does not accommodate innovation. As Strickland (1983) points out the aim is exact replication in every ritual. Tamu spent most of his childhood and early adulthood perfecting his techniques in order to attain this goal. Having achieved it he cannot repudiate it. The client's inability to fulfil the culturally specific patient role and the fact that he cannot innovate has led Tamu to comment on several occasions 'It is just too difficult to conduct rituals for Europeans.'

This theme of frustration also runs through Tamu's account of his experiences in the Gurkhas. He enters the army as a head shaman from a famous lineage, yet his leadership skills – an integral part of being a head shaman – are neither recognised nor valued. He remains un-promoted although his acquired skill in biomedicine and his existing skills in shamanic medicine are acknowledged by his clients. As a first aid instructor he should be a corporal but he is denied promotion.[8] This ambivalence in status is mirrored in his encounter with army doctors, which takes place on an unequal footing. He is only permitted to perform healing rituals after hours and outside the officially sanctioned institutions of biomedical healing. Despite his reputation as an expert healer among his own people he is considered by army doctors to be a practitioner of last resort: someone whose skills extend only to treating people labelled as hypochondriacs.

Interestingly, the army appeared to sanction his healing activities by allowing him to visit other camps in the evenings and providing him with transport. There remains, however, ambivalence, as Tamu does not fully know what the British officers who gave permission were told about his activities. His patients, on the other hand, greatly respected his work and rewarded it highly.[9] This went some way towards redressing the disappointments of his encounters with biomedical practitioners and it is why he continued to practice. Tamu considers his healing to be 'gods' work'. He cannot refuse to treat those in need. The esteem in which his clients held him, his awareness of his expertise, and his dedication to his profession may have partly redressed the rebuffs of biomedicine but they also created additional frustrations. Ultimately, Tamu could not convert his qualifications as a *pachyu* nor his successes in the informal arena of night time healing into success in the formal arena of an army career. Despite his abilities and achievements the public acclaim and prestige that accompany promotion were denied him. Frustrated and disappointed, Tamu left the army. In fact his army career was punctuated by attempts to leave but each time he was convinced otherwise by Nepali officers who pointed out the opportunities associated with army service. Finally he opted for voluntary retirement. When he left, Tamu carried with him the impact of his encounter with army hierarchy, biomedicine and British people, the implications of which continue to play themselves out in his life. In spite of his contemporary professional and personal successes in the UK, which has enabled some of the earlier experiences to be re-worked, the residues are still there and play a role in informing his present-day interactions with British people. He is irritated by his clients primarily because of their cultural 'ignorance' but contained within the equation is a deeper antipathy towards British people in general, and the 'officer class' in particular, at whose hands he feels he has suffered disrespect, disappointment and humiliation.

The emphasis in this chapter on transnational practice marks a new departure in the study of shamanic healing. By focusing on a shaman working cross-culturally attention is drawn to aspects of shamanic healing that do not usually attract examination such as the universalist nature of the worldview, the manner in which a shaman approaches clients from other cultural backgrounds and the influence of his previous experiences with that culture on his contemporary practice, the impact of 'ignorant' patients and the way in which he managed a largely covert practice. Our chapter also addresses issues of power and professional recognition and touches on the difficulties experienced by a shaman undertaking training in another healing tradition that devalues his expertise.

The picture that emerges from this work is complex and contradictory. According to Tamu the cosmos is universal and shamanic practice can be undertaken anywhere. Ritual space can be created as and when necessary, gods and ancestors travel and can be called across vast distances, all people have multiple souls and their astrological constellations can be accessed via Tamu astrological calculations. Numerous gods inhabit the landscape or townscape and demons that are prone to anger can create misfortune for those who live in the locality. Everyone has ancestors – even those that know little about them – who can protect their descendants or react with anger when neglected.

This reading of the English landscape and the bodies of the people who live in it is unproblematic as long as it remains Tamu's personal worldview. When European clients who do not share this worldview consult him and are required to act within it and cannot, Tamu faces a dilemma. Suffering is universal and it is his responsibility to provide assistance to those who request it. European clients, however, are often unable to adequately fulfil the patient role and this limits his ability to work with them. Tamu's practice is readily exportable and at the same time deeply rooted in a specific cultural world. By continuing to work transnationally – and by doing so in a manner that is as true as possible to his traditions – Tamu endures what he calls 'irritations'. He has been frustrated for a long time by foreign systems and has adapted as much as his tradition allows, but there is always an undercurrent of dissatisfaction.

ORTHOGRAPHY

Most non-English words in this chapter are *Chõ Kyui* (Tamu ritual language) which is an unwritten Tibeto-Burman language with no standard orthography. We have chosen to use a phonetic approach and render words in their simplest possible spelling. We have adopted the same approach to the small number of *Nepali* language words used.

Acknowledgements

We would like to thank the following people who commented on earlier versions of this chapter: Piers Vitebsky, Chris Evans, Mark Turin, Sandra Rouse, Martin Johnston and the editors of this volume. We are particularly grateful to Sharon Hepburn for her insightful comments and for suggesting the title.

Notes

1   There are traditional Chinese doctors and Tibetan doctors working transnationally, however, little or no academic attention appears to have been paid to their practices. An interview conducted with a Tibetan doctor based in Spain reveals that the major problems he faces concerns the difficulties Spanish people have following his dietary prescriptions and ingesting his herbal medicines (Gerke 2000).

2   'Tamu' is the singular of 'Tamu-mai', the ethnonym the people better known as 'Gurung' apply to themselves when they speak in their own language, *Tamu Kyui*.

3   There are two main types of shamans among the Tamu-mai: the *pachyu* and the *klehbri*. Although the belief system, cosmology and linguistic traditions of these shamans are essentially shared, they perform slightly different functions. The *klehbri* is primarily, but not exclusively, a death specialist and in some villages is intimately involved with the performance of certain calendrical rituals to village and clan deities. The *pachyu* is an exorcist, healer and death specialist. Both, but predominantly the *pachyu*, perform 'rituals of affliction' day-to-day rituals (*teh-mai*) which are involved with the removal or prevention of human 'misery' (Turner 1967: 9–16). Certain ritual activities overlap and either practitioner can perform some rites.

4   In the army Tamu acquired numerous qualifications in first aid. These included a series of regimental first aid training courses at different levels of advancement, a hygiene course and a first aid instructor's qualification. When stationed in the medical centre he worked as a doctor's assistant.

5   Tamu is not able to conduct major rituals in the United Kingdom as these inevitably involve animal sacrifice, a practice that it is not legal in the UK.

6   The *pye* [oral text] tells that in the past women were shamans and at one stage a woman saved the tradition from extinction.

7   In 1993 Tamu was awarded a small grant to bring a collection of Tamu shamanistic materials to the museum. For a discussion of this project see Herle (1994: 2–5).

8   Tamu's discharge certificate from the army states explicitly that he was unlucky not to be promoted. While he may not have had the necessary networks to facilitate promotion – and by his own admission had a reputation for being outspoken – clearly some of his senior officers recognised his leadership abilities. For whatever reason recognition did not materialise into reality and Tamu left the army deeply disappointed by the experience.

9   Although Tamu did not ask for payment, and was reluctant to accept it, his clients insisted and often paid him highly.

Bibliography

Atkinson, J.M. 1989 *The art and politics of Wana shamanship*, Berkeley: University of California Press.

Balzer, M. 1993 'Two urban shamans' pp. 131–164 in G. Marcus (ed.) *Perilous states: conversations and uncertain transitions*, Chicago: University of Chicago Press.

Bickel, B & Gaenszle, M. 1999 'Introduction' pp 247–270 (eds) in B. Bickel and M. Gaenszle (eds) *Himalayan space: cultural horizons and practices*, Völkerkundemuseum Press: Zürich.

Desjarlais, R. 1994[1992] *Body and emotion: the aesthetics of illness and healing in the Nepal Himalayas*, Delhi: Motilal Banarsidass Publishers.

Gerke, B. 2000 'The Tibetan medical diaspora in Spain: interview with Dr Lobsang Dhondup and Dr Pedro J.G. Arteagoitia', Tibetan Medical Centre, Bilbao, Spain *http://www.kreisels.com/ittm/lttm63.htm*

Herle, A. 1994 'Museums and shamans: a cross-cultural collaboration' *Anthropology Today* 10 (1), 2–5.

Holmberg, D.H. 1989 *Order in paradox: myth, ritual and exchange among Nepal's Tamang*, Ithaca: Cornell University Press.

Humphrey, C. 1999 'Shamans in the City' *Anthropology Today* 15 (3), 3–10.

Humphrey, C. with Onon, U. 1996 *Shamans and elders: experience, knowledge and power among the Daur Mongols*, Oxford: Oxford University Press.

Joralemon, D. 1990 'The selling of the shaman and the problem of informant legitimacy' *Journal of Anthropological Research* 46 (20), 105–118.

Kendall, L. 1996 'Korean shamans and the spirits of capitalism' *American Anthropologist*. 98 (3), 502–527.

Laderman, C. 1991 *Taming the winds of desire: psychology, medicine and aesthetics in Malay shamanistic performance*, Berkeley: University of California Press.

Mumford, S.R. 1990 *Himalayan dialogue: Tibetan lamas and Gurung shamans in Nepal*, Kathmandu: Tiwari's Pilgrims Book House.

Ortner, S. 1978 *Sherpas through their rituals*, Cambridge: Cambridge University Press.

Pettigrew, J. and Tamu, Y. 1994 'Tamu shamanistic possession (*Kh-hlye Kh-haba*): preliminary ethnographic notes' pp. 316–422 in M. Allen (ed.) *The anthropology of Nepal: people, problems and processes*, Kathmandu, Nepal: Mandala Book Press.

Pettigrew, J and Tamu, Y. 1999 'The Kohla project: studying the past with the Tamu-mai' *Studies in Nepali History and Society* 4 (2), 327–364.

Pettigrew, J. and Tamu, Y. (forthcoming) 'Sacrifice among the Tamu-mai of Nepal' in C. Evans and I. Hodder (eds). *Marshland communities and cultural landscape* Haddenham Project: Volume II. McDonald Institute of Archaeological Research: Cambridge.

Pignède, B. 1993[1966] *The Gurungs: a Himalayan population of Nepal*, Kathmandu: Ratna Pustak Bhandar.

Strickland, S.S. 1983 'The Gurung priest as bard' *Kailash, a Journal of Himalayan Studies* 10, 227–265

Turner, V. 1967 *Forest of symbols: aspects of Ndembu ritual*, Ithaca: Cornell University Press.

Villoldo, A. and Jendresen, E. 1990 *The four winds: a shaman's odyssey into the Amazon*, New York: Harper & Row.

Young, D., G. Ingram and Swartz, L. 1989 *Cry of the eagle: encounters with a Cree healer*, Toronto: University of Toronto Press.

9. The Xaghra shaman?

Simon Stoddart

This article is inspired by the need to interpret one of those discoveries, which for most people only occur once in a career. On the 25th September 1991, Andrew Townsend, working as part of a systematic excavation in the central area of the Brochtorff Circle near the village of Xaghra[1] on the island of Malta, uncovered a cache of nine carved figures (Figure 9.1; Plate 9.1). Six of these were stick figures, with decoration predominantly focused on the head, except for two, which had skirts typical of other contemporary sculpture. Further sculptures were a small head on a stand, a pig's head on a stick, and another head on a penannular ring. Later a small pot of ochre, a ceramic sieve and shell scoop were found in the same screened off area next to a large stone bowl. All these can be argued by virtue of shared context to form a related group from within the burial complex on the Xaghra plateau at the centre of Gozo, Malta, dating to the third millennium BC. These objects remain unique, but visibly adhered to the distinctive cultural identity of the period (Malone and Stoddart 1998, 247). The finds were loosely defined as those of a shaman (Stoddart *et al.* 1993). However, the question remains to what extent can this designation be justified? Or should a minimalist term of compromise such as 'technician of the sacred' be adopted in a vain attempt to avoid all difficult connotations?

SHAMANISM OR SHAMANISMS?

The concept of shamanism has gone through phases of enthusiastic support and post-modern rejection. As Price (2001, 6) points out, the term is an entirely externally imposed construction that covers considerable variation. Fortunately, for the purposes of this article, the term is undergoing something of current revival in anthropology (Atkinson 1992) and archaeology (Clottes and Lewis-Williams 1998). Nevertheless, the term has not escaped the continuing relativistic debate in social and cultural anthropology. Kehoe (2000; in press) is one of the most critical of the use of the term shamanism, specifically in the context of rock art by defining the practice as 'uncritical, reductionistic primitivism' that denies diversity. The term is, moreover, complicated by its relative usage in different traditions of anthropology (Lewis 1986, 78–79); it is more preferred in American Anglophone anthropology than in its British equivalent

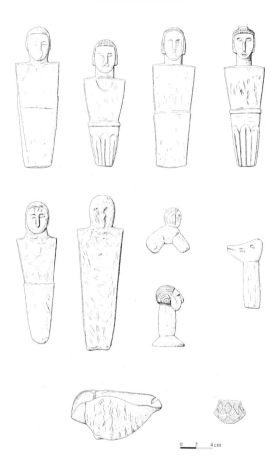

Figure 9.1 The shaman's cache and other paraphernalia. The upper nine figures in globigerina limestone were found as one "kit". The lower objects, a shell scoop and a small ceramic container of ochre were found nearby. Drawings by Steven Ashley.

where 'spirit possession' is the preferred term. Relativism is also complicated by the multivalency of shamanship, where an individual slips between different roles. In this circumstance, can scholars define sufficient common elements among shamanistic practice, or should we be defining the shamanistic practices of individual communities? A large number of modern authors stress that there is some common theme, which can be traced. Vitebsky (1995) defines 'astonishing similarities' between the different cultural contexts of shamanism, even if the linguistic origin can be traced to one cultural context, that of the Evenk of Siberia. Saladin d'Angilure (1996, 508) ends rhetorically with a statement that binds shamanism to humanity: 'is it not rooted in an immemorial prehistory which by way of the ideology of hunting was directly attuned to nature and the cosmos?' projecting a time depth shared by Balzer (1996, 1185): 'some humans need to reach deep, mythic, spiritual levels within ourselves.'

Plate 9.1. The shaman's cache at the moment of discovery. Photo by Simon Stoddart.

What does this shamanism, potentially so close to the essence, even the origins, of humanity comprise? Most authors stress the mediatory capacity of the shaman between this world and the next, and between the world of humans and animals. In the words of Saladin d'Anguilure (1996), the shaman is a 'mediator between the human world and the world of the spirits, between the living and the dead, between animals and human society.' In this role, the shaman can accompany the dead (Balzer 1996). In this status, the shaman frequently has an ambiguity of sex and role-play. A further key element is the performance of controlled trance, seeking knowledge through ecstasy. This transition frequently incorporates altered states of consciousness (Vitebsky 1995; Peters and Price Williams 1980) which allow access to the spiritual world, transcending reality through metaphor.

THE MATERIAL CULTURE OF SHAMANISM

The shaman's power may be derived from spirits but it can 'reside in objects, songs or actions, such as the beating of a drum' (Vitebsky 1995, 25). This linkage to the material is evidently an important part of shamanistic practice, even though it is given scant attention in most ethnographies. Vitebsky (1995, 82–84) does devote a section to shamanistic equipment. Musical instruments (especially drums), (exotic) rocks and crystals and parts of plants and animals are typical examples. One specific item, the Alaskan *kikutuk,* or animal effigy, is intriguing because it has a figurative quality which guides its use and interpretation. A fundamental aspect of all these objects is that they 'allow the shaman to perform associated action', and thus it is permissable to read the action, at least metaphorically, through the form of the object. These are objects of shamanistic power, where image reinforces action. It is also permissable to read the action through the posture of the participants, a detail often recorded in contemporary material culture. A final recoverable context of the shaman is the physical surroundings. Descent into the earth can be both a physical reality and a metaphorical point of the reference (Clottes and Lewis-Williams 1998, 28–29). This physical landscape is also frequently related to a shamanistic cosmology where entering the earth can comprise entry into the lowest level of that universe. Clearly this linkage to material culture in its broadest sense is crucial for any archaeological interpretation.

'Archaic' shamanism

Anthropologists are more cautious when they move outside the synchronic framework that lies beyond the vague psychological inheritance of humanity. The view of Balzer (1996, 1183) is typical: 'many arguments, however, concerning pre-written historical development of sorcerers, shamans and priests must remain unsolved.' However, Vitebsky (1995, 33) acknowledges that shamanism was most probably present in a large range of societies both past and present; although most prevalent among hunting societies, 'In societies with a more complex social organisation natural human anxieties about chance and misfortune shift from hunting to floods and crop failure ....passing exams and finding a job.' Some scholars also propose an inverse relationship between complex social structure and shamanism (Lewis 1986, 84; Douglas 1970, 97).

Vitebsky (1993) provides a highly stimulating analysis of one of these more complex societies in India (Table 9.1). The Sora are shifting cultivators on the edge of more complex kingdoms. The analysis of Vitebksy provides a detailed contextual analysis of shamanism relative to life and death, gender and numbers of participants (Table 9.1). This interlinkage between participants and performance, and explanation of the dialogues with the dead by the female shamans, provides a useful backdrop against which to consider the material culture of the Xaghra shaman.

Archaeologists have had much less temerity in assigning archaic shamanism, and have been criticised by some (e.g Kehoe 2000; in press). The most active field has been in the interpretation of hunter gatherer societies, concurring with the dominance of shamanism among such modern peoples. Interpretation has concentrated on the artistic products of shamanistic activities, a guide to the mind of the shaman whilst in a trance (Lewis-Williams and Dowson 1988; Clottes and Lewis-Williams 1998). Thus, cultural diversity is controlled by neurological similarity. Less attention has been addressed to

Table 9.1. Types of Sora shamanism.

Context	Underworld	Daily life
Ceremonies	Funeral	Divination
Shaman name	Kuran – Sanatang	Kuran – tedung
Importance	Great	Minor
Numbers of shaman type/village	2–3	12+
Shaman participation	Communal	Single
Gender	Female	Male

the tools of the shaman. One exception is the attribution by Piggott (1962a) of the grave of an individual accompanied by perforated bone pendants and natural hollow flint nodules to a shaman, drawing on similar interpretations of earlier periods of Siberia.

THE XAGHRA SHAMAN

In the course of the last half of the fourth millennium and the first half of the third millennium BC we can infer that a highly distinctive cosmological landscape developed in the Maltese islands, the most isolated archipelago of the Mediterranean, some 80km off Sicily. Perhaps we can press the evidence to interpret this tripartite landscape of life rituals (in structures normally designated *temples*), death rituals and domestic structures (Stoddart in press), all inscribed in local stone, in terms of the three cosmological levels suggested by the shamanistic ethnographic evidence: the celestial and exotic of the sky and beyond the seas; the land of temples and domesticity; the funerary and subterranean. The *upper cosmological level* can only be inferred indirectly from the material. For the congregation, the temples had an approximately common orientation towards Sicily, the ancestral origin of the islands (Stoddart *et al.* 1993). For the officiating priests, the complementary alignment out of the entrance of each temple towards celestial spheres could have been equally important (Foderà Serio *et al.* 1992). There are also some rare engravings which may refer to celestial bodies. One is the fragment of a (possibly) circular stone slab found at the Tal Qadi temple and engraved with radiating lines, 7-pointed stars and possibly a the depiction of a crescent moon (Evans 1971, Plate 34. 6; Pace 1996, 9). A further item is the 'solar wheel' sherd from Hagar Qim (Pace 1996, 9). The temples also contained the whittled down residual remains of exotic products from across the seas (greenstone etc). The skies and the lands beyond the seas formed layers of relative inaccessibility; power was credited to those who could claim access from this relatively isolated island. The middle terrestrial level was defined by six clusters of monuments which appear to have been the focus of the life rituals, each most probably focused on a central funerary monument (the lowest cosmological layer). The domestic structures, associated with these temples, were altogether more modest in size.

Table 9.2 Levels of Maltese cosmology.

Level	Definition	Occupants	Material culture
Upper	Celestial	Exotic ancestors and divine	Stars, exotic materials
Middle	Mundane	The living	Temples, houses
Lower	Spirits	The dead	Mortuary complexes

The clusters of temples were placed at the approximate centre of hypothetical territories, each most probably with an associated mortuary complex. Only two (one third) of the clusters have such a clear association. The presence of the Hal Saflieni underground mortuary complex in association with the temples of Tarxien and Kordin has been known since the beginning of the 20th century. The rediscovery of the Brochtorff Circle in association with the temples of Ggantija and Santa Verna on the Xaghra plateau in Gozo has been much more recent, and strengthens considerably our proposed understanding of Maltese landscape cosmology

These two clusters make an important and revealing cosmological comparisons. In each case, we can consider the funerary complex to form a naturally prominent monument on a physical eminence rising above the culturally prominent temples. There would have been approach routes which would almost certainly have been interconnected by processional ways, interlinking other megalithic markers in the landscape. For the Xaghra plateau on Gozo we can make a detailed reconstruction of the prominent features in this middle cosmological layer. This mesa-like plateau provided a natural setting for ritual action. An approach from low ground brings the Ggantija temples set on a prepared terrace into view just below the lip of the plateau. At least two significant locations link components of a ceremonial way from this temple complex to the circular mortuary structure (Brochtorff Circle) on the summit of the plateau. One is a cave (North cave) filled with the debris of ritual largesse. The other is a megalithic structure, which has some temple-like affinities (Ta Ghejzu). Beyond Brochtorff circle is a another definite temple structure (Santa Verna), which survey has shown to be the centre of a concentration of temple period debris, suggesting a residential complex encircling the megalithic remains.

These clusters of temples have generally been explained in terms of chiefly territorial behaviour (Renfrew 1976). However, we explain the presence of several contemporaneous temples of varying size and local history across the landscape, in association with a single funerary monument as the products of intense social networks (Bonanno et al 1990), following Boissevain (1965). The building stratigraphy of these temples is difficult to interpret, but it appears that monuments with open access, typical of public ritual structures, were subverted by the priestly class towards the end of the Tarxien period (3000–2500 BC), while secret knowledge was increasingly preserved in the inner parts of the temple. Transformations in the way temples were fitted out enabled parts to be selectively excluded from the eyes of the congregations outside.

Vision was a key factor in the control of knowledge both within and without the temples. The classic temples had a central line of rising sight to the main altar. Outside was generally a concave façade containing a paved or prepared area for what may be inferred to be the majority of participants. Activities could be brought in and out of

Table 9.3. Types of Maltese 'shamanism'.

Context	Underworld	Temple life
Ceremonies	Funeral	Divination
Shaman name	Unknown	Unknown
Importance	Great	Great
Numbers of shaman type/village	?	?
Shaman participation	Single ?	Communal
Audience participation	Smaller scale	Communal
Gender	?	?

sight across the main axis of vision of the congregation in this external vantage point. Inside many devices were employed to enhance the effect: screens, portholes, moving heads on static bodies, prominent areas of decoration, small objects indistinctly viewed from a distance, fire and smoke. Metonyms and metaphors abounded to give symbolic redolence to visual symbols of phalli, exotic valuables, human and animal representations. Certain colours of metaphorical value from bodily association were most probably prominent. Red ochre was clearly favoured, while white and black have also been recorded. This was one context of shamanistic practice, perhaps specifically related to divination (Table 9.3). Statuettes survive which present the distinctive seated posture of the 'shamans' with legs cocked to one side. Some of the vegetal art has qualities not dissimilar to that claimed for trance-like representations.

Sound was also key to this manipulation of secret shamanistic knowledge. Sound has recently been emphasised both in the wider context of megalithic monuments and their powers of resonance, and in the funerary rites of Malta. The importance of sound has long been appreciated underground at the Hal Saflieni monument, where a low-pitched voice achieves a high degree of resonance. However, these same principles have not yet been transferred above ground to the temples, which would require a computer reconstruction of potential roofing to achieve models of acoustic performance. However Watson and Keating (1999) make illuminating remarks about the effects of narrow constricted entrances on acoustic resonance, a resonance which might lead to altered states of mind, as suggested for shamanistic performance. They suggest the use of drums and other acoustic devices. Now that it appears from engineering experiments that the temples were most probably roofed, the full effect of a restricted entrance, a series of interlinked resonating chambers and smoke filled partial darkness would have been impressive in terms of controlling the mind, and thus restricted, specialist, arcane knowledge. Some stone vessels, usually interpreted as containers of liquids, could have been used as drums.

The lowest cosmological level was formed by burial complexes below ground. These below ground structures shared some of the material culture and practices of the shamanism in the temples above ground. Two monumental funerary complexes survive from the Tarxien period: Hal Saflieni and Brochtorff Circle at Xaghra. The first has been classically known as the hypogeum, a unique singular monument. The second was only rediscovered after the war and uncovered in the late 1980s and early 1990s. They share structural similarities. Both, as already outlined, are the focal points of temple clusters on high ground. Natural and cultural prominence coincide in this ritualised landscape. Both have megalithic structures that "watch over" circular incisions in the ground and which appear to provide access (proven at least in the case of Hal Saflieni) to lower storeys in the earth. Internally, both appear to have had central area for principal rituals and a range of peripheral areas for the more permanent placing of the dead. The central ritual area, in each case, comprised many temple-like constructional features, but not the axial emphasis of the above ground temples. Each site had an inner, screened-off area where at least in the case of the Brochtorff Circle, the symbolic artefacts of the shaman were kept. The peripheral burial areas in each case consisted of a series of modular compartments with different combinations of human bone, animal bone and figurative art. The shared material culture with the temples not only comprised the corpulent figurative art, but also offering bowls, stone spheres of varying sizes, varied fittings such as rope holes, hollows, portholes, and decoration in pecking and in paint. Only one characteristic aspect of material culture provides a profound contrast with the temples: the presence of human bone.

Over 200,000 fragments of human bone were recovered from the Brochtorff Circle at Xaghra, representing at least 700 individuals. This may represent one of the largest surviving samples of Neolithic populations in Europe, but it is of insufficient quantity to represent more than a small contributing community of about a hundred individuals living over about five hundred years. If our broader reconstruction of the landscape is correct, that this funerary monument was the focus of the whole human landscape of Gozo, then it is likely that Brochtorff Circle only served a subsection, most probably an élite of the prehistoric Gozitan landscape. Taking this further, less than 10% of an estimated 1400 individuals living in the Gozitan landscape had the right to formal burial in the Brochtorff Circle. If these assumptions are correct, then the arcane rituals, employing human bones as material culture, run in parallel to the arcane rituals without bones in the temple. Both trended towards exclusivity over the period of Tarxien.

Human bones as material culture: the shamanistic context

Secondary rites are a major part of both ethnographically observed burial rites and archaeologically encountered mortuary evidence. The classic studies of Hertz (1960) in Borneo, Bloch (1971) in Madagascar and Danforth (1982) in rural Greece illustrate the ethnographic prevalence of the reworking of human bones. These ethnographic observations have been extended back in time to prehistory. Studies of local landscapes in Neolithic Wessex have shown how this might have worked in the Avebury region. West Kennet chambered tomb (with an under-representation of skulls) (Piggott 1962b) was complementary to the causewayed enclosure of Windmill Hill (with a surfeit of skulls) (Smith 1965). A similar landscape distribution of body parts is difficult to demonstrate in the case of prehistoric Malta, because of the lack of excavation of different contexts, but a similar process can be proposed to have taken place within the confines of the mortuary enclosure of the Brochtorff Circle at Xaghra.

It is highly probable that a funerary procession, headed by the shaman, would have passed up the hill from the megalithic temple of Ggantija to the east. On arrival at the Brochtorff Circle at Xaghra, the participants would have entered a megalithic enclosure whose entrance was marked by two large monoliths (Bonello 1996). On entry, they would have crossed a megalithic threshold similar to those marking the entry to the temples. Just to the north was a setting of small monoliths standing over a cobbled closure to a pit within which a male had been recently placed, covered by the skull parts of what appear to be his own ancestors, and accompanied by food offerings. Every new corpse brought to the mortuary complex of Brochtorff Circle passed over this man and their collective predecessors before entering the deeper part of the cave. The funerary procession would then have descended steps into the open cave and the main complex of the mortuary enclosure.

Behind a screen shielded by piles of skulls to the left of the entrance, and presided over by a small image of twin seated corpulent individuals, significant items for the funerary ceremony undertaken by the shaman were kept. These significant items included a group of stick figurines, which appear to have been hand-held during ceremonies. The same objects represented the transition from life to death, since each was in a different stage of manufacture from roughout to finished figurine. The stylised form of the figurine only allowed detail in the expression of the facial features, and yet these themselves could be ascribed to no particular individual. One figurine appears to be a pig, an animal whose bones were found associated with the human deposits. Close by was a large stone bowl, probably employed for the washing of the newly deceased or for the cleansing of the disarticulated parts of previous individuals. Indeed the bowl itself contained a small figurative representation of a human leg. Other items included within this screened off area included a shell scoop, a small pot of red ochre and a ceramic strainer. These are all interpreted as the non-organic parts of the shaman's kit.

The rest of the cave was roughly divided into different modular compartments where bodies were distinctively treated and repackaged; these mortuary rites have been more fully described elsewhere and do not provide the focus of this article (Stoddart *et al.* 1999; Stoddart 1999). Definition of individual deposits is one matter. The reconstruction of the contributing funerary ritual is much more complex. We suggest that the vast majority of bodies were placed temporarily in the central area of the cave while shamanistic ceremonies took place, drawing on the ritual paraphernalia from the adjoining screened area. Many of these bodies were symbolically associated with clay figurines and/or small figured animal bones. At this stage each corpse retained its own individuality. Subsequently, these same deposits placed in the middle of the main routeway through the cave were redistributed. Some were placed as a collective undifferentiated group in the lowest part of the cave, inevitably concentrating the proportion of larger bones present in that area. These bodies lost their individuality and became part of the collective community. For others individuality was retained by the selection of the skull and other significant bones, placed as a package in key areas of the cave. For a few of these, the individuality of the bones was enhanced by association with animal skulls.

CONCLUSION

Can material culture alone be employed to identify a shaman? Or should we be content with the epithet of 'technician of the sacred'? It is ultimately up to the reader to judge. By the careful control of context at various nested scales (island, mortuary complex, screened off shamanistic area), I contend that the term shaman, at an appropriate level of generalisation, is helpful, since it opens the eyes of the archaeologist to levels of interpretation and meaning which would otherwise remain hidden. These steps do not, however, mean that I subscribe to a strongly prescribed definition of shamanism, since the ritual practitioners in prehistoric Malta were clearly radically different from the ritual practitioners in the cultural context of the Evenki for whose study the term was first defined.

Acknowledgements
I would like to thank Neil Price for commenting on this article in the light of his recent book on the Archaeology of Shamanism and for allowing me to see proofs of his introductory chapter prior to publication. To Andrew Townsend, I owe a double debt: the discovery and important comments on the interpretation made here and in previous discussion. To Gilly Carr, I owe the suggestion of tempting the limits of interpretation and by diplomatically reminding me of deadlines in the same way as I did when she wrote her doctoral thesis. I should also like to thank all those involved in investigating the Brochtorff Circle at Xaghra.

Notes
1   Pronounced 'shaara'

Bibliography
Atkinson, J.M. 1992 'Shamanisms today' *Annual Review of Anthropology* 21, 301–330.
Balzer, M.M. 1996 'Shamanism' pp. 1182–1186 in D. Levinson and M. Ember (eds), *Encyclopedia of cultural Anthropology*, New York: H. Holt.
Bloch, M. 1971 *Placing the Dead: tombs, ancestral villages, and kinship organisation in Madagasca*, London: Seminar Press.
Boissevain, J. 1965 *Saints and fireworks: religion and politics in rural Malta*, London, Athlone Press.
Bonanno, A., Gouder, T., Malone, C. and Stoddart, S. 1990 'Monuments in an island society: the Maltese context', *World Archaeology* 22(2), 190–205.
Bonello, G., 1996 'The Gozo Megalithic Sites: Early Visitors and Artists', pp. 19–30 in A. Pace (ed.), *Maltese Prehistoric Art 5000 – 2500 BC*, Fondazzjoni Patrimonju Malti in Association with The National Museum of Archaeology. Valletta: Patrimonju Publishing Limited.
Clottes, J. and Lewis-Williams, D. 1998 *The Shamans of Prehistory*, New York: Abrams.
Danforth, L. 1982 *The Death rituals of Rural Greece*, Princeton: Princeton University Press.
Douglas, M. 1970 *Natural symbols: explorations in cosmology*, London: Barry and Rockcliff.
Evans, J.D. 1971 *The Prehistoric Antiquities of the Maltese Islands: A Survey*, London: The Athlone Press.
Foderà Serio, G., Hoskin, M. and Ventura, F. 1992 'The orientations of the temples of Malta', *Journal for the History of Astronomy* 23, 107–119.

Hertz, R. 1960 *Death and the Right Hand*, London: Cohen and West.

Kehoe, A.B. 2000 *Shamans and religion: an anthropological exploration in critical thinking*, Prospect Heights Illinois: Waveland.

Kehoe, A.B. in press 'Emerging trends versus the popular paradigm in rock art research', *Antiquity*

Lewis, I.M. 1986 *Religion in context. Cults and Charisma*, Cambridge: Cambridge University Press.

Lewis-Williams, J.D. and Dowson, T. 1988 'The signs of all times. Entoptic phenomena in Upper Palaeolithic Art', *Current Anthropology*, 29(2), 201–245.

Malone, C. and Stoddart, S. 1998 'The conditions of creativity for Prehistoric Maltese Art' pp. 241–259 in S. Mithen (ed.), ea:*The prehistory of creative thought*, London, Routledge.

Pace, A., 1996 'Introduction. The Artistic Legacy of Small Island Communities: The Case of the Maltese Islands (5000–2500 BC)' pp. 1–12 in A. Pace (ed.), *Maltese Prehistoric Art 5000–2500 BC*, Fondazzjoni Patrimonju Malti in Association with The National Museum of Archaeology. Valletta: Patrimonju Publishing Limited.

Peters, L.G. and Price-Williams, D. 1980 'Towards an experiential analysis of shamanism', *American Ethnologist* 7, 397–413.

Piggott, S. 1962a 'From Salisbury Plain to Siberia', *Wiltshire Archaeological and Natural History Magazine* 58, 93–7.

Piggott, S. 1962b *The West Kennet long barrow: excavations 1955–6*, London: HMSO.

Price, N. 2001 'An archaeology of altered states: shamanism and material culture studies', pp. 3–16 in N. Price (ed.), *The Archaeology of Shamanism*, London: Routledge.

Renfrew, A.C. 1976 *Before Civilisation: the Radiocarbon revolution and prehistoric Europe*, Harmondsworth: Penguin.

Saladin d'Anglure, B. 1996 'Shamanism', pp. 504–508 in A. Barnard and J. Spencer (eds), *Encyclopedia of social and cultural anthropology*, London: Routledge.

Smith, I.F. 1965 *Windmill Hill and Avebury: excavations by Alexander Keiller, 1925–39*, Oxford: Clarendon Press.

Stoddart, S. 1999 'Mortuary customs in prehistoric Malta', pp. 183–190 in A. Mifsud and C.S. Ventura (eds), *Facets of Maltese Prehistory*, Mosta: Prehistoric Society of Malta.

Stoddart, S. in press 'Monuments in the prehistoric landscape of the Maltese islands: ritual and domestic transformations', in B. David and M. Wilson (eds), *Inscribed Landscapes: the archaeology of rock-art, place and identity*, University of Hawaii Press.

Stoddart, S., Bonanno, A., Gouder, T., Malone, C. and Trump, D. 1993 'Cult in an Island Society: Prehistoric Malta in the Tarxien period', *Cambridge Archaeological Journal* 3(1), 3–19.

Stoddart, S., Wysocki, M. and Burgess, G. with supporting contributions from Barber, G., Duhig, C., Malone, C. and Mann, G. 1999 'The articulation of disarticulation. Preliminary thoughts on the Brochtorff Circle at Xaghra (Gozo)', pp. 94–105 in J. Downes and A. Pollard (eds), *The loved body's corruption: archaeological contributions to the study of human mortality*, Glasgow, Cruithne Press.

Vitebsky, P. 1993 *Dialogues with the Dead. The discussion of mortality among the Sora of eastern India*, Cambridge: Cambridge University Press.

Vitebsky, P. 1995 *The Shaman*, London: Macmillan.

Watson, A. and Keating, D. 1999 'Architecture and sound: an acoustic analysis of megalithic monuments in prehistoric Britain', *Antiquity* 73 (280), 325–336.

10. Tobacco and curing agency in Western Amazonian shamanism[1]

Françoise Barbira Freedman

Besides the treatment of sickness, shamanism throughout Amazonia involves the wider management of relations between people, animals, plants and elements in a rainforest environment perceived as cosmos. Health and sickness are defined in terms of these relations, both among native minorities and, less expectedly, among the mixed Amazonian population, which is largely concentrated in towns and riverine settlements.

There is no activity in Amazonian shamanism that does not involve the use of tobacco; blowing smoke on people and objects is shamans' transforming action par excellence, and the ingestion of tobacco in various forms is essential in shamanic apprenticeship. Tobacco is used in all situations involving personal and/or social transformation: birth, initiation, annual cycle ceremonies, healing sessions and death. Hunters' success depends on 'medicine power', enhanced by plant-induced vision quests or dream quests undertaken by both hunters and shamans.

Pipes and cigars have been, both in pre-Columbian times and now, characteristic items in shamans' paraphernalia in most of the American continent, and their comparative study is of interest to ethnography. In this paper, however, my focus is on tobacco smoke as the main tool of Amazonian shamans. To Amazonians, this is the substance closest to soul matter and I argue that in all their activities including the treatment of sickness, shamans use tobacco smoke to cross, dissolve and re-draw boundaries between humans and the cosmos.

Although Wilbert singled out the cultural importance of tobacco in South America in his monograph (1972, 1975, 1987), tobacco has received comparatively little attention in recent anthropological research on Amazonian shamanism. Yet, as Reichel Dolmatoff and others have pointed out, 'the use of narcotic drugs by these Indians is an essential part of their culture'. 'Without a detailed knowledge of the role of these narcotics, any appreciation of social and religious customs would be very superficial indeed' (Reichel Dolmatoff 1975, xxi). Since the 1970s, ethno-botanists and anthropologists have taken a particular interest in the use of *Ayahuasca*[2] in Amazonian shamanic curing. The relationship between tobacco and 'plants of the gods' (Furst 1972; Schultes 1945, 1978; Schultes and Hofmann 1979, 1980; Schultes and Raffauf 1990) or 'plant teachers' (Luna 1986), is, however, mostly noted rather than investigated. For several thousand years, Amazonian shamans have used Nicotianas together with a range of other wild and domesticated psychoactive plants to intentionally control their body chemistry and induce altered states of consciousness. The overlap of tobacco use by hunters in the forest, by ordinary members of society during social assemblies and ceremonies, and by shamans in their specific activities as healers is greater than that of any other psychoactive plant used in Amazonia.[3]

I use the term shaman in the way the term is now commonly accepted in the anthropological literature on Amazonia. Shamans are defined by their control of spirit helpers in the forest as cosmos, their embodied practice in 'journeying' on behalf of patients, and their relational status in their communities. Rather than being a shaman or not, one is more or less shaman along a continuum between the agency of all male and female adults, male hunters, curers, ambivalent shamans and the agency attributed to powerful shaman outsiders.

My ethnographic focus is the Peruvian Upper Amazon and more particularly the Jakwash, also referred to as Lamista Quechua or Lamistos, a relatively large ethnic minority constituted from a mixed aggregate of forest people and Andeans around the colonial frontier town of Lamas (founded 1656). Long before Peru's independence (1821), there is considerable evidence that both native and either 'mixed blood' (Mestizo) or 'white' (Blanco) shamans from the Lamas province have been largely responsible for the historical diffusion of shamanism in the colonisation of the lowlands. S. *Vegetalismo*[4] is the name commonly given to this plant-based shamanic medical system, which is the main source of informal health care throughout Peruvian Amazonia. Quechua, the lingua franca of the colonisation of Western Amazonia,[5] has remained the idiom of shamanic curing in chants, spells and nomenclatures, long after it has ceased to be spoken. Luna (1986, 1991) has documented the cosmology and practice of *vegetalismo* among Western Amazonian urban shamans with Jakwash ancestry or trained by shamans from the Lamas region.

TOBACCO CULTIVATION: GENDER, HUNTING AND SHAMANISM

The categorical distinctions between village and forest, men and women, hunters, women and shamans, natives and colonists, are reflected in the growing, processing and consuming of tobacco in Amazonia. Tobacco, among all shamanic plants, straddles the Western categories of nature and culture the most. Tobacco plants are grown in the family gardens, yet in separate areas looked after individually by their owners, away from staples.

Shamans tend to their plants as extensions of their persons, like pets. 'Natural modelling', the symbolic representation of processes observable in nature, links together myths and modes of cultivation. Tobacco grows best in disturbed soil, on sites fertilized by ashes, grave sites, abandoned housesites and hollow tree stumps. This tallies with myths of origin of tobacco growing from humans' ashes. Among all cultigens, there is a collective awareness among the Jakwash that tobacco is the oldest 'teacher plant' (S. *planta maestra*), entrusted to native people as a special gift for humanity.

Jakwash shamans also 'manage' wild clusters of tobacco plants in areas of forest known to them. Wild specimens of *Nicotiana rustica* (which may have escaped from old gardens) are more highly valued for shamanic initiations and special treatments. The same continuum of use between cultigens and wild plants applies to *Ayahuasca* and some other shamanic plants. Besides *Nicotianas* found in the forest, the Jakwash recognise and value other plants as 'wild tobacco', (SQ. *sacha tabaku*). A mottled plant, SQ. *tigre tabaku* (unidentified) is thought of as the tobacco that jaguars and ocelots smoke in their houses in the spirit world. This plant, like others that are generically described as 'forest spirits' tobacco' (SQ. *supay tabaku*) is not transplanted.

Among the Jakwash, the preparation of tobacco nurseries in swiddens, the transplanting, weeding, supervision of young plants and harvesting of leaves after two to three months are all done by men, who smoke over young plants to ward off pests and encourage growth. Women are involved in tending the maturing plants, harvesting, removing the veins from harvested leaves and stringing the leaves to dry in stacks. Dried leaves are then wrapped in tubular bundles wrapped in bark, particularly *Tahuari* (*Couratari* sp), which is also beaten to make bark paper for cigars or rolled tightly with *Tamshi* vine. Honey from various bee species can be added if the bundle is to be compressed into a *maso* with a wooden press. When *Tahuari* is not available, dried banana leaves are used. Jakwash shamans prefer making curing cigars from whole dried leaves rather than from shredded tobacco and they also use tobacco leaves to cover cigars. Curing cigars are larger than hunters' cigars, often a foot long and half an inch thick; the Jakwash *S. Paleros* (bark shamans) also mix tobacco with powdered medicinal barks in these large cigars.

Shamanic use is marked by both the quality and quantity of tobacco consumed as well as by the form of consumption. In some areas, hunters may smoke large cigars, but only shamans drink tobacco juice; there may be different sizes of cigar for ordinary use and shamanic practice. Among the Jakwash and in S. *Vegetalismo*, only shamans, male or female, smoke pipes. If local pure '*rustica*' tobacco is unavailable, some shamans of mixed blood will use commercial cigarettes as a source of tobacco for curing, while others will not. Although the social patterns and modes of absorption of tobacco vary a great deal within the region e.g. by smoking, snuffing, drinking and enemas, there are shared understandings of the synergy between tobacco and other psychotropic plants among the Jakwash and other native minorities in Western Amazonia in shamanic apprenticeship and practice.

The prescribed consumption of tobacco in specified quantities and forms differentiates shamanic apprenticeship from herbalism. Without tobacco, the therapeutic use of medicinal plants, whether psychoactive or not, pertains to herbalists who are mainly women. While herbalists are expert in the use of medicinal plants for common ailments, the preparation of herbal remedies for more critical conditions pertains to initiated shamans and it is always accompanied by tobacco use. But in forest and in urban shamanism, tobacco use is inseparable from the preparation and consumption of visionary brews used in curing ceremonies and shamanic initiations. Tobacco by itself is also used in the form of infusion or syrup as a main plant-teacher for accessing altered states of consciousness in shamanic training, as a diagnostic tool and a therapeutic substance. As such, tobacco is one of five specialised paths recognised in *Vegetalismo*. S. *Tabaqueros* (tobacco specialists), are less numerous than *Ayahuasqueros*

(*Ayahuasca* specialists) or *Toeros* (specialists of *Toe, Brugmansia suaveolens*), but more widespread than *Paleros* (bark shamans) or *Perfumeros* (perfume shamans). According to the sayings of Lamista elders, these specialities corresponded to progressive stages of expertise, starting with *Ayahuasca* and tobacco juice, before accessing the more demanding use of barks and using subtle plant essences.

The training of a Lamista shaman is typically described as a lonely, isolated and lengthy procedure, which requires a long period of strict diet (Q. *sasiku-*, S. *dieta*) in seclusion under the supervision of a senior shaman or even on one's own, receiving directly the 'teaching of plants'. Although Western Amazonian shamans, whether native or non-Indians, do spend time 'dieting' in solitude, their training is also a social process that involves long distance relationships and elaborate inter-related geographical, cosmic and social maps. At the same time as they transform their bodies and acquire soul-power/knowledge (Q. *Yachay*), to a greater or lesser extent, all Western Amazonian shamans are involved in the dual process of expansion towards towns and towards remote forest or headwater areas.

Knowledge and power lie at the two extremes, which create polarities. Shamanic exchanges still take place at the confluence of rivers (Q. *urmana*), where there is archaeological evidence of ancient trade in stone, metal axes, shells and beads. Powerful shamans typically live near such places or near crossroads.

Tobacco and souls in Western Amazonia

Since Karsten's early attempts, inspired by Frazer, to account for Amazonian animism (1926), the understanding of souls and their relation to bodies in Amerindian cosmologies has fuelled several stages of anthropological discussion. Among recent interpretations, Viveiros de Castro's 'perspectivism' – that for Amerindians the world is inhabited by different types of subjects, all possessing souls, who apprehend the world from distinct points of views (1998, 470) – has moved this discussion forward. The contrast made by Viveiros de Castro (1996) between 'multinaturalism' and multicultural relativism is particularly useful. In the 'highly transformational' world of Amazonian cosmologies (Rivière 1974) humanity is constantly being produced from a wider universe of subjectivities. In both South and North America, Amerindian shamans are the agents of this production. In contrast with Euro-American categories of nature and culture, a focus on the total spectrum of relations that encompass social relations and implicate them (Strathern 1988) makes it possible to explore native categorical oppositions. The immanent quality of cosmic entities and the process of 'shape-shifting', the transformation of humans into other subjectivities and more particularly animals, are main aspects of Amerindian shamanism.

Tobacco smoke, which the majority of Amerindian shamans 'see as' a 'soul-like' substance, is instrumental in the fabrication of the 'soul-bodies'. Shamans can act as healers and sorcerers *because* they have effected changes in their perception and, simultaneously, altered their bodies. The repeated ingestion of psychoactive substances is perceived to result in a transmutation, a modification of bodily substance that can be seen by those who have already developed their extra-sensory perception. Vice versa, altering one's physical body, through body painting or the use of attributes pertaining to human or animal others, is thought to help bring about the desired transmutation.

Shape-shifting, which can be glossed as 'transmigration' of the shaman's soul into an animal body, also involves a process of trans-substantiation in that the shaman's body is forever transformed and partakes of the physical and ethological characteristics of the animal. This is the case whether or not animal parts are ingested deliberately by shamans, transferred to apprentices during initiation or transmitted malevolently by a sorcerer. Shamanic treatment often results in extracting animal substances lodged in the patient's body (fur balls, feathers, claws). My point is that Amerindian logic implies a modification of substance which most anthropologists have ignored because it does not fit with explanations of shamanism centred around the notion of metaphor.

The spirit allies that support the agency of shamans as healers or sorcerers are fed tobacco in order to make them 'relations' in terms of affinity and kinship (Vilaça 2000). All the interventions related to what Taylor calls 'the soul in the body' (1996), including the progressive socialisation of bodies in the life-cycle, amount to a substantial transformation of matter and bodies, by means of tobacco smoke, via the agency of a shaman.

'Seeing' what is invisible to others, knowing and acting are inseparable from one another in shamanic practice (Chaumeil 1983; Crocker 1985). Curers purge themselves with their patients and extend their own transmutation to them, while sorcerers invade the bodies of their victims or steal soul substance from them in a malevolent way. Curing the sick is an aspect of this broader shamanic agency upon boundaries between bodies (persons, social units) and subjectified processes of cause and effect in a relational cosmos. There is no changing of form without altering substance, no knowledge without experiential self-transformation, no curing without exchange relations with subjectivities in the cosmos.

The relationship between cognition and agency is the locus of shamanic power; this lies at the core of the difference between a hunter and a shaman using tobacco in the forest. Both are aware of cosmic subjectivities, but the hunter, unlike the shaman, is not able to incorporate the latter's identities – what Viveiros de Castro (1998) describes as 'perspectives' – including constellations of character and behaviour or 'ethograms', in an active inter-subjective process of transformation. As a counterpart to dietary proscriptions associated with shamanism throughout Amazonia, tobacco is an essential prescribed 'food' in the diet followed by shamans in isolation for physical and psychological preparation, both denoted by Q. *sasiku*. The synergy between avoidance of salt, hot pepper, sugar, fat and sexual activity – the most basic proscriptions in the shamanic diet – and the enhanced effect of nicotine in the human body still needs to be researched. From an anthropological viewpoint, what is of interest is not extra-sensory perception *per se*, but how it is used to create meaning in Amazonian cultures and society, using the specific effects of a wide range of plants, all with tobacco, within a pan-Amerindian hunting/shamanic ideology. The riddle remains that of linking shamans' explanations of corporeality to the socially meaningful patterns that can be unveiled by anthropological analysis, as well as to scientific explanations of associated neuro-physiological processes.

NICOTINE, TOBACCO AND SOULS

Nicotine was isolated at an early date (1868) and the effects of tobacco were understood before those of other alkaloid-rich plants. The various methods of tobacco consumption in South America procure the absorption of nicotine through internal – gastro-intestinal or respiratory – application. All possible methods, including chewing, drinking, drinking, licking, rectal enemas, snuffing, smoking, are used by Amazonians (Wilbert 1987, 6). The study of nicotine has revealed not only the psychotropic effects of strong doses of tobacco, but also its catalytic effects when used together with other psychotropic substances. Cigars of Nicotiana rustica have been shown to be strong enough to produce hallucinations and catatonia (Larson *et al.* 1961; Layten Davis and Nielsen 1999). Nicotine has also been shown to be capable of releasing serotonin from the brain commensurate in amount with the concentration of nicotine present (Martin *et al.* 1987)

It is tempting for anthropologists to draw a parallel between reports on the pharmacology of nicotine and Amazonian shamans' ideas about body boundaries. The speed with which nicotine invades the organism, reaching the brain in seven seconds from the onset of smoking, its actions on the adrenal medulla and the sympathetic ganglia and its structural similarity to the acetylcholine neurotransmitter are remarkable. According to Wilbert, these characteristics of nicotine 'have served (and still serve) the Indian to confirm basic tenets of shamanic ideology' (1987, 146– 148). Furthermore, nicotine interacts with other cholinergic transmitters and hormones, such as norepiphedrine, epinephrine, serotonin, dopamine (Armitage *et al.* 1969; Arneric and Brioni 1999; Conti-Tronconi 1987), furthering their distribution by increasing the permeability of cell membranes for transport of ions and transmission at synapses. At this stage, I do not have sufficient evidence to link shamans' assertion that tobacco smoke 'makes bodies permeable' with the pharmacology of nicotine, except in a general sense of having to do with permeability. There is, however, a contrast between the local common use of tobacco as an insecticide, a local analgesic, a wound disinfectant, an invaluable stimulant and appetite supressor in long forest treks by all people in the tropical forest, and its shamanic use. Shamans use tobacco smoke as a subtle substance that softens, even blurs, the boundaries between humans and a soul-abundant cosmos and yet helps maintain these boundaries. Jakwash shamans say that tobacco facilitates the visionary and dreaming effects of other psychoactive plants. All the shamans I have met were adamant that tobacco served them to modify their perception, either on its own or through its interaction with other psychoactive plants. Jakwash shamans also claim that smoking can re-activate the physiological effects of psychoactive susbtances used in the past together with tobacco in the minds of experienced shamans; these shamans are known as S.Q. *bancos* 'stools for the spirits', old diviners, working 'from the other side' in secluded spots within the cosmic landscape.

Tobacco smoke is the carrier of breath, intent, words, songs and spells with which shamans exert agency in the cosmos. This agency mostly consists in re-affirming and re-drawing boundaries after making them fluid and tractable with tobacco smoke. Diet and tobacco apply to times and spaces of social undifferentiation, which require

Figure 10.1. Francisco Montes, a shaman of mixed Capanahua and Jakwash origin, blows tobacco smoke into ayahuasca brew before a curing ceremony at his 'sacha mama' centre near Iquitos.

shamanic intervention in order to redefine a new status quo in the extended sense of Van Gennep's *rites de passage*: birth, initiation, shamanic initiation, sickness, death, feasts in the annual cycle. Conversely, physical unboundedness, for example of mentruating women, is considered both shaman-like and antithetical to shamanic agency since it is a passive and, therefore, dangerous open state. Shamans typically 'journey' with their patients and initiates through the undifferentiated phase of sickness or social limbo. The physical identification of relatives with sick household members, the couvade, mourning practices and the act of following a particular spirit's diet to gain shamanic power can be seen as related to the fact that shamans actually use their soul bodies (breath supported by tobacco smoke) to treat their patients as the first and foremost therapeutic action. Remedies are only given in the framework created by this action.

Vegetalismo constitutes a systematic exploration and codification of the experiential knowledge derived from psychoactive plants, in relation to the cosmos. The words that are always used to describe shamanic training are 'dieting' and 'studying the plants'. The plants are referred to as 'teachers' (S. *plantas muestras*). Throughout Amazonia, psychoactive plants are said to have 'mother-spirits' (S. *madres*). In forest

Quechua, the word *mama* (mother) is closely related to, if not co-terminous with, soul substance. SQ. *mamayar* means 'soul possess', glossed as 'hypnotise in the way of snakes' so that one loses all subjectivity and becomes a prey. The semantic field of *mama* overlaps with that of SQ. *amar* (associated in San Martin with S. *amo*, owner, boss) 'take possession of' *Mama* contrasts with the Spanish *alma*, Quechuicised as *alama*, which refers to the souls of the dead, separate from bodies (in the Christian tradition). Lamista shamans also use the terms 'owner' (S. *dueño*) and keeper (S. *guardian*) to refer to the spirits of plants. The differentiation between these two concepts of 'mother' and 'owner' appears to refer to an emphasis on either soul matter or control of territory and social relations, with connotations of feminine and masculine counterparts. The more psychoactive a plant – generally-speaking the more alkaloid-rich – the stronger its spirit. The dominant mother-spirits of plants are mainly animal predators and cosmic elements, which act as the spirit allies of shamans as they do throughout Amazonia yet without the mediation of plants that characterises *Vegetalismo*. The difference between *Vegetalismo* and other documented forms of Amazonian shamanism is the role of plants as ingested substance associated with entities, enabling diversified interaction between people and the cosmos. Shamanism is not only a purposeful cosmic journey 'under the influence', if it is ever that, but the 'study' of plants as guides to ecology and ethology in the cosmos. Through fight or seduction, victory, or death followed by revival, or other ways, rapid or slow, an active egocentric engagement with non-human entities in the cosmos creates humanising bonds. Although some cosmic entities are anthropomorphised in the way that they are in Indo-European legends and tales – and it is difficult to prove or disprove European influence – their agency is understood within the keenly observed rainforest ecosystem as cosmos. One of the puzzles of *Vegetalismo* is that urban shamans of mixed blood who have never learnt to hunt or even spent much time in a forest environment develop shamanic agency in relation to a very ecological cosmology. All interactions with entities in the cosmos are coloured by attraction or repulsion, resulting in assimilation through eating and sexual intercourse as a result of alliance or victorious fight. The shaman gains the favour of entities (Q. *munan-*, S. *te quiere*) or undergoes rejection. Favour is an expression of likeness that entails potential affinity and exchange. Frequently, friendly plant spirits make significant gifts (seeds, stones, patterns) as a token of this established affinity. Incubus/succubus relations with spirits lead to procreation and result in the formation of 'other world families', although only in the case of men. Tobacco is the standard medium of exchange, ever attractive to all spirits, mainly as smoke but sometimes as an offering to plants. In classic *Vegetalismo*, shamanic initiation requires the intake of tobacco juice after at least one week of shamanic diet in order to prepare the body for the ingestion of substances that are the attributes of one's allies, either physically or metaphorically: small live animals associated with animal spirits (being their food, or being a miniature version of them), quartz stones, and body parts of animal spirits. There is a relationship with cannibalism, which exceeds the scope of this paper. After communality of substance, – kinship – has been realised in some way, one is entitled to 'call upon' one's allies at any time in the same way as relatives can be relied upon. In localised kindreds, however, relatives, including children, stay as resident helpers only to the extent that the situation is attractive to them; they can leave at any moment. There is a scale of intimacy in shamans' perception of their familiar spirits as mere allies, as affines and as children. Brotherhood, however, does not seem to figure in the process of 'making kin' out of spirit allies.

HEALTH, SICKNESS AND BOUNDARIES OF HUMANITY IN THE FOREST

Besides having recognised prophylactic and therapeutic values, particularly in preventing infection of open wounds, the necessity of tobacco use in the forest cannot be separated from shamanic understanding. Jakwash men say that it is dangerous to venture in unclaimed forest areas without tobacco. Tobacco is both used to attract game animals and to keep animal predators at bay. There is a widespread belief that in relation to the distribution of soul matter, 'wild areas' are undifferentiated zones, which need shamanic intervention to become 'humanised. The first action of shamans in their role as founders of new settlements in newly colonised areas of forest is to blow tobacco smoke along the freshly opened paths. Sickness resulting from the malevolent or merely playful intervention of cosmic entities is potentially fatal. Inadvertent contact with them (through touch or mere vision) overrides human boundaries and results in the wasting away of one's soul-less body, through vomiting, diarrhoea and fainting, for example, unless one's 'skin'/human boundary can be restored through a shaman blowing smoke all over the sick body and in particular over its orifices. Not only is belief in this sickness powerful and widespread in the region, but it is reinforced by its association with the effects of certain plants which may cause unrelenting vomiting until tobacco is ingested as an antidote.[6] Sickness affects babies, children and women more readily than men and older people in relation to their soft/wet as opposed to hardened/dry skin, in the sense of body envelope and boundary. However, any sickness calls for the artificial creation of undifferentiatedness through a 'bland' shamanic diet, if there is time, and/or through tobacco/being smoked over by a shaman, before the appropriate ordinary boundedness can be restored or a new boundary created. At different stages in the life cycle for the individual, in the annual cycle for the local group, the boundedness that constitutes humanity is temporarily dissolved before being realigned anew or redrawn. Shamans blow smoke over young maize plants not only to ward off pests, but also because new maize stems are akin to human babies, soft and vulnerable. They blow smoke on freshly killed game in order to make it a fit food for humans, as meat that can be ingested neutrally without risk of imparting the markers of its species on the eaters.

Like their Aguaruna neighbours and the Shuar North of the Amazon river, the Jakwash have continued to mark the initiation of young men into manhood with the intake of psychotropic brews (*Ayahuasca* or *Toe*) with tobacco juice and the smoking of large cigars (Karsten 1926, 323). Tobacco has been used in the past and continues to be used to ensure good luck on hunts (Harner 1973, 60), as in many hunting societies, the Master of Game Animals (*Q. Sacha Runa*) needs to be pacified to release game. This is done through the use of tobacco, which also protects the humanity of hunters. The Jakwash have been famous for their sorcery and poison-making since colonial times.

Shamans use tobacco smoke as a support substance for spells and pathogens including the small palm wood darts – miniature version of blowgun darts – which are perceived to be the main tangible carriers of sickness throughout Western Amazonia (Tessmann 1930, 561–562).

There is a continuum from adult men to shamans in the deliberate control over the boundedness and unboundedness of self and others. It is not the capacity to access the forces through which we define humanity that differentiate shamans from ordinary people. Rather, it is their lesser or greater agency. They retrieve such forces on behalf of fellow group-members, incorporate them as a way of gaining familiarity with them, transfer the desired qualities to their patients and finally seal their patients' bodies so that they can be impervious to pathogens sent by humans or to attacks from cosmic agents. Tobacco smoke-breath is used at all the stages of treatment: blowing smoke, whistling after a long inhalation of tobacco smoke, sucking pathogens from patients' bodies after a deep inhalation of tobacco smoke, and interspersing actions with the singing of S.Q. '*icaros*' (songs conferring agency through particular plants and their mother-spirits.)

The shared use of tobacco creates a quasi-kinship social connection. The first gesture of the people who greeted Columbus and his men was to offer them tobacco. Wherever tobacco is used on the continent, one of its functions is to create an extra-ordinary social unity different from feasts that bring together people who are normally separated socially as well as spatially, for a short time and in a precarious way. Whether a pipe is passed around, or tobacco smoke is blown over the participants in a council, the sharing of this substance symbolises and creates consensus and social harmony. Tobacco smoking (and *Ayahuasca* drinking) create social bonds across ethnic (native and non-native) boundaries and between individual shaman partners in a different way from barter and gift exchanges on the one hand, patron-client and ties of ritual kinship (S. *compadrazgo*) on the other. These bonds are acknowledged to be different and they may lead to further exchanges that become cyclical, and to cultural change in the communities involved. Such change is due less to the introduction of new substances and practices in local shamans' modes of curing than in the gained awareness of new polarities, different from, yet related to, the awareness of 'further difference'. The presence of missionaries, anthropologists, agents on extractive fronts, government officials and NGOs contributes to create new polarities with which shamans have to contend. Popular syncretic cults and religious movements in Amazonia, although they may differentiate themselves from, and even oppose, shamanism, may also be interpreted in relation to this process.

SHAMANS' OBJECTS AND EMBODIED AGENCY

Both cigars and pipes are used in shamanic practice; whether Jakwash shamans use one or the other appears to be a matter of personal preference and availability. Hard tobacco from S. Q. *masos* rolls is sliced fine and rubbed between the hands to be used in pipes, while whole leaves are rolled in cigars. Trainee shamans are either given large cigars, or a *maso*, or a bundle of commercial *rustica* cigars which they have to smoke daily while ingesting their prescribed brews, learning to inhale lungfuls of tobacco smoke at rapid intervals as shamans do. The early use of pipes in contrast with cigars is not clear (Farabee 1922). Urban S. *Vegetalistas* use mostly cigars. At the time of Tessman's visit in the late 1920s, Lamista shamans used both cigars and pipes (1930, 332, 551). Huxley (1957, 192) notes the use of clay pipes among the Amahuaca. I have only seen wooden shamanic pipes in Western Amazonia. Their use is widespread and everywhere their making and decorating correspond to the cosmology. As a shamanic initiate I received my first pipe ceremonially 'cooked' in *Ayahuasca* brew after ingesting tobacco juice. The shamanic diet leading to this event consisted of plantains, certain fish and large cigars smoked while taking plant brews in the prescribed order. My pipe was made of Palo Sangre (*Brosimum sw, Moraceae*) in the common style of shamanic pipes in the area. It was decorated with geometrical designs, which were also used to decorate *Ayahuasca* cups, perfume pots, small calabashes for keeping pipe tobacco, and also as a face painting design by the people of the Sangama clan who hosted me. My second pipe was larger as an expression of my progress and was made in Aguaje wood (*Mauritia sp.*), associated with the water domain and fertility. The bowl was carved in the shape of a mermaid with a scaly tail base. Like the tube of my first pipe, its tube was made of the bone of the leg of a Tanrilla bird (*Eurypyga helias*). Preference was given to the use of the right leg, for which no explanation was available. There were sexual overtones about the fit between tube and bowl. The penis bones of Q *maki sapa* spider monkeys (*Ateles sp.*) and *achuñi* (*Nasua fusca*) are also used to make tubes for shamanic pipes. I was told that my second pipe marked the start of studying the water domain in the cosmos and together with it, I received a leaf rattle to shake while smoking during *Ayahuasca* ceremonies. Mermaid, bird bone and tree species with powerful mother-spirits gathered the three dimensions of the Amazonian cosmos perceived in *Vegetalismo* in this small functional object. Together with a tobacco pouch and disposable leaf rattles, this is all that Jakwash shamans encumber themselves with to go and visit their patients.

Pipes, rattles and decorated small calabashes are both an objectification of the various source of the power of shamans, displayed for those who can decipher them, and tools to journey in altered states of consciousness and access power of agency, whether for curing or sorcery. The pipes of hunters and shamans, like their wooden turtle shaped stools and their pouches made of anteater skin, their snail shell tobacco containers, partake of a shared symbolism the main aspects of which are widely known among the native people in the region within the 'culture of shamanism'. While hunters make use of symbolic objects as charms or protection to enhance their activity, shamans use them as personal attributes, which confer them agency in the cosmos. Eagle claws, jaguar or boa teeth and quartz stones can be either hunters' charms or 'magic rings' that shamans use to shape-shift and take on their animal skin/ personae.

The objects that Western Amazonian shamans use 'in relation to perspectival relativity' (Gray 1996) are only endowed with value as supports for shamans' relationships in the cosmos. The trade value of shamanic objects is in function of the agreed 'soul content' of the object, whether it is relatively rare – like small Incaic ceremonial metal axes – or quite common – like jaguar teeth. In order to release the potential agency located in these objects, rather than use them as amulets – as they are now sold in Amazonian market stalls – tobacco, alone or with psychoactive brews, has to be used, sometimes with particular songs or spells. Similarly, rattles, whether leaf, stick or seed rattles, only become journeying instruments, rather than mere objects, with humming, beating time and singing in obscurity, assisting shamans to anticipate and/or bring about the altered states of consciousness induced by plants. They have no trade value except as crafts made for tourists. Unlike shamans of the Northern Andes, who make altars in which they arrange insignia and objects of power symbolically, Amazonian shamans display their status and power on their bodies in ways that may only be transparent to initiates, those under the influence of psychotropic plant brews, or even at the limit to themselves.

The transfer of designs and patterns or phosphenes seen during plant induced hallucinations to objects of material culture, where they can constitute art forms, has been well studied in Amazonian ethnographies (Hugh Jones 1979; Reichel Dolmatoff 1975). The process by which the designs from men's visions are transferred to closely related women who then transfer them in pottery and weaving is, however, less clear (Gebhart Sayer 1984). Using both their songs and the blowing of tobacco smoke, shamans can guide and control the visions of those who take the plant potions and modulate effects as appropriate, either enhancing them or tapering them down if they prove overwhelming for participants. Smoke is blown onto the faces of patients, into the palms of their joined hands and more particularly on the crown of their heads, where the place of the fontanelles is held to be the main access and exit point of the soul in the body. The meanings of the patterns displayed on objects or garments used by shamans, or those given mentally to initiates, are then made visible during ceremonies. Under the influence of psychoactive brews, snakes, felines, birds of prey and other figures which are perceived as real emerge from these patterns, leaving profound impressions on patients. At other times, they merely function as semiotic devices, some for group members distinctively from neighbouring populations, others more universally within Amazonian cosmologies. The geometrical, zoomorphic designs that figure on Jakwash hunters' quivers and curare hunting poison tubes, on their belts woven by their sisters and wives and on the latter's water pots, are represented as petroglyphs on large liminal boulder stones in their territory. They were also stylised as ceremonial face paintings until the 1970s. Although there was the introduction of floral designs by missionaries, the demise of face painting and the development of new standardised 'Indian' designs by Mestizo entrepreneurs for the tourist trade in Amazonia have obfuscated shamanic patterns. They continue to be transmitted within the symbolism of *Vegetalismo* that relates to the esoteric overlay of the invisible on the visible in the cosmos. Each group's relational identity in Western Amazonia is associated with a distinctive set of symbolic meanings which need to be learnt in the same way as the group's language or dialect if shamanic training is undertaken among them. For instance, while the contrast between red and black (as in the Q. *wairuru* seed, *Erythrina sp.*) is used in shamanic medicine throughout the region, its values and its relation to white as a residual category vary from group to group. Among the Jakwash, in the same way that native hot and cold disease categories became intertwined colonial Hispanic medicine, colour categories have retained specific values within the wider Amazonian context. The black, red and white colour symbolism includes European values, yet the underlying logic is one of shamanic transformation rather than antagonism between black evil and white purity; black and white magic.

ETIOLOGY OF SICKNESS AND CURING

The cosmic in-between that shamans work in, so that ultimately they can identify with the rainbow-anaconda that encompasses all dualities, is a fluid space where relations of cause and effect in space/time are constantly negotiated socially, particularly in relation to the production of sickness and health. Among the Jakwash and more generally for all Western Amazonian shamans formed within the tradition of *Vegetalismo*, the spatial expansion, both through actual shamanic networks on the ground and through the acquisition of spirit allies in the cosmos, is inseparable from a personal pursuit of agency in this causal space. Although predators and particularly the jaguar are models of agency in the forest, they may have received undue importance in recent ethnography in relation to other animals, which are attributed great importance in Amazonian shamanism for intrinsic reasons. For example, *guacamayo* birds (macaws) are not predators but their soaring flight and loud cries over forest territories make them 'shaman-like' messengers. Certain species of beetles are also 'shaman-like' due to the iridescent quality of their hard backs ('skins') which is reminiscent of hallucinogenic effects. The maps that *Vegetalistas* trace in cosmic space/time are modelled on geography so that they travel along waterways from their houses, on or under the water, in the air or via imagined underground rivers, through territory which has both real and surreal landmarks. Jakwash shamans acquire their clusters of spirit allies on the model of expanding kindreds, so that newly contacted spirit allies aggregate to the first ones gained. All are then called in order, during each ritualised ingestion of psychoactive plants in curing ceremonies, and sung to as they appear. While the songs (S.Q. *icaros*) help shamans enliven and activate each relationship in turn as appropriate to the task at hand, tobacco smoke is thought to attract and feed the spirit allies. Hunters also use tobacco smoke in an ambiguous way in relation to the forest-cosmos boundary. On the one hand they disguise their human scent with tobacco, make themselves attractive to game animals in the forest and propitiate the spirit-masters of the animals. On the other hand, they use tobacco to safeguard their exposed human subjectivity from being taken over by greater soul agency in the form of forest spirits, were-animals and cosmic elemental forces. Unlike hunters, shamans use their human subjectivity to tackle, confront, snatch, pacify, integrate and master these forces through personal engagements. Hunters and shamans who fall prey to such forces need shamanic treatment which consists of recreating a bounded, 'tobacco-sealed' (Q. *arkana*) personal/social identity for the sufferer.

Q. *mamaya-* refers to the appropriation of a human being by a cosmic subjectivity, (Q. *amadu* if this subjectivity is an ancestor soul). This is a fatal illness if shamanic treatment is not available; Q. *cutipa* refers to the revenge action of animal species which redresses an imbalance between humans and other beings, particularly animals, in the cosmos. This revenge action is targeted to localised kindreds and like sorcery attacks, it is thought to move from stronger to weaker member until a prey is found. The Latin American folk syndrome of 'fright' sickness (S. *susto,* Q. *manchari,*) has been grafted on these Amazonian disease categories which both refer to breaches of the status quo and an inversion of power between people as hunters and animals as prey. Typically people are struck with these afflictions on the physical or social margins of villages, on the way to their gardens or when the integration of an in-marrying outsider is questioned. In all three cases the blowing of tobacco smoke by a shaman on the afflicted person's body is used as first aid. The most feared illness among the Jakwash Lamista, persistent bad luck at hunting, (Q. *afasi-ku*) results from the deprivation of agency that is concomitant with any of the 'attacks' above. This state of depression and apathy in turn affects the unlucky hunter's relationships with women, who do not receive meat for their families and may withdraw their sexuality in retaliation. A plant-induced visionary trance is then required to locate the origin of the suffering and reinstate normality. This condition is treated by the ingestion of large quantities of tobacco juice following a shamanic diet in seclusion and it is said to help the patient regain his keen motivation.

'TOBACCO IS THE FATHER OF ALL PLANTS'

The Jakwash gloss on the special place that tobacco occupies in the shamanic *materia medica* by saying that 'tobacco is the father of all plants'. My attempts to elucidate this statement invariably led to a labyrinth of circular arguments around animism in which the 'mother-spirits' of plants (S. *madres de las plantas*), the 'owners' of plants, animals and places (S. *dueño*) and souls were all mutually explanatory. The statement remained incomprehensible to me until I remembered to take it literally in terms of the native concepts of parenthood. Like other Amazonian people, the Jakwash do not have elaborate notions about the respective roles of men and women in conception. Male input is held to be necessary not only as a source of all semen but as a repeated contribution – by one or more men – in order to form and strengthen the soul of the growing foetus. All men who have sexual intercourse with a pregnant woman partake in the fatherhood of her baby and can claim paternity through performing the public rituals of couvade which involves fathers both physically and spiritually with their babies before and after childbirth (Metraux 1949a, 1949b; Rivière 1974). The couvade in South America refers to the ways in which both father(s) and mother contribute actively to the secure anchoring and formation of the soul in their baby's body in a physical way, using diet and a variety of behavioural prescriptions and proscriptions. The ritualised mimicking of childbirth by fathers is only one aspect of the couvade, which extends from early pregnancy through to the end of infancy. The continued importance of couvade behaviour among mixed Amazonian populations is reflected by the frequent calls made upon shamans to perform cures on babies with tobacco smoke to counteract parental breaches of taboos. There has been a recent ethnographic emphasis on the way in which couvade rituals progressively create a commonality of substance in mother, fathers and baby in households through acts of nurture (Rival

1998). Maternal nurture is not separate, but informed by paternal activity, to which the mother is also associated by way of sharing prescribed and proscribed foods during pregnancy as much as through sexual intercourse. As noted by Vilaça (2001), this nurturing process is quasi-shamanic in that it is a liminal state in which boundaries between humans and animals, between society and forces outside it or immanent to it, are fluid and require active realigning. The first intervention on a newborn is to blow smoke on his/her open fontanelles to close them day by day and seal the soul in the little body. Babies' souls which are ill-defined are particularly vulnerable to be possessed by animal souls (Q. *mamayadu*). Only shamanic treatment consisting of singing the song of the animal while blowing tobacco smoke is thought to be effective to address this common form of illness, whether medical treatment is also used or not. Fathers have a particularly important role in giving shape to their babies' souls through the couvade (Riviere 1974). By following social codes of behaviour, some of which transform their physical substance, fathers actively enhance the growth of their babies and their integration in the domestic and social groups. This physical association is enlivened at each time of crisis in the child's life until puberty; episodes of sickness may call for the re-enactment of couvade as locally codified.[7] While both paternal care and shamanic treatment involve transformation of physical substance, there is a crucial difference between the prophylactic ritualised behaviour of fathers in relation to their children and shamanic agency mediated by tobacco.

In the Amerindian shamanic logic that extends to all personal and social transitions, realignment is sought primarily through a transformation of bodily substance by way of dietary and behavioural changes. Through this transformation, the relationship of the agent with the subject is acted upon and as a result it is believed that the subject is also transformed. The first step in the quest for therapy when someone gets sick in a Jakwash household is twofold: seeking a cause and adhering to the basic shamanic diet. If an adult gets sick, close relatives and household members often associate themselves with him or her and follow the same diet. In Western Amazonia, being a shaman is a matter of degree. Each adult man is more or less a shaman, with approximately one in ten men identified by others as a 'strong shaman' (Q. *sinchi runa*), and one in twenty as Q. *sinchi yachak*, 'strong knower'. Any household head is likely to make a cigar and blow smoke on the body of a sick household member before the services of a more experienced shaman are sought. The greater the reputed power of the curer, the keener his capacity of diagnosis and the agency of his tobacco/breath. When they treat critically ill patients, shamans often associate themselves with the latter's diets. Blowing smoke is a transfer of the shaman's agency as subtle substance to the patient's body.

The Iakwash saying that 'tobacco is the father of all plants' can be understood in the light of the synergetic action between father and mother in the reproductive process. Pursuing native explanations also requires making sense of the relationship between tobacco as the father of a plant and the 'mother spirits' of plants that may have a noticeable effect on the human physiology. It is significant that the mother-spirit of tobacco is Q. *aya runa*, ancestor soul, in the sense of primeval ancestor. The Jakwash have few myths but, like other Amazonians, they associate the origins of humanity with tobacco. At the Eden Project's botanical garden in Cornwall, in August 2001,

Francisco Montes, a Peruvian shaman with Lamas ancestry, was invited to enrich the tropical greenhouse's Amazonian plant collection with rock paintings. At the centre of the paintings, he illustrated the myth in which the first shaman received simultaneously tobacco and *shacapa* (*Cerbera peruviana*) – the plant most commonly used to make rattles – the sources of the two main tools of the shamanic trade in Western Amazonia, before *Ayahuasca* became dominant in shamanic practice in the region. Further discussion with Francisco strengthened my hypothesis that mother-spirits and owners/guardians can be understood as differentiated, yet overlapping feminine and masculine sources of agency in the cosmos. The former are animal/cosmic and the latter humanised, anthropomorphic entities (*Sachamama/sacharuna*, forest female and male entities, *yakumama/yakuruna*, water female and male entities). In their multiple forms (the whirlwind, the rainbow) and through the animals associated with them, these entities are the primary sources of both disease and curing power. They are subjectified as calling upon shamans to take on their forms in order to interact with them. As noted by Viveiros de Castro, rather than thinking in terms of two worlds, mythical and human, we can see the cosmos as a pan-specific behavioural schema including humans: all shamanic animal and plant spirits have culture, the same culture as Amazonian people. They live in the same type of houses, go hunting, have wives and children, gardens, parties, and even get sick and need curing by fellow shamans, who smoke pipes. While the *runa* 'owners' smoke pipes, however, the '*mamas*' do not. They are rather latent subjectivities whose remoteness from humans is sometimes expressed in terms of 'grandmother (Q. *Yakumamay*, grandmother anaconda). Those spirits appear to be universal, generic parental figures, commanding many 'children' animal species which shamans can seek alliance with (otters, dolphins, rays in the case of *Yakumamay*) in contrast with humanoid forest genies and tricksters such as Q. *Chulla chaki – Curupira* or mermaids and mermen.

TOBACCO AND REPRODUCTIVE POWER

The plants that have S. *madres* (mother spirits) are typically those that make you 'see', 'know' and 'have power over' inter-relations in the cosmos. Shamanic plants are mainly defined in terms of their physiological effect on humans: if there is doubt on whether a plant has a mother spirit or not, synergy with other plants is used as a test. Secondarily, plants are evaluated in terms of their relationships with other systems (insects, vines, parasites, fungi, birds and mammals). Their power can be adverse or beneficial to humans according to how it is contacted. The focus is a practical one and the idiom, one of exchange and the creation of kinship bonds, including transmutation. Shamans' relations with cosmic entities can evolve from being their children to being their affines and their parents. Tobacco complements the shamanic diet in order to establish a commonality of substance with the cosmic entities: abstention of strong foods, salt and sexual activity aim at making bodies bland, receptive and permeable to the beings and ethos of impersonated animals or elements. When hunters and shamans forsake their human sexuality through dietary and behavioural prescriptions and proscriptions before entering the forest, so that they become as 'disembodied' as possible, they defer to the power of reproduction in the cosmos. Sexual power is then given to the masters of game animals in the case of hunters and used to relate to cosmic entities in the case of shamans. Whether seduction, actual copulation or fights with spirits are described, shaman's encounters with spirits are typically sexual and result in procreation and the creation of kinship.

The beginning of an affinity between a Jakwash shaman apprentice and an animal is seen by others to relate to the closeness between his/her behaviour and the animal's attributes. The apprentice will then be invited to follow the specific diet locally held as appropriate for ingesting particular plants associated with the animal. The shamanic diet 'actualizes' the relation between the apprentice and his/her familiar spirit-to-be in the same way that courting and sharing sexual substance create affinity. In the light of Viveiros de Castro's recent distinction between real, virtual and potential affinity in Amazonian Amerindian societies (2001), the role of tobacco in the shamanic diet is remarkable in instituting a quasi-consanguinisation of the virtual affinal relation between shaman and familiar spirit. Throughout this process, the animal, as mother spirit for these plants, is 'fed/attracted' with tobacco smoke until the apprentice gains sufficient familiarity of the animal's 'perspective', 'taming'it, 'seducing' it to the point of impersonating it. The relationship between shaman and animal 'mother-spirit' – in a male or female form – is initiated and implemented through the action of tobacco in a similar way to that of a father in human reproduction. Tobacco then activates the undifferentiated space of the 'ancestor world' or 'myth time' (S.Q. *ñaupa tempu*) in which communication is possible and transformation (of people into animals and vice versa) is a common occurrence. Nicotine makes a hunter or shaman like a 'super-conductive human' in the forest, the difference between them is that the shaman can embody, 'put on the coat of' his spirit allies, whom he has made into relatives. Tobacco 'makes visible' the manifest form of each species as a mere envelope that conceals an internal human form. This internal form is the locus of what Viveiros de Castro calls the 'subjectivity' of plants or animals. Within *Vegetalismo,* shamanic agency, rather than being deployed through a direct human/animal transmutation, requires the mediation of plants in order to achieve this transmutation. It is both the plants – which often have medicinal properties – and their mother-spirits – whose attributes make them dominant beings in the forest/cosmos – which confer curing power to shamans. Relationships with other shamans are constantly transformed over time through the ingestion of new psychoactive plants associated with particular 'owners' of the forest in different ways. Q. *yachay* (power/knowledge) describes this inter-subjectivity; its substance counterpart is a thick phlegm in the shaman's stomach that contains small animals related to his spirit allies. The codification of such associations is part of *Vegetalismo.* It is not revealed to novices as a body of knowledge but progressively disclosed to them as they receive visions and gain insights leading to their cultivation of relationships with specific plants, animals and their 'owners', which determine the development of their practice as healers, sorcerers or ambivalent shamans. At the same time, shamans must learn to harness their shifting into animal shapes and keep their spirit allies disciplined and tame in order to further their exploration of duality and difference, sources of their shamanic agency. Each relationship constitutes a 'medicine' that pertains to one of the cosmic domains (forest, water, underworld and sky) and carries with it a perspective from this domain in relation to the others. The most powerful medicines are those associated with the predators in each domain and those that bridge across domains. Shamans' tobacco-breath carries within it traces of all the inter-subjective relations that constitute their knowledge. In important treatments, when they initiate novices or, as the tradition has it, when they are about to die, shamans are able to regurgitate the objects or small animals (Q. *caruwa*) that dwelled in their phlegm, linking them substantially to their spirit allies.

Tobacco plants are often placed at the origin of culture as defined by gender relations among humans and presented as the dialectical outcome of gender. Numerous myths of origin of tobacco in Amazonia include the oppositions highlighted by Levi-Strauss between the female (menstruating)/male (hunter and men's councils), raw/cooked (smoking as different form), nature/culture (1970, 1978). Discussing the mental and social aspects of his comparison of such myths, Sperber pointed out that 'transformations in myths are concerned with the use of mythical thought' (1982, 113–114). Yet the study of myths in their social context, as a code which is not separate from the conditions of their communication, does not seem to be incompatible with comparison of themes. The first tobacco plants typically grew from the dead bodies of women or anacondas killed by men.[8] Besides, the ways in which native Amazonians scrutinise the forest environment for structure, for symbolic meaning, for associations and synthesis, deserves greater attention.

Tobacco enhances or restores the hunting power of men when endangered by women's sexuality as an aspect of their reproductive ability. Shamans abstain from both hunting and sexual activities when engaging in the 'capture' of soul power in the cosmos. While the relative and relational status of predator/prey have been perceived to be the fundamental dimension of perspectival inversions in recent ethnographies (Vilaça 2000), aspects of gender and kinship appear to be equally relevant. The exploration of gender differences by male human shamans through cosmic unions aims to create an 'in between' trans-sexual shamanic 'soul-body'. While the sexual symbolism of actual and cosmic rivers as vagina-paths, of mermaid-ridden waterfalls and pools, of foods and of houses have been emphasised in the Vaupés (S. Hugh Jones 1979; C. Hugh Jones 1979), it has received far less attention in Western Amazonia (except for Baer 1976). Hidden from repressive Christianity since colonial times, sexual symbolism has been transmitted mostly as esoteric knowledge, as trainee shamans explore the cosmos experientially through the ingestion of tobacco and plant brews. The rainbow, which is perceived to be a source of disease and also of phantom pregnancies in both the Andes and Western Amazonia, characteristically links cosmic domains with a high 'soul charge' which can affect exposed humans. These individuals can be hunters in the forest, socially marginated individuals and more particularly menstruating women in a similar way to thunder. The Anaconda/rainbow is the most powerful shamanic symbol in Amazonia. 'Mastering the rainbow' means encompassing gender differences in order to gain access to reproductive power in the cosmos.

Besides having 'spirit wives', male shamans can then incorporate the female identity of their spirit allies, experience pregnancy and generate spirit babies through their bodies in the way that women give birth. Jakwash shamans among others in Amazonia are not only concerned with hunting and ensuring an abundant supply of game animals for their group of reference. They also take responsibility for social reproduction more generally, including the initiation of boys and the successful reproduction of wild or semi-managed palm species that produce valued edible fruit during the annual cycle. Using tobacco smoke and spirit songs and spells, shamans claim to enhance the productivity of palm clumps that they are associating themselves with in a physical way by tending them, connecting with them as extensions of their persons.

From an evolutionary perspective, Amazonian shamanism is concerned with the survival and reproduction, both individual and social, of people in small societies of hunters and horticulturalists in rainforest ecosystems. Although in *vegetalismo* the emphasis is on the individual healing of urban residents, the action and rationale of blowing tobacco smoke on bodies or on palm clumps are not so different. I argue that, rather than casting the question in terms of the contrast between magic and empirical medicine, which have not changed since Rivers, looking at shamanic agency and particularly at the use of tobacco allows an exploration of how shamans understand curing efficacy. Admittedly there is a widespread use of social metaphor in shamanic curing in general. Taussig (1987) elucidated the redeeming power of the Indian shaman after the colonial condemnation of his works of the Devil in Colombian Amazonia. Post Rio 1992, Gow (1995) could write how 'curing identifies patients with the supreme domain of plant self-regeneration, the forest itself, the limitless extension of trees and vines'. In the enduring dialectics of colonial and post-colonial Amazonian society and shamanism, Indians are forever called upon to cure White evils. The constant source of curing efficacy, however, remains the transformation of patients' bodies through the removal of pathogens, the sealing of personal boundaries and the transfer of substances from one body to another with tobacco smoke.

SUBSTANCE AND METAPHORS

Shamanic healing and its inseparable obverse, harming are effected with blowing and/or sucking out actions on bodies, most of which require the use of tobacco. Whether the active principle in the cure is an identified organic chemical constituent in a plant or an active, positive identification of the patient with a self-generating plant or animal power is relevant to pharmacognosy, but not to shamanic logic. From the shaman's viewpoint, curing is effected through the transfer of power, by means of blown tobacco smoke supporting intent, with or without the words of a spell or a song. It is within this shamanic agency that bio-chemical compounds are thought to be effective and that, at the same time, metaphors become empowered and effective for healing. The power of the blower is different from his/her social status yet it is associated with social recognition of his role, whether as a marginal shaman, a sorcerer or a priestly sort of shaman. Learning to 'see' bodies is also to perceive the social dimension of power. At present to my knowledge there is no scientific way to account for the physical substrate of social consensus about shamans' power. Ethnographers can analyse the social dynamics of shamanic power contests, in which rival shamans compete to assess the power of their ' blowing', but elucidating the nature of such contests is another task altogether.

Native Amazonians' understanding of disease, in the wider context of Amerindian shamanism, is relational. There is no natural death in Western Amazonian native understanding. Death and disease are always regarded as resulting either from an intrusion of cosmic forces on the edges of human society, or from sorcery exercised by a human enemy. Sorcery can be carried out either directly or through the mediation of an agent manipulated in the cosmos as an extension of a shaman's subjectivity. Intervention is phrased in terms of a constant negotiation of balance in the cosmos through attack and revenge. Any illness has a cure, and any social ill can be redresssed, if only a shaman can find a channel of communication with the identified agents, which have caused it, neutralise them and 'seal' the patient with 'sealing substance' (Q. *arkana*) drawn from the shaman's body and manually or symbollically applied, using tobacco as a medium. In cures of sorcery (S. *mal de la gente, brujería, venganza,*), whether inflicted directly or through the mediation of a malevolent shaman paid for the job, the shaman first blows smoke over the patient's body to 'make it soft', then sucks the disease-carrying dart out of him/her, using tobacco and water, before finally 'sealing' the patient and usually sending the harmful dart back to its sender in counter-sorcery. The well cured person and his/her family is then freed to enjoy good health and good fortune. While the various tryptamine-rich plant brews give shamans 'vision' into cosmic space/time to locate sorcerers and estranged souls, tobacco is the operational tool that transfers shamanic agency from the cosmic plane onto the hut or house where the curing is taking place.

The physical journeys of *vegetalistas* along rivers and forest paths (now also including car, motor boat and plane travel) to shamans who have exchanged knowledge with them and become part of their networks provide reference pathways in the cosmic space where they have agency. Tobacco, visionary brews and the clairvoyance skills, which are developed as part of shamanic training, help shamans to explore their patients' relationships visually. This is no different from the way in which clairvoyant healers operate worldwide. However, what is relevant to anthropological discussion is the fact that all *vegetalistas*, whether native, Mestizos or Western foreigners, engage in this open-ended task of developing, maintaining and enriching their networks as operational bases which are at the same time physical, based in the landscape of Western Amazonia, and cosmic, inscribed in the social history of the region and its political and economic relations with the rest of the world. The pantheon of Peruvian Amazonian *vegetalistas*' 'spirit-allies' includes Christian saints, European doctors of past centuries, blonde fairies and Inca warlords in a consensual set which has been developed consistently since colonial times. *Vegetalistas*' networks are both individual and collective, as shamans from particular areas consolidate exchanges with those in specific areas through generations. Initiation and knowledge transfer give trainees potential access to their trainer's network. This network can be activated on the basis of acquired commonality of substance, if Q. *yachay* phlegm has been transmitted as the support matter for knowledge transfer. Tobacco is as essential to secure all knowledge transactions as it is to perform cures and 'seal' bodies.

The process of shamanic curing involves a transformation of the body as a soul-body constantly negotiating its boundaries through its interaction with others in the cosmos. In mixed Amazonian society, the focus is on individual bodies rather than on the collective 'body politic' of inclusive 'we-humans' – groups differentiated from animals and other people in a forest environment. In the perception of Western Amazonian shamans, there is no conceivable separation between empirical and metaphorical medicine because all *materia medica* is only perceived as active and only activated within a relational web of social-ecological relationships in the cosmos. For a Jakwash shaman, the efficacy of 'snake medicine' plants which save people's lives every day in Western Amazonia does not derive from the active ingredient *per se*. The understanding of the relationship between those plants and the snakes to whose venom they provide an antidote is essential to the treatment. The snakes, as mother-spirits of the medicine plants, may use them as food or as 'their' medicines. This 'cosmic ecology' fuses herbalism, spiritual healing and social relations in ways that are intractable to scientific enquiry as it is defined now; yet, shamanic curing takes place in the midst of these overlapping aspects.

Through exploring analogies and correspondences between their ecological observations of plants, animals and cosmic elements and human social relations, most particularly gender relations, shamans develop the skills to manipulate metaphors. Within particular regions, generic and particular metaphors are combined and constantly modified in response to inter-relationships with outsiders. In mixed Amazonian society East of the Andes, *vegetalismo* has contributed to both an extensive exploration of the medicinal properties of plants and to address the interface between Hispanic colonial medicine and native shamanism with the use of metaphors. At different times in the history of Western Amazonia, social metaphors have been used to express these relationships. These polarities are seen between town and forest, Mestizo and native, Catholicism and Amerindian shamanism and have been crucial to the definition of shamanic power in the colonial emergence of *vegetalismo* as the shamanic plant medicine of Western Amazonia. Shamanic networks in the region have been changing through history due to rivalries between missions, epidemics, wars, extractive booms and the dynamics of colonisation of the lowlands.

Sociality in Amazonia implies commonality of substance that is constantly acted upon shamanically in the 'making of kinship' among group members, in the integration of outsiders and also in the process of reproducing human society as a bounded, yet permeable entity. Blowing tobacco on bodies, places, crops, foods, brews is the most fundamental act of Western Amazonian shamans in their capacity as healers. In this paper, I have tried to show how tobacco is used in all activities of dissolving and the recreation of human/social boundaries, in the cosmic web of relationships between humans, animals, plants, stones and elements. Shamans are active in all situations that involve contact with the dimensions that inform society: the wild, the spirit world and ancestral souls. Powerful shamans are the only Western Amazonians whose souls are believed to remain differentiated after death as 'soul bodies' feeding on tobacco smoke within an undifferentiated pool of soul matter from which new individual souls are drawn by human parents in their babies' bodies.

At this point in time, when the use of *Ayahuasca* as a visionary brew is expanding in both Amazonia and in the capital cities of the West, it may be relevant to recall the primacy of tobacco in Western Amazonian shamanism. While nicotine may well act as a catalyst of the psychoactive plant mixtures used by shamans, the interpretation shamans offer is that tobacco smoke is the substance closest to soul and related to the power of differentiation and connection of subjectivities in the cosmos. Shamans, masters of the in-between, shape-shifters, have the task of aligning human agency with the cosmic order. They do this, including curing the sick, through manipulating the boundaries of their own and their patients' bodies and souls, as well as cosmic boundaries, using large quantities of tobacco while following an ascetic diet. The action of nicotine as a neurotransmitter, unknown to Amazonian shamans, might be an unwittingly powerful metaphor.

Notes

1   I am very grateful to both Gilbert Lewis and Stephen Hugh-Jones for their comments on an earlier draft of this paper, although the responsibility for the text is mine alone.

2   *Ayahuasca* generally consists of one of several species of *Banisteriopsis* woody vine, most commonly *Banisteriopsis caapi*, crushed and boiled in water with various plant admixtures generically called '*chacruna*' in Western Amazonia. A favoured '*chacruna*' is *Psychotria viridis*, which is rich in tryptamines and particularly in 2NN Dimethyltryptamine. The combination of *Ayahuasca* and *chacruna*, often described as male and female components of the brew, is necessary since without the Monoamine Oxidase inhibiting activity of the *Banisteriopsis*, the betacarbolines of the brew would be neutralised in the stomach and the psychoactive effects of the *chacruna* would not be felt. Other plants are added to the brew in idiosyncratic recipes, so that no two shamans in Western Amazonia use the same quantities of plant matter or the same plant combination in their brews.

3   This raises the question of whether the Western distinction between recreational and therapeutical uses of plant-derived drugs is applicable or not. In the same way as coca, the Amerindian uses of tobacco blur this distinction. In the case of tobacco, to a large extent this is a matter of both dosage and diet, as shamans ingest larger quantities of tobacco than other people in a codified controlled way that may enhance the potency of nicotine. All the shamans I have come across do not use tobacco as a regular intoxicant but take their cigars or pipes out for special treatments. They regularly complain about the taxing effects which ingesting large quantities of tobacco juice or smoking large cigars have on their bodies but see this as a prerequisite for treating their patients.

4   Here I am concerned mainly with the system that evolved in the region of Lamas in Peru, but comparable systems were developed in Ecuadorian Amazonia (Quijos) and in Colombian Amazonia (Sibundoy) at the same time, all originating from Hispanic colonial rule and developed further in the nineteenth and early twentieth centuries.

5   To account for the local usage of Spanish and Quechua, I use the letters S. to indicate Spanish words, Q. for Quechua words and S.Q. for words from either language used in either Spanish or Quechua speech or both in forms that may be hybrid.

6   These plants are more particularly those associated with the 'devil's gardens' (Q. *supay chacra*). These areas of forest are characterised by different trees and undergrowth from those in the surrounding forest. Some of the plants growing in these areas are toxic to humans and large mammals. Although it is suspected that fungi may be responsible for this phenomenon, to my knowledge it still awaits research.

7   Not only in the weeks and months following birth, but in some cases until puberty, the parents of a child will resume a quasi-shamanic diet whenever the child gets sick. Not doing so might incur the risk that their child's soul lose its anchoring in the young, still 'wet' body. By following a strict diet and smoking tobacco, the parents deliberately make

boundaries between humans and the cosmos fluid in order to re-draw them in conformity to social expectations. The father (or fathers) of the child avoid hunting (which requires a clear boundary between human as predator and animal as prey) and felling trees (which requires a clear boundary between human settlement or swidden and the forest as the abode of spirits).

8 The Gnau of New Guinea say that the first tobacco was grown from the decay debris in the skulls of ancestors (Gilbert Lewis, personal communication).

Bibliography

Armitage, A.K., Hall, G.H. and Sellers, C.M. 1969 'Effects of nicotine on electrocortical activity and acetylcholine release from the cat cerebral cortex' *British Journal of Pharmacology* 35(1), 152–160.

Arneric, S.P. and Brioni, J.D. 1999 (eds) *Neuronal Nicotinic Receptors: Pharmacology and Therapeutic Opportunities*, New York: Wiley-Liss.

Baer, G. 1976 'A particular aspect of Matsigenka shamanism (Eastern Peru): Male Female ambivalence', *Proceedings, 41st International Congress of Americanists* 3, 114–121.

Bruhn, J.G, Holmstedt, B., Lindgren J.-E. and H. Wassen, S. 1976 'The tobacco from Nino Korin: identification of nicotine in a Bolivian archaeological collection' *Arstryck 1976*, 45–48.

Chaumeil, J.-P. 1983 *Voir, Savoir, Pouvoir: le chamanisme chez les Yagua du Nord-Est péruvien*. Paris: Éditions de l'École des Hautes Études en Sciences Sociales.

Conti-Tronconi, B. and Raftary, M.A. 1999 'Brain and Muscle Nicotinic Receptors: Complex Homologous Proteins Carrying Multiple Binding sites' pp. 413–439 in William Martin *et al.* (eds) *Tobacco Smoking and Nicotine: a Neurobiological Approach*, New York and London: Plenum Press.

Crocker, C. 1985 *Vital souls; Bororo cosmology, natural symbolism and shamanism*, Tucson: University of Arizona Press.

Farabee, W.C. 1922 *Indian tribes of eastern Peru*. Papers of the Peabody Museum of American Archaeology and Ethnology (Vol 10), Cambridge: Harvard University Museum.

Furst, P T. 1972 (ed.) *Flesh of the gods: the ritual use of hallucinogens*, New York and Washington D.C.: Praeger.

Gebhart-Sayer, A. 1984 *The cosmos encoiled: Indian art of the Peruvian Amazon*, New York: Center for Inter-American Relations.

Gow, P. 1995 'River people: shamanism and history in western Amazonia' pp. 90–115 in Thomas, Nicholas and C. Humphrey (eds) *Shamanism, history and the state*. Ann Arbor: the University of Michigan Press.

Gray, A. 1996 *The Last Shaman: Change in an Amazonian Community*, Oxford: Berghahn Books.

Harner, M.J. 1973 (ed.) *Hallucinogens and shamanism*, Oxford: Oxford University Press.

Hugh-Jones, C. 1979 *From the Milk River: spatial and temporal processes in northwest Amazonia*, Cambridge: Cambridge University Press.

Hugh-Jones, S. 1979 *The palm and the Pleiades: Initiation and cosmology in northwest Amazonia*, Cambridge: Cambridge University Press.

Huxley, Francis 1957 *Affable savages: an anthropologist among the Urubu Indians of Brazil*, New York:Viking Press.

Karsten, S.R. 1926 *The civilization of the South American Indians, with special reference to magic and religion*, New York: Alfred A. Knopf.

Larson P.S., Haag, H.B. and Silvette, H. 1961 *Tobacco: Experimental and Clinical Studies: a*

Comprehensive Account of the World Literature, Baltimore: Williams & Wilkins (Supplement III, 1975).

Layten Davis, D. and Nielsen, M.T. 1999 *Tobacco: production, chemistry and technology*, Oxford: Blackwell Science.

Lévi Strauss, C. 1970 *The raw and the cooked*, London: Cape.

Lévi Strauss, C. 1978 *Myth and meaning*, London: Routledge and Kegan Paul.

Luna, L.E. 1986 *Vegetalismo shamanism among the Mestizo population of the Peruvian Amazon*, Stockholm: Almqvist & Wiskell International.

Luna, L.E. 1991 *Ayahuasca visions: the religious iconography of a Peruvian shaman*, Berkeley: North Atlantic Books.

Martin, W.R., Van Loon, G.R. and Layten Davis, D. (eds) 1987 *Tobacco smoking and nicotine: a neurobiological approach*, New York: Plenum Press.

Métraux, A. 1949a 'The Couvade' pp. 375–382 in J.H. Steward (ed.) *Handbook of South American Indians* (Vol. 5), Washington D.C.: U.S. Government Printing Office, Smithsonian Institution, Bureau of American Ethnology, Bulletin 143.

Métraux, A. 1949b 'Religion and Shamanism' pp. 559–599 in J.H. Steward (ed.) *Handbook of South American Indians* (Vol. 5), Washington D.C.: U.S. Government Printing Office, Smithsonian Institution, Bureau of American Ethnology, Bulletin 143.

Reichel-Dolmatoff, G. 1975 *The Shaman and the jaguar: a study of narcotic drugs among the Indians of Colombia*, Philadelphia: Temple University Press.

Rival, L. 1998 'Androgynous Parents and Guest children: the Huaorani Couvade', *Journal of the Royal Anthropological Institute*, 4(4), 619–42.

Rivière, P. 1974 'The Couvade: A Problem Reborn', *Man* 9(3), 423–35.

Schultes, R.E. 1945 'El Uso del Tabaco entre los Huitotos' *Agricultura Tropical* 1 (9), 10–22.

Schultes, R.E. 1978 'Plants and plant constituents as mind-altering agents throughout history' pp. 219–241 in L.L. Iversen *et al.* (eds) *Handbook of psychopharmacology*, New York: Plenum Press.

Schultes, R.E. and Hofmann, A. 1979 *Plants of the gods: origins of hallucinogenic use*, New York: McGraw-Hill.

Schultes, R.E. and Hofmann, A. 1980 *The Botany and Chemistry of Hallucinogens*,

Schultes, R.E. and Raffauf, R. 1990 *The Healing Forest*, Oregon: Dioscorides Press.

Springfield, Charles C Thomas (2nd edition).

Sperber, D. 1982 'Claude Lévi-Strauss Aujourd'hui', *Le Savoir des anthropologues*, Paris: Hermann.

Strathern, M. 1988 *The gender of the gift: problems with women and problems with society in Melanesia*, Berkeley: University of California Press.

Taussig, M. 1987 *Shamanism, colonialism and the wild man: a study in terror and healing*, Chicago: University of Chicago Press.

Taylor, A.C. 1996 'The soul's body and its states: an Amazonian perspective on the nature of being human' *Journal of the Royal Anthropological Institute* (ns) 2(2), 201–15.

Tessmann, G. 1930 *Die Indianer nordost-Perus. Grundlegende Forschungen fur eine systematische Kulturjunde*, Hamburg: Friederichen, de Gruyter.

Vilaça, A. 2001 'Making Kin Out of Others in Amazonia,' Seminar paper, Department of Social Anthropology, Cambridge, March 2001.

Viveiros de Castro, E. 1996 'Images of nature and society in Amazonian ethnology' *Annual Review of Anthropology* 25, 179–200.

Viveiros de Castro, E, 1998 'Cosmological deixis and Amerindian perspectivism' *Journal of the Royal Anthropological Institute* (ns) 4(3), 469–488.

Viveiros de Castro, E. 2001 'GUT feelings about Amazonia: potential affinity and the construction of sociality' pp. 19–45 in L. Rival and N. Whitehead (eds), *Beyond the visible and the material: the Amerindianization of society in the work of Peter Rivière*, Oxford: Oxford University Press.

Wilbert, J. 1972 'Tobacco and Shamanism: Ecstasy among the Warao Indians of Venezuela' pp. 55–83 in P. Furst (ed.), *Flesh of the Gods: the Ritual Use of Hallucinogens*, New York: Praeger.

Wilbert, J. 1975 'Magico-religious Use of Tobacco among South American Indians' pp. 439–461 in Vera Rubin (ed.), *Cannabis and Culture*, The Hague: Mouton.

Wilbert, J. 1987 *Tobacco and shamanism in South America*, New Haven and London: Yale University Press.

11. Magic, healing, or death?
Issues of Seidr, 'balance', and mortality in past and present

Jenny Blain

INTRODUCTION

This paper deals with magical/shamanistic practices within Northern European spirituality as it is being reconstructed in the present day, drawing on archaeological and saga evidence. In a series of publications (e.g. Blain 1999, 2002), I have examined discourse and practice within various strands of western paganism as constructed/reconstructed/reinvented spiritualities of post-modernity. In particular this involved an ethnographic study of religion derived from the Northern European writings and archaeology. Investigations led me to shamanistic practices known as 'seidr', indicated in the Icelandic sagas: for instance, the Saga of Eric the Red includes descriptions of a seid-woman's clothing, staff, talisman pouch and the platform on which she sits to practice divination. Archaeological finds have included staffs and talisman pouches, one including several hundred seeds of the psychoactive plant henbane, and there is considerable evidence for seidr as involving altered consciousness states and spirit helpers.

My work has involved tracing practices through the sagas and Eddas; and from these, via different forms of practice and (anthropological and practitioner) theory today, to comparison with Sámi and Siberian shamanisms. This work is auto-ethnography: engagement with the practices is required, and I read the saga and other evidence through my own relationship and familiarity with the cosmologies and practices, and discuss trance states and their uses as a practitioner with other practitioners. (See Wallis, forthcoming, Blain 2000 for theoretical discussions of auto-ethnography in practice.) It is also multi-sited, as the strands of discourse and practice lead me from place to place, group to group, one interpretation to another, and from past to present, reflexively. I use techniques of description and comparison in order to reach possible interpretations of seidr and its implications for practitioners' constitution of 'identity' and community, within specific contexts, social, political, religious - then and now.

In this paper I examine some evidence, past and present, for trance, healing and spirit-working in northern spiritual contexts. Seid-magical practices are referred to in the sagas with regard to divination and protection and for personal attack, with some instances which can be described as 'socially constitutive', bringing elements of the community into balance. Most practitioners seem to have been women. Today's seid-workers extend their practices to healing, or bringing 'a person' into balance, and instances of today's seid-healing are here outlined.

This work touches on some controversies. How were seidworkers regarded? Why is there suspicion in the sagas, particularly towards male practitioners? These controversies extend to the practices, use or significance of artefacts, and implications of seidr in the past and present, including questions of whether seidr could have been conducted for healing (there being little evidence for 'healing seidr' in the sagas) or whether it was regarded as 'evil magic'. If people use it for healing today, what may today's use indicate about past practices? Cursing and curing may be two sides of the same coin. Issues of the 'morality' of seid-workers, who act as mediators between human and spirit worlds, may be related to other contestations around shamanic or shamanistic practices, whether in the past or in today's seidr constructed for communities within post-modernity.

Today, practitioners emerge from at least two overlapping groups: 'Heathens' or those who derive religious identity from the cosmology of the North (the well of wyrd[1] and the world tree Yggdrasill) and the old goddesses and gods of Norse mythology (see Paxson, n.d. and in press); and 'Modern European shamanic practitioners' who began their explorations from within neo-shamanic contexts (e.g. Michael Harner's 'Core Shamanism'), and are working to 're-embed' their practices within landscape and legend (see Høst, forthcoming).

SEIDR AND THE SAGAS

The best-known account of shamanistic practice in the North comes from the *Saga of Eirík the Red*. When a Greenland farm (one thousand years ago) has fallen on hard times, it welcomes the visit of a seeress, to prophecy whether people will live or die. Her clothing and shoes, her staff and cloak, are detailed. She wears a hood of lambskin lined with catskin, and has white catskin gloves. Her gown is girdled with a belt of touchwood, from which hangs a bag to hold magical items. Her cloak is blue, fastened with straps and adorned with stones, and stones stud the head of her staff, which is topped with a large brass knob. Her calfskin shoes are tied with thick laces, with tin buttons on their ends. She is asked to predict the progress of the community; she eats a meal of the hearts of the farm animals, and a *hjallr*, a raised dais or platform used in this kind of magic, often translated as 'high seat', is made ready for her to sit, to foretell. The next day she sits on the platform, on a cushion stuffed with hen's feathers, to make her predictions. She engages in ritual practices known as *seiðr* (here transliterated seidr), which requires a special song to be sung to 'the powers' in order that she may gain their knowledge or assistance, in what appears to be ecstatic trance. She foretells an end to the famine and a good future for, among others, the woman Gudrid who has sung the song that enables the seeress to reach her trance state. She is described as a *spákona*, 'spae-woman', a woman who can prophesy: but the techniques she is using (seemingly requiring the assistance of spirits who are contacted within an altered consciousness state) are those of seidr, so that she is operating as a *seiðkona*. (The difference in name becomes important, because there is evidence that spae-women were mostly respected, but those who engaged with seidr viewed with more ambivalence and suspicion, as I discuss elsewhere (Blain, 2002)).

Archaeological evidence includes items such as staffs and pouches similar to those described for seeresses. Neil Price (*pers. comm.*) detailed for me an impressive list of sites in Scandinavia in which either staffs have been identified, or objects previously otherwise classified may be re-interpreted as 'shamanic' staffs, as Price discusses (in press, and forthcoming). Most are from burials identified as those of women, but one in Norway is of a man, and in several others either no attribution has been made, or the staffs are not in a burial context. Interestingly, the association of staff and seidworker within a burial context was present at the time of writing of the sagas: *Laxdaela saga* includes an account of the uncovering of a grave, deemed to be that of a seid-woman because of her staff.

The association of seeress, staff and magic can, however, be an uneasy one. The Laxdaela grave is uncovered because of dreams and other strange occurrences. The object of this excavation is the stopping of dreams in which the dead seid-woman protests about the behaviour of her living (and now Christianised) descendants. It results in the removal of her *blár* (blue) bones.[2] Seidr and seidworkers have not always been regarded happily, and the repertoire of seidr practice is disputed.

ACHIEVING TRANCE

Methods of achieving trance states are not detailed in the old material. In the *Saga of Eirík the Red*, we are told that women circled the seid-platform, and Gudrid sang the necessary chant or song *Vardlokkur*. Chanting is mentioned also in other examples. The Eiríks saga passage also includes a line that the seeress 'made her preparations', but we are not told what those were. Elsewhere, in the Eddic poem *Lokasenna*, Loki taunts the god Odhinn – described elsewhere as a practitioner of seidr – by saying:

> En þig síga kváðu
> Sámseyju í
> og draptu á vét sem völur,
> vitka líki
> fórtu verþjóð yfir
> og hugða eg það args aðal. (*Lokasenna* 24: Sigurðsson, 1998: 125)

Which may be translated as:

> Once you did seidr on Samsey
> and you beat on the drum as do völvas (seeresses)
> in the likeness of a sorcerer (vitki) you fared over the earth
> and I thought that showed you were *ergi*.

The translation of the obscure word *'vétt'* as 'drum' is difficult and disputed: it may or may not, therefore, refer to a shaman's drum (other suggestions have included a round lid (used as a drum) or a seid-platform on which the seer might possibly thump with a staff). But there are many indications of links with Sámi shamanism (indeed, Dubois (1999) sees seidr as a borrowing from Sámi practice, though reinscribed within Norse beliefs and worldview) and among the Sámi chanting was used in trance attainment, with the drum as a vehicle for the shaman's faring.

The word *'argr'* or *'ergi'* is worth a whole discussion in itself, for which there is not room here: but see Meulengracht Sørenson (1983) for a discussion of the word in the saga literature, and Blain and Wallis (2000) for an indication of its multiple meanings when applied to seidr, with emphasis on ways it may relate to 'third gender' locations, and how it is being interpreted by practitioners today. Suffice to say that this is one of the areas in which ambiguity surrounds the seid-worker's location and meanings, and hence ways in which practitioners are, or were, regarded by their communities. Further, there have been suggestions by historians and/or archaeologists that actual or symbolic sex practices accompanied or perhaps facilitated trance states – with a suggestion that the seeress' staff formed part of such practices – resulting in some dispute between historians and today's practitioners who tend to inscribe multiple meanings in staffs (including those of walking-stick, prop or support, being a branch of the world tree, forming a direct connection to earth or to other worlds, or becoming a conduit for energy).

Within 'traditional' shamanisms or contexts of altering consciousness a number of other methods of attaining altered-consciousness states are described. Shamanisms described within Eurasian contexts include use of a number of string and wind instruments (see e.g. Basilov 1997). Other common methods of achieving or assisting trance states include use of consciousness-altering substances such as alcohol, cannabis, and ergot (*Claviceps purpurea*) in Eurasian contexts, or tobacco, peyote, psilocybin mushrooms (*Psilocybe spp.*), *Ayahuasca*/yajé (*Banisteriopsis spp.*) and a variety of other plants in the Western hemisphere (see e.g. Ripinsky-Naxon 1993; Schultes and Hoffman 1992). Within seidr practice, whether in the past or today, a number of these may be relevant.

The most relevant substance for seidr practice in the past would appear to be Amanita muscaria, the red-and-white fly agaric. Its uses in Siberian shamanisms have been attested by a variety of writers (see e.g. Basilov 1997; Eliade 1964; Wasson 1971). There have been speculations that A. muscaria-induced trance has features similar to trance states described in sagas and other writings. For instance, in the description of the decision to become officially Christian, the Lawspeaker, Thorgeir, goes 'under the cloak' (Aðalsteinsson 1978) and remains thus in what is apparently a trance state – lying on the ground wrapped in his cloak – for a very long period of time before emerging to relate what he has 'seen' and propose a solution (see e.g. Blain 2002). The sagas, however, do not mention the use of any substance, in any context that I can discover: the special meal prepared for the seeress in *Eiríks saga rauða* is of the hearts of animals and is eaten the night before her seiðr is to occur. References to drinking in the Eddas (e.g. Mimir's well, the mead of poetry) are ambiguously metaphorical at best (though in a highly speculative mode, Leto (2000) suggests the use of both *A. muscaria* and the psilocybin mushroom *P. semilanceata* may be represented meta-phorically in various poems or sagas). Archaeology, however, does give some evidence, from several hundred henbane seeds found in the pouch of a burial considered to be that of a seeress (Price, *pers. comm*) and a very small number of cannabis seeds present in the Oseberg burial (often considered to be that of a seeress or a priestess), carefully placed between the cushions and feathers piled by the bed.

Today's practitioners most commonly refer to drumming, chanting or singing, and dancing to facilitate altering consciousness. Among some groups (today's European shamanic practitioners, or among those engaging in Heathen 'oracular seidr') these may be the only means used. Alcohol use tends to be limited before a 'shamanic' event, and is most likely to represent an offering to the gods or ancestors, though a group in California engaging in deity-possession have found that possessing entities may want 'to party', consuming copious amounts of alcohol which they are requested to 'take with them' when leaving the host (or 'horse' – a term borrowed from Umbanda).[3] Use of 'helper plants' tends to be restricted to smoke-smudge, often using mugwort (*Artemisia vulgaris*) or, in North America, prairie sage (*Artemisia ludoviciana*) or tobacco. In small-scale seid-workings and when the focus is healing or protection, rather than seeking knowledge for a group, drumming, rattling and chanting are still primary means of trance-induction, but plant-helpers may be used, whether in smudge or directly ingested or smoked – those most commonly reported being mugwort, wormwood (*A. absinthium*), the mushrooms *Amanita muscaria* and various Psilocybe species, cannabis, and various 'legal alternatives'. No practitioners have reported using henbane today. It should quickly be indicated that the purpose of helper plants is not simply to 'get high' or to 'trip', but to enable contact with entities including the plant spirits, to facilitate diagnosis and effect whatever kind of change is required.

HEALING-SEIDR?

Many of the saga references refer to gaining knowledge. Borovsky (1999) has, however, suggested that the seid-worker was not only 'seeing' along the strands of *wyrd*, in trance, but, assisted by her spirits, altering *wyrd*. Examples she gives are of the seidkona Thurid 'soundfiller', mentioned in *Landnámabók*, who in time of famine called fish into the bays around Norway before moving to Iceland as a notable settler, and the Greenland seeress Thorbjörg, who may not only be predicting a good future for the farm but in some way creating it, fixing its pattern within wyrd. It is this sense of the shaping of *wyrd*, the changing of potential patterns, that may relate to healing. I intend in this paper to outline two situations in which I have participated in 'healing seidr', and then give an account from a *seiðmaðr* or seid-man, one of the participants in my research.

First, though, a consideration of the Icelandic saga material. There are no references that I have found which relate specifically to healing. Rather, there are references to other ways in which *wyrd* is altered, affecting the futures of individual people in a variety of ways. These include cursing and calling an enemy to where he will be unsafe (e.g. in *Egils saga*) – but also giving protection against various ills, and removal of curses. (There are also a few instances of what Stephan Grundy calls 'socially constitutive seidr' (*pers. comm.*), in which a community is affected, such as the occasions referred to above, and the example of the seeress Thordís *spákona* who is called upon for her wisdom in legal cases, using her power to cause a wrongdoer to make restitutionin the *Saga of the Waterdalers*.) Many such 'individual' situations deal in illusion or shapeshifting. Anglo-Saxon material, though, is of a very different nature and contains a number of 'charms' or 'spells', many of which have 'healing' as their prime focus – e.g. 'against miscarriage', or against poison (the 'Nine Herbs Charm') (see e.g. Storms 1948).

While shamanic practice is not necessarily 'about' healing, it is clear that healing – and the socially constituted 'performance of healing' – is a part of what shamanic practitioners are expected to do, in various cultures and in the works of those who, like Eliade (1964) have attempted to define 'shamanism'. In this paper I am positing healing – like social change, like calling the fish into the sound, like affecting the environment – as a change in *wyrd*, fate, or *ørlög*, personal destiny/fulfilment, one that makes use of 'natural' or environmental factors with intent to effect a particular result. The lack of healing in the saga material can be theorised in several ways: notably that the use of seidr, or magic in general, is used as a plot element to further the story, and most often used *against* the protagonist, who is seen in a post-Heathen era[4] as standing against 'superstition' and Heathen mores. (This is notably the case in the *Kormáks saga*, where the hero defeats and subverts the attempt of the spákona Thordis to remove a curse that an earlier seid-woman had placed on him – which drives the plot of the saga.) However there is a possibility that some of the situations of protection have similarities with healing, and also I have speculated on the figure of Heidr in *Völuspá*, and whether she may be a bringer of relief to women in childbirth.

My speculations of seidr and healing extend to consideration of today's practices. Here people are engaging with healing, not because it is in the sagas or because they feel they 'should' do it to be 'shamans', but because they are inspired to do so, or driven by their spirits – i.e. members of the *non-human* communities in which they work – and by obligations to members of the human communities in which they work. I will give a brief account of a neo-shamanic healing, then two instances of seid-healing in which I participated.

In a neo-shamanic healing which I attended, the practitioner (Jonathon Horwitz) entered a trance state, facilitated by rattling and drumming, used the trance to find out 'what was wrong' and speak with a disease spirit, and reported back to the participant on the root of her ailment – a spirit-python that was causing her (very 'real' physical-health) problem – and how she could deal with it (by creating her own relationship with the spirit); which apparently she did, according to a report a few months later. The method of entering trance, negotiating with spirits, and returning to pronounce an effect, is well attested in the literature on shamanisms. Two 'seid' healings in which I have participated have taken somewhat different tacks. In one, a person who was diagnosed with schizophrenia had apparently entered an acute phase. He had stopped taking prescribed medications and was displaying symptoms, particularly dissociation, inappropriate talking about other realities, and inability to eat or sleep properly. His state was causing distress to other members of his community as well as the client himself. Before and at the start of the session, the client was talking in a very wild, dissociated fashion. He was persuaded to lie down and asked for the person 'protecting' the area to look behind him for some problem. After protective smudging, the two seidworkers entered a trance and undertook a journey, while the client lay quietly, sleeping or resting. One engaged in an argument with a dwarf who had something belonging to the client and reclaimed the item, the second investigated the area around, found a spirit-animal that seemed associated with the client, gave grain to feed it, and was given a talisman to give the client. On their return the client was woken. He was thoughtful, and finally said, 'you've given me a lot to think about.' He returned home, slept, and next day re-commenced taking his medications.

The second case was at a festival, where several attendees were disturbed by the appearance and account of a young man in attendance. He had earlier had an ailment for which he was given two medications. Taking both, he became unable to eat, lost one-third of his body-weight over several months, and his situation had since been diagnosed as created by the two mediations which should not have been given together and which had adversely affected his nervous system.

A respected seidkona was given a dream by the goddesses Sif and Freyja, to whom the young man had allegiance. She asked a number of seid-workers present to help. Two created a protected space. Two (the seidkona who was directing proceedings, and myself) provided energy for the event, drawing this from the earth. The healing was achieved through using runic energies, as she had been shown in her dream: the rune jera to 'see' the areas or nodes of the client's body, specifically within the nervous system, where healing was needed, the rune sowilo to exert energy directly to these nodes to shock them into functioning again. Two seidworkers shaped the 'sowilo' rune, two saw where it was needed and applied it, others provided warding throughout the experience. The experience was of an intently focused period of time – around two hours of 'clock time' – in which ten people worked as a purposeful team, were sure they had achieved an affect, and indeed that evening the client ate a reasonable meal and has since progressed.

It should be noted that neither of these is the account of the 'disease spirit' given by many accounts of shamanism, and by western practitioners such as Horwitz, as illustrated above. Both required some kind of restoration of balance or function. This does not necessarily mean a discrete distinction, but may refer to differences in the specifics of the cases. A more general view of healing-seidr comes from an account by the seidworker Bil Linzie (not present at any of these situations).

> I have been involved in a large number of healing sessions over the years. From a personal standpoint, I consider everything that I do 'healing.' Sometimes, I heal by eliminating an enemy which might be perhaps a 'disease' ghost, or it might be a physical person. Healing or health, in my mind, comes when the 'dust of turmoil or a crisis' settles – I think in terms of water an awful lot – so when the waves of storm calm.
>
> Healing or health, for me, takes place by making sure that the flow of the Waters is smooth and relatively unimpeded. Sometimes folks become so calm that the Waters stagnate like in a millpond where the outflow has become clogged (this is often expressed as disease with depression or psychosis); sometimes, the Waters dry up because the inlet above the pond is blocked and although it can be deadly it usually repairs up nicely. Sometime cruddy things take up residence in the pond and need to be tossed out;

sometimes, the individual (or a community for any of these) has pissed in its own Waters – having to unlearn bad habits often goes with this type of session.

I generally make a diagnosis with a form of spá. This is usually (though not always) the most difficult part. Sometimes, there are nasty or angry things which must be dealt with first before a diagnosis can even be made.

Usually, the healing ends with a sacrifice of some sort (though not always) – depends much on the overall picture.

Seid-work may inspired by spirits or deities, or calling on their assistance for diagnosis, for information, or for intervention. Who these spirits are varies with the person and the situation: Bil works with nine following 'ghosts', and several plant spirits which he described for me:

I make fairly extensive use of entheogens, in particular, Fliegepilz (amanita muscaria var. muscaria), toloache (datura inoxia), Johnson grass seed (stipa robusta) and several varieties of artemisia (a. lucoviciana; a. franserioides). All of which are legal. I use them to make seidh, both the healing kind and the protective kind. I don't recommend them to anyone, personally. Their ghosts are of their own mind and they will often volunteer their services. They will not be controlled, and toloache can be very dangerous although the others don't have the same personality that he does (which is fairly ruthless and occasionally bloodthirsty).

I only deal with these because they came to me during the period when the spirits had me. They showed me where they grow and how to use them (and still do). They make decisions in many cases and possess skills that I don't have. They can go places I've never heard of and can figure out things that I am unable to.

Most (or many of these plant-ghosts) can be very seductive, I suppose. I personally have never trusted any of them although I find the Fliegepilz to be friendly. All of them have a fairly ruthless side, though, including the Fliegepilz.

When I make a seidh, I work with a team of ghosts; different situations call for different team makeups. Inevitably, one of the members, for me, will be one (or more) of these. They lend power, control, intelligence, or clarity. They come together with others and act through me to make changes here on this Midgard. They maintain an interest here – their physical forms are here – but they are more like ghosts than plants. They are like the blackmarketeers of the ghost world. They can make shady deals, seem to know everyone, have their hands in everyone's cookie jar and are master string-pullers and button pushers.

I've definitely gotten into tight binds because of the way that they work, but they are thorough. They are able to make long range plans far better than I. Sometimes, I'd rather not work with them, but every time I've tried that option there were truly large messes to clean up afterwards.

I work with them because they were the ghosts who picked me up when I was dying. We have a bond, an understanding. They may eventually initiate the end of me as well – this I don't know. But while I live they are my staunchest comrades-in-arms.

But the focus of Bil's work, and others who have spoken to me of this, is not on 'healing' as such but on what Bil calls 'wholemaking', restoring balance – to a person, to a community, letting the waters flow freely – as Thordis spákona acted to bring redress and restoration of property. In the past this balance may have meant, at times, removing a person from the community. In the sagas, as said before, often magic is used against the protagonist: by those who protect their kinfolk or their local community. The ability to cure individual or community, from ill-health or social malaise, whether by shamanic or more conventional means, goes with the power to create disease, to summon spirits to a purpose others perceive as destructive. Further, seidworkers then and now deal with the dead: ancestors who are seen as a source of wisdom.

The unease and ambiguity many feel about these practices may colour the discourse of seidworkers. Bil refers to himself as 'dead'. Others may deal with death, visit places of death, be associated with death, and describe this ambiguity likewise. Here a seidworker describes a first visit to the place of the ancestors during an oracular seidr, where he had met a (dead) seeress who gave him information to relay to querants.

> as the time went by, whatever that was, it got increasingly easier and more and more vivid.. and I was more and more *there*. And at first I had some trouble negotiating being in that world and this world, being in the room and in Hel, but I found the staff very useful, and ended up clinging onto that for dear life quite a lot of the time. That was a good connection. ... And I, I heard – the seeress speak as much as I did 'see' things myself, and pick up, I don't know how else to put it, pick up and sense things from what people were asking ... And I went through [the gates] and it was just darkness everywhere. Loads of darkness. Which was actually very, very nice, because as much as it, you know, didn't feel very pleasant because it was a place of death it was also very pleasant because it *was* a place of death. Quite appealing and welcoming ...

Later he added:

> ... I should think under the wrong circumstances ... it would be very easy to stay there long term.

The seidworker exists between the worlds, part of each or neither. Questions of morality depend on the situation: they are relational, contingent, as are questions of the seidworkers' loyalties to the various communities to which they belong. The seidworker deals in uncertainty and ambiguity, negotiating with allies who one day may take their price.

CONCLUSION

Today people are drawing on evidence from the old literature of the north, and from archaeology, to create their own practical 'shamanisms' within the cosmological context of the well of *Wyrd*, the tree *Yggdrasil*, and the various beings that inhabit the

Nine Worlds. Among other uses, they engage with healing. Their uses, like those of 'shamans' in more 'traditional' societies, are inventive and creative (see Greene, 1998), and they draw on 'shamanistic' practices from elsewhere (though chiefly Sámi and Siberian practices) to recreate ways of relating to their world and ways of benefiting the communities among whom they work. They create practices for today. Rather than viewing these as an attempt to create what might have been or state what is, I relate them as revealing possibility. For seidr practitioners, the past in the imagination of the present creates potentialities, worlds, 'realities'. Conversely, for those, whether seidworkers or academics, who attempt to understand the past, the present gives potential for awareness, not necessarily of historical 'truth', but of complexity, diversity and multivocality.

Notes

1   'Wyrd' is 'fate', or perhaps more accurately the construction of what is and what may result. The Well of Wyrd lies at the roots of Yggdrasill, the world tree, and contains what has been, what is, and what may result.

2   The seid-woman complains that her descendant Gudrun is making a terrible noise over her head and dropping wax on her! Gudrun has become christian, and the area above the seeress' grave serves as her chapel. Here the solution is to remove the bones. The description of the bones as 'blár' – translated variously as blue, black, or blue-black – may connect them in other ways with magic, the otherworlds, and here, of course, death. The cloak of the Greenland Seeress is also 'blár'.

3   Robert Wallis reminds me that they also consume 'extensive quantities of tobacco', as he has described (e.g. Wallis, 1999 and forthcoming).

4   The sagas were written about 200–400 years after 'conversion' to Christianity.

*Research on which this article was based was enabled by a grant from the Social Sciences and Humanities Research Council of Canada.

Bibliography

Mediaeval literature referenced

Eiríks saga rauða:Eirik the Red and other Icelandic sagas trans. G. Jones 1961 Oxford: Oxford University Press.

Egils saga: Egils saga trans. C. Fell 1975 London: J.M.Dent & Sons.

Kormáks saga: The story of Kormak the son of Ogmund trans. W. Morris and E. Magnússon, London: William Morris Society, 1970.

Landnámabók: The book of settlements trans. H. Pálsson and P.G. Edwards 1972 Winnipeg: University of Manitoba Press.

Laxdaela Saga trans. H. Pálsson and M. Magnusson 1969 Harmondsworth: Penguin.

The Vatnsdalers' Saga trans. G. Jones 1973 Princeton: Princeton University Press.

Modern literature referenced

Aðalsteinsson, J.H. 1978 *Under the cloak,* Acta Universitatis Upsaliensis 4, Uppsala: Almqvist & Wiksell.

Basilov, V.N. 1997 *Shamanic worlds: rituals and lore of Siberia and Central Asia,* pp. 3–48 in M.M. Balzer (ed.) Armonk, NY and London: North Castle Books.

Blain, J. 1999 'Seidr as shamanistic practice: reconstituting a tradition of ambiguity' *Shaman* 7(2), 99–121.

Blain, J. 2000 'Speaking Shamanistically: seidr, academia, and rationality', DISKUS. Online. Available HTTP: *http://www.unimarburg.de/religionswissenschaft/journal/diskus/#6*

Blain, J. 2002 *Nine worlds of Seid-magic: ecstasy and neo-shamanism in North European paganism,* London: Routledge.

Blain, J. and Wallis, R.J. 2000 'The 'ergi' seidman: contestations of gender, shamanism and sexuality in northern religion past and present' *Journal of Contemporary Religion,* 15(3), 395–411.

Borovsky, Z. 1999 'Never in public: women and performance in Old Norse literature' *Journal of American Folklore* 112(443), 6–39.

Dubois, T. 1999 *Nordic religions in the Viking Age,* Philadelphia: University of Pennsylvania Press.

Eliade, M. 1964 *Shamanism: archaic techniques of ecstasy,* New York: Pantheon.

Greene, S. 1998 'The shaman's needle: development, shamanic agency, and intermedicality in Aguarina Lands, Peru' *American Ethnologist* 25(4), 634–658.

Høst, A. forthcoming 'Exploring seidhr: a practical study of the seidhr ritual', forthcoming in *Religious practises and beliefs in the North Atlantic area,* Center for North Atlantic Studies, Århus University.

Leto, S. 2000 'Magical potions: entheogenic themes in Scandinavian mythology' *Shaman's Drum* 54, 55–65.

Meulengracht Sørenson, P. 1983 *The unmanly man: concepts of sexual defamation in early Northern society,* trans. J. Turville-Petre, Odense: Odense University Press.

Paxson, D. n.d. 'The return of the Völva', Online. Available HTTP: *http://www.hrafnar.org/seidh/seidh.html*

Paxson, D. in press 'Oracular seidh, past and present: a functional analysis' in *Proceedings of the Viking Millennium symposium,* L'Anse aux Meadows, Newfoundland, September 2000.

Price, N.S. in press 'The archaeology of Seiðr: circumpolar traditions in Viking pre-christian religion', in *Proceedings of the Viking Millennium symposium,* L'Anse aux Meadows, Newfoundland, September 2000.

Price, N.S. forthcoming *The Viking way: religion and war in the later Iron Age of Scandinavia,* Uppsala University Press, Uppsala.

Ripinsky-Naxon, M. 1993 *The nature of shamanism. Substance and function of a religious metaphor,* Albany (NY): State University of New York Press.

Schultes, R.E. and Hofmann, A. 1992 *Plants of the gods: their sacred, healing and hallucinogenic powers,* Healing Arts Press.

Sigurðsson, G. (ed.) 1998 *Eddukvæði,* Reykjavík: Mál og menning.

Storms, G. 1948 *Anglo Saxon magic,* The Hague: Martinus Nijhoff. Rpt. Folcroft Library Editions, 1975.

Wallis, R.J. forthcoming *Shamans/neo-Shamans/Autoarchaeology: Druids, Heathens, Pagans or 'plastic' medicine-men.* London: Routledge.

Wallis, R.J. 1999 'Auto-archaeology and neo-shamanism: the socio-politics of ecstasy', PhD Thesis, Dept. of Archaeology, Southampton University.

Wasson, R. G. 1971 *Soma, divine mushroom of immortality,* New York: Harcourt Brace Jovanovich.

12. Of crystal balls, political power, and changing contexts: what the clever women of Salerno inherited

Christopher J. Knüsel

INTRODUCTION

Ritualists, those whose social role includes the performance of ceremonies, are often depicted in popular magazines, periodicals, and films, yet we know very little about the appearance of them and the objects which supported their role in the poorly documented later prehistoric and early medieval periods. We have ample represent-ations of priests for the High and Late Medieval period of Europe, yet the origins of their paraphernalia are murky and are likely to draw on, to some unspecified extent, pre-Christian practice and practitioners. For example, what was the appearance of the bishop who accompanied Bertha in the sixth century AD to Kent at her marriage to Ethelbert and what sort of ritual practitioners did he encounter who were, presumably, already there? It seems that the latter were formidable enough for Ethelbert to prefer an open-air meeting with the legate Augustine '... by reason of an old superstition [that would not] suffer him to come unto him in any house, lest, if they were skilful in sorcery... [they]... deceive him and prevail against him' (Bede, *Historia Ecclesiastica* I. 25). This paper sets out to aid the reconstruction of the practice and appearance of pre-Christian ritualists from material remains. It highlights the funerary record as supremely informative because of its relationship to social structure and due to its supremely ritualised (van Gennep 1960) and potentially socially contentious character as survivors vie for the status, rights, and privileges of the deceased (cf. Mauss 1990). In this contribution, the related healing and apotropaic aspects of the ritualist are emphasised and examined through the changing funerary contexts of objects that accompany burials in the Early Medieval period.

RITUAL IN EARLY MEDIEVAL EUROPE

There has been hesitancy in archaeological enquiry to address the question of pre-Christian ritual during the Early Medieval period. Wilson (1992), for example, writes that he finds it '...impossible to name the religion practised, the gods worshiped, or the ritual which preceded burial' (p. 3). Wormald echoes this assessment, writing '...a crisis of confidence has overtaken the study of Anglo-Saxon pre-Christian culture' (1993, 939). Wood (1987, 53) comments on the difficulty of defining both Christianity and paganism in the period, noting that the sources of pagan practice are '... infinitely more difficult to use. The Norse legends recorded in later periods may reflect the cosmology of Scandinavians in the ninth century, but they tell us nothing about how religion functioned.' Part of this difficulty arises from attempts to identify and define such concepts through the direct historical approach in which analogies drawn from later medieval society encompass a more institutionalised and uniform social organisation than was present in much of the Early Medieval period (see, for example, discussion in Steuer 1989).

The distinctive features of the world religions, including Christianity, are both doctrinal and social organisational in that they rely on regularised clerical roles, a standard ritual, and formal doctrine, all of which contribute to an authoritative, all-encompassing cosmology and worldview which 'act as social mechanisms for the authoritative control of identity, community, and knowledge across time and space' (Hefner 1993, 122). The success and dissemination of these religions lies in their 'political and moral mechanisms for defending the Word against the babble of disparate truths' (Hefner 1993, 122). This structural homogeneity contrasts markedly with traditional ritual practices and belief systems, which are not institutionalised, have no sacred texts, and are centred on the individual practitioner and his or her personal skills and attributes (James 1952, 33–35; Barker 1993, 214; Hamayon 1994, 81; Hugh-Jones 1994, 33–35). This means that traditional folk religions tend to be ethnocultural rather than doctrinal (Russell 1994, 48). Because early medieval texts are few and, those that do exist, written by unabashedly ecclesiastical hands (cf. Wormald 1978), we are presented with an often inimical and insensitive view of pre-Christian ritual, its performers, its development, and its regional variation. Early Medieval society should be treated as a protohistoric one, much like European later prehistory. It is necessary, then, to rely on analogies and models drawn from pre-state societies, as well as later historical developments, in order to identify and understand pre-Christian ritual and ritualists.

HISTORICAL SOURCES

Within Christianity, there is a strong association between the ritualist (i.e. the priest), healing and miraculous cures. In some cases, this association is so strong that the corporeal remains of the deceased, often recognised as saintly relics, become the subject of veneration. At the turn of the fourteenth century Pope Boniface VIII repeatedly issued Papal Bulls against the practice of defleshing the remains of the saintly in order to retrieve the bones for use as relics of veneration (Brown 1981). In AD 1220 Stephen Langton, Archbishop of Canterbury, on the occasion of the translation and consecration of the tomb of his predecessor, Thomas Becket, distributed remains of the saint to ecclesiastical and temporal potentates present at the event (Butler 1995, 23). Geoffrey Chaucer alluded to the healing powers of this shrine and the remains it housed: '... from every shire's end/ Of England, down to Canterbury they wend/To seek the holy blissful martyr, quick/To give his help to them when they were sick' (*Prologue* Ll. 15–18).

We know, in this case, how Becket was dressed before his interment because the Archbishop had presciently organised the apparel for his burial beforehand.

> 'He had to hand the very garments in which he had been ordained eight years and more before, the alb, a simple 'superhumeral', his mitre, stole and maniple, and the chrismatic (the bandeau set around his head at his episcopal anointing to catch the sacred oil). They left on him the haircloth garments and the monastic robe as decided, and arrayed him in his priestly vestments. Then they added his archiepiscopal tunic, the dalmatic, chasuble and the pallium, which they pinned into position on the shoulders. The gloves were drawn on to his hands. In his right hand they placed a chalice. On his finger outside the glove was set his archiepiscopal ring, and the fingers on his left hand were closed about his pastoral staff' (Urry 1999, 146).

Thus, Thomas was clothed as both a cloistered and secular prelate, arrayed to sing Mass, and as a penitent. The symbols (the *insignia*) of his office (the *dignitas*) were also included. In the High Middle Ages, the mortuary chalice and paten would become a veritable *sine qua non* of priestly burial (see, for example, Stroud and Kemp 1993; Daniell 1997). These enduring symbols of priestly status distinguish these individuals even in the absence of other perishable materials.

There are no similar descriptions of the burial of ritualists from the preceding Early Medieval period, yet – as we shall see below – ethnographic analogy, in addition to historical texts and archaeological remains, would suggest that such individuals might be equally, although differently, apparelled and accompanied in burial. Ethnohistoric sources do provide some tantalising glimpses of pre-Christian practice and ritual paraphernalia.

Gregory of Tours makes few explicit mentions of pre-Christian ritual, but does refer to the 'idolatrous' practices of the Germanic peoples, fashioning '... idols for themselves out of the creatures of the woodlands and the waters, out of birds and beasts ... and to these they made their sacrifices' (*Historia Francorum* II. 9, 125). He also relates the events surrounding a visit of an 'impostor' to Tours who was found to possess '... a big bag filled with the roots of various plants...mole's teeth, the bones of mice, bear's claws and bear's fat ... recognised ... as witchcraft' (IX. 6, 485). This description is very similar to the contents of a bag carried on the belt of a seventeenth-century Finnish sage or shaman[1] (*Tietäjä*). This pouch, which hung from the waist of the *Tietäjä*, contained bones, bear's teeth, and other similar objects said to be connected with healing and protection. The Finnish shaman dressed distinctively for healing ceremonies, wearing a shirt, belt, and cap with animal parts from a diver or squirrel sewn onto it (Siikala 1992a, 71). Siikala notes that this dress resembled an ancient witch's dress. Although these costumes are variable, they are identifiably different enough for them to be unusual within societies (see below). The garments and objects, though, recall similar themes, such that they have been associated with descriptions of individuals from earlier periods.

Thorbjörg, meaning 'the little prophetess' in Old Norse (Simek 1993, 326), the seer of *Eirik the Red's saga*, adorned herself with a necklace of glass beads, catskin gloves, and a lambskin hat lined with white cat's fur. She also carried a staff with a brass-bound knob studded with stones and a pouch in which she kept charms. She ate with a bronze spoon and a knife with the tip broken off (Anon., *Eirik's Saga* 4, 81–88). Although the charms in this pouch are not described, they have been equated with those found with Bronze Age Scandinavian interments. This bag may, thus, have contained '... a piece of amber bead, a small conch shell, ... a small cube of wood, a flint flake, a number of dried roots, a piece of bark, the tail of a grass snake, a falcon's claw, a small, slender pair of tweezers, a bronze knife in a leather case, a razor with a horse's head handle ... a small flint knife stitched into a an intestine or bladder, a small, inch-and-a-half-long leather case in which there was the lower jaw of a young squirrel and a small bladder or intestine containing several small articles ...' (Glob, cited in Glosecki 1989, 99).

Female participation in ceremonies as ritualists, although still hotly contested in today's churches, is attested in pre-Christian rituals. Tacitus writes that the Germans 'believe that there resides in women an element of holiness and a gift of prophecy; and so they do not scorn to ask their advice, or lightly disregard their replies' (*Germania* 8). Although this assertion may simply be a means by which Tacitus chose to represent the 'otherness' of these peoples, there are other sources that support the association he described. The Scandinavian *Seidr*, a seance or a 'sitting' to commune with spirits, was performed by women in a trance, and it was considered unmanly for men to behave in a similar capacity (Glosecki 1989, 97; Siikala 1992b, 81–82). In the eighth-century Lombardic *Leges*, 'soothsayers' are defined as both male and female and are involved in divination and providing answers (Hillgarth 1986, 109). Female 'magicians' are also found in the Later Medieval and post-Medieval periods in Hungary and are considered to have existed in the pre-Christian period (Dömötör 1984). We know the names of some of these individuals, such as the Bructerian Veleda, an unmarried woman who, in AD 69, prophesied the destruction of Roman legions and, as a result, 'enjoyed wide influence over the tribe of the Bructeri' (Tacitus, *Histories* IV, 61).

In a review of Anglo-Saxon witchcraft and magic, Meaney (1989, 30) notes that the prescriptions seem largely to relate to 'young women looking for lovers, wives trying to win the favour of their husbands, or to produce a live baby, or mothers anxious for the health of their children.' Perhaps, then, it is to the realm of female interments and their grave goods that we should turn to find ritual objects and ritualists. Unfortunately, we have no adequate descriptions of how Veleda or any other ritualist, male or female, looked or what objects supported their role in AD 69 or thereafter. Thus, we must turn to ethnographic analogy in order to create an image of how such individuals might have appeared and how this and their ritual acts might be displayed in the material remains of the past.

ETHNOGRAPHIC ANALOGY

Symbols are said to make the shaman (Hoppál 1992, 127). Manipulation of these symbols in the performance of ceremonies contributes to the popular support of individual shamans. In animistic societies natural features and processes can symbolise social processes, rather than being metaphors generated by society from natural features and events, as is often assumed to be the case (Humphrey 1996, 55). The effect is to mystify social processes rather than the natural world. This situation suggests that to control the acquisition and meaning of symbols could have the effect of altering social processes at the same time, as well as perspectives of the natural world, its landscapes, and its resources. Herein resides an implicit power of ritualists and also confers upon them a potentially ambivalent disposition. They are both defenders against evil and misfortune and casters of malicious spells.

The shamanic costume is replete with the symbols of shamanic status. Objects typical of such costumes include distinctive clothing, such as ornately decorated belts; hats, which often incorporate antlers or horns and other animal parts; and gloves, sometimes with an odd number of fingers. Other decorations include crystals, metal, shell, and bead accoutrements, metal rings, bells, and animal and human figures (Djakonova 1978; Graceva 1978). Shamanic rites also often incorporate tambourines or drums, sieve-spoon drumsticks, mirrors, and wooden wands or staves that in some cases may resemble a horse (Eliade 1964) or contain parts of animals, such as a hoof (McGregor 1943). Some of these items may function as utilitarian household objects in other contexts (Siikala 1992c, 8), but in the hands of the ritualist they take on other, more profound meanings. Animals and parts of animals symbolise the helpers that aid the transformative process of moving between worlds (Vitebsky 1995).

Due to differences in topography, climate, cultural inclination and social and economic disposition (Winkelman 1990), these symbols vary from one region and time to another, especially when the objects are related to the idiosyncrasies of individual ritualists (cf. Humphrey 1996). The rigours of archaeological preservation means that the perishable materials are unlikely to be recovered, leaving only the more resilient ornaments. Among these many and varied objects, crystals are reported to make up part of the paraphernalia of ritual specialists worldwide; although their specific meanings differ somewhat from one society to another. Despite being polysemic, in many societies they have a spiritual importance. For example, the crystal ball, so popularly associated with fortune telling and mystical vision, today, is identified as 'symbolic of the divine world of light before the creation of the earth' in Ferguson's (1961, 175) *Signs and Symbols in Christian Art*. Kieckhefer (1989) notes that crystal-gazing was used in the Later Medieval period as a means of divination, sometimes in conjunction with a mirror or other reflective surface to conjure supposedly evil spirits.

Eliade (1964, 350) notes the significance of crystals when he writes, 'The *Manang* [shaman] has a box containing a quantity of magical objects, the most important of which are quartz crystals, *bata ilau* (the 'stones of light') by the help of which the shaman discovers the patient's soul'. Illness is understood to result from the flight of the soul from the patient's body (soul flight). Further evidence of the crystal's importance comes from the Cobeno of South America where the shaman introduces crystals into the novice's head so that these may eat out the brain and eyes, replace these organs, and become his strength (Eliade 1964, 52).

Among the Kwakiutl of the North West Pacific Coast, Boas (1966, 136) reported that 'A small pouch is often attached to the neck ring [a shaman wears], in which small objects are kept.... these are worn by him permanently. The quartz crystal representing the super-natural power is used by many shamans.' Barbeau (1958) records that a novice shaman on the Pacific Northwest Coast of North America of high social standing received an amuletic crystal from a crane in order to cure a chief's foot injury.

Alternatively, crystals might also have a negative connotation. In Australia, the evulsed central incisors of a boy who had undergone initiation were not to be carried with crystals, which were considered magical substances. If the teeth came into contact with the crystals they would absorb magic and bring injury to the boy (Frazer 1993, 38). It is apparent from these descriptions that the crystals provide the ritualist with curative powers that may also play a part in his or her rite of passage to become a healer, as well as symbolising a protective force. Ritualists act in a world that is '… in constant danger of attack by numerous evil spirits causing sickness and death and is, in fact, actually attacked by them. If there is one person who is powerful enough to defend the human world against them, it is the shaman who is acquainted with a variety of spirits. He is the virtuoso in the world of spirits. He "knows" the ways and strategies of evil spirits causing sickness and death, and he alone is endowed with the capacity to "see" the spirits' (Waida 1992, 234).

ANGLO-SAXON ENGLAND AND POST-ROMAN EUROPE

In her review of burial inclusions in Anglo-Saxon graves, Meaney (1981, 1989) has argued that many of the objects interred with the dead had amuletic and curative properties that were intended to confer protection on the owner/deceased. Most prominent among these are groups of objects found in the vicinity of the pelvis and thigh along the left side of the interments of females (see Meaney 1981; Knüsel and Ripley 2000). Among them are: staves; sieve-spoons; cowrie shells; animal teeth, claws, antlers and horns; girdle-rings; 'toilet implements' such as earscoops; model implements; 'Hercules Club' pendants; keys; girdle-hangers; and workboxes; as well as crystal beads and balls. Meaney (1989, 9–10) identifies three of these as being most commonly connected with women in archaeological contexts. These are crystal balls, usually in metal slings, cylindrical bronze boxes hung on chatelaine chains with inclusions of fabric and herbs, and a group of artefacts found beside the left side of the body, perhaps remnants of a bag, which contained broken glass, rings of bronze and iron, curated heirlooms and animal remains. The contents of these containers seem to suggest some of the same types of inclusions as those described by Gregory of Tours and that he found so deviant (see above). Like the ones described by Gregory, some of these may have had medicinal or apotropaic associations.

During the Anglo-Saxon period, crystal balls often occur with perforated spoons of Roman design, sometimes without their handles, in a minority of female burials. Meaney (1981, 86) records 78 instances of crystal balls; although this number has no doubt increased in the intervening years. These objects follow a distribution through the Upper Rhineland and northern France into central Europe and along the Danube into Eastern Europe and the Crimea (Roes 1958; Hinz 1966), where the earliest occurrence is in a 4th–3rd century BC Greco-Scythian grave context and the latest in the Viking period at Birka (Rice, cited in Meaney 1981, 84). In England burials with crystal balls and spoons cluster in Kent; although they do occur sporadically elsewhere (Meaney 1981). This distribution and dating would suggest a pre-Christian significance or meanings, depending on their context, for these objects, especially since Scandinavia was one the last areas of Europe to be Christianised. Burials containing these objects have never been adequately explained, although they have been considered to be amuletic, symbolic, an ethnic marker, an indicator of high status, or a combination of these (Meaney 1981; Speake 1989; White 1988, 1990). The assemblages also include girdlehangers, knives, brooches, necklaces, buckles, pottery or metal vessels, and weaving battens in a variety of combinations. Similar objects have also been found in Iron Age and Roman burials and amongst ritual site assemblages (Kirk 1949; Woodward 1992). Although the individuals involved are said to be women in all instances, in many cases no reference is made as to how this assessment was determined; although grave good associations appear to be the salient indicator in many. Fausett first recorded some of these objects in the 1880's, which has occasioned Shephard (1979) and Huggett and Richards (1990) to question the accuracy and rigour of the age and sex assessments.

It is obvious from these assessments that there is considerable debate over the meaning of these enigmatic objects (see Knüsel and Ripley 2000), but their wide spatial and temporal distribution would indicate that they are unlikely to be ethnic markers as they have previously been considered (see also discussion in Lucy 2000). Some are indeed found in well-accompanied burials of then, presumably, high status individuals (see below). Equally, they appear not to be entirely related to the sex of the deceased (cf. Lucy 1997; Knüsel and Ripley 2000; and below). Rather, they seem to represent something about the interred that relates either to their lives or their deaths that the living considered to represent in the funerary context and during the laying out of the deceased.

SOME SPECIFIC EXAMPLES

This section reviews some of the interments that have crystals and/or spoons incorporated among their grave inclusions. It is beyond the scope of the present paper to consider all such occurrences. In some of these burials, it may be that the objects relate to a simple symbolic protection of females, as is the case for objects such as beads and coins worn by women in the Near East today and in the recent past. For example, green cornerless cube agate beads are considered to neutralise the effects of menstruation blood upon women in childbirth. Thus a woman who has experienced difficulties in childbirth may have these beads included in a necklace. Alternatively, cowrie shells, triangular mother-of-pearl pendants, and black glass beads are considered to ward off the 'evil eye' (Mershen 1991). Among the burials discussed in this contribution are some of the most distinctive excavated from the Early Medieval period; they have been selected because their interments and the combination of objects they contain provide a context for the crystals, which suggest potential meanings for these objects.

The sixth-century Burial 45, at Chessel Down on the Isle of Wight, contained a

Figure 12.1. The crystal ball and silver sling from Chessel Down, Isle of Wight Burial 45 (Reproduced with permission of the British Museum).

crystal ball in a silver sling (Fig. 12.1) and spoon combination between the knees, among other grave inclusions distributed throughout the burial, including parts of a gold braid; an iron key; three brooches, one square-headed, one disc, and one short-long brooch; a bead necklace; a knife; a buckle; and three buckets at the foot end of the grave (Arnold 1982). There was also an iron weaving sword or batten, the presence of which might simply suggest that this instrument had a female connotation. In other contexts, this object has been interpreted as a symbol of a craft specialisation or as representative of 'the goddess who weaves', a depiction found on bracteates (coins) (though not included in the burial of Chessel Down 45) from Scandinavian and Continental sources in the post-Roman period. The goddess depicted on these bracteates also holds a crystal ball with a cross atop it that resembles royal and imperial insignia (e.g. an orb). It may also be an allusion to the peace brought between peoples through marriage alliances (Enright 1990).

A crystal bead, which was part of a necklace, accompanies Grave 49 at Sewerby, East Yorkshire, that of a female aged about 20 to 25 years of age at death, who was buried in the late fifth to sixth centuries AD. This individual was 'by far the most lavish in the part of the cemetery dug' (Hirst 1985, 39). A cairn and two postholes identified the place of burial of this young female. Her interment was the only one at the site to be adorned with a cairn. The grave inclusions included an unmatched pair of square-headed brooches with intricate designs, the remains of a box, in addition to a bronze cauldron, and a ring from a purse or bag found in the vicinity of the left femur. Above her were the remains of an older woman, G41, buried in a prone position with a sooty fragment of a beehive quern over the pelvic area. This individual is argued to have been interred alive (Hirst 1985, 39–40), but may, in fact, have died in a fire (Anderson 1994). The skeleton certainly has the 'pugilistic pose' of a fire victim in which the contraction of the flexor muscles in the hands, arms, thighs and legs in the heat of the fire produce a posture similar to that of G41 (Bass 1984, 160; Knight 1991, 285–287 and Figs. 11.4 and 11.8). This assessment does not indicate intent (see discussion in Lucy 2000, 78–80); this individual may have been exposed to fire either accidentally or intentionally. Above these two burials, a wooden vessel had been placed. This vessel may relate to an offering to the deceased, indicating that the cairn was visited sometime after the interment was made.

A disturbed seventh-century tumulus burial at Swallowcliffe Down, Wiltshire, lay on the highest point on the Down within a previously existing Bronze Age barrow. This female burial was placed on a decorated wooden bier (referred to as 'bed burial') and contained an iron pan, a bucket, the remains of a decorated satchel, a tapered rod thought to be a spindle, and two glass palm-cups. In addition, there were also remnants of a wooden box or casket that contained two knives, a bone comb, amber and glass beads, four silver brooches, a tin-bronzed strapmount and, in close proximity to one another, a bronze sprinkler or strainer and a silver spoon. The silver spoon is a unique object, decorated as it is with head of a bird from whose open mouth springs the handle. Speake (1989) has suggested that the close proximity of these two objects is similar to other burials that contain a spoon and crystal ball, although in this case the crystal ball is replaced by the sprinkler/strainer. The burial was marked with a post-hole at the northeast corner of the grave, suggesting that it was perhaps a landmark. Being located on a later parish boundary and within a Bronze Age barrow, with other tumuli at some remove from it, makes this burial a liminal one.

The burial of a diminutive female, only 4' 7" (139.7 cm) tall, and dating to before AD 550, was excavated from an annex some 18' (roughly 5 m) beneath the floor of Cologne Cathedral in Germany. The individual lay within a tomb made of stone slabs, accompanied by a large group of gold and cloisonné jewellery, including a gold-mounted crystal ball, a silver bulla or amulet box, and a cloth or leather purse containing glass and crystal beads, and two silver coins of Theodoric and Athalaric (AD 526–534), respectively. At the foot end of the grave was a lime-wood box that contained a leather slipper, a leather bottle with a wooden cork, a pottery spindle whorl, fragments of gold brocade, wool and fabrics, hazelnuts, a walnut, and a date-stone. The woman was interred wearing a cloak held in place by strap ends of garnet within the designs of which one can see the form of a cicada, a symbol Werner associates with eternal life and 'royal dignity' (1964, 202).

The decoration on of these strap ends is reminiscent of the 300 gold insects identified variously as cicadas by Werner (1964) or bees by Kazanski (1997) found in the tomb of Childéric, who was interred beneath a tumulus measuring 10 x 40 m, in the year AD 481–482 in Tournai, in what is today Belgium. This burial was arranged by his son,

Clovis, the first Christian ruler of the Franks (see Moorhead (1985) for a discussion of Clovis' religious persuasions). The burial goods, recovered in 1653, when the tomb was excavated, were for the greater part stolen in 1831 and lost or destroyed. Among them, though, was jewellery consisting of red garnets mounted in gold cloisonné, some in the shape of a horse's head, and others, including a signet ring bearing Childéric's image and his name; weapons, including two swords decorated with gold, a scramasaxe, a lance, and a hatchet. In addition, this burial contained the head of a horse with its horse harness and 200 silver and 100 gold coins minted in Constantinople between AD 476 and 491, these last being found in a purse (Werner 1964; Kazanski 1997). An object originally identified as a stylus is now considered to be gold cross-bow fibula, similar to those worn in the Late Roman period by imperial officials (James 1992). An unmounted rock crystal ball also made up a part of this elaborate and varied assemblage (Kazanski 1997, 66, depicted in Meaney 1981, 87). Childéric's tumulus was found some distance from the church of Saint-Brice, which was founded later, in an extensive burial ground that developed around Childéric's tumulus after its creation. Several ditches, about 15 to 20 m from the burial, contained the remains of horses, mostly stallions and some geldings, numbering over 20 animals (Brulet et al. 1988).

These interments, all dating from the fifth to seventh centuries AD provide an outline of the changing circumstances under which crystals have been found. All but one is a female burial, and the male burial, that of Childéric, shares its tumulus with that from Chessel Down and Swallowcliffe Down and probably with the Sewerby burial, while the female from Cologne Cathedral comes from what would later become a sacred building. Given the provenance of this burial, though, it may be that it differs from Childéric's tumulus only in that it became incorporated into the fabric of the later Cathedral. The occurrence of the crystals, though, joins what may seem otherwise to be unrelated interments.

A RITUAL CONTEXT FOR THE HEALING ARTS

Recent interpretations of female interments with crystals have concentrated on their being apparently associated with '"high status", possibly royal, graves' (Pollington 2000, 48). This assessment would seem to draw support from the inclusion of the rock crystal ball in Childéric's burial. This interpretation, though, does not explain what aspect of this presumed high status role such inclusions represented. The origin of this interpretation comes from the crystal balls being associated with sieve or perforated spoons. Meaney (1981) interpreted these perforated spoons as strainers for skimming wine, a presumed activity of wealthy women at table in the feasting hall, an ascription which would support the notion of these being female aristocrats. More recently, Speake (1989) has dismissed this interpretation. He notes that the perforations of such spoons are too large and too small in number to have been used as strainers of liquid. In addition, he argues that this function does not explain why these spoons should be found with crystal balls. Rather, Speake (1989) believes that they may be associated with the sprinkling of aromatic liquids to disguise offensive odours.

Figure 12.2. The rock crystal charm in its silver mounting of the Stewarts of Ardsheal (MOSP53). (Reproduced with permission of the National Museum of Scotland).

Legend has it that a curative concoction was made of water in which a crystal sphere had been washed or boiled. 'On May Day in Scotland cattle were sprinkled with water in which a crystal ball had been washed' (Speake 1989, 41). A similar 'rock crystal charm' with a silver mount attached to a silver chain resides in the National Museum of Scotland (MOSP53). This object once belonged to the Stewarts of Ardsheal and was 'dipped in drinking water as a protection against disease and death' (Fig. 12.2).

Speake (1989, 41) believes that the sprinkler from Swallowcliffe Down may have been filled in a hanging bowl. Perhaps the bucket found at the foot-end of the grave served this purpose. When filled with water, this vessel or the iron pan, also found in the burial, could produce a reflective surface. Crystal balls and spoons, then, may be associated with a protective or healing rite and, possibly, one involving divination of spirits to aid in these procedures.

There are other pieces of evidence to support the idea that these objects are part of a ritualist-healer's accoutrements. During the rite of passage undertaken by Odin in his bid to attain greater wisdom, the god learns a series of chants, including a thirteenth that reads, 'If I sprinkle water over a child he will never fall in the thick of battle nor falter and sink in the swordplay' (Crossley-Holland 1993, 17). Furthermore, Bonser (1963, 154) emphasises that a bronze spoon makes up part of the regalia of Thorbjörg during her *seidr*, a séance commenced with a chant, designed to prophesy when a famine would relent in *Eirik the Red's Saga*. The function of the spoon in this passage seems only to do with eating a meal consisting of gruel and the hearts of various animals. That this spoon, though, is mentioned specifically with a knife from which the tip had broken might suggest that it had significance beyond being a mere utensil. Lvova (1978) notes the spoon's function in the healing séance among the Chulym Turks, being used to stir food from which evil spirits were fed, and then also as a source of a divination rite in which the spoon was thrown over the shaman's shoulder and, if landing bottom up, the patient would be cured.

Although Meaney (1981) rightly questions the ascription of the perforated spoons as Christian elements used to celebrate the Eucharist, she discounts this interpretation because of the object's association with women. She argues that this would militate against such a ritual association. She did not consider the possibility that they functioned in pre-Christian rites that involved women that would only later become the prerogative of men, however. The perforated spoons and sprinkler may be argued to have been, in essence, examples of the *aspergillum*, a brush or a perforated globe holding a sponge that is used by Christian priests to sprinkle the altar, clergy, and parishioners with holy water; 'it symbolizes the purification from and the expulsion of evil' (Ferguson 1961, 162) – essentially exorcism. Thus, in AD 601 Bede reports that Pope Gregory advised Bishop Mellitus to resist destruction of pagan temples, but rather to asperse them with holy water to purify them from the worship of demons and to prepare them for Christian liturgy in a setting familiar to the local populace (Bede, *Historia Ecclesiastica* I. 30). Aspersion also often functioned in the funerary domain. Myrc's *Liber Festivialis*, a collection of sermons for the higher festivals of the Christian year, describes sprinkling to deprive fiends of power in the grave (Erbe 1905, 295). Misuse of such measures was associated with witchcraft in the Later Medieval period. Myrc's *Instructions for Parish Priests* makes specific allusion to the excommunication of 'all that make expiments [i.e. experiments] or witchcrafte or charmes with oynements of holy chirch' (Ll. 733–735). A variety of sources document the sprinkling of the grave and the deceased in the Later Medieval period (see, for example, illustrations of a priest using an *aspergillum* in Basing 1990, 104 and Binski 1996, Plate V), a practice which continues today in Roman Catholic funerals. Similarly, the earlier Visigothic liturgies recommend sprinkling the body and the grave with the *aspergillum*, an act designed to protect the grave from attacks from the devil (Ariès 1981, 141). Since healing rites often involve the casting out of unwanted spirits, this seems a related function.

A similar motivation – to cast out or protect from evil – may explain the figure of the Virgin Mary that stands on the mantelpiece in the kitchen of the later medieval hospital, Hôtel Dieu, at Beaune in Burgundy. She, too, holds an *aspergillum* (Fig. 12.3). This figure, in the context of a hospital, again suggests the association of such objects with healing and, possibly, protection. The question, then, remains: were these symbolic objects actually used in healing or were they simply symbols associated with protection from evil influences, perhaps including sickness, in the Anglo-Saxon period? Speake notes that the bowl of the silver spoon in the Swallowcliffe Down burial exhibits scratches that suggest use. Furthermore, this spoon was repaired in antiquity, probably employing some perishable material to join the two pieces of the broken handle. It seems that these burials may relate to the role of a ritualist-healer at least in

Figure 12.3. Figure of the Virgin Mary holding an aspergillum *from the kitchen of the medieval hospital at Beaune, Burgundy (author's photograph).*

some instances, and perhaps to the protection against illness that such objects conferred in others. In these contexts the crystal ball and sieve-spoons may have been used together to asperse water that warded off evil, including the evil that inhabited the sick.

When addressing the people engaged in healing Meaney (1989), Rubin (1989) and Pollington (2000) note that there is little literary evidence dating to the Early Medieval period that relates to women (or men, for that matter) acting as healers; although Meaney notes that the seventh-century *Pseudo-Ecgbert Penitential* prescribes penance for women who treated their children with 'witchcraft'. Previously, only one inhumation has been interpreted, potentially, as that of a female healer in England. Dickinson (1992) identifies a burial from the northern fringe of a later fifth to early sixth century burial ground at Bidford-on-Avon, Warwickshire, as possibly represent-ative of one of these individuals because of the odd inclusions found in what appears to be a decayed leather bag found between the left forearm and hip. It contained two rings, one of copper alloy and the other of iron with a twill weave in animal fibre; a small, worn disk-headed bronze stud; and an antler cone. These oddments lay in close proximity to a knife with a handle made of animal bone and decorated with a double ring and dot motif. Dickinson believes this individual to have been a 'cunning woman', the abilities of whom Pollington (2000, 45) associates with herbal knowledge. This burial, like those discussed above, is unique, but does not contain the spoon and crystal ball combination. It seems that some females in the Early Medieval period were interred with materials used to effect cures, perhaps one aspect of a number of women's roles in the period. In this context, the crystal bead found with Sewerby 49 and the crystal ball in the female burial in Cologne Cathedral may be representative of protective charms. The female burials from Swallowcliffe and Chessel Down with their crystal balls and perforated spoons may thus be more suggestive of the performance of a healing and protective rite. These women may have been perceived as pre-eminent in their ability to harness curative and protective powers.

THE INHERITANCE OF THE CLEVER WOMEN OF SALERNO

Salerno, in Italy, developed as a centre of medicine by the 900s and, by the tenth and eleventh centuries, many clergy and the 'women of Salerno' became associated with the place. At this early date their skill was more in practice than in textual medicine, but by the twelfth century, with the role of medicine becoming more prominent and training more rigorous, the study of medicine became more formal with an established curriculum. These successors of the early practitioners began, by then, to contribute to treatises on the subject. Medical training and practice was limited to men for the most part, as it was until comparatively recently. However, among these early practitioners were women. Some 24 names of women active as surgeons are known from Naples between 1273 and 1410. The most famous of these learned female practitioners was Trota or Trotula, of Salerno, who flourished in the twelfth century and, although much maligned in later centuries as a charlatan, did write a general work on medicine (Siraisi 1990; Rawcliffe 1995). Dame Trotula, who became famous and legendary for expertise in the healing arts, appears as Empress or Queen of Mid-Wives, holding the symbolic orb (Jones 1998, 28) (Fig. 12.4).

By this date, women formed a small minority involved in formalised healing, although many women were likely engaged in healing arts but have left no literary trace of their existence, nor, it seems, did their contemporaries record them. Jones (1998) notes the scarcity of depictions of women in the illuminated manuscripts of the Later Medieval period. He writes:

> 'The pictures must give a misleading idea of the scale of the activities of women, as well as of their importance. In rural communities 'wise women' and midwives no doubt did much of the prescribing and treatment required, without help of books. But there were women who achieved the status of recognised practitioners, with a proper knowledge of the medical authorities, particularly in Italy. Still more women practised strictly within the circle of their family of household, where books in the vernacular could play a vital role in passing down a modicum of medical knowledge from generation to generation' (1998, 28).

This later medieval involvement of women in healing begs the question of earlier precedent. Given that some women such as those from Swallowcliffe Down and Chessel Down received such marked and elaborate burials, why did they draw so little attention from the chroniclers of the time? Hamayon (cited in Humphrey 1994, 193–194) observes that '...shamanism in any hierarchical system, let alone a state, becomes marginalised, feminised, and fragmented.' Early Medieval Europe is clearly

Figure 12.4. Dame Trotula holding the orb as 'Empress of Mid-Wives' (reproduced with permission of the Wellcome Trust, University Collge London).

dominated by the process of state formation, first in Merovingian Gaul and then in more northerly regions (Hodges 1986), therefore, one might expect ritualists following a pre-Christian tradition to have been affected in a similar manner. It is also possible that ritual knowledge was hidden from missionaries and ecclesiastics due to its secret nature, as has been the case more recently (Sokolova 1989), perhaps even out of fear for the practitioners and their powers among members of the indigenous group (Yengoyan 1993, 242). Even where the ritualist's role has survived the acculturative process they have often been derided as being much inferior to those of the past (Eliade 1964, 67, 249 *passim.*). Instead of assuming, though, that these omissions are a happenstance of the past, it is equally likely, if not more so, that these women also fell prey to the social and political transformations of early medieval society.

The demise of ritualists plays a role in the disintegration of pre-state society and culture as a whole. The ritualists act as the keepers of a type of knowledge and practice in preliterate societies that makes them a threat to emergent rulers and administrators as they contend for social, political, and economic control within society (cf. Fisher 1992; Humphrey 1994; Knüsel forthcoming). That ritualists were integral to their societies and central to the political and social circumstances makes them targets for suppression in the process of state formation when spiritual and political roles are increasingly combined in a single personage (cf. Humphrey 1994). This association would have been a threat to the functioning of pre-Christian ritualists in Europe, as it has been demonstrated to be elsewhere.

Support for this argument comes from near contemporary sources. The seventh-century *Penitential* ascribed to the Archbishop (of Canterbury) Theodore recommends penance for those who engaged in incantation and divination. In the later, much less benign ninth-century Laws of Alfred, we read the following: 'Do not allow the women who are accustomed to receive enchanters [e.g. those who use incantations], magicians [e.g. those who use illusion] and witches [*wican*] to live' (quoted in Meaney 1989, 20). In the course of early medieval state formation, these individuals and the objects that supported their role became debased, perhaps only mere decoration for the emergent élites. The paramounts, their emissaries, and their followers usurped their original functions and the roles they supported. Proselytizing Christian missionaries aided this process through syncretic mixing of pre-Christian and Christian concepts, ensuring the survival of the former, despite the adoption of Christianity (Maxwell-Stuart 2000). The non-Christian healer may thus have gone underground beneath the pressure of emerging rulers who linked Christianity with powerful political allies. It is informative, in this light, to note that Charlemagne, beneath the guise of Christian piety, prohibited the conquered Saxons from burying under mounds and destroyed the Irminsul, a sacred place and depository for gold and silver, in his hegemonisation of Saxon lands (Collins 1998, 48). This prohibition and destruction struck at those places that supported the regional paramounts and their followers whom Charlemagne would vanquish. It is likely that the activities of ritualists were also placed under proscription as part of the old order. In this case, objects associated with pre-Christian healing were essentially destroyed in the act of burial, which may have appeared or had been interpreted as – at least outwardly to some – an act of commemoration.

A more recent example of how political changes make their impression in the ritual realm demonstrates how such a scenario is played out. During China's Cultural Revolution a *Yadgan* or shaman decided not to pass on his ritual knowledge because he believed that, if he did so, he would only become 'a nail in the eye of other people and meat in the mouths of other people' (Humphrey 1996, 212). He bundled up his shaman costume and instructed that it be put away in the granary, a high place, which previously had meant a cliff or a mountain, the usual places in which such objects were abandoned. With this he ended his line. Subsequently, the costume was buried to avoid it being plundered during the unrest of the Cultural Revolution. As a consequence, though, many of his descendants were said to have committed suicide.

That Childéric's burial was made in the old style – beneath a mound, rather than within a church – with numerous elaborate and unique grave inclusions and later surrounded by other burials may represent his role as the protector of his people. Germanic sacral kingship involved the paramount acting as the mediator with the divine and saw the tribal fortunes associated with his person (cf. de Vries, cited in

Figure 12.5. The shrine of Charlemagne from Aachen Cathedral (Reproduced with permission of Aachen Cathedral). The crystal ball in a mount appears in the centre of the five ornaments that decorate the top of the shrine.

Russell 1994, 173, note 142). The crystal ball, then, perhaps represents a symbol of sacral protection within the burial. Furthermore, it seems clear that Clovis, armed with the new religion and styled as 'Consul' or 'Augustus' according to Gregory of Tours (*Historia Francorum*, II. 38), removed the symbols of his father's authority with the burial. Clovis had abandoned notions of divine decent (Russell 1994, 175) and, unlike his father and in a manner similar to Constantine the Great, he was interred, it seems, in the church of the Holy Apostles, later re-dedicated to St. Geneviève, in Paris (Périn 1992).

Later in time, the crystal ball, this time mounted in gold, makes another appearance atop the twelfth or thirteenth century gold-bedecked shrine that covered the tomb of Charlemagne (d. AD 814) in the Cathedral he founded at Aachen (see Schleifring and Koch 1989) (Fig. 12.5).

Einhard (1969, 84) records the inscription that adorned the tomb: 'Beneath this stone lies the body of Charles the Great, the Christian Emperor, who greatly expanded the kingdom of the Franks and reigned successfully for forty-seven years. He died when more then seventy years old in the eight hundred and fourteenth year of our Lord, in the seventh tax-year, on 28 January.' Einhard notes that Louis the Pious succeeded his father 'by divine right' (1969, 90). The tomb was opened by Otto III in the year 1000 to find the Emperor's body, nearly uncorrupted, seated on a sort of throne wearing a gold crown and holding a sceptre in gloved hands (although see Dierkens 1991). Thus the crystal ball may have retained its association with divine protection, but now it was associated with the ruler; it had been co-opted from the realm of females to one associated with monarchy, empire, and dynastic aggrandisement.

This transition is similar to the one that saw the Emerald Buddha of Thailand develop from a religious relic to become enshrined within the grounds of the royal residence at Bangkok 'as patron and guardian, at one and the same time, of the Chakkri dynasty and the country over which it rules' (Tambiah 1984, 214–215). A later development, in the seventeenth and eighteenth centuries, saw divine right kings in France and England touching for the king's evil or *mal le roi*, which was considered an effective cure for scrofula (i.e. a form of tuberculosis affecting the lymph nodes in the neck). This tradition of the king's touching as a cure, documented for the first time among the early Capetian and Norman kings of France and England, respectively, may descend from an earlier tradition (Bloch 1973). Gregory of Tours relates how a woman clandestinely snipped a few threads from the cloak worn by the Merovingian King Guntram (AD 561–592), steeped them in water, and administered them to her son as an infusion that brought about a cure for a recurrent fever (*Historia Francorum* IX, 21) (see also Bloch 1973, 16–18). Healing became a royal prerogative and an extension of the sacral character of monarchs, a testament to their closeness to the divine and to God.

The changing contexts of the crystal ball shows it now to be a symbol of mystical vision, then symbolic of healing and protection, and again a symbol of temporal power. The clever women of Salerno indicate a pattern of female participation in healing that was considerably older, if equally underplayed. The close association between medicine and the clergy combined to mix therapeutic treatment with care for the soul through prayer as ministered by men to the exclusion of women, even holy women, who required a male priest to perform the sacrament. This mix of therapy with submission to the supernatural would not seem out-of-place in the apparently animistic world of the Early Medieval period. The inheritance of healing rites seems to have been bilateral through a syncretic mixing of practices and concepts.

Acknowledgements
My thanks go to Gilly Carr and Patty Baker for organising the session on Medical Anthropology and Archaeology at Magdalene College, Cambridge, from which this contribution sprang. John Robb and Joanna Sofaer-Deverenski arranged for the presentation of a version of these 'non-skeletal' ideas as part of their material culture seminar series in the Department of Archaeology, University of Southampton. For their and their colleagues' comments I am grateful. I also thank Miranda Green, Gilly Carr, and Sam Lucy for their reviews of the manuscript and suggestions for its improvement. This piece benefited greatly from Carol Palmer's reading, editing and remembrances of her grandmother and her 'funny ideas'. As usual, however, the responsibility for the final form and content of this contribution rests with the author.

Notes

1   In order to clarify the potential, contentious associations of this term, the word shaman is
     intended here in a general way to identify a ritualist in pre-state societies. The word
     'priest' or 'priestess' is not used because these ritualists gain their power from their office
     (the *dignitas*), which relates to their position in a well-established hierarchy. There is no
     suggestion that pre-state Europeans recognised such hierarchies. To invoke them, then, is
     potentially anachronistic. The term shaman is used to describe individuals who have
     some connection to a spirit world or spirits. It seems that Tacitus and Bede referred to
     these individuals as *sacerdotes*, although this general term may relate to a myriad of
     individual distinctions for which we have lost the original significance. The term shaman
     is used in modern anthropological discourse to describe individuals known by many
     names, most of which have no equivalent in European languages. These names when
     rendered as 'witch', 'diviner', 'soothsayer', 'sorcerer', 'medicine man', 'prophet' or
     'magician' were often used in a pejorative or an inexact manner to describe indigenous
     ritualists and their activities. The term 'shaman', derived from a Tungusian (i.e. Siberian)
     word 'hammas' or 'saman' (Eliade 1964, 4) avoids the negative connotations often
     associated with these terms.

Bibliography

Anderson, T. 1994 'Palaeopathology: more than just dry bones' *Proceedings of the Royal College
     of Physicians of Edinburgh* 24, 554–580.
Anonymous 1996 *The vinland sagas: the Norse discovery of America*, Translated by Magnus
     Magnusson and Herman Pálsson. Harmondsworth: Penguin Books.
Ariès, P. 1981 *The hour of our death*, Translated by Helen Weaver. New York: Vintage Books.
Arnold, C.J. 1982 *The Anglo-Saxon cemeteries on the Isle of Wight*, London: The British Museum.
Basing, P. 1990 *Trades and crafts in Medieval manuscripts*, London: The British Library.
Barbeau, M. 1958 *Medicine men on the North Pacific Coast*, Ottawa: National Museum of Canada
     Bulletin No. 152, Anthropology Series No. 42.
Barker, J. 1993 "We are Ekelesia': conversion in Uiaku, Papua New Guinea', pp. 199–230 in
     R.W. Hefner (ed.) *Conversion to christianity: historical and anthropological perspectives on a
     great transformation*, Berkeley: University of California Press.
Basing, P. 1990 *Trades and Crafts in Medieval Manuscripts*, London: British Museum Press.
Bass, W.M. 1984 'Is it possible to consume a body completely in a fire?' pp. 159–167 in T.A.
     Rathbun and J.E. Buikstra (eds) *Human identification: case studies in forensic anthropology*,
     Springfield (IL.): Charles C.Thomas.
Bede, The Venerable 1994 *Ecclesiastical history of the English nation*, Volume 1. Translated by J.E.
     King. Cambridge, MA: Harvard University Press, Loeb Classical Library.
Binski, P. 1996 *Medieval death*, London: The British Museum Press.
Bloch, M. 1973 *The royal touch*, London: Routledge and Kegan Paul.
Boas, F. 1966 *Kwakiutl ethnography*, Chicago: University of Chicago Press.
Bonser, W. 1963 *The medical background of Anglo-Saxon England*, Oxford: Oxford University
     Press.
Brown, E.A.R. 1981 'Death and the human body in the later Middle Ages: the legislation of
     Boniface VIII on the division of the corpse' *Viator: Medieval and Renaissance Studies* 12,
     221–270.
Brulet, R., Coulon, G., Ghenne-Dubois, M.-J. and Vilvorder, F. 1988 'Nouvelles recherches de
     la sépulture de Childéric' *Revue Archéologique de Picardie* 3/4, 39–43.

Butler, J. 1995 *The quest for Becket's bones: the mystery of the relics of St. Thomas Becket of Canterbury*, New Haven and London: Yale University Press.

Chaucer, 1979 *The Canterbury tales*, Harmondsworth: Penguin Books.

Collins, R. 1998 *Charlemagne*, London: MacMillan.

Crossley-Holland, K. 1993 *The Penguin book of Norse myths*, Harmondsworth: Penguin Books.

Daniell, C. 1997 *Death and burial in Medieval England*, London: Routledge.

Dickinson, T.M. 1992 'An Anglo-Saxon 'cunning woman' from Bidford-on-Avon' pp. 45–54 in M.O.H. Carver (ed.), *In search of cult: archaeological investigations in honour of Philip Rahtz*, Woodbridge: Boydell Press.

Dierkens, A. 1991 'Autour de la tombe de Charlemagne' *Byzantion* 61, 156–180.

Djakonova, V.P. 1978 'The vestments and paraphernalia of a Tuva shamaness' pp. 325– 339 in V. Diòszegi and M. Hoppál (eds), *Shamanism in Siberia*, Translated by S. Simon. Budapest: Akadémiai Kiado.

Dömötör, T. 1984 'The problem of the Hungarian female *Tàltos*' in M. Hoppál (ed.) *Shamanism in Eurasia* 2, 423–429.

Einhard 1969 *Two lives of Charlemagne*, Translated by Lewis Thorpe, Harmondsworth: Penguin Books.

Eliade, M. 1964 *Shamanism: archaic techniques of ecstasy*, London: Arkana.

Enright, M.J. 1990 'The goddess who weaves: some iconographic aspects of bracteates of the Fürstenburg type' *Frühmittelalterliche Studien (University of Munster)*, 24, 54–70.

Erbe, Theodor (ed.) 1905 *Mirk's festial*, Early English Text Society Extra Series 96.

Ferguson, G. 1961 *Signs and symbols in Christian art*, London: Oxford University Press.

Fisher, R. 1992 *Contact and conflict: Indian-European relations in British Columbia, 1774–1890*, UBC Press: Vancouver.

Frazer, J. 1993 *The golden bough: a study in magic and religion*, Hertfordshire: Wordsworth.

Glosecki, S.O. 1989 *Shamanism and Old English poetry*, New York and London: Garland Publishing.

Graceva, G.N. 1978 'The Nganasan shaman costume', pp. 315–323 in V. Diòszegi and M. Hoppál (eds) *Shamanism in Siberia*, Translated by S. Simon. Budapest: Akadémiai Kiado.

Hamayon, R. 1994 'Shamanism in Siberia: from partnership in supernature to counter-power in society' pp. 76–89 in N. Thomas and C. Humphrey (eds), *Shamanism, history, and the state*, Ann Arbor: University of Michigan Press.

Hefner, R.W. 1993 'Of faith and commitment: Christian conversion in Muslim Java' pp. 99–125 in R.W. Hefner (ed.) *Conversion to christianity: historical and anthropological perspectives on a great transformation*, Berkeley: University of California Press.

Hillgarth, J.N. (ed.) 1986 *Christianity and paganism, 350–750: the conversion of Western Europe*, Philadelphia: University of Pennsylvania Press.

Hinz, H. 1966 'Am Langen band getragene bergkristallanhänger der Merowingerzeit' *Jahrbuch der Romisch-Germanische Zentralmuseums Mainz* XIII, 212–230.

Hirst, S.M. 1985 *An Anglo-Saxon inhumation cemetery at Sewerby, East Yorkshire*, York: York University Archaeological Publications, No. 4.

Hodges, R. 1986 'Peer polity interaction and socio-political change in Anglo-Saxon England' pp. 69–78 in C. Renfrew and J. Cherry (eds) *Peer polity interaction and socio-political change*, Cambridge: Cambridge University Press.

Huggett, J. and Richards, J. 1990 'Anglo-Saxon burial: the computer at work' pp.107–124 in E. Southworth (ed.) *Anglo-Saxon cemeteries: a reappraisal*, Gloucester: Alan Sutton.

Hoppál, M. 1992 'Shamanism: an archaic and /or recent system of beliefs' pp. 117–131 in A-L. Siikala and M. Hoppál (eds) *Studies on shamanism*, Budapest: Akadémiai Kiadó.

Hugh-Jones, S. 1994 'Shamans, prophets, priests, and pastors', pp. 32–75 in N. Thomas and C.

Humphrey (eds) *Shamanism, history, and the state*, Ann Arbor: University of Michigan Press.

Humphrey, C. 1994 'Shamanic practices and the state in Northern Asia: views from the centre and periphery' pp. 191–228 in N. Thomas and C. Humphrey (eds) *Shamanism, history, and the state*, Ann Arbor: University of Michigan Press.

Humphrey, C. with Urgunge Onon 1996 *Shamans and elders: experience, knowledge, and power among the Daur Mongols*, Oxford: Oxford University Press.

James, E. 1992 'Royal burials among the Franks' pp. 243–254 in M.O.H. Carver (ed.) *The age of Sutton Hoo: the seventh century in North-west Europe*, Woodbridge: Boydell Press.

James, E.O. 1952 *The nature and function of priesthood*, London: Thames and Hudson.

Jones, P.M. 1998 *Medieval medicine in illuminated manuscripts*, London: The British Library.

Kazanski, M. 1997 *Les Francs: Precurseurs de l'Europe*, Paris: Musée du Petit Palais.

Kieckhefer, R. 1989 *Magic in the Middle Ages*, Cambridge: Cambridge University Press.

Kirk, J.R. 1949 'Bronzes from Woodeaton, Oxon.' *Oxoniensia* 14, 1–45.

Knight, B. 1991 *Forensic pathology*, New York: Oxford University Press.

Knüsel, C.J. and Ripley, K.M. 2000 'The Man-Woman or 'Berdache' in Anglo-Saxon England and Post-Roman Europe' pp. 157–191 in W. Frazer and A. Tyrrell (eds) *Social identity in Early Medieval Britain*, Leicester: Leicester University Press.

Knüsel, C.J. forthcoming. 'More Circe than Cassandra: the Princess of Vix in ritualised social context' *Journal of European Archaeology*.

Lucy, S. 1997 'Housewives, warriors and slaves? Sex and gender in Anglo-Saxon burials' pp. 150–168 in J. Moore and E. Scott (eds) *Invisible people and processes: writing gender and childhood into European archaeology*, Leicester: Leicester University Press.

Lucy, S. 2000 *The Anglo-Saxon way of death*, Stroud, Gloucestershire: Sutton.

Lvova, L. 1978 'On the shamanism of the Chulym Turks' pp. 237–244 in V. Diòszegi and M. Hoppál (eds) *Shamanism in Siberia*, Translated by S. Simon. Budapest: Akadémiai Kiado.

Mauss, M. 1990 *The gift: the form and reason for exchange in archaic societies*, Translated by W.D. Halls. London: Routledge.

Maxwell-Stuart, P.G. 2000 *Witchcraft: a history*, Stroud, Gloucestershire: Tempus.

McGregor, J.C. 1943 'Burial of an early American magician' *Proceedings of the American Philosophical Society* 86(2), 270–298.

Meaney, A.L. 1981 *Anglo-Saxon amulets and curing stones*, Oxford: British Archaeological Reports (British Series) 96.

Meaney, A.L. 1989 'Women, witchcraft, and magic in Anglo-Saxon England' pp. 9–40 in D.G. Scragg (ed.) *Superstition and popular medicine in Anglo-Saxon England*, Manchester: Manchester Centre for Anglo-Saxon Studies.

Mershen, B. 1991 'The Islamic cemetrey of Abu en-Naml' pp. 135–141 in S. Kerner (ed.) *The Near East in Antiquity: German contributions to the archaeology of Jordan, Palestine, Syria, Lebanon and Egypt*, Amman: Al Kutba.

Moorhead, J. 1985 'Clovis' motives for becoming a Catholic Christian' *Journal of Religious History* 13(4), 329–339.

Myrc, J. 1868 *Instructions for parish priests*, edited by Edward Peacock. London: Early English Text Society, Trübner and Co.

Périn, P. 1992 'The undiscovered grave of King Clovis I' pp. 255–264 in M.O.H. Carver (ed.) *The Age of Sutton Hoo: the seventh century in North-west Europe*, Woodbridge: Boydell Press.

Pollington, S. 2000 *Leechcraft: early English charms, plantlore, and healing*, Norfolk: Anglo-Saxon Books.

Rawcliffe, C. 1995 *Medicine and society in Later Medeival England*, Stroud, Gloucestershire: Alan Sutton.

Roes, A. 1958 'Origine et déstination des cuilliers perforées de l'époque Mérovingienne' *Revue Archéologique de l'Est et du Centre-Est* IX, 88–96.

Rubin, S. 1989 'The Anglo Saxon physician' pp. 7–15 in M. Deegan and D.G. Scragg (eds) *Medicine in Early Medieval England*, Manchester: Manchester Centre for Anglo-Saxon Studies.

Russell, J.C. 1994 *The Germanization of Christianity: a sociohistorical approach to religious transformation*, New York: Oxford University Press.

Schleifring, J.H. and Koch, W.M. 1989 'Rekognoszierung der Gebeine Karls des Grossen im Dom zu Aachen' *Archäologie im Rheinland* 1988, 101–102.

Shephard, J. 1979 'The social identity of the individual in isolated barrows and barrow cemeteries in Anglo-Saxon England' pp. 47–79 in B.C. Burnham and J. Kingsbury (eds) *Space, hierarchy, and society*, British Archaeological Reports International Series 59, Oxford.

Siikala, A.-L. 1992a 'Singing of incantations in Nordic tradition' pp. 68–78 in A.-L Siikala and M. Hoppál (eds) *Studies on shamanism*, Budapest: Akadémiai Kiadó.

Siikala, A-L. 1992b 'Shamanic themes in Finnish epic poetry' pp. 79–86 in A-L Siikala and M. Hoppál (eds) *Studies in shamanism,* Budapest: Akadémiai Kiadó.

Siikala, A.-L. 1992c 'Siberian and Inner Asian shamanism' pp. 1–14 in A.-L Siikala and M. Hoppál (eds) *Studies on shamanism*, Budapest: Akadémiai Kiadó.

Simek, R. 1993 *Dictionary of Northern mythology*, Cambridge: D.S. Brewer.

Siraisi, N.C. 1990 *Medieval and Early Renaissance medicine: an introduction to knowledge and practice*, Chicago: The University of Chicago Press.

Sokolova, Z.P. 1989 'A survey of the Ob-Ugrian shamanism' pp. 155–164 in M. Hoppál and O.J. Sadovszky (eds) *Shamanism: past and present*, Budapest and Los Angeles/Fullerton: ISTOR Books.

Speake, G. 1989 *A Saxon bed burial on Swallowcliffe Down*, London: Historic Buildings and Monuments Commission for England, Archaeology Report No. 10.

Steuer, H. 1989 'Archaeology and history: proposals on the social structure of the Merovingian kingdom' pp. 100–123 in K. Randsborg (ed.) *The birth of Europe: archaeology and social development in the first millennium AD*, Rome: L'Ermadi Bretschneider.

Stroud G. and Kemp R.L. 1993 *Cemeteries of St. Andrew, Fishergate*, The Archaeology of York: The Medieval Cemeteries 12/2, York: Council for British Archaeology for York Archaeological Trust.

Tacitus, C. 1986 *The histories*, Translated by Kenneth Wellesley. Harmondsworth: Penguin Books.

Tacitus, C. 1970 *Germania*, Translated by E.M. Hutton and revised by E.H. Warmington. Loeb Classical Library, Cambridge (MA): Harvard University Press.

Tambiah, S.J. 1984 *The Buddhist saints of the forest and the cult of amulets*, Cambridge: Cambridge University Press.

Tours, Gregory of 1983 *The history of the Franks*, Translated by Lewis Thorpe. Harmondsworth: Penguin Books.

Urry, W. 1999 *Thomas Becket: his last days*, Stroud, Gloucestershire: Sutton.

van Gennep. A. 1960 *The rites of passage*, Chicago: University of Chicago Press.

Vitebsky, P. 1995 *The shaman: voyages of the soul, trance, ecstasy and healing from Siberia to the Amazon*, London: Duncan Baird Publishers.

Waida, M. 1992 'Problems of Central Asian and Siberian shamanism' *Numen* 30, 215–239.

Werner, J. 1964 'Frankish royal tombs in the cathedrals of Cologne and Saint-Denis' *Antiquity* 38, 201–216.

White, R.H. 1988 'Roman and Celtic objects from Anglo-Saxon graves: a catalogue and an interpretation of their use', *British Archaeological Reports*, British Series 191, Oxford.

White, R.H. 1990 'Scrap or substitute: Roman material in Anglo-Saxon graves' pp. 125-152 in E. Southworth (ed.) *Anglo-Saxon cemeteries: a reappraisal*, Stroud, Gloucestershire: Sutton.

Winkelman, M.J. 1990 'Shamans and other 'magico-religious' healers: a cross-cultural study of their origins, nature, and social transformations' *Ethos* 18(3), 308–352.

Wilson, D. 1992 *Anglo-Saxon paganism*, London: Routledge.

Wood, I. 1987 'Christians and Pagans in ninth-century Scandinavia', pp. 36–67 in B. Sawyer, P. Sawyer, and I. Wood (eds) *The Christianization of Scandinavia*, Alingsäs, Sweden: Viktoria Bokförlag.

Wood, P. 1993 'Afterward: boundaries and horizons' pp. 305–321 in R.W. Hefner (ed.) *Conversion to Christianity: historical and anthropological perspectives on a great transformation*, Berkeley: University of California Press.

Woodward, A. 1992 *Shrines and sacrifice*, London: Batsford.

Wormald, P. 1978 'Bede, 'Beowulf', and the conversion of the Anglo-Saxon aristocracy' pp. 32–95 in R.T. Farrell (ed.) *Bede and Anglo-Saxon England*, British Archaeological Reports (British Series) 46.

Wormald, P. 1993 'Review of Anglo-Saxon paganism' (1992: Routledge, London) by David Wilson *Antiquity* 67, 939–940.

Yengoyan, A.A. 1993 'Religion, mortality, and prophetic traditions: conversion among the Pitjantjatjara of Central Australia' pp. 233–257 in R.W. Hefner (ed.) *Conversion to Christianity: historical and anthropological perspectives on a great transformation*, Berkeley: University of California Press.

13. Lithic therapy in early Chinese body practices[1]

Vivienne Lo

INTRODUCTION

Treatments that use different forms of 'stone' (shi 石) were central to many early Chinese body practices. Whether the bodies concerned were alive, sick or already dead, different forms of lithic therapy could effect alchemical transformations designed to heal, and delay the processes of decay. In order to understand the transformative power of stone in Chinese medical culture it is necessary to bring together evidence from many sources, drawing from received and excavated texts and other archaeological discoveries from the late Warring States (475 BC to 221 BC) and early imperial period (from 221 BC). Stone could cut, cool and hot press the body. It could also be a dwelling place for spirits, a protective and generative force as well as a stimulant. Despite the many different techniques identified in this paper, we will find that there were recurring features of early lithic therapy which ultimately came to bear on the transformation of medical technology using lancing stones (bian 砭) during the course of the Han dynasty (202 BC to AD 220).[2] Thinly veiled in the innovative principles and practice of acupuncture (here defined as piercing the skin with stone or needle to normalise the body's inner essences) of that time we will find a substantial inheritance of the older medical traditions.[3]

Jade was a most highly prized stone and will serve as one model for understanding the role of stone in early body practices. When mortuary ritualists, as well as technical and medical writers of the Warring States and early imperial period, dressed the body in jade and metaphors of jade they meant to concentrate all the qualities of the most refined form of stone for the benefit of the body. In time jade became an important substance in the traditional Chinese materia medica, used for the treatment of 'heat in the stomach', respiratory difficulties and more generally for lightening and rejuvenating the body.[4] Similarly we will see that the wushi 'five stones' are a feature of early mythology about the saving of the universe, of mortuary practice as well as one Han physician's drug repertoire. Five stone remedies are also a feature of later pharmacology. While it is abundantly clear that one cannot assume that ideas about the relationship between the body, its essence, spirits and souls are consistent throughout every aspect of medical and mortuary culture, we will see that there are significant similarities where the body is subject to the application of stone.[5] In the course of this paper I will give an account of overlapping networks of stone-based mortuary, medical and self-cultivation technologies whereby the body's health, integrity, longevity and immortality are guarded and defended. What unifies the practices is the construction of the body that they are dealing with. Vestiges of these early treatments also remain enshrined in transmitted medical literature and surviving traditions of medical practice where the body is thought of as a physiological entity made up of the triad qi (氣 the fundamental stuff of life), shen (神 a manifestation of the 'spirits') and jing (精 'essences').[6]

SPIRIT OF STONE

What, then, was the significance of stone in early Chinese culture? Political, philosophical and scientific treatises do not canonise stone as one of the 'five agents' (wuxing 五行) which include the powers of wood, fire, earth, metal and water. The five agents, together with the complementary aspects of Yin and Yang, were at the foundation of Chinese correlative thinking throughout imperial times.[7] Nevertheless we should not overlook the importance of stone in early Chinese attitudes to the mysteries of life and death, especially in those centuries around the turn of the millenia when classical medical thought was in its formative period.

Stone as a generative force and, unusually, as aligned with the agents of water, wood, metal, earth and fire, is evident in the Book of the Generation of the Foetus (胎產 書 *Taichanshu*), one of the silk manuscripts excavated from the Mawangdui burial site.[8] Each agent rules a one month period of foetal development beginning with water in the fourth month, following the five agents' cycle 'of conquest' (克 ke) but, exceptionally, culminating with stone in the ninth month. Stone, here, is a phase which corresponds to the growth of filament hairs.[9] The gestation period ruled by stone marks the maturation of the body's shape and form and precedes the tenth month when it is vitalised with qi. Since it is clear that the concept of stone in early China referred to more than simply the crude material, or pieces of rock, we are well prepared to embrace the many meanings of shi 石 as they emerge in different medical contexts.

From the Records of the Historian (史記 *Shiji*) and History of the Former Han (漢書 *Hanshu*) biographies, Zhang Liang's (張良) (d. 187 BC) natural patience and respect were severely tested by an old man who turned out to be the manifestation of a stone spirit, normally resident in a yellow stone beneath Jibei Gucheng (濟北穀城山) mountain. The old man gave Zhang Liang the *Taigong bingfa* (太公兵法) a book on military strategy, instructing him to, 'read this and become a king'. Towards the end of his life Zhang Liang renounced the world and all his riches to 'roam with the famous recluse Master Red Pine,' a patron of esoteric practices concerned with lightening the body and, perhaps, with the pursuit of immortality. He was eventually interred with the yellow stone.[10] It was not uncommon to find spirits and deities bound to certain places and people might identify and mark these places with propitiary goods.

The Stone Spirit (石神 *shishen*) itself was one of seven medical treatises, given to the former Han physician Chunyu Yi (淳于意) (fl 154 BC), by his teacher Yang Qing (陽慶), and recorded in *The Record of the Historian*, but it is not extant.[11] A first avenue of approach to the nature of the *Stone Spirit* would read shi as the prescription of mineral drugs (藥石 yaoshi), as distinct from either lancing stones or plant products. Chunyu Yi criticises his colleague Sui (遂), physician to the King of Qi (齊), who misuses a prescription known as wushi. Physician Sui quotes the legendary half-bird, half-man physician, Bian Que (扁鵲), 'Yin stones are used to treat Yin illnesses, Yang stones to treat Yang illnesses,' and expounds a simple analysis of his symptoms wherein Yin and Yang match cold and hot and are applied to remedy excesses of the opposite quality accordingly.[12] Chunyu Yi accuses Sui of superficial diagnosis, stressing the value of a complex diagnosis arrived at from the sum of the pulse, complexion and a knowledge of the depth of illness. He diagnoses that Sui's illness comes from heat in the centre and adds that when the centre is hot and you can't pass water wushi is contra-indicated. Misuse of such potent medicines will lead to a disruption of Yin and Yang and eventually lead to perverse qi (邪氣 xieqi) and abscesses (疽 ju). Sui ultimately dies from in-growing abscesses.

The wushi were not always simply a medical prescription for sores and heat. Documentary records and archaeological finds from a number of different periods attest the pervasive importance of 'five stones' and five colour stones (wuse shi 五色石 i.e. five stones, each a different colour) in the cultivation of long life, cure of illness and the prevention of decay.[13] The five minerals that make up the five stones vary, but the number five links the stones to the five agents and their five correspondent colours are one guiding theme in the selection of each particular group. In the mythological account of how the goddess Nuwa (女媧) saved the universe she uses the five stones to mend the heavens.

> 'Gong Gong struggled with Zhuan Xu to be Son of Heaven but was not victorious. He was furious and struck Bu Zhou mountain. And heaven's column was snapped and the cords of earth were severed. Nu Wa smelted the five colour stones to mend the azure heavens. She broke off the sea turtle's feet to erect the four poles'.[14]

On the theme of the five stones Wang Chong (王充 27 – ca. 100) adds,

> Using the five colour stones to mend heaven, still could be called the five stones seeming to be like medical stones to cure illness.[15]

At the most basic level of health care the five stones were topically-applied mineral preparations used to heal sores. The *Zhouli* states, 'in all cases of treating sores use the five du (毒) to attack them'.[16] Du is normally translated 'poison', but in this case it refers to the potency, or the active ingredient, of the medicine. Zheng Xuan (鄭玄 127–200) then notes, 'the du is the du of the medicine'. He goes on to record the medicines with the five du (五毒之藥 wudu zhi yao)[17]. A similar combination can be found in Ge Hong's account of 'yellow white techniques' (黃白朱 huangbai shu) one hundred years later, but this is a different medicine. It seems that people practising yellow white techniques took a similar combination of minerals over a long period of time in order to strengthen the body and make it less susceptible to illness, weakness or decay. Amongst other minerals Ge Hong lists cinnabar (丹沙 dansha), realgar (雄黃 xionghuang), alum (baifan 白礬), stratified malachite (曾青 cengqing) and magnetite (cishi 磁石), a selection of wushi 'five stone' minerals which represent the five colours, red, yellow, white, green/ blue and black and therefore conveys all the potency of the five agents into the remedy.[18]

By Wei/Jin times (3rd century) wushi remedies were fashionable as a stimulant.[19] It is possible that Chunyu Yi and his colleagues were already aware of their effect and that his criticism of Sui was not only of Sui's crude diagnosis, but also obliquely aimed at an incipient addiction. Warming medicines may induce a feeling of comfort. Perhaps in the long term, or in large amounts, they may have had a pleasant and exciting effect that served to blind the addict to a simultaneous slow and insidious degeneration of the body. Sun Simiao (581–682?) finds good reason to criticise their use warning his readers to 'eat calming wild ge (葛) and don't take the five stones'. He regarded it as a ferocious poison and urged people to burn the prescription.[20] Despite his censure (and perhaps in tribute to the long-standing prescription which undoubtedly had its medical uses) he included the recipe for 'Five stone powder prescription for restoring life' (五石更生散方 wushi geng sheng san fang) in *Qianjin yifang* 千金翼方, and attributed it to a Marquis of He 何侯.[21] However according to the chemist Wang Kuike (王奎克)'s speculation, Sun modified the original recipe replacing arsenolite (yushi 礜石) (which contains arsenic) with the benign shiliuhuang 石硫黃.[22]

Sun Simiao was reacting to a cult of taking the five stones associated with the scholar the Marquis of He (何宴 He Yan), who was represented in later literature as a dissolute wastrel. According to Yu Jiaxi (余嘉錫 1883–1955), He (何) himself said that Five Stone Powder was not originally a stimulant used in the 'arts of the bedchamber', but was a medical prescription that could also stimulate 'an illumination of the spirit and the clarity of heaven'.[23] The pursuit of this elusive state was apparently responsible for the death of millions of literati in the three centuries from Wei/Jin (third century) to Sui/Tang (sixth/seventh centuries). Wang believes that the Han recipe contained arsenic in the form of yu (礜) and that there was a common confusion between this character and the benign alum (礬 fan) which rendered the later prescription harmless. The circumstances of the Wei/Jin scholars' death (reduction in digestion, febrile symptoms, dryness and scabbing of the skin including rot, nerve poisoning, lapses in consciousness, weakness and heart paralysis, whole body numbness delusions diarrhoea and death) is consistent both with some of Sui's symptoms and with long term arsenic poisoning.[24]

He Yan's practice may have been purely hedonistic, or perhaps both hedonistic and aimed, fatally, at preserving his life. But he was neither first nor last to condition his body with the properties of 'stone'. There is evidence that Han elite took minerals to preserve their bodies, if not also for pleasure. Traces of lead, mercury, cinnabar and arsenic were found in the corpse of the near perfectly preserved countess of Dai, buried in the Mawangdui burial mound in 168 BC.[25] She had taken all of these minerals for a long period during her lifetime. Her clothes were also soaked in cinnabar. Another well preserved corpse excavated at Fenghuangshan (風凰山) tomb 168 had been filled with cinnabar after death. From as early as the New Stone Age Longshan culture (ca first half of second millennia BC) wealthy families commonly used cinnabar in their burial practices. In one tomb at the Erlitou (二里頭) site (ca nineteenth – sixteenth century BC?), for example, six centimetres of cinnabar were spread thickly over one corpse alone.

Cinnabar clearly had a disinfecting and rot preventing function. Yet other stones could confer the power of permanence and preservation from their very presence in the tomb. Scattered in an orderly fashion around the King of Nanyue's Han tomb (c. 122 BC) were all kinds of medicinal minerals. More unusually, at the base of southern wall on the western side of the coffin chamber, were five coloured stones.[26] They are not decorative stones such as the necklace of agate, crystal, amber and other coloured and presumably precious stones found in the well endowed Western Han tomb at Maquan (馬泉), Xianyang in modern Shaanxi.[27] Interred stones and ores undoubtedly had a demon-quelling influence.[28] But the stones from the King of Nanyue's tomb have added significance. Of these five, zishuijing (紫水晶: purple), sulphur (硫礦 liuhuang: yellow), turquoise (綠松石 lusongshi: green), ochre (赭石 zheshi: red) and realgar (雄黃 xionghuang: yellow), only realgar is also listed in Zheng Xuan's note to Zhouli or in Ge Hong's list of wushi in 'jindan'. Even though these minerals are not a complete set of colours corresponding to the 'five agents', they are surely chosen with the influences of the five agents in mind and the benefits they would bring to the corpse or soul of the occupant.[29] They are also ores which, when refined, produce a more potent essence, a process which resonates with the hopes and expectations of refining the essence of the corpse itself.

By the six dynasties period the burial of five colour stones was no longer a prerogative of the rich. *Laughing at the Dao* (笑道論 *Xiaodao lun*) describes the burial requirements for salvation, '… The emperor (also requires) five ounces of gold for the fashioning of dragons, while the common people rely on iron or five stones of different colours, on which the jade script is inscribed.'[30] In time, it seems, that the stones became a part of the geomancer's arsenal for quelling demons. Convincing evidence of atropaic medical tools comes from a number of prescriptions from 52 Remedies (五十二病方 *Wushier bingfang*), the longest medical text excavated from the Mawangdui site. One remedy for swellings in the groin requires shooting arrows from a peachwood bow. Another, for a form of groin swelling involves the Pace of Yu, a ritual step, controlling the spirits with a stone and beating the patient over the head with an iron mallet: 'on the sixteenth day of the month when the moon first begins to deteriorate, perform the Pace of Yu thrice. Say 'Moon is matched against sun' and 'Sun is matched against

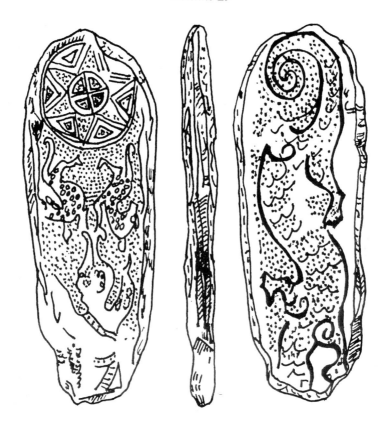

Figure 13.1. The Rainmaster Stone (after Ma Jixing and Zhou Shirong 1978, 82).

moon' – three times each. 'Father is perverse, Mother is strong. Like other people they bore Sons, and only bore swellings in the groin. Perverseness desist. Grasp the hammering stone and strike your Mother. Immediately, exorcistically beat and hammer the person twice seven times with an iron mallet. Do it at sunrise, and have the person with the swelling in the groin face east'.[31]

With an increased vulnerability to spirits and demons beyond death, stones and pottery tiles interred along with other mortuary items, may well have had an atropaic medical function. One intricately engraved pottery tile, that Chinese historians often link to early hot-pressing techniques, was excavated from a Warring States tomb in Hebei, Yi (易) county (Fig. 13.1).

On the front at the top is a six-pointed star formation set into a circle, towards the handle end is the upper body of a man with two arms raised. His lower body on the handle end is damaged. Just above each of his hands and with one foot pointing towards the figure's head are two leopard or dragon-like beasts in profile, upside down with their tongues sticking out. On the back is the body and legs of another scaly dragon. Unfortunately its head is damaged. The dragon design has lead scholars to associate the figure on the tile with the Rain Master (雨師 yushi), for dragons were thought to be rain-makers. Shi Shuqing quotes the Canon of Mountains and Seas 山海經 (*Shanhai jing*), 'the Rain Master ... in his two hands each grasps a snake, at the left ear there is a black snake and at the right ear there is a red snake' and a number of commentaries to demonstrate that the Rain Master was an important figure in Warring States and Han ritual. Han Feizi, states 'when the Yellow emperor was with the ghosts and spirits on Tai mountain, Wind Uncle went ahead and cleared the way and the Rain Master washed the road.'[32]

Chinese medical historians have suggested that the tile, being flat and oval, and fitting neatly into the palm of the hand, is a good size for massage or hot pressing.[33] Its lavish decoration also suggests that it also had a role in assisting ritual incantation, perhaps in ridding the patient of disease, such as we have seen in the Wushier bingfang remedy quoted above. We can assume that the tile carried the power of the 'Rain Master' and his techniques into the tomb and could, just like the interred stones described above, serve to draw a boundary around the corpse and protect the body in death.

Under the auspices of exploring early Chinese 'stone' culture we can slip quite naturally from discussing the use of minerals to preserve and enhance the body, both live and dead, to stones for controlling demons and spirits. In both these areas we can see a remarkable similarity in medical and mortuary culture where the body is treated and protected with different forms of stone. In the next section we will see how the construction of bodies of stone in Han times drew upon all the atropaic, nourishing, vitalising and transformational qualities that have accrued by that time to the concept of stone.

THE JADE BODY

Stone in its purest form, its most refined essence, was thought manifest in jade: Han elite used powdered jades, and especially powder from antiques, to prepare elixirs of life.[34] And when related to the human body, whether through the use of crafted jades or through metaphor, we will find that the conception of a body bounded and shaped and even made with jade had a technical reality which recurs through different Han body cultures.

Whereas in life, 'jade had been essential to the full representation and protection of members of the elite', in death it also seems to have kept the spirits at a distance.[35] From as early as Liangzhu culture we can see large quantities of a type of jade girdle ornament (組佩飾 zupeishi) blanketing the corpse, such as the 755 pieces found in Fuhao's (婦好) tomb at Yinxu (殷墟) and two Eastern Zhou period (770 BC to 256 BC) jade face nets (Fig. 13.2).

Jades are apparently already graded at the Liangzhu (c. 3,200–2,200 BC) sites; jade discs found covering the bodies of the dead were of a higher quality than those stacked at their feet. And as a medium for directly addressing the spirit world, the large and

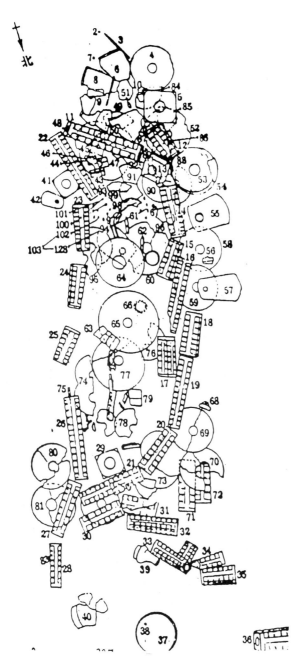

Figure 13.2. The 755 Jades covering Fu Hao's body (after Lu Zhaoyin 1981).

varied deposits of precious jades found at two Shang (c. 1600–1045 BC) sites such as Guanghan (廣漢) Sanxing dui (三星堆) and Shenmu (神木) Shimao (石峁), appear to contain jade buried as offerings to spirits. There is both archae-ological and textual evidence that suggests that jade was still given in offerings to the spirits right through to the imperial sacrifices of the Han dynasty.[36]

Stone, and jade in its own distinctive way, determined a sacred space wherein the body would not decay. Jade funerary clothing (玉衣 yuyi) reached its logical conclusion in Han times with the twenty-two suits of jade, at one time made for the emperors, but later bestowed on favoured kings and ministers between the mid second century BC and AD 222. Recent excava-tions show that similar burial suits were in use as early as the eastern Zhou period and we can therefore extrapolate that by Han times the image of the elite 'body of jade' was embedded in popular imagination.[37] Five of the Han suits are in perfect condition and are best represented by the suit of Prince Liu Sheng (劉勝 d. 113 BC) and his wife Dou Wan (竇綰) excavated from tomb M1 at Hebei Mancheng (滿城) in 1968.

In the progression from the outer part of the Mancheng tomb (which, unlike pre-Han tombs, is cut into the rock of mountain cliffs) through to the burial chamber itself, Wu Hung finds a transition from wood, to stone, culminating in the jade of the suit itself; this progression may reflect the ancient Chinese belief that the most beautiful jades are naturally concealed within stone boulders.[38] The corpse was protected with several layers of jade; jade orifice plugs and jade bi originally forming part of some kind of shroud were followed by a complete representation of his body. The coffins themselves were also lined with jade. And finally placed between two of Liu Sheng's coffins there was a small, seated jade figure inscribed with the words 'ancient jade person' (古玉人 gu yu ren), surely the most distinctive image of the potential for Liu Sheng's immortality.[39]

Where other jade suits are made of rough jades with only the uncovered body parts fashioned smoothly, the jade covering of Liu Sheng was all smooth and well crafted, fashioned after his naked body with a care for anatomical accuracy, a basic nose and genitals. His wife's covering even had jade ears. Wu Hung argues coherently that this is not a suit, but a 'jade body', one which would somehow facilitate posthumous transformation.[40] Liu Sheng's virtual body was made of 2,498 small plaques of bowenite, a form of grey, green stone that is softer than true jade (Fig. 13.3).[41]

Corpse preservation jades, such as the han (琀) and zhen (瑱) were used in Han times to plug the orifices after death. The covers for the eyes seem to have been slightly concave discs, often penetrated by small holes, perhaps originally to secure a face net. Those for the nose were small solid cylinders. Similarly the plugs for the ears and anus were cylindrical jades with eight facets, the latter being larger. The plug placed in the mouth was most commonly in the shape of a cicada, although two excavated from the Mancheng site are, unusually, half-moon shaped with a round stopper shaped teat to fit

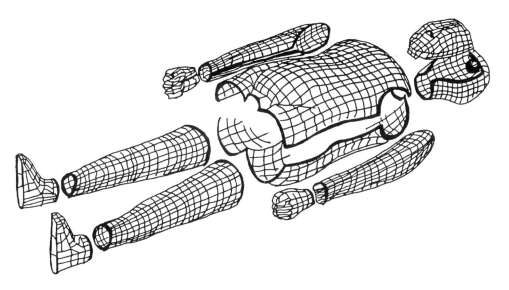

Figure 13.3. Prince Liu Sheng's Jade Body from Mancheng Hanmu fajue baogao (after Li Ling 2000, 313).

between the lips.[42] Perhaps the plugs themselves, as the most material manifestation of the atropaic quality of stone, served to protect the orifices from infestation by worms or demons. Alternatively, or perhaps simultaneously, they must have prevented leakage of the body's vital essence. But to really appreciate the meaning of jade in mortuary culture it is essential to look at the relationship of jade and the human form as it was constructed in second century B.C. China.

Jade came to be a complex metaphor with multiple and sometimes conflicting associations accruing to different grades and qualities through context and usage.[43] *Zhuangzi*, attacking the Confucian sage, his morality, pomp and ritual, likens white jade to simplicity, the Way and the virtue, the true form of the inborn nature ...

> And so the sage arrives, limping along after humaneness, urging on to do right, and the world feels doubt for the first time; making a big thing of music, beating his breast over rites, and the world is divided for the first time. Thus, if the pure, unworked substance had not been destroyed, how would there be any sacrificial goblets? If the white jade had not been re-fashioned, how would there be any jade tallies? If the Way and its Virtue had not been abandoned, wherein the assumption of humaneness and right? If the inborn nature had not been deserted, wherefore rites and music? If the five colours had not confused men ...[44]

In a passage also found in *Liji*, *Guanzi* and *Xunzi*, *Shuowen* provides us with a five-fold gloss for jade which gives us a clue to its value in Han times:

> Jade, the most beautiful of stone, has five virtues: through its smooth and moistness it is warm, that's the bearing of humaneness; through the shiny patterned outer layer one can know the centre, that's the bearing of rightness; through its sound reverberating and rising with perfect pitch it is heard from afar, that's the bearing of wisdom; if you try and break it by bending it does not give, that's the bearing of courage; that it is sharp and incorruptible, yet not (stubborn or extreme), that is the bearing of (purity) ... [45]

The appearance of jade, far from eulogising such simple, guileless purity as eulogised by Zhuangzi, evokes the classical Confucian virtues, desirable moral qualities, courage and wisdom – a combination that reflects the priorities of *Xunzi*, *Guanzi* and Xu Shen (許慎 *c.* 55–*c.* 149), the author of *Shuowen*. Xu Shen's principle motivation was to elucidate the language and thereby the wisdom of the ancient classics, for the benefit of strong central government and the moral and social order that it could underpin.[46] Yet there are qualities that *Zhuangzi* and Xu Shen both mean to convey by evoking images of jade. Altogether jade epitomises excellence, the best of human nature – its purity, modesty and mildness, combined with the potential for strength and endurance. With these qualities in mind we are better placed to understand the meaning of jade when it refers to the body in early Chinese medical literature.

With some understanding of the use of jade in mortuary culture and the qualities associated with jade in the early Chinese mind can explore references to a jade body (玉體 yuti) in literature, both excavated and received, which begins in the Warring

States.[47] *Zhanguoce* (戰國策) 21 uses the term as an honorific epithet for the Queen mother's body, 'I fear that Queen Mother Zhao's 'jade body' has a fissure, so I am willing to look on her from afar'. And *Hanshu* refers to a technique to purify the mind, 'with the soft and fragile 'jade body' to withstand the toilsome harbouring of malicious thought'. In both cases the jade body seems to be a vision of perfection against which to measure deterioration and debasement. It may also imply a means to healing. The jade body can also be the image of a beautiful woman. Sima Xiangru's (司馬相如) 'Fu on lust' Haose fu (好色賦) reads, 'her flowery bearing offers itself, her jade body lounges on the bed.'

The term jade body (yuti 玉體) appears in the fourth text of *Maishu* (脈書), a manuscript in six texts excavated at the Zhangjiashan burial site, which collectively represent the earliest extant treatise to set out the principles and practice of acumoxa.[48] Acumoxa in later periods is 'acupuncture and moxibustion' [zhenjiu 針灸], where moxibustion (jiu 灸) specifically refers to burning artemesia vulgaris (mugwort) over the body. However, it should be noted that early references to jiu (灸) in the texts cannot be definitively linked to the use of the same herb, and should be translated simply as 'cautery'.

In contrast to the 'jade body' of received literature, the authors of the *Maishu* acumoxa texts refer to a perfect body which is a physiological entity with a technical reality that borrows from ideas originating in self-cultivation culture. The 'jade body' in this context is a specialist term and not necessarily part of a common vocabulary. But we will see how elements of the construction of this physiological body as well as references to body parts made of jade keep recurring in contemporary and later medical and hygienic treatises.

> Now the reason that flowing water does not stagnate and a door that pivots does not get woodworm is because of movement. When there is movement then it fills the four limbs and empties the five viscera; when the five viscera are empty then the 'jade body' will benefit. Now one who rides in a carriage and eats meat must (fast and purify themselves?) in Spring and Autumn. If they do not (fast and purify themselves?) then the mai will rot and cause death.[49]

The recommendations for exercise, diet, and moderation in this passage share little with the other five *Maishu* texts except for one short passage about treatment principles which I translate below. Mostly, *Maishu* concerns the course of the mai, the word I translate 'channels', and related pathology.[50] In the directive that 'fills the four limbs and empties the five viscera' we have testimony to the influence of yangsheng (養生) 'nurturing life' culture, and in particular daoyin (導引) 'guiding and pulling', early Chinese therapeutic exercise and breath-cultivation, and dietetics, on early Chinese medical ideas. In order to understand the reference to the jade body and its care we must therefore consult the literature that describes techniques of breath, sex and daoyin cultivation. A twelve sided, late Warring states piece of jade (c. 380?) brings together the themes of precious stone and techniques to refine the essences of the body.[51] It is not clear whether the jade itself had a practical purpose. One end is hollowed, but the hole does not pierce the top and scholars have speculated that it is a hilt, a walking stick handle or a scroll end. Nine trisyllabic phrases in zhuan (篆) script decorate its sides and give instructions for xing qi (行氣) 'moving qi'. Once qi is taken into the body, the adept projects it down through the body, before it returns heavenward (Fig. 13.4).

The original function of the jade is still uncertain as is the transcription of the characters. Here is Harper's tentative translation of the four concluding phrases:

> Swallow, then it travels; travelling, it extends; extending, it descends; descending, it stabliszes; stabilizing, it solidifies; solidifying, it sprouts; sprouting, it grows; growing, it returns, returning, it is heaven. Heaven – its root is above; earth – its root is below. Follow the pattern and live; go against it and die.[52]

Figure 13.4. Caption: 'Xing qi' Jade (after Li Ling 2000, 343).

Articulating the verse was probably the outward expression of a technique to nurture the movement of qi within the body and served to refine and intensify each stage of the process.

The Mawangdui breath-cultivation texts and parts of Yinshu, a manual of daoyin exercises excavated together with *Maishu* from the Zhangjiashan tomb site, are textual expansions of the jade breathing technique first described on the Warring States jade. In *Ten Questions* (十問) the Yellow Emperor asks the question, 'what is the essential ingredient for life?' Rong Cheng's answer centres on the correct way to ingest qi and consciously project it into the limbs:

> The way to breathe qi: it must reach to the extremities … Breathing must be deep and sustained. Fresh qi is easy to hold on to, qi that has been kept over night is ageing, fresh qi creates long life. The one who is good at putting the qi in order causes the qi that has been kept overnight to disperse during the night and fresh qi to collect in the morning by penetrating the nine orifices and filling the six cavities.[53]

Following this technique, the adept must both consciously direct fresh qi to fill the six bowels (腑 fu) as well as disperse old qi through the extremities. Other techniques of the same period record slightly different priorities in cultivating qi in the body: in the *Maishu* (4) quotation above we found that movement 'fills the four limbs and empties the five viscera' to benefit the jade body. On the one hand the breathing technique refers to breathing qi outwards into the limbs and on the other, to filling the body and inner bowels through the orifices. What we have is a rudimentary temporal and spatial rotation of qi, not yet an integrated circulation. The two techniques stress the importance of internal movement. The concern to empty the inner organs is a physiological underpinning of the more general concern to empty the mind/heart of distractions and the search to align human being with underlying patterns of the universe.[54] Here are two exercises taken from a daoyin 'leading and guiding' manual found in the same tomb as *Maishu*. Both promote the flow of qi away from the head and inner organs outward through the limbs:

> When suffering with there being less qi in the two hands, both the arms cannot be raised equally and the tips of the fingers, like whirling water, tend to numbness. Pretend that the two elbows are bound to the sides, and vigorously swing them. In the morning, middle of the day and middle of the night. Do it altogether one thousand times. Stop after ten days?

> Ailing from [liquor?]. The prescription for pulling it: grasp a staff in the right hand, face a wall and do not breathe; with the left foot tread on the wall, resting when tired; likewise with the left hand grasp the staff, with right foot step on the wall, likewise rest when tired. When the qi of the head flows downwards, the foot will not be immobile and numb, the head will not swell, and the nose will not be stuffed up. Whenever there is free time practice it frequently.

Another term found in both breath and sexual-cultivation, 'the jade closure' (玉閉 yubi) may refer to a location within the body, although there is some controversy over exactly where it might be. Some annotators relate it to the passes (關 guan) of later Han and Daoist self-cultivation, a barrier located near to the navel which stored qi and jing. 'Closure' (bi 閉) in later Daoist literature emphasises the act of enclosing an inner space and containing and accumulating the body's essences within. Yubi, this act graced with the metaphor of jade, must refer to sealing the body's fluids and essences. With the link between jade and the orifices already established, one suspects that the act of sealing happens at the orifices and, by implication, also the skin. Many early breathing techniques also involve contracting the anus to move inner qi.[55] Here *Ten Questions* describes how to sustain vigour, and ensure longevity by absorbing a woman's essences into the body:

> In the cultivation of lengthening life secretly use the jade closure. At that movement when the jade closure opens, the illumination of the spirit arrives and accumulates. As it accumulates, it will be manifest. When the jade closure firms the quintessence, this will make the jade spring imperturbable. Then the hundred afflictions will not increase and thus you can live long.[56]

The technique is repeated in *Tianxia zhidaotan* which then describes the stages in the arrival of spirit illumination beginning at the first level with the orifices, then secondly moving to the voice (emitting from a third orifice), thirdly the external body becomes radiant and then working inwards through the spine, muscles, fluids and ultimately towards stimulating a feeling of inner strength and spiritual empowerment.

> When you are on the point of cultivating it, you must examine the word; move with the jade closure, and you can become one with the immortals. With the first movement, ears and eyes are keen and bright; with the second movement, the sound of the voice radiates; with the third movement, skin and hide shine; with the fourth movement, the spine and bones are strong; with the fifth movement, buttock and thigh are square; at the sixth movement, the waterways move; with the seventh movement through strength one achieves absolute sturdiness; with the eighth movement, though rising up the will becomes proud; with the ninth movement, you move in accord with the heavens; the tenth movement, engenders an illumination of the spirit.[57]

The body enclosed with jade is radiant and substantial, brimful of essence and moisture. Here we have the arrival of spirit illumination (神明 shenming) a quality that we have already met in connection with the later application of the five stone drugs. Images of jade brought to descriptions of the body, just like the body made or dressed in jade at death may seem to infer a hypothetical, idealised, body. Perhaps, for the people of the second century BC that body had no reality accept as a metaphor for unattainable physical excellence. Yet for groups of people that seriously pursued the attainment of physical immortality the ideal was associated with a technical and potential reality. At least for the author(s) of *Maishu* (4), the jade body could derive direct benefit from proper training, diet and sexual cultivation.

Despite the fact that *Maishu* (4) recommends moderation and movement in caring for the mai of the 'jade body', *Maishu* is not a treatise on self-cultivation. It simply uses self-cultivation priorities to model new medical techiques. After *Maishu* (4) there is a short text differentiating body constituents, followed by *Maishu* (6) which gives us the earliest extant reference to acupuncture (in so much that acupuncture can be defined as body piercing to normalize the flow of qi).

> The channels are valued by the sages. As for qi, it benefits the lower body and harms the upper; follows heat and distances coolness. So, the sages cool the head and warm the feet. Those who treat illness take the surplus and supplement the insufficiency. So if qi goes up, not down, then when you see the channel that has over-reached itself, apply one cauterisation where it meets the articulation. When the illness is intense then apply another cauterisation at a place two 'Chinese inches' above the articulation. When the qi rises at one moment and falls in the next pierce it with a stone lancet at the back of the knee and the elbow.

Thus, the sage physician draws qi down and out through the limbs by applying cautery or lancing stones to open the channels at the joints. Corrected, the flow moves in a downward direction through the limbs. Here we have the technical elements of self-cultivation embraced within new medical ways to project qi away from the head and body. At first impression there seems to be a contradiction between the crude nature of the intervention (surgery with stone) and the object of intervention (qi). Sharpened stone tools seem appropriate for petty surgery, but would certainly leave wounds that are incommensurate with the subtle nature of acumoxa. Indeed the very next passage in *Maishu* is exclusively conerned with lancing abscesses. We are left with idea that medical technology had not quite caught up with changes in theory.[58] Despite the *Maishu* juxtaposition of petty surgery and physiological medicine, it is certainly not possible to identify a monolinear development from petty surgery with stones to the modern acupuncture needle and this is a point stressed by both Yamada Keiji and Paul Unschuld.[59] It may be that in the course of experimentation with petty surgery, some physicians made observations and hypotheses concerning the potential of stone to treat the body at a deeper level. But we should not underestimate either the variety or the potency of stone in early Chinese medical culture.

Yamada points out that of the compound terms used in the *Huangdi neijing* compilation, the work widely acknowledged as the canon of acumoxa, a contrast is made between different types of lancing stones and 'piercing and cauterising' (刺灸 ci jiu).[60] His point is that where the combinations 'moxibustion and acupuncture' are contrasted to 'techniques with lancing stones' (砭法 bianfa), acupuncture is classified as more akin to moxibustion than surgical techniques – a feature well-illustrated in the excavated channel texts from Mawangdui and Zhangjiashan which, on the whole, refer to 'cauterisation' (久 = 灸 jiu) to treat the channels and not stone.

Where *Maishu* (6) uses both cautery and stone bian to normalize the movement of qi and writes of opening the channel at the joints with a stone lancet does this necessarily mean breaking the flesh? Since stone in Han culture had a way of defining and containing the most precious and vitalising essences of the body could a specially chosen stone not open the channel and influence the movement of qi itself, with the power of its very presence? Or when Bian Que states that needle and stone treat at the level of the blood and channels, and we envisage piercing through the skin, should we not also entertain the idea that specially selected or crafted stones were used to heat, press and massage the channel?[61] Whether *Maishu* refers to body piercing to move qi or not, many contemporary records testify to the use of hot stones, massage and cautery for treating different medical conditions.

In the words given to the Yellow Emperor written in *Lingshu*, we see the new theories and technology matched,

> I wish not to employ poisonous herbs; to be without applying bianshi 'stone lancet.' I wish to use small needles to connect the jingmai and adjust blood and qi, to lay out the meeting places (會 hui) where it comes in and out and flows smoothly or inversely. So that it may be transmitted to posterity, that they will use this method in an enlightened way, … I will for the first time establish the Needle Canon (鍼經 *Zhenjing*).[62]

Here we have a rejection of lancing stones in favour of small needles applied to a body imagined in physiological terms, where qi and jing flow smoothly along routes known as the jingmai and where the qi comes and goes at 'meeting places'.[63] With the advent of metal needles we can also find a parallel sophistication in the aim of medical intervention.

We saw in the discussion of the 'jade closure' techniques, that self-cultivation cultures were often intent on achieving a state of shenming 'illumination of the spirits'. Shenming, in this context, is consistent with an acuity of the senses and a visible brightness which corresponds with having successfully cultivated or 'received' (接 jie) Yin.[64]

The code for successful cultivation in the Mawangdui self-cultivation texts reads, 'the qi arrives, blood and qi flow freely, the ears and eyes are keen and bright, the skin gleams, the voice is clear, the back, thighs and buttocks are sturdy and you get through to an illumination of the spirit'. In *Lingshu* 9 we find similar outcomes for acupuncture needling:

> In all cases the way of needling entails stopping when the qi is adjusted: tonify
> the Yin and sedate the Yang, the voice and qi become increasingly clear, the
> ear and the eye become keen and bright, if one goes against this the blood, the
> qi will not flow freely.[65]

From the first century AD there are increasing references to acupuncture with needles. Medical texts excavated from a tomb at Wuwei (武威) provide us with the earliest datable detail about the site of needle insertion and manipulation technique.[66] The Wuwei site (*c.* first century AD) is contemporary with or just subsequent to latest theories about the date of the *Huangdi* compilations. We can therefore be reasonably certain that significant and rapid changes had taken place in both theory and technology around the time of, or shortly after, the closure of the Mawangdui (168 BC) and Zhangjiashan (*c.* 186–154 BC?) tombs and before the time of the closure of the Wuwei tomb.

JADE BODY PARTS

As the stone lancet was replaced by metal needles in acupuncture therapy, references to jade and stone were retained in the construction of the new physiological body. Jade, as glossed by Xu Shen and translated above, combined hardness and durability with an appearance of glossiness – a shining quality which also conveys the illusion of moistness. *Huainanzi* (to 139 BC) strengthens the association of jade and moisture when it records the belief that jade lying beneath a mountain will stimulate luxuriant growth. Mountains were thought to be the source of clouds and rain. It is the resonance of these qualities of strength, radiance and secretion with youthful sexuality that definitively links jade with the ability to sustain sexual competence into old age and therefore with long life itself. Increasing dryness of the body and, in particular, the sexual and reproductive emissions in both male and female, match easily failing strength and frailty and contrast to the physical qualities of valour and vigour. Images of jade in late Warring States and Han medical literature are clearly related to the preservation of vital fluids and youthful vigour. But once again we find the metaphorical body of jade first appearing in self-cultivation literature: 'jade spring' (玉泉 yuquan) identifies a source inside the body where qi accumulates and transforms and which is part of the physiology of accumulating 'essence' (精 jing).[67] 'Jade hole' (玉竇 yudou) and 'jade whip' (玉策 yuce) were euphemistic identifications of the vagina and penis respectively in Mawangdui sexual literature.[68] Anxiety about loss of fluid and the dryness of old age and deterioration seems to have brought the metaphor of jade to the mouth and the reproductive organs. The idea of metaphorically sealing the body with orifices of jade to create a bounded inner space full of heavenly fluids is reminiscent of the use of jade stoppers in burial culture to plug the orifices of a corpse.

Zhenjiu jiayi jing gives us the earliest acupoints explicitly associated with stone and jade. On the abdomen above the navel and at the eighteenth point along the kidney channel is a location known as the 'stone pass' (石關 shiguan). On the belly we have the 'stone gateway' (石門 shimen); on the chest there is the 'jade hall'(玉堂 yutang) and at either side of the base of the skull we rest on the 'jade pillow' (玉枕 yuzhen).[69] Under the tongue on the lateral sublingual vessels, and directly linked to the 'jade spring', the pool of saliva that is a source of nourishment and transformation in breath meditation, are two acupoints known as 'jade fluid' (yuye 玉液) and 'golden saliva' (jinjin 金津). With the advent of steel needles technical developments caught up with theoretical changes in the construction of the body. The object of acumoxa treatment, like self-cultivation, could finally be trained on perfecting a physiologically conceived body, perhaps even the 'jade body' as it was imagined by the author of *Maishu*(4) who brought together self-cultivation and acumoxa theory. Through locations on the body, some likened to jade itself, it was possible to control the physiological essences and spirits of the body qi, jing and shen. This is a trend that we have seen beginning in the self-cultivation of excavated manuscripts dating to late third/early second centuries BC and that is elaborated and partially systematized in the medical physiology of the *Huangdi neijing* corpus.

CONCLUSION

An examination of early Chinese lithic therapy has found recurring patterns in the techniques of mortuary, self-cultivation and medical theory and practice. Mineral prescriptions such as cinnabar, arsenic, mercury and jade were thought to preserve the body in life and in death. And scattered around the corpse, minerals and stones served to delineate a sacred space free from deterioration or threat from malevolent spirits. In the jade burial suits, now known to have been used since the Eastern Zhou period, we have evidence of the widespread belief that bodies treated with jade could transcend the decay of normal death. In the *Maishu* acumoxa texts we see the same qualities of stone come to bear in innovative medical ideas. Care of the 'jade body' also involved creating a protected internal space by emptying the viscera and filling the limbs – a priority pervasive in daoyin, breath and sexual cultivation, drafted into the principles and practice of the acumoxa therapy. Jade in self-cultivation is always linked to the transformative power of the triad qi, jing and shen. Thus where *Maishu* refers to the 'jade body' it is followed by the earliest extant reference to acupuncture practice, where a lancing stone normalizes the movement of qi, bringing it down through the body and out to the limbs.

There is a paradox between lightness and density that runs through early Chinese perceptions of the nature and potency of stone. Different kinds of medical stone might protect the body from harmful influences and working at or towards the extremities, make it light, rhythmically filling and emptying its organs so that it can become a channel for qi, jing and a comfortable dwelling place for the spirits. But it is precisely from this condition of mobility, lightness and emptiness that it derives the potential to solidify, strengthen and sustain the material nature of the body, its blood, vessels, skin, bone and muscles. It is this body dressed in all the rare qualities of jade that increasingly became the target of sophisticated medical attention during Han times.

GLOSSARY

Jing (精) is a term which is frequently found in medicine and self-cultivation in a triad with shen 神 'spirit' and 氣 qi (see below). In sexual-cultivation jing may refer directly to semen. At other times jingqi 精氣 seems to refer to the finest quality of qi which is the universal vitality out of which things condense and into which they dissolve.

Mai (脈) Harper translates 'vessel', which draws out the early association with the arteriovenous system. I prefer to follow the contemporary analogy with du 瀆 'channel' or 'canal' found in the *Maishu* 脈書 (Channel document). The translation 'channel' also serves to emphasize the relationship of the mai to the superficial anatomical channels as defined by muscle and bone, as they were understood before the more elaborate theories of the jingluo and jingmai found in the *Huangdi neijing* 黃帝內經 (*Yellow Emperor's inner canon*). Jingluo or jingmai has been variously translated as 'conduit', 'meridian', 'circulation tract' etc.

Qi (氣 popularly rendered ch'i) is a complex and changing concept which defies simple lineal histories. In the mid-Warring States references to qi tend to refer to atmospheric and environmental conditions, especially those moist vapours – clouds and mists – and, by analogy, to formless, clustering qualities that can be discerned with careful observation, like smoke, ghosts or the vibrant, martial aura of an army. By the mid fourth century qi often indicates the fundamental stuff in nature which both promotes and indicates vitality in the phenomenal world. It may enter the body in various ways – through the orifices and the skin – but its movement within the body is not formalised. Some historians translate qi as 'vapour' and, in doing so, underline the amorphous watery qualities of steam and mist which are formative influences in the early period and are an enduring feature of the concept. As qi begins to be applied to the phenomena of the inner body, the ideas, although never totally distinct from the early versions go through significant transformations. Rather than replacing the old meanings the range of meanings grow inclusively – a process that is continuous to the present day. I have not translated the term, and shall refrain from doing so because of the substantive changes that take place as qi itself begins to figure in the inner body.

Shen (神) in Warring States literature such as *Guanzi*, *Zhuangzi* and the *Zuo zhuan*, often designates spirits and divine entities that dwell outside the human body. Elsewhere shenming comes to mean characteristics of divine beings that allow them a spirit-like wisdom, a sharpness and clarity of perception rather than a mechanical or analytical intelligence. In Warring States and Early Imperial self-cultivation the shen began to refer to the spirit in-dwelling in the human body, conceived as an individual entity. The term continued to convey the qualities of a mysterious and radiant intelligence as represented in its earlier meaning.

Wuxing (五行) has been variously translated as 'five agents', 'five phases',' five processes' or 'five elements'. The five 'xing' refer to the concepts of wood, fire, earth, metal and water, although they are not equivalent to the elements of early western philosophic thought. The translation 'elements' refers to a material constituent and lacks the dynamic of quality and movement inherent in the early concept of xing. 'Phases' concentrates exclusively on division of time and the passage of the seasons – and 'process' seems to bring a mechanistic quality to what is fundamentally a natural metaphor. 'Agents' refers generally to their influence in a process of transformation and avoids the pitfalls of time and substance inherent in the other translations.

NOTES

1 The research for this paper was carried out thanks to a generous grant from the Wellcome Trust. This paper was originally prepared for the March 2000 meeting of AAS in San Diego. I am grateful to the other members of the panel, 'Embodying Perfection: Self Cultivation Traditions in Pre-Modern China', for their encouragement and to Donald Harper, Li Ling and Mark Lewis for providing me with important research material. I am also indebted to the two readers, Tim Barrett and Charlotte Furth, for their invaluable comments and criticism. All remaining errors are naturally my own responsibility.

2 The most comprehensive discussions of bian and related subjects are in Ma Jixing 馬繼興 and Zhou Shirong 周世蓉. 1978 'Kaogu fajuezhong suojian bianshi de chubu tansuo',考古發掘中所見碥石的初步探索 *Wenwu* 11, 80–82, and Yamada Keiji 1998 *The origins of acupuncture, moxibustion and decoction*, Kyoto: International Research Centre for Japanese Studies.

3 *Huangdi neijing* 黃帝內經 is the work most famous for its exposition of classical acumoxa theories. It is a corpus now extant in three recensions, the *Taisu* 太素(Great Basis), the *Suwen* 素問 (Plain Questions) and the *Lingshu* 靈樞 (Divine Pivot). Each of these is a compilation of small texts dealing with separate topics which may reflect the thinking in a distinct medical lineage. It is thought that the earliest texts were set down during the first or at the earliest the second century BC Collectively they represent the kind of debate through which classical medical concepts matured.

4 Li Shizhen 李時珍. *Bencao gangmu* 本草綱目 (comp. 1552–1593, pr. 1596) Taibei: Hongye shuju 1979.

5 Ken Brashier demonstrates that ideas differentiating souls, the hun 魂 and po 魄, developed independently within the medical field before they were applied in mortuary culture. See Brashier, K. 1996 'Han thanatology and the division of souls', *Early China* 21, 125–158.

6 See glossary

7   See glossary. See also the discussion in Graham, A. 1989 *Disputers of the Tao*, La Salle, Illnois: Open Court, 340–356.

8   The Mawangdui burial mound is located in the northeastern section of Changsha 長沙, Hunan, formerly the Western Han Kingdom of Changsha, and was excavated in the early 1970s. It contains three tombs. Tombs no. 1 and no. 2 belonged to the Lord of Dai Li Cang 利 蒼, and his wife (who was buried in tomb no. 1). Tomb no. 3, from which the manuscripts were excavated, was occupied by one of their sons, who died in 168 BC at the age of about 30.

9   Translated in Harper, D. 1998 *Early Chinese medical literature: the Mawangdui medical manuscripts*, London: KPI, 371–384. It is remarkable that the sequence of the agents correlated to stages of fetal development follows the cycle of conquest, rather than the cycle of generation. Both cycles were known by the second century BC, although some of the correllations do not match later formulations. See *Early Chinese medical miterature*, 379.

10   Zhang Liang's biography is *Shiji* 史記 55, Sima Qian 司馬遷 (*c.* 145–86 BC) References to Beijing: Zhonghua shuju, 1962, 2034–5 and 2046. *Hanshu* 漢書 juan 40, di 10 (comp. AD 58–76) Ban Gu 班固 (32–92), SBBY vol. 55, fasc. 15, 2.

11   *Shiji* 105, 2798.

12   *Shiji*, 2810–11. Bian Que is depicted on Han reliefs as a human headed bird. Liu Dunyuan relates this to similar myths about physicians in the Indian subcontinent and speculates that there was maritime contact. Some Japanese scholars believe that Bian Que belonged to a group of shamans who roamed East China dressed like birds. See the references and discussion in Unschuld, P. 1985 *Medicine in China: a history of ideas*, Berkeley: University of California Press, 97 and 374 n.69.

13   Li Ling has written several articles which bear upon the nature and use of the five stones. See 'Li Ling. 1998 'Wushi kao' 五石考 *Xueren* 13, Jiangsu wenyi chubanshe, 397–405. and 1997, 'Yaodu yijia' 藥毒一家, pp. 77–84, in *Dushu* 讀書 3 and 1993 *Zhongguo fang shu kao* 中國方書考, Beijing: Zhongguo Renmin, 283–309. Also see Rudolph Wagner, 'Lebensstil und Drogen im chinesischen Mittelatler, in *T'oung Pao* 59, 1973, 79–178.

14   Wang Chong 王充 (27–c. AD 100), *Lun heng* 論衡. *Lun heng zhushi* 論衡注釋 Beijing: Zhonghua shuju, 1979, vol. 2, 603.

15   ibid 608.

16   These are huangwu 黃堊, zhishidan 置石膽, dansha 丹沙 'cinnabar', xionghuang 雄黃 'realgar', yushi 礜石 'arsenolite' , cishi 磁石 'magnetite'. Zhouli juan 1. See *Concordance to the Zhouli*, DC Lau and Chen Fong Ching (eds). 1993 Hong Kong: Commercial Press, 9, 1.19.

17   As listed in Li Ling, 'Wushi kao', 400. See also Ge Hong 葛洪 (AD 283–343) *Baopuzi* 抱朴子, juan 4, 'jindan' 金丹, (Beijing: Zhonghua shuju, 1980), 69 and Needham, J. 1976 *Science and civilisation* V.3 Cambridge: Cambridge university press, 1976, 86, and 96, noted.

18   Many of these minerals are the same as those used to colour early paints. See Li Ling, 'Wushi kao', 401.

19   A number of late Qing and early twentieth century scholars have documented the partiality of Wei/Jin period scholars for the use of stimulants. Yu Jiaxi 余嘉錫, for example, describes the odd behaviour of elite users when experiencing the internal heat generated by the prescription. Their outrageous behaviour was mimicked by those envious, less wealthy young men who are documented as falling about writhing on the ground in the market places. See 'Yu Jiaxi 余嘉錫. 1996. 'Hanshisan kao' 寒食散考, pp. 362–404 in *Zhongguo xiandai*

xueshu jingdian: Yu Jiaxi yu Yang Shuda , Liu Mengxi 劉夢溪 (ed.), Hebei: Hebei jiaoyu chubanshe, 362–404. See Li Ling. 1997 'Yaodu yijia' 藥毒一家, pp. 81–81, in *Dushu* 讀書 3.

20 Li Ling (1993).

21 Sun Simiao 孫思邈. (*c*. 581–682 AD), *Qianjin yifang*, 千金翼方, juan 22. Reference to *Qianjin yifang jiaoshi* 千金翼方校釋 (Beijing: Renmin weisheng, 1998), 339. The recipe includes zishiying 紫石英, baishiying 白石英, jishizhi,赤石指 , zhongru 鍾乳 and shiliuhuang 石礦黃. Sun Simiao adds ren shen 人參 and fuzi 附子. In later medical literature remedies of a similar name were used for restoring consciousness from a comotose or prostrated state.

22 *Qianjin yifang*, juan 23 and 24, also mentions the 'Five stone powder prescription for curing cold and changing your life' that was taken by the Marquis of He and Huang fu shian 皇莆仕安 (Huangfu mi 215–82).

23 Yu Jiaxi, 'Hanshisan kao', 366.

24 Wang Kuike speculates that He's original five stone powder (hanshisan 寒石散 also called cold stone powder) is consistent with two recipes – one of cao 草 'herbal substances' and the other of shi 石 'minerals', for resolving wind and cold respectively, taken from Zhang Zhongjing's *Jinkue yaolue* 金匱要略 and recorded by Chao Yuanfang 劁元方 in *Zhubing yuanhou lun* 諸病源候論 (the former which contained yushi 礜石). Chao is quoting from Huangfu Mi. The prescriptions are recorded in *Zhubing yuanhou lun* juan 6, as hanshi san fa hou 寒食散發侯. See Chao Yuanfang 劁元方, *Zhubing yuanhou lun* 諸病源候論 (AD 610). References to *Zhubing yuanhou lun jiaozhu* 諸病源候論校注, Beijing: Renmin weisheng, 1991, 166–170. See Wang Kuike 王奎克, 'Wushi san' 五石散 in *Zhongguo gudai huaxue shi yanjiu*, ed. Zhao Kuihua 趙匱華 (Beijing: Beijing daxue chubanshe), 85–87. His argument is summarised in Li Ling, *Wushi kao*, 398–399.

25 A photograph of the Countess of Dai's newly excavated body is in Fu Juyou 傅舉有 and Chen Songchang 陳松長. 1992 *Mawangdui Han mu wenwu* 馬王堆漢墓文物, Changsha: Hunan 42–43. Since the excavations she is deteriorating.

26 I am grateful to Li Ling for a photograph of the stones.

27 *Kaogu* 1979.2, 134–5. Uncut precious stones have also been found in Tang tombs. See, for example, the sapphires, rubies, topaz and chalcedony found in the bottom of a silver pot containing miniature dragons and a golden leaf. Here we have stones that match four of the colours of the wuxing. *Wenwu* 1972.1, 32. Also see Michaelson, C. 1999 *Gilded dragons*, London: British Museum Press, 121.

28 Morgan, C. 1996 'Inscribed stones', *T'oung-pao* 82, 317–346 traces the history of incribed stones in Song and Tang burial practice with reference to the burial ritual as described in different editions of the the *Lingbao* canon. For a description of a pottery vessel inscription of Eastern Han date (193 AD) see 'Inscribed stones', 338–339. An inscription on the jar reads '(Let) those who practice the Dao bury five stones whose essences will pacify the tomb (and thus) benefit sons and grandsons.' The ore in question has not been identified with certainty. One opinion is that it is yushi 礜石 (arsenolite) known for its demon quelling properties. See Wang Yucheng 王育成 1991. 'Dong Han daofu shili' 東漢道符釋例, *Kaogu xuebao* 1, 54.

29 *Xihan Nanyuewang mu, shang* 西漢南越王墓上. 1994 Beijing: Wenwuchubanshe. 141.

30 Compiled by Luan zhen 鸞甄 (570). tr. Carole Morgan (1996), 327. During the Tang and Song periods passages of Daoist sacred texts, in particular of the *Lingbao liandu wuxian anling zhenshen huangzeng zhang fa* 靈寶煉度五仙安靈鎮神黃繪章法 (Lingbao Method for Salvation

through Sublimation:Yellow Precepts of the five Immortals for Pacifying tombs) of the *Lingbao* canon, were written on stone in cloud seal script, a talismanic script, thought to derive from the initial in creation. These stones then carried the power of the script as well as the alchemical power of their own potential for refinement into the grave to aid in the re-birth of the deceased. See Carole Morgan, 'Inscribed stones', 318 and 326. cf. Livia Kohn, *Laughing at the Dao* Princeton: Princeton University Press, 1995, 74.

31   Mawangdui Hanmu boshu zhengli xiaozu, (ed)., 1985. *Mawangdui Hanmu boshu* 馬王堆漢墓帛書, vol. 4. Beijing: Wenwu, 1985, 52. tr. Harper, *Early Chinese medical literature*, Mawangdui medical literature, 261.

32   Shi Shuqing 史樹青. 1962. 'Gudai keji shiwu sikao' 古代科技事物四考, *Wenwu* 3, 47–48. *Hanfeizi* juan 3, pian 10 'shi guo' 十過. SBBY vol. 173, fasc. 1, 3b.

33   This tile and two others from the same site were originally thought to be some kind of unfired cosmetic or cleansing utensil for scrubbing the skin, with related medical functions. See An Zhiming 安志敏. 1957 'Gudai de caomian taoju' 古代的糙面陶具, *Kaoguxuebao* 4, 1–12. Shi Shuqing reinterprets them as bianshi. Shi Shuqing, 'Gudai keji shiwu sikao' *Wenwu* 1962 3, 47.

34   Li Yu, the Grand General of the Later Wei, used an ancient recipe containing jade powder which preserved his corpse. *Hou Weishu*. cited in Wu Hung. 1997 'The prince of jade revisited' pp. 147–169, Rosemary E. Scott (ed.) in *Chinese jades, colloquies on art and archaeology in Asia No. 18,*. London: Percival David Foundation of Chinese Art. and Li Fang 李方 (925–96). *Taiping yulan* 太平御覽. References to, Siku quanshu vol. 900, 193. Sima Qian also records that Han Wudi took jade powders to strengthen and preserve his body

35   Rawson, J. 1995 *Chinese jade from the Neolithic to the Qing*, London: British Museum Press, p. 74.

36   Jessica Rawson *Chinese jade from the Neolithic to the Qing*, 55

37   I am indebted to Donald Harper for pointing out the jade suit discovered in tomb D9M1 at a Wu 吳 site in Suzhou at Zhenshan 真山. See *Zhenshan Dong Zhou Mudi* 真山東周墓地. 1999. Suzhou bowuguan, Beijing: Wenwu.. It was thought that body suits began between the time of the Han emperors Jingdi 景帝 and Wudi 武帝 and there are non recovered after the third year of the huangchu 黃初 reign period of the Wei king Wendi 文帝. See Mancheng Hanmu fajue baogao, 滿成漢墓發掘報告 1980. Beijing: *Wenwu*, p. 378. SeeLu Zhaoyin. 'shi lun liang Han de yuyi' 試論兩漢的玉衣, *Wenwu* 89.10, pp. 51–58 and 'zai lun liang Han de yuyi' 再論兩漢的玉衣 *Kaogu* 81.1, 60–67.

38   Wu Hung. 1997 'The Prince of Jade Revisited' 147–169 , in R.E. Scott (ed.) *Chinese Jades, Colloquies on Art and Archaeology in Asia No. 18*, London: Percival David Foundation of Chinese Art.

39   All mentions of yuren 玉人 in received literature up until the end of the Western Han period refer to jade workers, rather than people of jade.

40   Wu Hung, 'The Prince of Jade Revisited', 158–164.

41   It seems that jade took on a new significance in the burial rituals of Liangzhu culture. The numbers of jade pieces excavated at burial sites from at that time dramatically increased. Good quality nephrite discs were placed on the stomach and chest of the wealthy while lesser quality jades were found elsewhere or in smaller tombs. Michaelson, C. 1996. 'All excellent qualities: Chinese Jade from the Neolithic to the Han' p. 180, in Silk and stone, London: Hali Publications.

42   Xia Nai 夏鼐. 1983 'Handai de yuqi' 漢代的玉器, *Kaogu xuebao* 2, 133–136.

43   Jessica Rawson describes some of the jade metaphors applied in *Shijing*. She also gives an account of how jade was thought to have been used in the idealisation of Zhou ritual preserved retrospectively in *Zhouli*. *Chinese Jade from the Neolithic to the Qing*, 54–56.

44   *Zhuangzi* 莊子 juan 4, pian 2 ('Mati' 馬蹄). See *Sibu beiyao* (SBBY) vol. 176, fasc. 2. 7b–8.

45   *Shuowen* 1A, 19. See Duan Yucai 段玉裁 (1735–1815). *Shuowen jiezi zhu* 說文解字注. References to Shanghai: Guji, 1981, 10.

46   Boltz, W.J. 1993 'Shuo wen chieh tzu', p. 430 in *Early Chinese texts: a bibliographical guide*, ed. Michael Loewe, Berkeley. SSEC.

47   Collected in Morohashi, vol. 7, 803. See *Concordance to the Zhanguoce*, D.C. Lau and Chen Fong Ching (eds) 1992 Hong Kong: Chinese University of Hong Kong, Institute of Chinese Studies, Commercial Press, 1992: *Zhanguoce* 21, 262. Hanshu juan 72, di 42. SBBY, vol. 56, fasc. 24, 3b.

48   Jiangling Zhangjiashan Hanjian zhengli xiaozu. 1989 Jiangling Zhangjiashan Hanjian *Maishu* shiwen' 江陵張家山漢簡〔脈書〕釋文, *Wenwu* 7, 74. (hereafter '*Maishu* shiwen'). I follow Harper who divides *Maishu* into six core texts which he describes as 'Ailment List', 'Eleven Vessels', 'Five Signs of Death', 'Care of the Body,' 'Six Constituents' and 'Vessels and Vapor'. His titles indicate well the content of each text. See *Early Chinese medical literature*, 31.

49   '*Maishu* shiwen', 74.

50   The word mai is difficult to translate. See Glossary. See Donald Harper, *Early Chinese medical literature*, Prolegomena: Section 3, 13–14 and Sivin, Nathan. 1987 *Traditional medicine in contemporary China*, Ann Arbor: Center for Chinese Studies, The University of Michigan., 34, 122 n. 11; and Paul Unschuld 1985 75, 81–83.

51   Opinions about dating are based on the style of the script which closely resembles that on an inscription of 380 BC See Guo Moruo 郭沫若. 1972 'Gudai wenzi zhi ban de fazhan' 古代文字之辨的發展, *Kaogu* 3 for the earliest report and transcript. Alternative transcriptions are in Chen Shou 沈壽 and Mao Liang 毛良. 1980 *Zhonghua yishi zazhi* 10.2 and 1982.12.2 and Li Ling, Zhongguo fang shu kao, 321.

52   Donald Harper, *Early Chinese Medical literature*, 126.

53   *Mawangdui Hanmu boshu* , vol. 4, 147. The viscera appear to fill and empty at different times and in different stages of breath cultivation. The six cavities are identified later as the Yang viscera or hollow organs, the gall bladder, stomach, large intestine, bladder and 'triple burner.' See *Huangdi neijing suwen* juan 1, pian 4 'Jinkui zhenlun' 金匱真論, SBBY, vol. 204, fasc. 1, 16a.

54   Roth summarises evidence from *Guanzi*, *Zhuangzi*, *Lushi chunqiu* and excavated texts from Mawangdui in Roth 1997.

55   These are described in Harper 1995.

56   Also translated in Harper *Early Chinese medical literature*, 390–91 and n2.

57   Also translated in Harper, *Early Chinese medical literature*, 427.

58   I have matched archaeological and textual evidence of medical stones. See 'Spirit of stone: technical considerations in the treatment of the jade body' in Lo *BSOAS* 65, 1 (2002) 99–128.

59   Paul Unschuld, *Medicine in China – A history of ideas*, 95.

60   Yamada Keiji, *The origins of acupuncture, moxibustion and decoction*, 24.

61   *Shiji* 105, 2793. The statement is a modified version of one in *Hanfei zi* juan 7, pian 21. SBBY, vol. 173, fasc. 2, 2b–3.

62   *Lingshu* juan 1, pian 1 'Jiuzhen shier yuan'. SBBY vol. 205, fasc. 1, 1–4. The *Zhenjing* is one of

the medical canons listed in the Yiwenzhi, the bibliographical treatise of the *Hanshu* and was a nine juan text used by Huangfu Mi (215–282) and associated with a nine juan *Suwen* (Basic Questions). Historians have identified these two texts as the earliest known elements of the *Huangdi neijing*. However, it is impossible to know whether there was ever a Han text known as *Huangdi neijing* or what collection of texts it might have been.

63 For jingmai see glossary under mai.

64 For shen and shenming see glossary. A discussion of the terms can be found in Knoblock, J. 1988 *Xun zi A translation and study of the complete works* Vol 1. 1–6, Stanford: Stanford University Press, 252–254. The concept of shen in the *Guanzi* and the *Huainanzi* is the subject of a paper by Roth, H.D. 'The early Chinese concept of shen: a ghost in the machine?', 11–24 in *Sagehood and systematizing thought in Warring States and Han China*, (Asian Studies Program: Bowdoin College). See also Harper's discussion of shenming in *Early Chinese medical literature*, Prolegomena: Section 4, 10–11.

65 *Lingshu* juan 2, pian 9 'Zhongshi' 終始. SBBY vol. 205, fasc. 1, 10b.

66 Zhang Yanchang 張延昌 and Zhu Jianping 朱建平. 1996 *Wuwei Handai yijian yanjiu*. 武威漢代醫簡研究, Beijing: Yuanzineng chubanshe, 1996, 21–23.

67 *Mawangdui Hanmu boshu*, vol. 4, 146. The passage is translated and discussed in Harper, *Early chinese medical literature*, Translation: MSV1A.3, 8 n.33.

68 There are five references to the jade whip in Mawangdui yangsheng literature. See *Tianxia zhi dao tan, He Yinyang* and *Yangsheng fang* 養生方 where substances are rubbed on to the penis to enhance sexual intercourse. *Mawangdui Hanmu boshu*, vol.. 4, 107, 108, 145, 152, 156.

69 *Zhenjiu jiayi jing* 針灸甲乙經 3, ed. 1979, pp 407, 404, 390 and 336, Beijing: Renminweisheng.

BIBLIOGRAPHY

An Zhiming 安志敏. 1957 'Gudai de caomian taoju' 古代的糙面陶具, *Kaoguxuebao* 4, 1–12.

Boltz, WJ. 1993 'Shuo wen chieh tzu', pp. 429–442 in. Michael Loewe (ed.) *Early Chinese texts: a bibliographical guide*, Berkeley: SSEC.

Brashier, K. 1996 'Han thanatology and the division of souls' *Early China* 21, 125–158.

Chao Yuanfang 劊元方 1991, *Zhubing yuanhou lun* 諸病源候論 (AD 610) *References to Zhubing yuanhou lun jiaozhu* 諸病源候論校注, Beijing: Renmin weisheng.

Chen Shou 沈壽 and Mao Liang 毛良. 1980 *Zhonghua yishi zazhi* 10(2) and 1982 volume 12(2).

Duan Yucai 段玉裁 (1735–1815) 1981 *Shuowen jiezi zhu* 說文解字注. References to Shanghai: Guji.

Fu Juyou 傅舉有 and Chen Songchang 陳松長 1992 *Mawangdui Han mu wenwu* 馬王堆漢墓文物, Changsha: Hunan.

Ge Hong 葛洪. (AD 283–343) 1980 *Baopuzi* 抱朴子, Beijing: Zhonghua shuju.

Guo Moruo 郭沫若. 1972 'Gudai wenzi zhi ban de fazhan' 古代文字之辦的發展, *Kaogu* 3.

Hanshu, 漢書 1962 (comp. AD 58–76) Ban Gu 班固 (32–92), Zhonghua shuju.

Harper, D. 1995 'The bellows technique in Laozi V and Warring States Macrobiotic Hygiene' *Early China* 20, 381–391.

Harper, D. 1998 *Early Chinese medical literature: The Mawangdui medical manuscripts*, London: KPI.

Huangdi neijing 黃帝內經 (comp. C. first century AD) (*Lingshu, Suwen* and *Taisu*). References to Sibu Beiyao (SBBY) edition.

Huangfu Mi 皇甫謐. *Zhenjiu jiayi jing* 針灸甲乙經 (3 ed.) 1979 Beijing: Renminweisheng.

Hunansheng bowuguan and Zhongguo kexueyuan kaogu yanjiusuo. 1974 'Changsha Mawangdui er, sanhao Hanmu fajue jianbao' 長沙馬王堆二，三號漢墓發掘簡報, *Wenwu* 7, 39–48.

Jiangling Zhangjiashan Hanjian zhengli xiaozu. 1989 'Jiangling Zhangjiashan Hanjian *Maishu* shiwen' 江陵張家山漢簡〔脈書〕釋文, *Wenwu* 7, 72–74.

Knoblock, J. 1988 *Xun zi a translation and study of the complete works vols 1. 1–6*, Stanford: Stanford University Press.

Kohn, L. 1995 *Laughing at the Dao*, Princeton: Princeton University Press.

Lau, D.C. and Chen Fong Ching (eds) 1993 *Concordance to the Zhouli*, Hong Kong: Commercial Press.

Lau, D.C. and Chen Fong Ching (eds) 1992 *Concordance to the Zhanguoce*, Hong Kong: Chinese University of Hong Kong, Institute of Chinese Studies, Commercial Press.

Li Fang 李方 (925–96) *Taiping yulan* 太平御覽, References to Siku quanshu.

Li Ling 李零. 1993 *Zhongguo fang shu kao* 中國方書考, Beijing: Zhongguo Renmin.

Li Ling. 1997 'Yaodu yijia' 藥毒一家, Dushu 讀書 3, 77–84.

Li Ling. 1998 'Wushi kao' 五石考 *Xueren* 13, Jiangsu wenyi chubanshe, 397–405.

Li Ling 2000 *Zhongguo fangshu kao*, Beijing: Dongfang chubanshe.

Li Shizhen 李時珍 1979 *Bencao gangmu* 本草綱目 (comp. 1552–1593, pr. 1596), Taibei: Hongye shuju.

Lo, Vivienne. (forthcoming 2002) 'Spirit of stone: technical considerations in the treatment of the jade body' in *Bulletin of the School of Oriental and African Studies*.

Lu Zhaoyin 盧兆蔭, 1981 'zai lun liang Han de yuyi' 再論兩漢的玉衣 *Kaogu* 1, 60–67.

Lu Zhaoyin 1989 'shi lun liang Han de yuyi' 試論兩漢的玉衣, *Wenwu* 10, 51–58.

Ma Jixing 馬繼興 and Zhou Shirong 周世蓉. 1978 'Kaogu fajuezhong suojian bianshi de chubu tansuo', 考古發掘中所見砭石的初步探索, *Wenwu* 11, 80–82.

Mancheng Hanmu fajue baogao, 滿成漢墓發掘報告 1980. Beijing: Wenwu.

Mawangdui Hanmu boshu zhengli xiaozu, (ed.), 1980 *Mawangdui Hanmu boshu* 馬王堆漢墓帛書 1, Beijing: Wenwu.

Mawangdui Hanmu boshu zhengli xiaozu, (ed.), 1985 *Mawangdui Hanmu boshu* 馬王堆漢墓帛書 4, Beijing: Wenwu.

Michaelson, C. 1996 'All excellent qualities: Chinese jade from the Neolithic to the Han' pp. 176–85 in, Jill Tilden (ed.) *Silk and stone*, London: Hali Publications.

Michaelson, C. 1999 *Gilded dragons*, London: British Museum Press.

Morgan, C. 1996 'Inscribed stones', *T'oung-pao* 82, 317–346.

Morohashi, Tetsuji 1957–60. *Dai Kan-Wa Jiten* 大漢和辭典. 13 vols, Tokyo: Taishukan shoten.

Needham, J. 1976 *Science and civilisation* Vol. 3 Cambridge: Cambridge University Press.

Rawson, J. 1995 *Chinese jade from the Neolithic to the Qing*, London: British Museum Press.

Roth, H.D. 1997 'The early Chinese concept of shen: a ghost in the machine?' pp. 1–24 in *Sagehood and systematizing thought in Warring States and Han China*, Asian Studies Program: Bowdoin College.

Roth, H. 1997 'Evidence for stages of meditation in early Daoism', *Bulletin of the School of Oriental and African Studies* 60(2), 295–314.

Shiji 史記. Sima Qian 司馬遷 (*c*. 145–86 BC) 1962 Beijing: Zhonghua shuju.

Shi Shuqing 史樹青 1962 'Gudai keji shiwu sikao' 古代科技事物四考, *Wenwu* 3, 47–48.

Sivin, Nathan. 1987 *Traditional medicine in contemporary China*, Ann Arbor: Center for Chinese Studies: The University of Michigan.

Sun Simiao, (*c.* AD 581–682) 1998 *Qianjin Yifang*, 千金翼方. References to Qianjin yifang jiaoshi 千金翼方校釋, Beijing: Renmin weisheng.

Taiping yulan 太平御覽, References to Siku quanshu vol. 900, 193.

Unschuld, P. 1985 *Medicine in China: a history of ideas*, Berkeley: University of California Press.

Wagner, R. 1973 'Lebensstil und Drogen im chinesischen Mittelatler' *T'oung Pao* 59, 79–178.

Wang Chong 王充 (27–c. AD 100) 1972 *Lun heng* 論衡. Lun heng zhushi 論衡注釋 Beijing: Zhonghua shuju, vol. 2.

Wang Kuike 王奎克. 'Wushi san' 五石散 pp. 85–87 in Z. Kuihua (ed.), *Zhongguo gudai huaxue shi yanjiu* 趙匱華, Beijing: Beijing daxue chubanshe.

Wang Yucheng 王育成 1991 'Dong Han daofu shili' 東漢道符釋例, *Kaogu xuebao* 1, 54.

Wu Hung. 1997 'The prince of jade revisited' pp. 147–169 in R.E. Scott (ed.) *Chinese Jades*,. London: Percival David Foundation of Chinese Art.

Xia Nai 夏鼐 1983 'Handai de yuqi' 漢代的玉器, *Kaogu xuebao* 2, 133–136.

Xihan Nanyuewang mu, shang 西漢南越王墓上. 1994 Beijing:Wenwuchubanshe.

Yamada Keiji. 1979 'The formation of the Huang-ti Nei-ching' *Acta Asiatica* 36, 67–89.

Yamada Keiji. 1998 *The origins of acupuncture, moxibustion and decoction*, Kyoto: International Research Centre for Japanese Studies.

Yu Jiaxi 余嘉錫. 1996. 'Hanshisan kao' 寒食散考, pp. 362–404 in L. Mengxi 劉夢溪 (ed.), *Zhongguo xiandai xueshu jingdian: Yu Jiaxi yu Yang Shuda*, Hebei: Hebei jiaoyu chubanshe.

Zhang Yanchang 張延昌 and Zhu Jianping 朱建平 1966 (eds) *Wuwei Handai yijian yanjiu*. 武威漢代醫簡研究, Beijing: Yuanzineng chubanshe.

Zhang Zhongjing 張仲景 (AD 196–220). *Jinkue yaolue* 金匱要略.

Zhenshan Dong Zhou Mudi 真山東周墓地. 1999 Suzhou bowuguan, Beijing: Wenwu.

Zhuangzi 莊子 (fourth to second centuries BC) References to Sibu beiyao vol. 176, fasc. 2.

14. Kill or cure: Athenian judicial curses and the body in fear

Ralph Anderson

The inclusion of curses in a volume on medical archaeology and anthropology might, at first sight, appear incongruous. They are, on the face of it, intended to cause harm, and belong more to studies of magic and religious belief than to accounts of healing practices. However, the curses examined here, from fifth- and fourth-century Athens and its territory of Attica, draw on contemporary popular notions of mind, body and self for their effectiveness. Further, they may have had therapeutic properties, in certain circumstances, both for those using them and, paradoxically, for those who believed they had suffered from their effects, providing a means to handle the acute anxiety generated by the court cases which the curses seek to influence.

Cursing is treated here not as a single operation involving two people, but as two different operations, namely cursing and perceiving oneself a victim, in which only one person participates actively – in the first case, the curser, in the second, the victim – whereas the other party is present only imaginatively. The language of the extant classical Athenian curse tablets is examined, revealing that curses aim to produce internal paralysis in their victims. Although hardly a new finding, this is re-examined in the light of Ruth Padel's work on popular Greek conceptions of consciousness in order to uncover its precise implications in Greek terms. These are considered first from the victim's perspective, through accusations of magic, and then from that of the person using the curse, through the archaeological evidence for cursing. Accusations of magic appear not simply as devices by which humiliated litigants could save face after an unexpected defeat, but as a means of handling the experience of crushing public failure. They offer a link between the internal, private (and in this case, painful and isolated) world of personal experience and the external, public world. A similar double function is identified for the curser, for whom curses act to remove his pre-trial anxieties both by disabling his opponent, as he believes, and by acting directly on his internal state through the activities involved in performing a curse.

The theoretical framework of the paper is drawn from Kapferer's (1997) work on Sri Lankan sorcery ritual and the formal exposition of this broad approach to human consciousness by Csordas (1990). Although the use of Kapferer's Sri Lankan material as a framework for understanding Greek practices emphasises similarities rather than differences between the two cultures, this is not intended to equate the magical and religious practices and beliefs of the two societies. Kapferer's analysis instead provides an instructive guide for the exploration of Greek practices which seem in some respects to manifest dynamics similar to those at work in Sri Lankan sorcery belief and practice. This paper does not seek to explain every instance of judicial cursing, nor does it assert that uniform motivations and experiences were shared by all cursers and all victims. The Greek magical and religious symbolic system was capable of embracing and giving meaning to vast ranges of divergent individual experience. This paper presents some potential uses of aspects of that symbolic system under particular circumstances.

Greek curse tablets are typically composed of a thin sheet of lead, inscribed and folded or rolled up, pierced with one or more nails, and left either in the sanctuary of a chthonic (earthbound or underworld) deity, or in or near a grave (Figure 14.1. cf. Jordan 1988; Voutiras 1998). Many tablets are so brief that the context of their use cannot be reconstructed, as they bear only a name, presumably that of the intended victim. Others are more elaborate, including details such as the victim's occupation, his relationship with the curser and a description of his intended fate, together with various cursing formulae. In the classical period (500–323 BC), curses were used against rivals in a range of spheres of activity, including business, public performance (oratory, athletics, drama) and erotics, and for seeking redress against thieves. The most frequent context for the use of curses in this period, as reflected in the extant curse tablets, is that of lawsuits in the popular courts of democratic Athens (Faraone 1991, 10–11; Versnel 1991, 60–63). In these 'judicial curses', one litigant seeks to hinder the other's performance in the hearing through the use of a type of curse also known as a binding spell. It is on this type of curse that this paper focuses.

Binding spells, *katadesmoi*, derive their name from the typical verb of magical cursing found on the tablets, *katadeō*, 'I bind, tie down, imprison'. A common alternative was *katekhō*, 'I hold back, keep back, restrain'. The tablet *DTA 107*, for example, from early-fourth-century Attica, reads:

> Let Pherenikos be bound (*katadedesthō*) before Hermes of the underworld and Hekate of the underworld. I bind (*katadeō*) Galēnē, Pherenikos' [girl], before Hermes of the underworld (*khthonios*) and I bind (*katadeō*) her before Hekate of the underworld (*khthonia*). And just as this lead is worthless and cold, so let that man and his property be worthless and cold, and those who are with him who have spoken and counselled concerning me.

> Let Thersilokhos, Oinophilos, Philōtios, and any other judicial supporter (*sundikos*) of Pherenikos be bound (*katadedesthō*) before Hermes of the underworld and Hekate of the underworld. Also Pherenikos' soul (*psukhē*) and mind (*nous*) and tongue (*glōtta*) and plans and the things that he is doing and the things that he is planning concerning me. May everything be contrary for him and for those counselling and acting with him.
>
> *Defixionum Tabellae Atticae (DTA)* 107 (Gager 1992, 127 trans., modified)

The use of the word *sundikos*, which refers specifically to a supporter at a trial, whether a co-litigant, witness or backer, shows that this curse belongs to a judicial context. Other examples of the binding idiom include *DTA* 49 and 50 (Attica, 4th cent. BC), two of a group of four tablets written by the same person and pierced through with a single nail. Both seek to bind (*katadeō*) the *psukhē* and *glōtta* of their victims. *DTA*

Figure 14.1. Unrolled curse tablet, probably 4th century BC Attica (Peek 1941, pl. 24, by permission of the German Archaeological Institute).

84 (Attica, date uncertain) binds 'the wicked tongue (*glōtta*), the wicked heart (*thumos*) and the wicked soul (*psukhē*)' of two separate rivals of the curser. *DT* 69 (Attica, 4th cent. BC) binds the mind (*nous*) and 'wits' (*phrenes* – see below) of its victim.

In each of these examples, the curses do not simply attack their victims in a general sense, as whole persons, but anatomise them. While some of the specific target areas, such as the tongue, are obvious choices in a judicial context, the targetting of other areas suggests a more penetrating attack on the being of the victim, beyond his performance in court. The inscriptions suggest that curses attempt to manipulate the consciousnesses of their victims. Some consideration of Greek concepts of consciousness is therefore in order.

The terminology of mind and body used in the tablets suggests that the popular understanding of consciousness in classical Greece was very different from our own, especially regarding the division between mind and body. This division has been taken for granted in much Western thought on consciousness (see e.g. Gardiner 1998, Csordas 1994 for discussion), but in popular Greek thought such a dualistic split in the nature of human beings may either not have existed or not have been so pronounced. Greek terms relating to elements of the mind or body frequently display a high level of overlap between the psychic and the somatic. The general term *splankhna* (singular *splankhnon*), for example, describes 'the inward parts, especially the heart, lungs, liver, kidneys' (*LSJM*) yet it can also refer to what *we* might want to call 'character' or 'personality'. At Euripides *Medea* 221, it is said to be unfair to dislike someone before you 'clearly learn their *splankhnon*'. Ruth Padel has argued persuasively that it is anachronistic to regard such usages as metaphorical and thus unreal: centuries of movement away from Greek conceptualisations have furnished us with alternative conceptions of the body, the mind and what it is to be human, which leave the Greek originals, and the phrases we use which hark back to them, as metaphorical and poetic alternatives to reality. For the Greeks, Padel argues, *splankhna* always carried the baggage of the full field of its meanings as both entrails *and* personality, even where one sense was contextually privileged over the other (Padel 1992, 9–13, 39).

A more specific example of this overlap and fusion of senses is provided by one of the targets of *DT* 69 (above), the *phrenes* (singular *phrēn*). These form a mind/body organ with both a role in consciousness and a place in the body. On the one hand, the *phrenes* appear to function like our 'mind' and are credited with a role in thinking and feeling. For example, the early poet Hesiod advises his audience to lay up his myth of the generations or races of mankind in its *phrenes* (*Works and Days* 106–7). *Logos* (thought/speech) comes from the *phrēn*, and tears pour from it (Aeschylus *Choephoroe* 107, *Seven against Thebes* 919). On the other hand, the *phrenes* had a physical existence in the body. At *Iliad* 16.480–1, *phrenes* refers to the midriff, lungs or diaphragm: Patroclus' spear strikes Sarpedon 'where the *phrenes* press close about the throbbing heart'.[1] This ambiguity is both summed up and attacked by the anonymous author of the fifth-century BC Hippocratic text, *On the Sacred Disease*. His tirade against the idea that the *phrenes* could be intelligent suggests that this was a popular view at the time, while testifying to the concrete nature of the *phrenes* as part of the physical body: 'I do not know, myself, what power *phrenes* have to think and be intelligent, except that if someone is unexpectedly overjoyed or upset, they leap and make the person jump. This is because of their fine texture and very wide extension in the body' (*On the Sacred Disease* 20, Loeb 2.178–181, Littré vol. 6, p. 392). It would make little sense for us to describe our own minds as having a fine texture and wide extension in our bodies, or to describe a spear piercing someone's mind in anything other than a figurative sense. That the Greeks could speak in such terms suggests a view of consciousness as embodied, that is, that the category of the psychic was not separated from and opposed to the somatic.

Other terms commonly found on curse tablets, *psukhē* and *nous*, are clearly more psychic than somatic, yet, as Padel argues, they too are conceived of as literally 'inside' us. They 'share profoundly in the learning, feeling, thinking … attributed to innards. … The question is not what actual physical reference they might have, but how the words behave' (Padel 1992, 27). That is, we should not attempt to map the Greek terms on to our own vocabulary of consciousness but should instead look at the uses to which the Greeks themselves put the words.

In terms of its historical development, *psukhē* initially shared in the physicality of the *splankhna*, referring to actual breath, especially breath as a sign of life, as at *Iliad* 22.466–7, where Andromache gasps out her *psukhē* as she faints. By the fourth century, however, especially in prose and above all in philosophy, it had come to mean 'soul', the essence of a person (e.g. Plato *Meno* 81b. Cf. Vernant 1983, 333–5; Padel 1992, 31). However, the important point here is the function of *psukhē* as an inalienable part of a human being. Padel calls it the 'sensual, emotional, purposeful self' (1992, 30). It is involved in perceiving the world: the sight of the lock of Orestes' hair is stamped upon his sister Chrysothemis' *psukhē* (Sophocles *Electra* 902–3). It is a seat of emotion and desire: Phaedra's *psukhē* is subjugated by *erōs*, sexual passion (Euripides *Hippolytus* 505, 527). It is the force of embodied consciousness directed into the world: in battle, a fighter is 'strong in hands and *psukhē*' (Pindar *Nemean* 9.38; cf. Lysias 20.29, where *psukhē* is 'courage' or 'spirit'). It leaves the body at death or when consciousness is lost (e.g. Hyperenor's death at *Iliad* 14.518 and Andromache's fainting, above).

Nous captures the sense of consciousness directing itself into the world. The most common translation, 'mind', does not bring out its full range of applications, which includes attention, intelligence and purpose (Handley 1956, 209–10). In the phrase *prosekhein ton noun*, 'to attend to, pay attention to', *nous* indicates critical attention, and with it perception (e.g. Thucydides 7.19.5, Lysias 10.10, 28.7). The command *deuro noun ekhe*, 'pay attention', is literally 'have/hold your *nous* hither' (Euripides *Orestes* 1181). Because his *nous* is turned elsewhere, Eteocles fatally does not notice that his dying brother and enemy Polyneices still holds his sword (Euripides *Phoenissae* 1418). When Oedipus impugns the seer Teiresias' prophetic art, he calls him 'blind in ears and *nous* and eyes' (Sophocles *Oedipus Tyrannus* 371). To 'have *nous*' is to have sense, to be right (e.g. Aristophanes *Ecclesiazusae* 433, 747; Plato *Laws* 887e). A deed that has *nous* is a sensible one (e.g. Sophocles *Electra* 1328; Euripides *Hippolytus* 920). To act *kata noun*, 'according to *nous*', is to act with purpose (Aristophanes *Knights* 549). To have something in your *nous* is to have a plan, purpose or idea (Aristophanes *Knights* 499, *Peace* 762). In some traditions, *nous* appears as an intentional, constitutive force: for Parmenides and Heraclitus, it created the world, and yet is inside human beings (Padel 1992, 33; Parmenides fr. 16; Heraclitus fr. 17DK). If *nous* is 'mind', it is a planning mind directed towards a specific end, or a perceiving mind addressing a particular object. It is practical and applied, not simply 'mind' in the abstract.

Such, then, are the targets of binding in judicial curses. The overlap between psychic and somatic exhibited by these terms, in particular the *phrenes*, suggests a conception of consciousness – mind, thought and feeling – in Greek popular thought as embodied. A potentially useful framework for the concept of embodied consciousness is elaborated by Kapferer in his analysis of Sri Lankan sorcery beliefs and practices. In this tradition, it is considered 'that consciousness is embodied but also transcends its embodiment' (1997, 226), a belief which is manifested in the ceremonies Kapferer studies. This addresses an important dynamic of embodied consciousness, its orientation towards the world around it, termed intentionality (not an intention, but the state of having intentions) by some scholars (see Kapferer 1997, 4–5, 305 n. 1). As Kapferer puts it, 'body and world form a relatively balanced sensory unity or flow together' (1997, 222). Consciousness does not originate solely in the human organism but is an emergent property of the involvement of the body in its world. Sri Lankan anti-sorcery rituals use this framework in their treatment of intense human anguish, which is seen as an attack by sorcery and frequently felt as acute fear or anxiety. This isolates the victim from his social and physical environment, which can come to be experienced by the victim as dominated by the hostile sorcery and thus itself threatening and hostile (Kapferer 1997, 227–35). The sorcery seen as underlying the victim's suffering is conceived of as binding the victim in its coils. For the most elaborate anti-sorcery rite, the Suniyama, the patient begins in a wretched, pre-language condition, on the margins of the human world, bound in coils representing the hostile sorcery and which make manifest his near-solipsistic isolation. The rite progressively severs these coils while restoring the patient to the centre of the human world, oriented outwards towards its horizons.

In the Greek context, *phrenes, psukhē* and *nous* can be seen as manifestations of the consciousness and intentionality of a human being, that is, his or her outwards extension towards the environment. They may be seen as particular cultural expressions of the way embodied consciousness directs itself into the world and transcends the physical boundaries of the organism through perception, speech and action. On this analysis, to bind the *phrenes, psukhē* and *nous* is to deprive the victim of his intentionality, that is, to prevent his consciousness transcending the boundaries of its own body and apprehending and interacting with its world. The loss of intentionality can be minor (to lose one's thread or have one's mind go blank) or more radical (including both sleep and unconsciousness and, in the Sri Lankan case, the traumatised withdrawal of sorcery victims).

The potential for connecting one form of loss of intentionality, unconsciousness, with binding in Greek thought is suggested by certain uses of verbs such as *pedaō* and *xumpodizō*. Though not found in the curse tablets, these are relevant here because both refer to binding, meaning respectively 'bind, shackle, or fetter' and 'tie the feet together, bind hand and foot' (*LSJM*). *Pedaō* even appears to have functioned as a poetic literary equivalent of *katadeō* in Pindar *Olympian* 1.75–78 (Faraone 1991, 11). At *Odyssey* 23.16, for example, sleep binds (*epedēse*) Penelope's eyelids. To awaken is to be freed from sleep's shackles, as at Sophocles *Ajax* 675–6, where 'all-powerful Sleep releases those he has bound' (*ho pankratēs hupnos / luei pedēsas*). In Plato's *Republic* (488c), mutineers 'bind' (*xumpodisantas*) a ship's captain with drink or drugs.

In the courtroom, it is possible that a loss of intentionality would take the form of an attack of paralysing fear or 'stage fright' that would prevent a litigant from speaking.[2] A fragment of Euripides' *Alcmeon*, for example, describes how 'Fear (*phobos*), when someone has been brought before the court to speak on a charge of murder, stuns the mouth (*stoma*) of men and shuts up the *nous*, so he cannot say what he wants (*ha bouletai*)' (Frg. 67 Nauck). The sense of fear as a loss of intentionality is seen also in Theophrastus' discussion of cowardice (*deilia*), which he calls 'a sort of yielding (*hupeixis*) of the *psukhē* due to fear' (Theophrastus *Characters* 25). The verb *hupeikō*, from which *hupeixis* is derived, means to retire or withdraw, or to yield something to another person. Its usages suggest a loss of agency, or the subordination of one person's will to that of another. At Xenophon *Cyropaedia* 8.7.10 and *Memorabilia* 2.3.16, for example, it describes young men deferring to their elders. In Plato *Crito* 51b it describes yielding to one's country's commands. A fear-inspired *hupeixis* of the *psukhē*, one of the manifestations of a human being's intentionality, may be taken as a withdrawal from the world and a failure of the self to extend into an environment which has become too much to bear.

That the vocabulary of binding could also capture the experience of fear is suggested by a passage of Euripides' *Ion*. Here, Creusa explains why she attempted to kill her son, Ion, as a baby: 'My son, I was bound by fear when I cast away your life. I killed you against my will!' (*en phobōi, teknon,/katadetheisa san apebalon psukhan./ekteina s' akous'* – 1497–99). In this example, the verb of being bound, *katadetheisa*, is a passive form of the verb of binding found on many curse tablets, *katadeō*.

A more complex example is found in Aeschylus' primordial courtroom drama, the *Eumenides*, when the Erinyes (Furies) sing their 'binding hymn' (*humnos…desmios*) to shackle Orestes' *phrenes* (*desmios phrenōn* – *Eumenides* 306, 331–2, 345–6). Faraone (1985) argues that the hymn is of a piece with the courtroom setting of the *Eumenides* as a whole, and should be considered as a literary rendering of a judicial binding spell. While the hymn may be seen as inflicting internal paralysis and a loss of intentionality on Orestes, the manifestation of this as fear is not explicitly marked in the text. Such a manifestation would, however, be consistent with the terrifying effect the Erinyes have on mortals throughout the play. The Pythia, the priestess of Apollo at Delphi, is literally brought to her knees by fear at the mere sight of the Erinyes sleeping in the temple: 'I have no strength left in me nor can I go upright. I run with the aid of my hands … for an aged woman, overcome with fright, is a thing of naught…(*deisasa gar graus ouden* – 36–8)'. Orestes is warned by his protector, Apollo, not to let fear of the Erinyes conquer his *phrenes* (*memnēso, mē phobos se nikatō phrenas* – 88). At 407, even Athena feels the need to assert that she is not afraid of them, merely startled by their strange appearance. Significantly, this assertion comes immediately after the choral passage in which the Erinyes perform their *humnos desmios*, at the end of which they ask who among mortals does not stand in awe of them or fear them (*hazetai* – 389; *dedoiken* – 390). If the Erinyes inspire fear in all who encounter them, their 'binding hymn' may be thought of as representing the sudden, overwhelming onslaught of that fear on its victim.

In classical Athens, lawcourts could inspire fear in those appearing before them, even outside the doom-laden world of tragedy. A lawcourt was an unpredictable and dangerous arena. Defendants risked heavy punishments, even death, for some offences. Prosecution too could prove hazardous. In some types of lawsuit, plaintiffs who failed to secure a certain proportion of the vote would themselves be punished. Any case could have ramifications beyond the particular lawsuit: legal action in Athens was frequently motivated as much by feuding behaviour as by the pursuit of justice (Cohen 1995, ch. 5). Since all suits were brought by private individuals, a plaintiff, whether successful or not, ran the risk of becoming personally embroiled in a judicial feud with the defendant's family and friends (Osborne 1985, 1–6 traces one example). The potential gains and losses of a trial were clearly enormous in the high-status trials represented by the preserved speeches of the Attic orators, but even in low-profile cases the pressures on litigants could be considerable. For those who had little, like the litigants in the majority of cases, even small penalties could be disastrous.

In addition to the hazards inherent to legal action, the lawcourt was itself an intimidating place. Athenian juries often comprised several hundred jurors, who were not obliged to sit still and listen, but could – and did – heckle, talk among themselves, interrupt with awkward questions, object to the order of points in a speech, or simply jeer an unpopular litigant from the court (Bers 1985). Crowds of spectators were frequently in attendance (Lanni 1997). Litigants had to face all this in person, as each man represented himself.[3] There were no lawyers, and no judges to control the proceedings.

Not only was the case itself at stake in a trial, but each litigant also stood to gain or lose face from the proceedings. In an intensely agonistic society such as Athens, in which male identity was constructed through public competition, injury to self-esteem and public standing might be as deeply felt as the loss of the case (Versnel 1999, 149). Humiliation of the unsuccessful was a staple of Greek culture. Pindar describes an unsuccessful athlete's 'hateful homecoming' and disgrace, his slinking down back alleys and shunning of hostile eyes (*Olympian* 8.69, *Pythian* 8.86–87). In the *Iliad*, fear of ridicule forced Hector to remain outside the walls of Troy and face Achilles (22.99–130). The Sophoclean hero's greatest fear was the triumphant laughter of his enemies (Knox 1964, ch. 2). Quite apart from the exultation of the victor at the unsuccessful litigant's expense, juries themselves delighted in mocking a loser (Demosthenes 18.138; Versnel 1999, 156). Such mockery alienated the victim from his immediate social context, as spectators united in public derision of him and his associates, and was a thoroughly crushing experience in its own right.[4]

Faced with such high stakes in such an unpredictable and pressurised setting, even an experienced speaker could lose his nerve, as happened to the renowned fifth-century orator Thucydides, son of Melesias (i.e. not the historian), in an incident discussed by Faraone (1989). An ancient commentary on a reference to the event in Aristophanes' *Wasps* tells us that, having heard his accusers speak, this 'excellent orator' found himself unable to utter a word in his defence, 'just as if he had a tongue (*glōtta*) which had been bound (*enkatekhomenēn* – from a compound of *katekhō*) from within'. He was convicted (*Wasps* 946–48 and scholion). Another version, however, in Aristophanes' *Acharnians*, presents a picture of Thucydides simply being outgunned by the flashier rhetoric of his younger adversaries (*Acharnians* 703–18). Faraone infers that two interpretations of events had been in circulation. On one side, the victors attributed their success to their superior rhetoric, which had bewildered an old man. On the other side, those more friendly to Thucydides 'suggested that some kind of mysterious paralysis intervened which prevented such a famous public speaker from defending himself' (Faraone 1989, 151).

Faraone interprets such allegations of magic-use as face-saving exercises. Following Brown (1970, 25), he states that 'the acknowledged use of magical rituals in the community often provides professional performers with an easy opportunity for face-saving in the event of a radically poor performance' (Faraone 1989, 154). The opportunity to employ such tactics was enhanced by the circumstances under which public opinion was formed in Athenian society, in particular the 'somewhat wider social acceptance of mendacity' in Greek society generally (especially where honour was at stake) and the absence of an 'authoritative empirical science which could rule out incredible claims' (1989, 159 and n. 29). While allowing that dishonest or cynical accusations could be made, to evaluate all such accusations against a modern scientific tradition in this way denies the possibility that an unexpectedly defeated litigant could make an accusation of magic that was neither dishonest nor self-deluding but instead reflected his felt experience. What would it mean for a defeated litigant genuinely to accuse his opponent of cursing him, and what role does the curse play in the accuser's experience?

If we take an accusation as reflecting actual experience, the accusation of cursing may be seen as the objectification and externalisation of the victim's experience of paralysis and fear. Unlike in cases of 'voodoo death', which are commonly analysed in terms of the power of suggestion (a position discussed by e.g. Davies, for a Haitian context – 1986, 131–142), there is no evidence from classical Greece that the victim was deliberately made aware of the curse (Graf 1997, 161–169; Faraone 1985, n. 7). However, this is immaterial to the self-perception of the victim. The existence of the curse, for the victim, is founded on and proved by his own experience – his humiliating and inexplicable failure and the internal experience underlying it. What matters is that the victim *feels* as if he has been cursed. That is, that he experienced the collapse of his intentionality, manifested as a sudden inability to speak or think clearly at a crucial moment, leaving him profoundly isolated from other human beings, in an exposed and vulnerable position before them, internally frozen and unable to extend himself towards those around him. Where this paralysis and isolation was due to fear, the aversiveness of the experience would be particularly potent, and the urgency of externalising it proportionately increased.

In such circumstances, to level accusations of cursing could be a step towards exorcising the experience, since the accusation contains the implication that the language of the curse tablets has been successfully imposed on the victim's consciousness. Because this language provides a model of the victim's experience which captures his experience while at the same time being comprehensible to others, the curse, as it appears in the accusation, can provide a 'verbal object' for the accuser's experience. It lifts the experience of feeling oneself cursed out into the world, overcoming the victim's isolation by rendering his experience visible to and shareable with others (cf. Scarry 1985, 15–16).

The therapeutic benefit of the accusation does not depend solely on its being believed, although it would be greatly enhanced by such acceptance. The act of objectification of experience which underlies the accusation and makes it possible is in itself restorative of the victim's intentionality. In apprehending his loss of intentionality as a state of cursedness resulting from his opponent's action, the victim constitutes his all-pervading subjective state as an object of reflective thought, separating it from the self it had previously inhabited and dominated, and putting the victim, to some extent, in control of his condition.

This process of objectification is in itself an achievement, since the preceding state of loss of intentionality (a paralysis of the 'organs' of consciousness) was an inability to apprehend the world and form the objects of consciousness. That is, the pressure in the courtroom temporarily overwhelmed the ability of the victim to form experience out of the raw sensations of being in the world. In the act of objectification, then, the victim to some extent begins to transcend the experience of loss of intentionality, and finds a way to escape and manage a condition which he would otherwise be forced passively to endure (cf. Lienhardt 1961, 170). In the act of naming his condition, the victim is reconnected to the world through the act of placing it out into the world as an object (rather than experiencing it as coterminous with the self) and by perceiving things which happen inside himself as originating externally.[5]

What, however, of the curser? There are many potential motivations for cursing. One is that the curser believes that cursing represents his only chance of success. Faraone argues that the person most likely to use a binding spell is someone who 'doubted his or her ability to win without it, that is ... the [curser] was the perennial 'underdog'... protecting himself against what seemed to be insurmountable odds' (Faraone 1991, 20). Many early Attic judicial curses feature the names of prominent Athenian orators and politicians, such as Demosthenes and Lycurgus (*DT* 60 – Wünsch 1900, 63; Faraone 1991, 16 and n. 76 cites many further examples). This supports the idea of the curser as underdog, as it suggests, first, that some of the trials concerned were high-profile, high-risk ventures, and second, that, to the curser, the opposition did indeed appear overpowering.[6] Despite the democratic and egalitarian ethos of the courts, wealthy citizens had significant advantages over their poorer counterparts. They could afford the services of professional speech-writers, for example, and may well have performed a range of (expensive) public services which would testify to their polis-friendly characters and buy them favour with the jury (Ober 1989). A person perceiving himself to be faced with insuperable opposition may already have a threatened or constricted intentionality. He may come to perceive the future as no longer open but already determined. Anticipating an encounter he has no hope of winning, he may feel himself irrevocably locked into a course of events which he is powerless to influence (through ordinary means) and which will lead him inevitably to public defeat and humiliation.[7]

Should a person in such a state of dread or acute and sustained anxiety choose to inflict a curse on his opponent as a way of evening the odds, the curse may act on his condition in two ways. First, the curse restores the curser's intentionality by, in his own eyes, removing the threat at source. In the curser's belief, his performative verbal and material acts choke off the intentionality of the opponent so that *he* will be the one who cannot speak. Second, since the curser is caught in a state of threatened or restricted intentionality, the composition of the curse, which depicts a similar state, may be seen as an objectification and externalisation of the curser's own state. In a similar way to that in which the curse as it appeared in the accusation functioned as an externalisation of the victim's experience, the curse as it is performed by the curser externalises his own experience of fear or dread. The orientation of the curse towards the pragmatic source of the curser's anxiety, his opponent, aids the process of objectification and externalisation because it grounds it in the curser's real concerns. That this objectification is accomplished by means of the powerful, performative language of magic aids the propulsion of the harmful experience it encapsulates away from the body and into the world.[8]

The production of the material element of the curse, the tablet, is crucial to the process of objectification and to the feeling of the efficacy of the curse. The tablet as a physical object does more than simply carry the words of the cursing formula. As mentioned earlier, many curse tablets are inscribed simply with the victim's name, suggesting that it was enough to recite the name and the cursing formula over the tablet as it was twisted and perforated. The tablet is the physical embodiment of the curse and the guarantor of its longevity. Anecdotes from the later history of magic bear this out. The fourth-century AD orator Libanius, for example, recovered his health and his lecturing voice when the apparatus of a binding spell, a mutilated chameleon, was removed from his lecture room (Bonner 1932; Libanius *Oration* 1.243–50). More explicitly, a Greek curse tablet from a late Roman cemetery in Savaria, Pannonia, promised it would remain effective for as long as the tablet lay with the corpse with which it was buried (Gáspár 1990). In these examples, the physical component of the curse was vital. The creation of that physical component involves symbolically loading the sheet of lead that will become the tablet with the image of the fear and anxiety of the curser, either by engraving it into the surface or by speaking the formula over it as it is folded and pierced. The curser's fears are converted into a weapon to attack his opponent.

The curser with his curse seeks to release himself from his inhibitory state of feeling himself 'bound' and disadvantaged. On one level, the curse achieves this by, in the curser's belief, rendering his opponent helpless through the imposition of a paralysis of the 'organs' of consciousness which will prevent him from speaking or taking effective action.[9] On another level, the curse frees the curser by objectifying his own state, naming and distancing his fear, and thus restoring his sense of personal agency. The two modes of action are integral to each other. The objectification of the curser's experience in itself reinstates his intentionality, but it is the role of the tablet in this process of objectification that makes the curse an effective weapon in the curser's eyes. As a weapon, the curse is intended to inflict a loss of intentionality on its victim, and this is meaningful for the curser because he knows only too well what a loss of intentionality feels like. The manipulation and reconstitution of the curser's internal, emotional state is essential to the creation of the curse, just as the creation of the curse is essential to the reconstitution of the internal state.

The manipulation of the curser's internal state during the performance of the curse is shaped and directed by the places chosen for the ritual. Normal practice in fifth- and fourth-century Athens was to deposit the tablet either in the sanctuary of a chthonic deity, such as Hekate, or in or near a grave. In particular, graves of the 'untimely' dead, the *aōroi*, were sought out. Where it has been possible to estimate the age of the deceased in graves containing curse tablets, the person has been found to have died young (Faraone 1991, 3 and 22 n. 6; Gager 1992, 118; Jordan 1988, 273). The characteristic of the *aōroi* dead is to have died 'incomplete', that is, without having achieved the *telos* (goal) of their lives. The clearest example of this was for a woman to die unmarried and childless, and thus not 'really' a 'proper woman'. Similarly, the graves of murder-victims, the *biaiothanatoi*, were selected.[10] Being 'incomplete' in life, the untimely and violently dead were equally 'incomplete' in death. They formed an ambiguous, liminal category of the dead, believed to be unable to enter the underworld completely, and to wander the earth as ghosts for the duration of their 'natural span' (Johnston 1999, chs. 4–5; cf. Tertullian *De Anima* 56.4).

A grave, especially the grave of an *aōros* or a *biaiothanatos*, had properties which were important in generating and directing the energies of a curse. Two main features stand out, liminality and pollution. A grave is, by its nature, a liminal space. It occupies an ambiguous and unstable position between the worlds of the living and the dead, located in the world of the living but simultaneously part of the underworld. As with other markers of the boundaries between realms, it appears stable only as long it is not scrutinised in its own right. When examined directly, it dissolves into a state of flux and instability, oscillating between the categories it separates, belonging to each in equal measure while being truly part of neither (Johnston 1991, 217f; cf. Handelman 1981, 324–34). The ontological liminality of graves is matched by their spatial liminality. Athenian burials normally took place outside but not far from the city walls. The main cemetery, the Kerameikos, for instance, lay immediately outside one of the main gates, in the margin where city and country meet. Even within the human world, the place of the dead was an ambiguous space.

Sanctuaries of chthonic deities are also liminal. As sanctuaries, they lie between the worlds of gods and mortals. As shrines to underworld deities in particular, they hover between the worlds of the living and the dead. Spatially, they often occupied liminal zones. A fifth-century shrine to Hekate, for example, has been tentatively identified at a crossroads just outside the boundary of the Athenian Agora, itself a sacred space (Camp 1986, 78; *LIMC* VI.986).

To enter a liminal space is to court confusion and endanger one's intentionality. Pindar, at a loss as to how to finish an ode, described himself as having been 'whirled at the path-shifting crossroads' (*Pythian* 11.38). By going to a grave or a chthonic sanctuary, places at the edge of the human world, the curser takes up a physical position which reflects his personal state. This position mirrors the marginal position within its own life world taken up by the body in fear, which finds itself unable to participate in human society.

Liminality, however, is a multi-directional property. While a liminal site may be marginal and a place of confusion and indecision, as Pindar complained, its existence in the margins of the ordered world can give it a creative aspect as a place that refuses to be definitively categorised. It is a place of potential and a place from which to start afresh. Its position betwixt and between the categories of the ordered world may, in some sense, bring it alongside the liminal phase of a rite of passage, in which initiands may undergo a symbolic social death in order to be reborn into new identities.

Chthonic deities virtually embody this double-edged potential. They bring 'the terror of destruction' (Burkert 1985, 200) but also life and prosperity: 'The corn comes from the dead', and a farmer should pray to Demeter and chthonian Zeus (Hippocrates *On Regimen* 4.92, Loeb 4.442–3, Littré vol. 6, p. 658; Hesiod *Works and Days* 465). Hades, the ruler of the dead, is also Pluto, the bringer of wealth (Burkert 1985, 200). Even the chthonic Erinyes of Aeschylus' *Eumenides* have a benevolent aspect: by the end of the drama, they have been persuaded to become the Eumenides of the title, the 'kindly-minded ones'. Hekate, one of the deities most commonly invoked in cursing, has not only an association with malignity, death and pollution but also a benign and protective aspect (Parker 1983, 222–23; Johnston 1990, 21–28).

In cursing, the curser goes to a place which is simultaneously both a marginal place mirroring his own marginal state and a place of unformed and potentially regenerative energy. These balanced potentialities are set in motion by the second major feature of graves of the *aōroi*, their pollution. On top of the taboo against interfering with graves, or more generally against loitering in cemeteries, the graves of the 'restless' dead might be expected to exercise an additional repulsion (Johnston 1999, chs. 4 and 5; Parker 1983, 38–9). Chthonic sanctuaries may be thought to have exercised a similar repulsive force due to the potentially destructive and polluted aspects of their patrons.[11] The essential element in this is aversiveness. Pollution and danger concentrate around beings, places and substances that defy the categories established by human society for ordering the world. The encounter with such beings and places can engender feelings of disgust, an immediate and potent sensation which operates on a visceral level prior to that of reflective thought, inspiring its subject to reject and recoil from contact with the source of the pollution (Kapferer 1997, 247; cf. Kristeva 1982).[12] This moment of recoil mobilises the ambiguous potential latent in liminality in the direction of regeneration. It forces the curser back from the margins of the human world, reorienting him towards society and its norms by calling upon deep-seated cultural aversions instilled into him as part of his membership of that society.

The curse itself, in its aspect as an attack on the victim rather than a restorative measure for the curser, invokes the destructive potential of the margins of the world. Victims are to be bound before the gods of the underworld (*DTA* 107), or for as long as the tablet lies in the grave (Gáspár 1990), or are to have everything become useless for them, as the corpse in the grave is useless (*DT* 68). The victim's consciousness is to be bound fast, reducing it to a marginal state mirroring that of the grave. The status of graves and chthonic sanctuaries as gateways to the underworld transmits the destructive forces of the curse away from its creator and towards the powers who will carry the curse out. The act of depositing the tablet in a location that is at once on the margins of society's world and repulsive to the curser separates the destructive forces embodied in the tablet from him, flinging them towards his victim at the same moment that he himself is thrust back from those margins and towards the centre of the human world.

What conclusions can be drawn? Cursing draws on popular beliefs about what makes a human being (consciousness, the human organism and its relationship with the world). The texts that dominate our picture of ancient medicine and are the foundation of the history of modern Western medicine – the Hippocratics, Galen, and the like – denigrate this popular tradition as senseless and irrational (Lloyd 1987). However, an examination of cursing reveals this tradition as being far from senseless but rather as demonstrating a subtle and inventive use of the resources provided by the Greek symbolic system to manipulate consciousness.

This paper does not attempt to explain all cursing under the same rubric, as this would deny the versatile inventive power of Greek religion, which was critical to its role in the shaping of lived experience. It would also require that all those who used curses shared the same motives and all victims perceived themselves identically. I hope at least to have shown that there can be more to cursing than the intention to inflict harm (although this is clearly a central element), and more to accusations of magic than a straightforward concern with face-saving. The acts both of cursing and of perceiving oneself the victim of a curse can have therapeutic and regenerative implications for the curser and the self-perceived victim respectively, offering them responses to and means to grasp problematic and distressing experiences.

Acknowledgments
I would like to thank my graduate supervisor, Prof. Paul Cartledge, for his support and comments on several versions of this paper. I would also like to express my gratitude to various members of the graduate community in the classics faculty, in particular Ashley Clements for introducing me to (and explaining) the work of Kapferer, Lisa Bendall for her detailed comments on several late drafts and Coulter George for checking over an earlier version of the paper. I would also like to acknowledge a sizeable debt to the respective oeuvres of Christopher Faraone and Hendrik Versnel, who have done much to open up the field of ancient magic in recent years. Finally, I would like to thank the two reviewers for their criticisms and comments on the paper. Any imperfections, misjudgements and outright errors that still remain I freely claim as my own.

Notes

1   Janko (Kirk (ed.) 1992, 379–80) interprets *phrenes* as 'lungs', as opposed to 'diaphragm', used by the Loeb translator, Jones. *LSJM* gives *phrenes* as midriff.

2   This should not be taken as equating 'stage fright' with the complete mental breakdown witnessed in sorcery victims in Kapferer's account. Sorcery is an extreme example, and appears here because it offers a dramatic illustration of the dynamics of embodied consciousness.

3   Although various legal 'consultants', including professional speech-writers, were available, they could not take the litigant's place in court.

4   Cf. *Eumenides* 155–59, where reproach is likened to a goad, striking under the *phrenes*. David 1989 details laughter as deliberate humiliation in Sparta.

5   There is a further benefit to this, in that, since the victim now perceives his failure as originating externally, he is freed from potentially corrosive self-recrimination regarding his ability to live up to male ideals of public competitiveness.

6   The underdog motif is visible in what Faraone (1991, 11) considers possibly the earliest example of a binding spell, Pindar *Olympian* 1.75–78, where Pelops, hoping to avoid the fate of all Hippodameia's previous suitors, who were killed by her father after being unable to beat him in a chariot race, appeals to Poseidon to 'bind/block' (*pedason* – from *pedaō*) the older man's spear.

7   We might compare the cases of Olympic Games victors who won '*akoniti*', literally 'without dust' – their opponents caved in before the contest had even begun.

8   A caveat is necessary as to whether the tablet is deposited by the curser himself or by a professional acting on his behalf. The simple language of the early *katadesmoi* requires little or no specialist knowledge beyond basic literacy, in contrast with the highly elaborate formulae of later magic. Both material and textual evidence are ambiguous. Four bound, lead 'voodoo dolls', encased in lead boxes containing curses, found in two graves in the Kerameikos dating to around 400 B.C., appear to be the work of the same person(s), providing perhaps the earliest material evidence for a professional magician in Greece (Faraone 1991, 4). However, another tablet, dating from only a few years later suggests that magic, like religion, was not solely in the hands of professionals: it contains frequent spelling corrections which suggest some self-consciousness about certain non-standard features of the author's own speech (Jordan 1999, 116f, no. 1, Ashmolean Museum inv. G.514.3). This could indicate a less than practised author. As far as textual evidence goes, Plato *Republic* 364c refers to wandering magicians who offer their services to the wealthy,

suggesting the professionalisation of magic. Against this, when Plato sets out punishments for those harming others with spells, at *Laws* 933d–e, he distinguishes between 'prophets and diviners' and 'those without knowledge of the prophetic art', suggesting that both 'professional' and 'amateur' practitioners co-existed. It is possible that, in the classical period, magic had not been monopolised by a professional class but could, at least in its simpler forms, be practised by a wide range of people. The elaboration of Greek magic, which took it out of reach of the non-specialist, was a later phenomenon conditional on Alexander's conquests and the subsequent transmission to the Greek world of the developed magical lore of Babylonia and Egypt (Gordon 1999, 248). For the purposes of this paper, I assume that at least some cursers, if they did not compose the tablets themselves, at any rate deposited them in person. For *katadesmoi* made or placed by professional magicians, I would suggest that a similar process of reorientation and regeneration of the curser takes place, but that the reconstitution of his intentionality is achieved initially through the social contact with the *magos* inherent in the act of consultation and then through the action that he knows the *magos* has taken on his behalf.

9   How this will manifest itself is left open and is largely unimportant as long as it *does* manifest itself somehow. This flexibility helps support the belief in the efficacy of curses, as it allows a wide range of phenomena to be interpreted as signs of the curse's taking effect.

10 The term *biaiothanatos*, literally 'violently killed person', does not apply to the war-dead. Death in battle was the heroic *telos* par excellence.

11 Cf. a late third- or early fourth-century A.D. Greek magical handbook which advises the magician to flee after reciting a spell at a crossroads, 'for it is there that she [Hekate] appears' – PGM LXX 16–17 (Betz 1986, 297–98).

12 Kapferer 1997, 238–47 describes a similar dynamic in cursing in Sri Lankan. Sorcery shrines are characterised by both liminal location and pollution. The more potent shrines lie in 'marginal geographical, ethnic, social and political locations, at boundaries of transgression and conversion' (239), often at the edges of cities. The original shrine to Suniyam, the main sorcery demon, lies in an area where Sinhalese-speaking communities give way to Tamil-speakers (240). One famous shrine is crowded with mangy and flea-bitten dogs, which are loathsome to the local (Muslim) population. The pot used in cursing is itself conceived as holding disease and pollution, as its spouts represent cobra hoods (242–43). Suniyam himself is an ambiguous being, embodying both destructive and creative potential (261–62).

Abbreviations

DT   Audollent, A. *Defixionum Tabellae*, Paris, 1904.

DTA   Wünsch, R. *Defixionum Tabellae Atticae*, IG 3.3, Berlin 1897, in A.N. Oikonomides (ed.), *Inscriptiones Graecae IG I², II/III² paraleipomena et addenda*, Chicago: Ares Publishers, 1976.

LIMC   *Lexicon Iconographicum Mythologiae Classicae*, 9 vols. in 18 pts., Zurich: Artemis, 1981–

LSJM   Liddell, G. and Scott, R. *A Greek–English Lexicon*, 9th edition, revised by Jones, H. S. and Mackenzie, R., Oxford, 1940.

PGM   Preisendanz, K. *Papyri Graecae magicae: Die griechischen Zauberpapyri herausgegeben und übersetzt von Karl Preisendanz*, 2 vols., Stuttgart: Teubner, 1973–4

Bibliography

Bers, V. 1985 'Dikastic *Thorubos*' pp. 1–15 in P.A. Cartledge and F.D. Harvey (eds) *Crux: essays in Greek history presented to G.E.M. de Ste. Croix on his 75th birthday*, London: Duckworth.

Betz, H.D. (ed.) 1986 *The Greek Magical Papyri in Translation*, Chicago and London: University of Chicago Press.

Bonner, C. 1932 'Witchcraft in the Lecture Room of Libanius' *Transactions of the American Philological Association* 63, 34–44.

Brown, P.M. 1970 'Sorcery, Demons and the Rise of Christianity' pp. 17–45 in M. Douglas (ed.) in *Witchcraft Confessions and Accusations* London: Tavistock.

Burkert, W. 1985 *Greek Religion: Archaic and Classical*, Oxford: Blackwell. Translation by J. Raffan of *Griechische Religion der archaischen und klassichen Epoche*, Stuttgart: Verlag W. Kohlhammer, 1977.

Camp, J.M. 1986 *The Athenian Agora: excavations in the heart of Classical Athens*, London: Thames and Hudson.

Cohen, D. 1995 *Law, Violence and Community in Classical Athens*, Cambridge: Cambridge University Press.

Csordas, T.J. 1990 'Embodiment as a Paradigm for Anthropology' *Ethos* 18, 5–47.

Csordas, T.J. 1994 'Introduction' pp. 1–24 in T.J. Csordas (ed.) 1994 *Embodiment and Experience: The existential ground of culture and self*, Cambridge: Cambridge University Press.

David, E. 1989 'Laughter in Spartan Society' pp. 1–25 in A. Powell (ed.) *Classical Sparta: Techniques behind her success*, New York and London: Routledge.

Davies, W. 1986 *The Serpent and the Rainbow*, London, Collins.

Faraone, C.A. 1985 'Aeschylus' ὕμνος δέσμιος (*Eum.* 306) and Attic Judicial Curse Tablets' *Journal of Hellenic Studies* 105, 150–54.

Faraone, C.A. 1989 'An Accusation of Magic in Classical Athens (Ar. *Wasps* 946–48)' *Transactions of the American Philological Association* 119, 149–160.

Faraone, C.A. 1991 'The Agonistic Context of Early Greek Binding Spells', pp. 3–32 in C.A. Faraone and D. Obbink (eds) *Magika Hiera: Ancient Greek Magic and Religion*, Oxford and New York: Oxford University Press.

Gager, J.G. (ed.) 1992 *Curse Tablets and Binding Inscriptions from the Ancient World*, Oxford and New York: Oxford University Press.

Gardiner, M. 1998 '"The Incomparable Monster of Solipsism": Bakhtin and Merleau-Ponty', pp. 128–144 in M.M. Bell. and M. Gardiner (eds) *Bakhtin and the Human Sciences*, London, Thousand Oaks, New Delhi: Sage Publications Ltd.

Gáspár, D. 1990 'Eine griechische Fluchtafel aus Savaria' *Tyche* 5, 13–16.

Gordon, R. 1999 '"What's in a list?" Listing in Greek and Graeco-Roman malign and magical texts', pp. 239–78 in D.R. Jordan, H. Montgomery and E. Thomassen (eds) *The World of Ancient Magic: Papers from the first International Samson Eitrem Seminar at the Norwegian Institute at Athens 4–8 May 1997*, Bergen: Norwegian Institute at Athens.

Graf, F. 1997 *Magic in the Ancient World*, Cambridge, Mass.: Harvard University Press. Translation by F. Philip of *Magie dans l'antiquité gréco-romaine*, Paris: Belles Lettres, 1994.

Handelman, D. 1981 'The Ritual Clown: Attributes and Affinities' *Anthropos* 76, 321–70.

Handley, E.W. 1956 'Words for 'Soul', 'Heart', and 'Mind' in Aristophanes' *Rheinisches Museum für Philologie* 99, 205–25.

Johnston, S.I. 1990 *Hekate Soteira: A study of Hekate's roles in the Chaldean Oracles and related literature*, Atlanta: Scholars Press.

Johnston, S.I. 1991 'Crossroads' *Zeitschrift für Papyrologie und Epigraphik* 88, 217–224.

Johnston, S.I. 1999 *Restless Dead: Encounters between the Living and the Dead in Ancient Greece*, Berkeley, Los Angeles and London: University of California Press.

Jordan, D.R. 1988 'New Archaeological Evidence for the Practice of Magic in Classical Athens' pp. 273–77 in *Praktika of the 12ᵗʰ International Congress of Classical Archaeology*, Athens, September 4–10, 1983, vol. 4.

Jordan, D.R. 1999 'Three Curse Tablets' pp. 115–124 in D.R. Jordan, H. Montgomery and E. Thomassen (eds) *The World of Ancient Magic: Papers from the first International Samson Eitrem Seminar at the Norwegian Institute at Athens 4–8 May 1997*, Bergen: Norwegian Institute at Athens.

Kapferer, B. 1997 *The Feast of the Sorcerer: Practices of Consciousness and Power*, Chicago and London: University of Chicago Press.

Kirk, G.S. (ed.) 1992 *The Iliad: a commentary*, vol. IV: books 13–16, commentary by R. Janko, general editor G.S. Kirk, Cambridge: Cambridge University Press.

Knox, B.M.W. 1964 *The Heroic Temper*, Berkeley and Los Angeles: University of California Press, and Cambridge and London: Cambridge University Press.

Kristeva, J. 1982 *The Powers of Horror: an essay on abjection*, New York and Guildford: Columbia University Press. Translation by L.S. Rondiez of *Pouvoirs de l'horreur*, Paris: Editions du Seuil, 1980.

Lanni, A.M. 1997 'Spectator sport or serious politics? Οἱ περιεστηκότες and the Athenian lawcourts' *Journal of Hellenic Studies* 117, 183–189.

Lienhardt, G. 1961 *Divinity and Experience: The Religion of the Dinka*, Oxford and New York: Oxford University Press.

Lloyd, G.E.R. 1987 *The Revolutions of Wisdom: Studies in the Claims and Practice of Ancient Greek Science*, Berkeley, Los Angeles and London: University of California Press.

Merleau-Ponty, M. 1962 *Phenomenology of Perception*, London: Routledge and Kegan Paul. Translation by C. Smith of *Phénoménologie de la perception*, Paris, 1945.

Ober, J. 1989 *Mass and Elite in Democratic Athens: rhetoric, ideology and the power of the people*, Princeton: Princeton University Press.

Osborne, R. 1985 *Demos: The Discovery of Classical Attika*, Cambridge: Cambridge University Press.

Padel, R. 1992 *In and Out of the Mind: Greek Images of the Tragic Self*, Princeton, New Jersey: Princeton University Press.

Parker, R. 1983 *Miasma: Pollution and Purification in early Greek Religion*, Oxford: Oxford University Press.

Peek, W. 1941 *Kerameikos: Ergebnisse der Ausgrabungen; Bd. 3: Inschriften, Ostraka, Fluchtafeln*, Berlin: Deutsches Archäologisches Institut, W. de Gruyter.

Scarry, E. 1985 *The Body in Pain: The Making and Unmaking of the World*, Oxford and New York: Oxford University Press.

Vernant, J.-P. 1983 *Myth and Thought among the Greeks*, London, Boston, Melbourne, Henley: Routledge and Kegan Paul. Translation of *Mythe et pensée chez les Grecs*, Paris: Librairie François Maspero, 1965.

Versnel, H.S. 1991 'Beyond Cursing: The Appeal to Justice in Judicial Prayers', pp. 60–106 in C.A. Faraone and D. Obbink (eds) *Magika Hiera: Ancient Greek Magic and Religion*, Oxford and New York: Oxford University Press.

Versnel, H.S. 1999 'Κόλασαι τοὺς ἡμᾶς τοιούτους ἡδέως βλέποντεσ "Punish those who rejoice in our misery": On curse texts and *Schadenfreude*' pp. 125–62 in D.R. Jordan, H. Montgomery and E. Thomassen (eds) *The World of Ancient Magic: Papers from the first International Samson Eitrem Seminar at the Norwegian Institute at Athens 4–8 May 1997*, Bergen: Norwegian Institute at Athens.

Voutiras, E. 1998 *ΔΙΟΝΥΣΟΦΩΝΤΟΣ ΓΑΜΟΙ: Marital Life and Magic in Fourth-Century Pella*, Amsterdam: J.C. Gieben.

Wünsch, R. 1900 'Neue Fluchtafeln' *Rheinisches Museum für Philologie* 55, 62–85 and 232–71.

15. Etruscan female tooth evulsion: gold dental appliances as ornaments

Marshall Joseph Becker

INTRODUCTION

The anthropological data on tooth evulsion, including both ethnographic and archaeological examples, is not extensive (see Becker 1995b) but does indicate that the deliberate removal of incisors is an ancient as well as modern behaviour known from many cultures around the world. Tooth evulsion was not common in Europe, but recent research (Robb 1997) has indicated that it existed during the Neolithic period in Italy among at least some of the ancient peoples of that period. Seeking evidence for cultural continuities in this behaviour has yet to reveal conclusive evidence, largely because cremation burial became popular among the Iron Age populations throughout much of Europe. The mortuary programs involving cremation destroy almost all the evidence that we would need to demonstrate that tooth evulsion was practised, a fact that may explain why we have almost no known European examples of this behaviour.

Recent studies of gold dental appliances used in ancient Etruria has provided the data needed to infer that tooth evulsion survived in at least one small part of Italy into the Classical era. Much of what we know about women in ancient Greece and Rome derives from their images and roles as depicted on works of art (cf. Bonfante 1975). Women's social relations also are inferred from surviving texts (Fantham *et al.* 1995). Relatively new is the use of anthropological models of culture to interpret these artistic and textual depictions of women. The application of techniques from physical anthropology to identify the sex of skeletal remains and to investigate gender differences in health and disease incidence has recently become another means by which we can learn more about the lives and status of ancient women. Combining these approaches enables us to understand more clearly the lives of women in antiquity, and to differentiate among the varieties of cultures in which they lived.

Ancient gold dental appliances now have been studied in detail as an interesting category of artefact (e.g. Becker 1999b, 2000). This research, combined with recent discoveries in physical anthropology, archaeology, the ancient literature and social anthropology, enables us to re-examine and to understand better the functions of these appliances and the role they played in the lives of South Etruscan women. The dynamics of social change in Etruria during the period of Romanization is also revealed by this new information.

Numerous references to gold dental appliances appear in the classical literature.

These comments were well known long before the first actual example was recovered from an archaeological context toward the end of the 18th century (Böttiger 1797). Etruscan goldsmithing skills are well documented from objects found in their elaborate tombs, but Etruscan primacy in applying these arts to 'dentistry' had remained almost unknown. Now we can document that more than 2,600 years ago skilled Etruscan goldworkers first applied their talents to fashioning complex dental appliances (Waarsenburg 1994). Two sets of skills were needed to make these pontics: knowledge of goldsmithing and knowledge of the teeth around which appliances were fitted. As will be discussed later, the fabrication of dental appliances at that time appears to have been an activity of skilled goldsmiths or other crafters, rather than the work of barbers or physicians.

During the end of the 19th century the systematic mining of Etruscan tombs revealed most of the known examples of ancient dental appliances. Since 1885 an extensive literature has emerged dealing with the score of ancient Etruscan dental appliances that are known. These appear in an impressive variety of shapes and sizes (Becker in preparation a). While often noted by archaeologists, these ancient prostheses were a subject more frequently examined by dental or medical historians. The work of Clawson (1934) and Johnstone (1932a, 1932b) provide the best early descriptions. The many poor descriptions of these appliances allowed numerous errors to infiltrate the literature, a problem exacerbated by the many copies made of these early examples of 'dentistry.' Authors mistook duplicates for originals, rarely examined the actual appliances, and often generated error-filled 'inventories' (Deneffe 1899, Sudhoff 1926, Casotti 1947). Tabanelli (1963) attempted a true catalogue (see also Emptoz 1987), but not until the important review by Bliquez (1996) do we find specific and accurate information regarding the history of these prostheses. Bliquez also offers some of the best available photographs of these appliances.

MATERIALS AND METHODS

With the recent discovery of a 'new' appliance in a museum collection there now are twenty examples of Etruscan gold dental appliances known from Italy (cf. Bliquez 1996, see also Becker 1999b). Another example was recovered from excavations at Tanagra in Greece (Becker in preparation a). These all are distinct from the type of Near Eastern dental appliances that were developed a bit later in antiquity (Becker 1995–96). All of the surviving examples in Italy, England and Denmark have been examined in detail (e. g. Becker 1992a, 1994a–d) with the specific intent of under-standing where in the mouth they were placed, and to infer their function or functions. The ancient literature also was reviewed to determine what could be learned from the texts in which dental appliances are noted. The relationship of medical practitioners to those who performed dental extractions (Becker in preparation a) also helps us to understand the social context in which these appliances were made and worn. The minimal archaeological evidence associated with these pieces (see Cozza and Pasqui 1981; Waarsenburg 1994, Becker 1999a) was also surveyed to determine if relevant information could be gleaned from the few notes associated with their excavation.

Dentistry

An historical summary helps place these dental appliances in the context of medical developments relating to the mouth. The earliest records of dental care appear in Egyptian medical papyri of the seventeenth and sixteenth centuries BC (see Badre 1986). Guerini (1909, 28) notes that the Egyptians may have decorated teeth with gold after death, but concludes that they produced no dental prostheses before 500 BC (see also Emptoz 1987, 546, fig. 1; Becker 1994c). Dental prostheses first emerge in the Etruscan world in the seventh century BC (Johnstone 1932b, 448; see also Bliquez 1996 n. 18, Hoffmann-Axthelm 1985, 28–31, 38–39). By 630 BC (Becker in preparation a: no. 18) a high status resident of ancient Satricum was buried wearing a complex and sophisticated dental appliance. Over the next few hundred years the proliferation of gold prosthetic devices in Etruria is indicated by the numbers of examples that survive, as well as the frequency of reference to them in Roman texts. These texts (Bliquez 1996) suggest that such appliances were still being made after 200 BC, but no examples of gold bridgework are known from the period of the later Roman Republic or of the Empire. The earliest Near Eastern dental prostheses, made from gold or silver wire, appear in the fifth century BC (Becker 1995–96; see also Masali and Peluso 1985). The use of wire prostheses to hold loose teeth in place extended into the twentieth century. Several ancient sources refer specifically to the use of dental appliances for the preservation of loose teeth, as well as for the replacement of 'missing' teeth (Bliquez 1996). The relevant section of the Hippocratic texts (Hippocrates *Dentition* 1. 32; Jones 1946, 1953) provide no basic information on dentistry other than the references to the 'wiring' of loose teeth, suggesting an origin for the Near Eastern type of appliance. In fact, the Hippocratic section labelled 'Dentition' is not an independent text at all, but quite clearly an early scribal error (Hippocrates 1923: 317–319) that relocated this brief section from Aphorisms III to a place between sections 25 (teething) and 26 (children's tonsils: see Hippocrates *Aphorisms* 3. 25).

Hippocrates (*On Joints* 30–34) notes that teeth displaced or loosened through an injury to the jaw could be braced with gold wire until they re-established themselves in place. Loose teeth generally are a consequence of poor dental hygiene, of dental disease or the result of trauma, such as a blow to the mouth. The simple band type appliance could help to stabilise teeth loosened by a blow or by periodontal disease. While most of the known dental prostheses appear to be cosmetic, the simple band variety might also have served to hold in place teeth that were loosened by a blow or by disease. The possibility that such simple bands may have been purely ornamental is strong.

Dental pontics, or bridges, include those appliances with one or more false teeth that are held in place to form a device meant to replace one or more missing teeth. Even these cosmetic appliances, designed to fill the gap left by 'lost' teeth (see below), would serve to maintain the remaining teeth in their correct places. This would ensure continued proper articulation of the teeth and their continued efficient function, one of the principal goals of modern orthodontistry. At best this was but an incidental function. The suggestion that these soft gold appliances could be used in straightening teeth (Corruccini and Pacciani 1989) has been noted elsewhere (Becker 1995b). Martial

(AD 40–104) notes that in Italy various materials were used to replace missing teeth, including bone, ivory, and even the tooth of an ox. Pine and boxwood, often claimed to have been used for the dentures of President George Washington but never documented, are also said to have been used by the Romans (see Bliquez 1996: Text 10). Martial's observation suggests Roman use of dental appliances, yet only one of the known examples derives from a context that might have a Roman origin.

TOOTH EVULSION AND SOUTH ETRUSCAN PONTICS

After nine years of detailed studies, a consistent theme emerged regarding where these ancient pontics were placed in the mouth. Almost all were designed to replace one or both of the upper central incisors of the women who wore them. However, during the 1980s studies of the entire skeletal population at Tarquinia, in South Etruria (Becker 1990, 1993, in preparation b), revealed that incisors were rarely lost, or were the last teeth to be lost by old adults. Incisors are the most common teeth still in place at death at Tarquinia. Women under 60 years of age almost never lost their incisors, and the more common early loss of the flanking teeth would make it impossible to wear an appliance. Therefore, the probability of an adult woman having lost one or both upper central incisors by natural means and being able to wear a pontic is improbably low.

Leprosy, which includes as a symptom the early loss of upper central incisors, was considered as an alternate possible reason for the absence of these teeth in Etruria. The leprosy theory can be rejected since no evidence of that disease is found in the surviving skeletal remains of the Etruscan period. Even if we posit that the interesting social relations and proximity between Etruscan males and females generated unusually high levels of violence (cf. Robb 1997), the skeletal evidence demonstrates that these women did not lose incisors in the process. Loss due to violence would be detectable in the skeletal record and also might be expected to remove left front teeth, as most Etruscan males may be assumed to have been right-handed. In fact, where a single tooth is replaced it invariably is a right central incisor. Tooth loss due to a task-specific activity that was part of 'women's work' also has been ruled out since no activity can be specified either in the ethnographic database or by inference regarding a specific behaviour.

TOOTH EVULSION: THE SOCIAL ANTHROPOLOGY OF RITUAL REMOVAL

Wearing an Etruscan pontic obviously requires the absence of one or both incisors, but the presence of the flanking teeth is essential for installation. Thus, one must infer that healthy teeth were deliberately removed from these Etruscan women in a process anthropologically documented from around the world (cf. Suzuki 1982) and referred to as 'tooth evulsion' (Becker 1995b).

Evulsion is the term used when one or both incisors, usually but not always the upper central, are deliberately removed. This most commonly is a ritual procedure, often compared with circumcision as a rite of passage (see Beidelman 1987). The term 'avulsion' (or luxation) is used when one or more teeth are accidentally knocked out, due to injury, or removed prematurely as in the case of a child's deciduous dentition that would soon fall out naturally.

The parallels between tooth evulsion and circumcision generally involve rituals associated with coming of age, or puberty rites. No study has tabulated the correlation between male and female circumcision and gender associations with tooth evulsion. Simply the ability to endure pain is one element in this ritual process, but other complex cognitive associations may be inferred. While widespread throughout the world, tooth evulsion only remained common in parts of Africa and Australia through the twentieth century. Modern replacement of healthy incisors with gold teeth exists among certain social classes and ethnic populations in the western world today. However, since the removal of healthy teeth violates most contemporary dental ethics the subject has not been studied.

No historical reference to tooth evulsion exists from any part of the classical world and no examples of tooth evulsion are known from the existing skeletal remains from Greece or Rome. In fact there had been no evidence from any place in Europe, from any period of time, where tooth evulsion has been documented (cf. Suzuki 1982) prior to John Robb's sophisticated study of Neolithic period dentition in Italy (1997). Robb's evaluation of the data led him to conclude that tooth evulsion had been practised among some Neolithic period groups in Italy.

The evidence associated with Etruscan dental appliances provides direct archaeological and biological evidence for the deliberate removal of one or both upper central incisors among high status Etruscan females expressly for the purpose of wearing a dental pontic (cf. Becker 1995b). I believe that deliberate removal or evulsion of upper central incisors was being practised by these South Etruscan women in order to replace the deliberately removed tooth with a gold-work substitute. Some of these deliberately removed teeth may have been 'recycled,' or used by these Etruscans to serve as the 'false' teeth in dental pontics. This recycling would solve the cosmetic problem of matching size and colour (Becker 1995b). In cases where damage to the extracted tooth was extensive, a replacement tooth might be required.

During the Iron Age the various Etruscan peoples, as most Italic peoples, uniformly practised cremation of the dead. This cultural behaviour masks the possibility that tooth evulsion also was practised during that period. Although no evidence has been found from this period, the *ossilegium* (cremated remains) of these peoples should be carefully inspected for traces of gold. The earliest known pontic, from Satricum, has been dated to approximately 630 BC (Waarsenburg 1994, Becker 1994d). By the seventh century BC inhumation had become common throughout central Italy, but the use of large open tombs created situations that were not conducive to skeletal preservation (Becker 1993). Careful reviews of the existing skeletal material from this region may provide some support for Robb's conclusions as well as for my own.

EVIDENCE FOR DENTAL EVULSION IN SOUTH ETRURIA

We know about ancient dental extractions from a considerable classical literature on this aspect of medicine. In the early nineteenth century Carabelli (1831) searched the classical texts for information which relates to ancient dentistry. More recently, Heyne (1924) focused research on dentists and dentistry in the classical literature. Many authors reading the early Greek texts and the Latin translations that followed, underestimate just how much Roman medicine had been influenced by the Etruscan tradition in surgery and dentistry (Tabanelli 1963, 74–89), and ignore the possible influences of Egyptian and Phoenician knowledge (Saunders 1963). Medicine in ancient Rome had reached a high degree of sophistication by the second century BC when almost all aspects of general dentistry as it is now known, with the exception of tooth repair and orthodontistry, had become common medical knowledge.

Skilled practitioners of dental extractions probably operated for hundreds of years before the first known reference to a dental forceps appears. The proper removal of a tooth is a very skilled operation, and all instructions direct the tooth puller to cut the gum down and work the tooth loose manually to be certain that the root is withdrawn intact. Any bit of root remaining within the jaw after an unsuccessful extraction prevents proper healing and can have fatal consequences, a fact that ancient dentists knew quite well. The use of scaling instruments and specialised blades for cutting the gum and bone surrounding the tooth, to expose and loosen the root and to get a better grip with fingers or with an instrument, was common by the first century BC (see Jackson 1990). Indirect evidence for the practice of tooth extraction in antiquity derives from references to dentists on tombstones, or the occasional depiction of what some scholars believe may be a dental forceps (Lanciani 1892, 353). Numerous surviving examples of instruments believed to be dental forceps are known (see Künzl and Weber 1991). L. Bliquez (*pers. comm.*) believes that the first reference in a text to an *odontagrisi*, which is translated as a 'tooth-forceps' (Hippocrates *Peri Ihtrou* 9.2) in which Jones places at 'a date later than 400 B.C.' (Hippocrates 1995: 297–298). In this text note is made that the *odontagra*, like the uvula-forceps, are such simple tools that 'anyone can employ [them], since their use appears to be straightforward.'

Now we also have one archaeological site providing unequivocal evidence for the 'professional' practice of tooth extraction in antiquity. Excavations by a Danish team that was part of an international program co-ordinated by Dr. Irene Iacopi (Archaeological Superintendent for the Roman Forum) focused on the large Temple of Castor and Pollux in the Forum Romanum. Their excavations revealed an important series of small shops, or *tabernae*, built into the main temple platform and main stairway of the temple (see also Strong and Ward-Perkins 1962, 25). One of these *tabernae* yielded large numbers of human teeth indicating that dental extractions were one aspect of the trade conducted there (Nielsen and Zahle 1987; Guldager and Slej 1986, 33; Guldager 1990; Poulsen 1992, 56; Nielsen 1992, 109–111, Becker in press a). The effectively extracted diseased teeth found here demonstrate that dentistry was associated with the pharmaceutical aspect of the medical trades. This shop provides the best archaeological evidence for dental extractions known from the ancient world.

A DENTAL PONTIC NOW IN COPENHAGEN

Perhaps one of the best known Etruscan gold dental appliances is in the collections of the Danish National Museum, Copenhagen (Becker 1992a, 1994b, 1995a; Fig. 15.1). This example represents one of the four types of Etruscan dental appliances; the ring-constructed variety (Becker in preparation a). The ring-constructed type uses a complex variation of the simple band technique (cf. Becker 1996) but is designed to hold a 'false' tooth in place. The surviving human teeth associated with the Copenhagen specimen provides evidence for comparative dental wear and tooth size that enables us to identify this pontic as worn by a female (see Table 15.1) who died at between 30 and 50 years of age. The Copenhagen appliance was fashioned for placement in the upper jaw of this adult female.

The Copenhagen appliance is formed from three distinct, small, seamless gold rings ('loops') that were cold-welded into a series. The two lateral loops surrounded the healthy 'anchor' teeth in the jaw while the central loop held the false tooth in place between them. The lateral loops were fitted over the upper left central incisor (I1 – first incisor) and the right lateral incisor (I2). Each of the loops is seamless, having been formed by drawing out a ring from a solid piece of gold rather than by making a loop from a strip of gold. The three loops of the Copenhagen appliance, each custom-designed to fit around one tooth, are joined by invisible cold welds. The lateral loops were curved in such a way as to encircle the base of each living dental crown, with specific fitting done after the false tooth had been set into the band and the appliance was ready to be inserted.

The lateral loops of the Copenhagen appliance were designed to conform to the contours of the natural teeth. The central band was made to hold an artificial right central incisor (I1) by forming a sharply rectangular enclosure to prevent the squared base of the replacement tooth, of ivory or bone, from slipping in this collar. The false tooth set into this 'box' would have been a 'crown' only, with its upper and exposed portion carved to mimic the tooth that it replaced. The lower part or base of the false tooth would have been square-cut to fit into the 'box.' No rivet (pin) is needed in this type of appliance since the false tooth was held in place the way a gemstone is fixed into a setting. A small band was made and then fitted with the false tooth in the same fashion that a goldsmith would make any bezel setting. The rectangular setting prevented rotation and facilitated a good fit. The false tooth was secured in place by pressing the gold tightly around it. With the lateral loops attached the bridge is completed, a design remarkably similar to modern dental pontics. The bridge was inserted into the mouth by fitting the lateral bands around living teeth using pressure to mold the extremely pure, and therefore soft, gold band securely in place. This appliance was meant to be a permanent fixture.

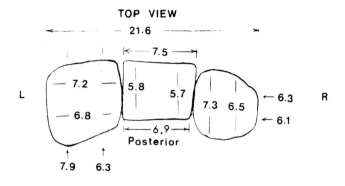

TOP VIEW

21.6

7.5

L   7.2   5.8   5.7   7.3 6.5   ← 6.3   R
     6.8   ← 6.1

6.9
Posterior

7.9   6.3

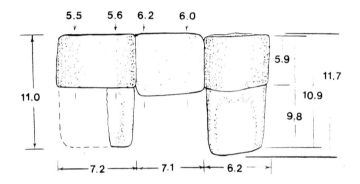

5.5   5.6   6.2   6.0

5.9

11.0   11.7
                            10.9
                            9.8

7.2   7.1   6.2

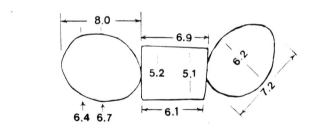

8.0

6.9

6.2

5.2   5.1

7.2

6.4 6.7   6.1

BOTTOM VIEW

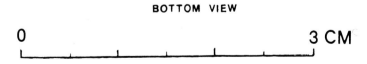

0   3 CM

Figure 15.1. The Copenhagen dental appliance.

Table 15.1. Odontometric data.

Mesial-distal and buccal-lingual diameters

	I2 M-D / B-L	I1 M-D / B-L	1I M-D / B-L	2I M-D / B-L
Orvieto/ CPN	6.1 / 7.1	7.2 / 5.6	7.2 / 7.1	- - / - -
Valsiarosa	6.0 / 6.0	7.5 / 6.1	7.7 / 6.1	6.1 / 6.0
Bruschi III	7.2 / 6.9	6.1 / 5.9	5.3 / 5.3e	(7.9 4.5)
Liverpool I	? / ?	6.2 / 7.2	6.9 / 7.5	? / ?
Liverpool II	5.5e / -	7.0e/ -	[8.7* / -]	

( ) bent and distorted band (possible error in measurement)
  e Estimation
[ ] dimensions of the "false" tooth.
 * Appears not to be original tooth in this appliance.

Only the M-D length is important as an indicator of the space to be filled by the false tooth, presumably to M-D length of the tooth removed.

SOUTH ETRURIA ONLY

A distribution map of ancient dental appliance find spots (Becker in preparation a) demonstrates that this technology was concentrated in South Etruria. The archaeo-logical locations where these appliances originated suggest that their use was specific to this small region only, and that the use of dental appliances was not a cultural custom employed throughout the Etruscan realm (cf. Becker 1992b). South Etruria can be defined as the region immediately north of Rome between the Tiber and Arno rivers and from the Tyrrhenian Sea and the Appenine Mountains. This zone has been identified as culturally distinct in many aspects. Art forms, burial customs, and many other traits specific to this region have led many archaeologists to consider South Etruria as a distinct territory within the general 'Etruscan' realm. Unless there were radically different mortuary patterns in the areas generally identified as Central and Northern Etruria – patterns that might involve the removal of gold appliances from the mouth of the deceased – we must conclude that this technology was a part of the ornamentation used only by women in South Etruria. The few examples found beyond the borders of this specific zone of ancient Etruria can be explained by two factors relating to the movement of the high status Etruscan women who might be expected to wear such appliances. Rather than suggesting that women in cultures outside South Etruria might be emulating the fashions of that region, I believe that these Etruscan women had moved beyond their native territories through two possible processes. First, high status marriage alliances made between upper class Etruscan mercantile families and foreign trading partners may have led women wearing these pontics to live far from home. A second possible explanation is that these women found with Etruscan pontics were accompanying their Etruscan husbands beyond their homeland while the men were conducting the business that made the Etruscans wealthy.

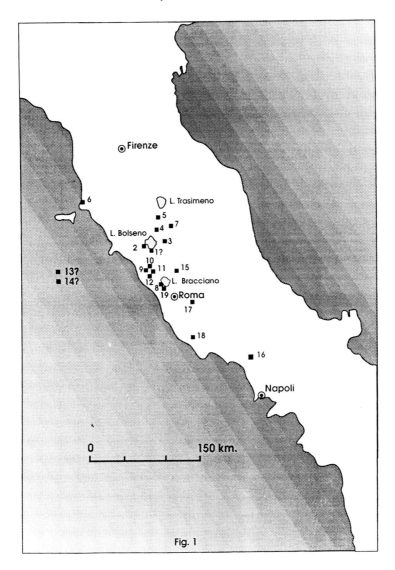

Figure 15.2. Map (Distribution of Find Sites).

TOOTH SIZE AS AN INDICATOR OF SEX

The evidence supporting my conclusion that only women used these dental pontics derives from direct measurement of the surviving teeth and/or of the gold bands of these appliances. These ring-shaped bands tightly fitted around specific teeth that have rotted away reflect the actual tooth dimensions (see Table 15.1). The long history of odontometric study demonstrating sexual dimorphism in human teeth (see Goose

1963, Brace and Ryan 1980, also the note by Brace *et al.* 1991, 36–37) has been surveyed by Kieser (1990, 65–70). The field studies of Ditch and Rose (1972) first demonstrated that dental size alone can be used to correctly evaluate sex in 93% of available examples. Rösing (1983) found accuracy ranging from 90 to 97% in sexing non-adults using tooth size. In a similar study Owsley and Webb (1983, 184) find that teeth 'do not allow sex determination at the level of accuracy achieved by conventional indicators…'. However, even Owsley and Webb conclude (1983, 181) that 'Dental descriminant functions are applicable to forensic science cases if used with caution.' The consensus is that odontometrics have been useful in evaluating sex in skeletal populations.

Sexual dimorphism in tooth size also has been tested using a large sample of dental data from the south Etruscan city of Tarquinia (Becker 1990, 1993, in preparation b), a site from which the greatest concentration of these dental appliances has been recorded. The finding that tooth size can be used to evaluate sex at a 90% level of accuracy in a population specific to south Etruria, suggests that sexual dimorphism in tooth size is sufficiently clear to permit relatively accurate assessment of sex in the people represented.

These findings regarding the relationship between tooth size and sex have been duplicated for a central Italian population of the first millenium BC (Becker and Salvadei 1992, 59–64, 113). At Osteria dell'Osa bone preservation was poor, but femurs provided a highly reliable indicator of sex (over 92%, cf. MacLaughlin and Bruce 1985) except in the case of males under the age of 25 years. For young adult males, a very small percentage of the total population, the lesser development of muscalature reduced predictive use of the femur to just over 60% (Becker and Salvadei 1992: 63). Bones and/or teeth were recovered from 602 graves and were evaluated by Becker and Salvadei independent of grave goods. In the 135 cases where associated tomb offerings provided an extremely good indication of gender, agreement with sex was found in 89.6% of these examples (Becker and Salvadei 1992, 61).

Although the evaluation of gender from associated grave goods is a problematical procedure, when selectively practiced this approach has been demonstrated to be as accurate a method as skeletal analysis only when applied to certain large skeletal populations that include clear bimodal artifact distributions. Thus, Toms' (1986) study of grave goods from the Etruscan period cemetery at Veio is probably highly accurate despite the lack of confirming skeletal analysis. Where gender evaluation based on grave goods has been compared with direct skeletal analysis, as at Osteria dell'Osa (Becker and Salvadei 1992) or at Pithekoussai (Becker 1995c). Independent skeletal analysis confirms the archaeological inference regarding gender based on associated grave goods by linking the meaning of the dichotomy in the sets of grave goods found with individuals at these sites to specific sex evaluations achieved by study of the skeletons. Therefore we also may use grave assessments to confirm the consistency of our independent skeletal analysis. The 10% of problematical cases reflect the overlap between robust females and small males common in any population, and also reflect the significant percentage of errors made in any society in assigning gender at birth. As evident from our studies, incisors within the population at Osteria dell'Osa have relatively little metric variability (Becker and Salvadei in preparation; see Tables 15.2

and 15.3 below). Nevertheless, we find that averages for the breadth of the central incisor diverge between males and females in this central Italic population; a population that was contemporary with the nearby and contemporary Etruscan Iron Age population (cf. Becker 2000).

Actual measurement of the teeth of individuals who wore these gold appliances are not available, but may be derived from the pontics in which individual teeth were encircled by gold bands (Becker unpublished a). These individual bands were so carefully fitted to the teeth that they encircled that the gold provides a mold-like cast enabling us to recognize which teeth were bound and where on the teeth these appliances were fitted (Becker 1996, 1999a). The long bands that girdled several teeth do not reveal clear metric evidence for sex. In addition to the odontometric data indicating that all of the multiple-ring appliances were worn by women, we have archaeological data that supports the same conclusion. The limited archaeological data for the Satricum appliance (Waarsenburg 1994, cf. Becker 1994d) and also the Valsiarosa appliance (Cozza and Pasqui 1981; Becker 1994a, 81–85) indicate that the people in these graves were adult females (see also Becker 1999a, in preparation c).

A GREEK CONNECTION

The discovery of an Etruscan type gold dental appliance at Tanagra in Greece can now be understood in terms that more specifically reflect ancient trade and social behaviours. The presence of this typically South Etruscan artefact reinforces the hypothesis that the people from Tanagra had trade relations or other dealings with Etruscans. Assuming that the wearer of this appliance actually died at Tanagra we may infer that Etruscan people were resident at the site and possibly engaged in trade. The linkage of these dental appliances with females reinforces the idea that ancient, and not so ancient, trade was facilitated by marriage alliances (Buchner and Ridgway 1993). The discovery that these appliances were only a South Etruscan phenomenon helps us to focus on the most probable origin for the woman buried at Tanagra whom I believe to have worn this ancient appliance, in life and in death.

To imply, as some readers have, that foreign women would simply 'copy' or mimic Etruscan customs such as tooth evulsion for the wearing of dental prostheses is to misunderstand fundamental cultural behaviours as they have been understood through a century of anthropological research. Modern urbanites, lacking 'cultural' borders in any anthropological sense, may spawn children who pierce, puncture and tattoo in emulation of their peers and 'role models' as defined by Hollywood. These aspects of complex society are not comparable with the intact cultural systems of antiquity, and indeed with most of the world in the Christian year 2001.

SOUTH ETRUSCAN BEHAVIOUR: EATING AVOIDANCE

The wearing of gold dental appliances by South Etruscan women relate to other Etruscan social behaviours noted in the ancient texts. Several ancient Roman authors

Table 15.2. Measurements of incisors.

Correlation between Maxillary Central Incisor M-D length and sex at Osteria dell'Osa (10th–8th centuries BC; from Becker and Salvadei Ms. A, using Salvadei's odontometric tables).

Tomb Number	M-D Length L	M-D Length R	Sex	Gender[1]
17	9.1	–	M	M (Becker and Salvadei 1992: 113)
28	–	8.6	F???	F
59	7.5	–	F?	F
62E	–	9.5	M???	M (Becker and Salvadei 1992: 815)
62Cel/E	–	8.2	F	F
107	9.5	9.3	M	M
117	8.1	8.1	F?	F
125	9.5	9.5	M	M
134	–	9.0	M	M
140	7.8	7.7	F	F
141	–	(8.6)	F	F
145	(8.3)	(8.3)	F	F
153	8.6	8.4	F??	F
156	8.5	8.5	F	F
157	9.0	8.8	F	F
163	8.6	8.6	F??	F
170	7.6	7.6	F	I
187	8.8	8.9	F???	I
188	8.2	–	M???	I
191	8.4	8.4	F??	I
222	–	8.6	F?	F
223	–	8.8	F???	F
242	9.1	9.0	F???	F
243	8.6	8.4	F?	F
246	8.9	8.9	F	F
249	–	8.7	F	F
250	–	7.6	F	F
251	8.6	–	F?	F
253	8.1	8.3	M???	M
254	–	8.8	M	M
256	–	8.9	M	M
261	8.5	–	F	F
262	–	8.9	F	M
263	–	9.2	F?	F
266	8.5	–	M???	M
274	6.8	–	F???	F
278	9.4	9.3	M??	M
282	–	7.7	F??	F
293	–	8.3	F	F
303	–	8.7	F	F

Tomb Number	M-D Length		Sex	Gender[1]
	L	R		
309B	7.9	5.8	F	I
311	9.1	9.2	F???	M
313	7.5	7.7	F	F
317	9.1	8.9	M	F
319	(8.4)	–	M??	M
325	8.0	–	M???	F
328	7.1	7.0	F	F
334	8.3	8.1	F?	F
337	8.0	–	F	F
339	9.0	9.1	F?	F
342(ad)	7.6	–	M???	F
342(ch)	9.5	9.3	M	M
345	8.7	8.6	M???	F

N=53 N=37 N=42 See notes.
I = gender not determined

1   Gender has been determined on the basis of tomb offerings found with the skeleton (Bietti Sestieri 1992, passim). This line of study has been discussed in the above text. For analytical purposes the archaeological gender assignments here will be given precedence over the sex evaluations derived from the study of the osteometric data. Two children under the age of five years have been eliminated from this list. T. 12 has a right central incisor first evaluated as 'F' (Becker and Salvadei 1992, 113) and later identified as 'M.' Since there were two people in this tomb the source of this tooth remains unclear.
2   Of these 53 individuals sex evaluation agrees with gender assignment (see Note 1) in 47 cases (90.4%). Of the five other cases, four were nearly correct (e.g. Tomb 325 = M???) and only the evaluation of T. 262 is problematical as the person in Tomb number 262 was evaluated as 'female' (F), but the artifacts suggest a male gendered person.

indicate that Etruscan husbands and wives dined together in public, reclining together in their public life as they intended to lie together in death. Etruscan gender relationships were quite different from those of Romans and Greeks, both of whom practised gender 'avoidance' while eating and in other contexts. To the Romans the 'unusual' Etruscan social behaviour of polite men and women dining together generated considerable 'ethnographic' commentary. Men dined only with men, with lewd women and servant girls in attendance. Mixed gender dining was perceived as an abhorrent custom by both the classical period Greeks and to some extent by the Romans. Rowland (2001, 12) succinctly notes that the Greeks and Romans found the freedoms of gender associations among the Etruscans 'shockingly so.' Since polite Etruscan women normally dined together with their husbands, and often with other men in public, the physical appearance of these women at dinners attended by Romans and/or Greeks provided an important reflection of family status. Gold dental appliances, like gold jewellery and elaborate clothing, provided important items of conspicuous consumption for these women. The Etruscan use of decorative dental

Table 15.3. Central incisor breadth and assignment of sex at Osteria dell'Osa (Note that the considerable degree of overlap).

| | Female | | Male | |
	Left	Right	Left	Right
5.8		X		
6.8	X			
7.0		X		
7.1	X			
7.5	XX			
7.6	XX	XX		
7.7		XXX		
7.8	X			
7.9	X			
8.0	XX			
8.1	X	XX	X	
8.2		X	X	
8.3	XX	XX		X
8.4	X	XXX	X	
8.5	XX	X	X	
8.6	XXXX	XXXX		X
8.7	X	XX		
8.8	X	XX		X
8.9	X	XX		XXX
9.0	XX	X		X
9.1	XX	X	X	
9.2	X			X
9.3				XXX
9.4		X		
9.5		XXX	XX	
N=	27	29	9	13
Ranges	6.8-9.1	5.8-9.2	8.1-9.5	8.3-9.5
Averages	8.26	8.29	8.91	9.04

appliances, like the use of written Etruscan, disappeared during the first century BC as the Etruscan chiefdoms were absorbed into the Roman state.

MAKERS OF PONTICS: NEITHER DENTISTS NOR PHYSICIANS

Possible makers of these Etruscan gold dental appliances are discussed by Bliquez and others (Guerini 1909, 102; Hoffman-Axthelm 1985, n30). Treggiari (1979, 82 n11) interprets texts of the early Roman period to suggest that some of the goldsmiths of the period may have been women. Gender may have been a factor of importance in the intimate contact needed for the fitting of dental appliances in the mouths of Etruscan women. Goldsmiths, ivory carvers, and other artisans fabricated these appliances, and I suggest that the makers fitted or applied these devices as a branch of cosmetology. Evidence from excavations at the Temple of Castor and Pollux in the Roman Forum indicates that cosmetologists operated as professionals distinct from dentists, who did extractions (Guldager 1990; Becker in press a), and from physicians, who prescribed treatments for diseases of the mouth. These professions are distinguished in the Roman literature, and the various shops excavated in the Forum represent distinct areas where these several trades were plied.

Brown (1936) provides a review of the literature relating to people called 'dentists.' The earliest contemporary reference to a dentist may have been made about 409 or 408 BC by Aristophanes (Deneffe 1899, 10). Bliquez (1996) reviews the ancient texts that specifically make note of dental appliances. The status of Roman dentists (tooth pullers?), possibly even lower than that of physicians, has often been discussed. Bliquez notes that Pliny may exaggerate in calling medicine a Greek discipline, but the low status of the field would not have attracted Romans of high social standing. Lanciani's (1892, 353) note of the discovery in 1864 of the tombstone of the dentist Victorinus (or Celerinus), decorated with an instrument which may be a dental forceps, also provided an early clue as to means by which the status of some of these ancient practitioners could be inferred. Lanciani also noted the name of a general surgeon as well as an 'Alexander' who is shown with a plier-like tool. This reference to a general surgeon led Jackson (1988, 119) to infer that dental extractions were performed by physicians and surgeons, but this tool may have been a surgical forceps. Jackson (1988, 119), in this revision of his earlier evaluation, suggests that by 100 BC Romans were taking over these medical trades from Greek immigrant families or that these Greek physicians were assuming Roman names. The status of these 'new professionals' may have improved during this period.

The question to be asked here relates to the possibility that females performed extractions as well as made gold appliances. Women who were practising as 'doctors' and/or 'physicians' are noted in ancient Rome, in categories that are clearly distinct from midwives (Lefkowitz and Fant 1982, 161–163; Flemming 2000). The specific activities of these female physicians remain unknown, but given the gender avoidance practised by the Romans one can infer that they may have treated women. Treggiari's (1978, 162–164) intensive examination of the literature referring to the activities and the status of labourers in ancient Rome, focusing on jobs that the upper classes described as common and sordid, identified 225 specialised trades. For example, Cicero notes that numerous tasks were unsuitable for a free person, including unskilled manual work, retail trades, workshop employees, and providing pleasure (entertainers, food sellers, perfumers). These trades usually were conducted from workshops (*officina*) or shops or inns (*tabernae*). Obviously people without formal establishments, such as street venders and some prostitutes, had even lower status. Treggiari (1980, 48) uses these texts to infer a low social status for people in the category of *opifices*, those who practised manual arts (writing, building, healing), and this category may have included physicians. She concludes that the surgeons and dentists, who were involved with blood and gore, probably occupied the lower end of this bottom end of the social scale

Discussion and summary

The extensive documentation of Roman medical practices that survives reflects their complex and literate society. During that period the 'emerging states' in Etruria rarely employed writing for more than ritual and related religious purposes. The writing system needed to support such a socio-economic development also led Roman authors to incorporate into their texts whatever had been the medical and dental oral tradition among the Etruscans as well as that of the Greeks.

In ancient Etruria the social relations between women and men, and the power and prestige of the former in various Etruscan cities, is only now the subject of archaeological investigation as practised by anthropologists (Nelson 1997). Gender inequality as represented by different decorative procedures has been investigated among the prehistoric peoples of the Pacific Northwest coast (Moss 1996). Her studies of labrets (ornaments inserted through incisions in the lips or cheeks) indicate that the size and materials used in making them have direct status implications (Moss 1999). The patterns of dental wear created by these labrets indicate both location and size of these ornaments, even when the actual ornament is not found. These data provide important suggestions regarding how dental appliances may be identified in the record using only teeth, and how these data may be interpreted. Thus our attention may now shift from direct evaluation of Etruscan gold dental appliances to the teeth on which they were worn (cf. Becker 1996)

As Rowland (2001, 12) observes, 'four hundred years of unrelenting warfare' gradually led to the collapse of Etruscan political resistence to Rome, along with the ultimate abandonment of use of written Etruscan. No Roman or other woman would embark on the complex decorative mode that would compromise her identity as a Roman, or lead her to emulate behaviours of a society no longer viable.

Conclusions

1. Those Etruscan dental pontics which include replacement teeth were worn as decorative replacements for healthy teeth that were deliberately removed (tooth evulsion) to provide space.
2. Dental evulsion and replacement by the use of pontics were limited to South Etruria, as indicated by the distribution of find sites. The concentration of these appliances in and around Tarquinia suggests that their use may have been even more limited to the women from Tarquinia.
3. In ancient South Etruria, where dental appliances were worn, only women used them. This type of female adornment was a regional marker for the culture.
4. Residents of 'Etruscan' cities in the central and northern parts of ancient Etruria may have married women from the Tarquinia area only infrequently.
5. Simple gold band appliances, those with no false teeth attached, could have had functional aspects, such as preventing the movement or loss of teeth loosened by a blow or by periodontal disease. However, the use of these appliances in south Etruria appears to have been purely decorative.

Acknowledgements
My most sincere thanks are due Dr. Gillian C. Carr for her kind invitation to participate in this publication and her considerable editorial efforts, along with those of Dr. Patty Baker, to improve upon the original manuscript. Thanks also are due to Dr. Loretana Salvadei and to the many people who facilitated my study of Etruscan dental appliances at museums throughout Europe, and to E. Kursh for editorial assistance. Special thanks are due Prof. L. Bliquez and Dr. A. M. Haeussler for their considerable aid in this research and for their useful comments on the manuscript. This paper was completed while the author was a Research Associate of The University Museum of Archaeology and Anthropology of the University of Pennsylvania. My sincere thanks are due Prof. Jeremy Sabloff, Museum Director, and Prof. Donald White of the Mediterranean Section for their encouragement and support of this research, and to Dr. S. Tomaskova for comments on an earlier version of this paper.

A generous grant from The National Geographic Society allowed the field portion to be completed at Tarquinia. The ideas presented and the accuracy of information transmitted is solely the responsibility of the author.

Bibliography
Badre, L. 1986 'Machoire (No. 349),' pp. 266 in E. Gubel (ed.) *Les Pheniciens et Le Monde Mediterraneen* [Exhibition Catalogue], Brussels: C. Coessens.
Becker, M.J. 1990 'Etruscan social classes in the VI century B.C.: evidence from recently excavated cremations and inhumations in the area of Tarquinia,' pp. 23–35 in H. Heres and M. Kunze (eds) *Die Welt der Etrusker*, Berlin: Akademie-Verlag.
Becker, M.J. 1992a 'An Etruscan gold dental appliance in the collections of the Danish National Museum: evidence for the history of dentistry' *Tandlaegebladet* (Danish Dental Journal) 18 (96), Cover, 599–609.
Becker, M.J. 1992b 'Cultural uniformity during the Italian Iron Age: Sardinian nuraghi as regional markers' pp 204–209 in R.H. Tykot and T.K. Andrews (eds) *Sardinia in the Mediterranean: a footprint in the sea*, Sheffield: Sheffield Academic Press.
Becker, M.J. 1993 'Human skeletons from Tarquinia: a preliminary analysis of the 1989 Cimitero site excavations with implications for the evolution of Etruscan social classes' *Studi Etruschi* LVIII [for 1992], 211–248.
Becker, M.J. 1994a ' Etruscan gold dental appliances: origins and functions as indicated by an example from Valsiarosa, Italy' *Journal of Paleopathology* 6 (2), 69–92.
Becker, M.J. 1994b 'Etruscan gold dental appliances: origins and functions as indicated by an Example from Orvieto, Italy, in the Danish National Museum' *Dental Anthropology Newsletter* 8 (3), 2–8.
Becker, M.J. 1994c 'Spurious "examples" of ancient dental implants or appliances' *Dental Anthropology Newsletter* 9 (1), 5–10.
Becker, M.J. 1994d 'An analysis of the cremated human remains from Tomb XVII of the 1896 excavations at Satricum, Italy' pp. 147–148 in D.J. Waarsenburg (ed.) 1:*The Northwest necropolis of Satricum: an Iron Age cemetery in Latium Vetus*. Doctoral Dissertation, Faculty of Letters, University of Amsterdam.
Becker, M.J. 1995a 'Female vanity among the Etruscans: the Copenhagen gold dental appliance' Vol. II, pp. 651–658 in A.C. Aufderheide (ed.), *Actas del I Congreso Internacional de Estudios sobre Momias, 1992*, Santa Cruz de Tenerife: Museo Arqueológico y Etnológico de Tenerife.

Becker, M.J. 1995b 'Tooth evulsion among the ancient Etruscans: recycling in Antiquity' *Dental Anthropology Newsletter* 9 (3), 8–9.

Becker, M.J. 1995c 'Human skeletal remains from the pre-colonial Greek emporium of Pithekoussai on Ischia (NA)' pp. 273–281 in Neil Christie (ed.) *Settlement and Economy in Italy 1500 BC to AD 1500*, Leicester, UK: Oxbow Monograph 41.

Becker, M.J. 1995–96 'Early dental appliances in the Eastern Mediterranean' *Berytus* 42, 71–102.

Becker, M.J. 1996 'An unusual Etruscan gold dental appliance from Poggio Gaiella, Italy' *Dental Anthropology Newsletter* 10 (1), 10–16.

Becker, M.J. 1999a 'The Valsiarosa gold dental appliance: Etruscan origins for dental prostheses,' *Etruscan Studies* 6: 43–73.

Becker, M.J. 1999b 'Etruscan gold dental appliances: three newly "discovered" examples', *American Journal of Archaeology* 103, 103–111.

Becker, M.J. 1999c 'Ancient "dental implants": a recently proposed example from France evaluated with other claims' *International Journal of Oral & Maxillofacial Implants* 14, 19–29.

Becker, M.J. 2000 'Reconstructing the lives of South Etruscan women' pp. 55–67 in A.E. Rautman (ed.) *Reading the body: representations and remains in the archaeological record*, Philadelphia: University of Pennsylvania Press.

Becker, M.J. In press a 'Dentistry in ancient Rome: direct evidence based on an analysis of the teeth from the excavations at the Temple of Castor and Pollux in the Roman Forum' pp. 218–231 in S. Sande and Jan Zahle (eds) *The temple of Castor and Pollux*, Volume II, Roma: Edizione De Luca.

Becker, M.J. Unpublished a 'Two dental appliances in the Liverpool Museum and 2 in the Villa Giulia Museum, Rome', (field notes, May-June 1988), Manuscript on file, Anthropology Section, West Chester University of Pennsylvania. West Chester, PA 19383 USA.

Becker, M.J. In preparation a 'Ancient dental appliances: a corpus and typology' Manuscript on file, Anthropology Section, West Chester University of Pennsylvania. West Chester, PA 19383 USA.

Becker, M.J. In preparation b 'An analysis of human skeletal remains from recent excavations at Tarquinia, Italy,' Paper presented at the Quinto Encontro di Studi Etrusci (2000). Manuscript on file, Anthropology Section, West Chester University of Pennsylvania. West Chester, PA 19383 USA.

Becker, M.J. In preparation c 'Skulls and teeth associated with Etruscan dental appliances: an evaluation of the Poggio Gaiella Example,' Manuscript on file, Anthropology Section, West Chester University of Pennsylvania. West Chester, PA 19383, USA.

Becker, M.J. and L. Salvadei 1992 'Analysis of the human skeletal remains from the cemetery of Osteria dell'Osa' pp. 53–292 in A.M. Bietti Sestieri (ed.) *Osteria dell'Osa*, Rome: Quasar.

Becker, M.J. and L. Salvadei in preparation 'Correlation between maxillary central incisor M-D length and sex at the Iron Age Site of Osteria dell'Osa, Italy,' Manuscript on file, Anthropology Department, West Chester University of Pennsylvania. West Chester PA 19383, USA.

Beidelman, T.O. 1987 'Circumcision' pp. 511–514 in Mircea Eliade (ed.) *The Encyclopedia of Religion*, New York: Macmillan Publishers.

Bliquez, L.J. 1996 'Prosthetics in classical antiquity: Greek, Etruscan, and Roman prosthetics' pp. 2640–2676 in W. Haase and H. Temporini (eds) *Aufstieg und Niedergang der römischen Welt, Part II: Principate*, Vol. 37 (3).

Bonfante, L. 1975 *Etruscan dress*, Baltimore: Johns Hopkins University Press.

Böttiger, K.A. 1797 *Griechische Vasengemälde. Mit archäologischen und artistischen erläuterungen der originalkupfer.* Volume I, Weimar: Industrie-comptoir.

Brown, L.P. 1936 'Appellations of the dental practitioner' *Dental Cosmos* 78, 246–258, 378–389, 481–495.

Brace, C.L. and A.S. Ryan 1980 'Sexual dimorphism and human tooth size differences' *Journal of Human Evolution* 9, 417–435.

Brace, C.L., S.L. Smith and K.D. Hunt 1991 'What big teeth you had Grandma! Human tooth size, past and present' pp. 33–57 in M.A. Kelley and C.S. Larson (eds) *Advances in dental anthropology*, New York: Wiley-Liss.

Buchner, G. and D. Ridgway 1993 *Pithekoussai I. La Necropoli: Tombe 1–723 scavate dal 1952 al 1961*, Roma: Giorgio Bretschneider Editore.

Carabelli Edlen von Lunkaszprie, G. 1831 *Systematisches Handbuch der Zahnheilkunde* (First volume), Wien: A Doll's Universitätsbuchhandlung.

Casotti, L. 1947 'L'odontotecnica degli Etruschi' *Rivista Italiana di Stomatologia* 2, 661–678.

Clawson, D. 1934 'Phoenician dental art' *Berytus* 1, 23–31.

Corruccini, R.S. and E. Pacciani 1989 '"Orthodontistry" and dental occlusion in Etruscans' *Angle Orthodontist* 59 (1), 61–64.

Cozza, A. and A. Pasqui 1981 'Carta Archeologica D'Italia (1881–1897): Materiali per Agro Falisco,' *Forma Italiae*, Serie II, Documenti 2. Firenze: Leo S. Olschki for Unione Accademica Nazionale.

Deneffe, V. 1899 *La Prothése dentaire dans l'Antiquité*, Anvers: H. Caals.

Ditch, L.E. and J.C. Rose 1972 'A multivariate dental sexing technique' *American Journal of Physical Anthropology* 37, 61–64.

Emptoz, F. 1987 'La Prothése Dentaire dans la Civilisation Étrusque' pp. 545–560 in *Archéologie et Médecine*: VII Recontre Internacionales d'Archéologie et d'Histoire (Antibes 1986). Juan-les-Pins: Editions A.P.D.C.A.

Fantham, E., H.P. Foley, N. Boymel Kampen, S.B. Pomeroy and H.A. Shapiro (eds) 1995 *Women in the classical world.image and text*, Rome: Giorgio Bretschneider.

Flemming, R. 2000 *Medicine and the making of Roman women: gender, nature, and authority from Celsus to Galen*, Oxford: Oxford University Press.

Goose, D.H. 1963 'Dental measurement: an assessment of its value in anthropological studies' pp. 125–148 in D.R. Brothwell (ed.) *Dental Anthropology*, New York: Pergamum.

Guerini, V. 1909 *A History of dentistry*, Philadelphia: Lea and Febiger.

Guldager, P. 1990 'En tandklinik og skønhedssalon i Rom' *Tandlaegebladet* (Danish Dental Journal) 94 (10), 422–426.

Guldager, P. and K. Slej 1986 'Il Tempio di Castore e Polluce' *Archeologia Viva* 5 (4), 24–37.

Heyne, R. 1924 *Zähne und Zahnärzliches in der schönen Literatur der Römer*, Doctoral Dissertation. Leipzig.

Hippocrates 1923/31 *Hippocrates: ancient medicine*. Volumes 1, 2 and 4, translated by W.H.S. Jones. London: William Heinemann (Reprinted 1967).

Hippocrates 1928 *Hippocrates: ancient medicine*. Volume 3, translated by E.T. Withington. London: Willian Heinemann.

Hippocrates 1995 *Hippocrates*, Volume VIII, edited and translated by Paul Potter. Cambridge, MA: Harvard University Press (Loeb Classical Library 482).

Hoffmann-Axthelm, W. 1985 *Die Geschichte der Zahnheilkunde* (second edition), Berlin: Quintessenz Verlags-GmbH.

Jackson, R. 1988 *Doctors and diseases in the Roman Empire*, London: British Museum Publications.

Jackson, R. 1990 'Roman doctors and their instruments: Recent research into ancient practice' *Journal of Roman Archaeology* 3, 5–27.

Johnstone, M.A. 1932a 'The Etruscan collection in the free public museums of Liverpool' *Annals of Archaeology and Anthropology, Liverpool* 19, 121–137.

Johnstone, M.A. 1932b 'The Etruscan collection in the public museum of Liverpool' *Studi Etruschi* 6, 443–452.

Jones, W.H.S. 1946 *Philosophy and medicine in Ancient Greece*, Baltimore: Johns Hopkins Press.

Jones, W.H.S. 1953 'Ancient documents and contemporary life, with special reference to the Hippocratic Corpus, Celsus and Pliny' pp. 100–110 in E. Ashworth Underwood (ed.) *Science, medicine and history*, London: Oxford University Press.

Kieser, J.A. 1990 *Human adult odontometrics. the study of variation in adult tooth size*, Cambridge: Cambridge University Press.

Künzl, E. and T. Weber 1991 'Das spätantike Grab eines Zahnartztes zu Gedara in der Dekapolis' *Damaszener Mitteilungen* 5, 81–118.

Lanciani, R. 1892 *Pagan and Christian Rome*, New York: Benjamin Blom [Reissued in 1967].

Lefkowitz, M.R. and M.B. Fant 1982 *Women's life in Greece and Rome*, London: Duckworth.

MacLaughlin, S.M. and M.F. Bruce 1985 'A simple univariate technique for determining sex from fragmentary femura: its application to a Scottish short cist population' *American Journal of Physical Anthopology* 67, 413–417.

Masali, L. and A. Peluso 1985 'L'odontoiatria nell'antico Egitto' pp. 51–66 in G. Vogel and G. Gambacorta (eds) *Storia della odontoiatria*, Milan: Ars Medica Antiqua.

Moss, M.L. 1996 'Gender, social inequality, and cultural complexity: Northwest Coast women in prehistory' pp. 81–88 in D.A. Meyer, P.C. Dawson and D.T. Hanna (eds) *Debating Complexity*, Calgary: Archaeological Association of the University of Calgary.

Moss, M.L. 1999 'George Catlin among the Nayas: understanding the practice of labret wearing on the Northwest Coast' *Ethnohistory* 46 (1), 31–65.

Nelson, S.M. 1997 *Gender in archaeology: analyzing power and prestige*, Walnut Creek: Alta Mira Press.

Nielsen, I. 1992 'The Metellan temple' pp 87–117 in I. Nielsen and B. Poulsen (eds) *The temple of Castor and Pollux I*, Rome: De Luca for the Soprintendenza Archeological di Roma.

Nielsen, I. and J. Zahle 1987 'The temple of Castor and Pollux on the Forum Romanum. Preliminary report on the Scandinavian excavations 1983–1985' *Acta Archaeologica* 56 (1985), 1–30.

Owsley, D.W. and R.S. Webb 1983 'Misclassification probability of dental discriminant functions for sex' *Journal of Forensic Sciences* 28, 181–185.

Poulsen, B. 1992 'The written sources' pp. 54–60 in I. Nielsen and B. Poulsen (eds) *The temple of Castor and Pollux I*, Rome: De Luca for the Soprintendenza Archeological di Roma.

Robb, J. 1997 'Violence and gender in early Italy' pp. 43–65 in A.O. Kosloski-Ostrow and C.L. Lyons (eds) *Troubled Times: Osteological and Archaeological Evidence of Violence*, New York: Routledge.

Rösing, F.W. 1983 'Sexing immature human skeletons' *Journal of Human Evolution* 12, 149–155.

Rowland, I. 2001 'Etruscan Secrets', *New York Review of Books* 48 (11), 12–17.

Saunders, J.B. de Cusance Morant 1963 *The transitions from ancient Egyptian to Greek medicine*, Lawrence: University of Kansas Press.

Strong, D. Emrys and J.B. Ward-Perkins 1962 'The temple of Castor in the Forum Romanum' *Papers of the British School at Rome* 30 (17), 1–30.

Sudhoff, K. 1926 *Geschichte der Zahnheilkunde* (second edition), Leipzig: Johann Ambrosius Barth.

Suzuki, H. 1982 'Skulls of Minatogawa Man' pp. 7–49 in Man H. Suzuki and K. Hanihara (eds) *The Minatogawa*, Tokyo: University of Tokyo Press.

Tabanelli, M.N. 1963 *La Medicina nel Mondo degli Etruschi*, Firenze: L.S. Olschki.

Toms, J. 1986 'The relative chronology of the Villanovan cemetery at Quattro-Fontanili at Veii' *Archeologia e Storia Antica* 8, 42–97 [AION: Napoli, Istituto Universitario Orientale].

Treggiari, S.M. 1978 'Rome: urban labour' pp 162–165 in [no editor noted] *Seventh International*

Economic History Conference, Edinburgh 1978 Tonbridge, Great Britain: Lewis Reprints, Ltd.

Treggiari, S.M. 1979 'Lower class women in the Roman economy' *Florilegium* I: 65–86.

Treggiari, S.M. 1980 'Urban labour in Rome: mercennarii and tabernarii' pp 48–64 in P. Garnsey (ed.) *Non-slave labour in the Graeco-Roman world*, Cambridge: Cambridge Philological Society, Supplementary Volume no. 6.

Waarsenburg, D. 1994 *The Northwest necropolis of Satricum: an Iron Age cemetery in Latium Vetus.* Doctoral Dissertation, Faculty of Letters, University of Amsterdam.